The
McNamara
Years
at the
World
Bank

Published for the World Bank
The Johns Hopkins University Press
Baltimore and London

The McNamara Years at the World Bank

Major Policy Addresses of Robert S. McNamara 1968–1981

With Forewords by Helmut Schmidt, Chancellor of the Federal Republic of Germany, and Léopold Senghor, former President of Senegal

The Johns Hopkins University Press
Baltimore, Maryland 21218, U.S.A.

Library of Congress Cataloging in Publication Data

McNamara, Robert S., 1916-
    The McNamara Years at the World Bank.

    Includes index.
    1. Underdeveloped areas — Addresses, essays,
lectures. 2. World Bank-Addresses, essays,
lectures. I.World Bank. II. Title
HC59.7.M37   338.9′009172′4   81-3743
ISBN 0-8018-2685-3   AACR2

CONTENTS

FOREWORD

by Helmut Schmidt,
Chancellor of the Federal Republic of Germany

In the thirteen years that Robert McNamara served as President of the World Bank, he transformed that institution into the world's largest and most important single source of international development assistance. When he took office in 1968, the Bank was lending about a billion dollars a year. By 1980, that figure had grown to $12 billion. In his final year, this one development agency was supervising over 1,600 projects, with a total value of some $100 billion, in more than a hundred developing countries.

Those are impressive statistics. But they do not reveal the full dimensions of Mr. McNamara's achievement.

That becomes clear if one peruses what has now been collected together here for the first time in one volume: his major policy addresses as an international civil servant.

In effect, this volume constitutes a careful, reasoned, and sometimes impassioned commentary on the human condition of late twentieth-century man—and what the international community can and ought to do about it.

What I believe Mr. McNamara has really demonstrated during his thirteen years of leadership at the World Bank is that there is no inherent contradiction between the careful, prudent investment of scarce resources and the direct pursuit of greater social equity. As he has often reminded us, accelerated economic growth and the reduction of absolute poverty are the twin complementary goals of international development. Both are necessary. Both are achievable.

These pages reveal Robert McNamara as a hard-headed manager, a warm-hearted humanist, and a man whose disciplined mind ranges philosophically far beyond the precise statistics he is so fond of quoting.

I will not suppress the fact that, besides his tasks as President or his achievements as a political and economic orator with a moral consciousness, he also has been an always unselfish personal adviser to many people all over the globe—including myself. Therefore, I am among those who have good reason to be thankful. I wish this book a wide range of readers and, also, I wish recognition of Robert McNamara as having impartially served the world.

PREFACE

par Monsieur Léopold Sédar Senghor,
Ancien Président de la République du Sénégal

Rassembler, en un livre, l'ensemble des discours de M. Robert McNamara, Président du Groupe de la Banque mondiale, est une heureuse initiative. Ces textes montrent comment un homme de lucidité, mais de foi, a essayé de soulever des montagnes pour aider à l'instauration d'un *nouvel ordre économique mondial,* parce que fondé sur une plus grande justice dans les relations des pays du Nord et du Sud. Comment il a pu, en grande partie, réussir son audacieux pari d'accroître, très sensiblement, l'aide du Groupe de la Banque mondiale aux pays en développement. Il n'est pas un seul domaine essentiel— agriculture, infrastructures, industrie, énergie—qui n'ait fait l'objet de la sollicitude de M. McNamara. Il a suffi, à chaque fois, que les pays du Sud fussent concernés pour que, lui-même, se sentît responsable et agît en conséquence. A ce titre, les pays pauvres lui doivent beaucoup, et c'est l'occasion, pour moi, de lui exprimer notre profonde reconnaissance.

Cependant, au-delà de l'action "économique" de M. McNamara, j'ai été frappé par sa vaste culture et sa sensibilité de poète. C'est ainsi qu'il nous est arrivé, à lui et à moi, de discuter sur les poètes d'origine celtique.

A sa manière, en effet, M. McNamara est un poète. Son activité, intense, en faveur du développement du Tiers-Monde m'est apparue comme celle d'un homme d'action inspiré, ou, mieux, comme celle d'un poète de l'action. Pour cela, il fallait une intelligence fine, doublée d'une intuition fulgurante, qui fait saisir l'avenir, qui, à l'occasion, fait entreprendre des actions qualifiées d'utopistes, et qui ne sont que les réalités de demain.

C'est ainsi que l'an dernier, à la XIe Session de l'ONU, il a fait dire, par la Banque mondiale, qu'on ne pouvait résoudre les problèmes économiques sans examiner leurs aspects culturels. Une telle attitude suppose une grande générosité : une foi qui trouve ses fondements dans les racines profondes de la religion. Toutes qualités que l'on trouve chez le président du Groupe de la Banque mondiale. Dès lors, il était normal que son oeuvre, en définitive, fût ce que nous savons : une oeuvre de paix et de fraternité parce qu'une oeuvre à la fois économique et culturelle, voire spirituelle.

FOREWORD

by Léopold Sédar Senghor,
former President of the Republic of Senegal

To bring together, in one volume, the major addresses of
Robert McNamara, President of the World Bank Group, is a
welcome initiative. His words show how a man of sharp in-
tellect and of faith has sought to move mountains to help establish a *new world economic order,* built on greater justice in the
relations between the countries of the North and the South.
They show how, in large measure, he made good on his bold
challenge to increase very appreciably the aid given by the
World Bank to the developing countries. There is not a single
essential area—be it agriculture, infrastructure, industry, or
energy—that has not been Mr. McNamara's concern. Whenever
the countries of the South were troubled, he felt a sense of
responsibility and acted accordingly. The poor countries rightly
owe him much, and I take this occasion to express to him our
profound gratitude.

Yet, beyond Mr. McNamara's activities in the "economic"
sphere, I was struck by his vast culture and by his poetic sensitivity. Thus have our talks turned, on occasion, to a discussion
of the poets of Celtic origin.

In his own way, Mr. McNamara is indeed a poet. His intense
efforts to help the Third World develop were to my mind those
of an inspired man of action, or, better still, those of a poet of
action. For this, great intelligence is needed, intensified by
flashes of intuition that perceive the future and lead—on occasion—to actions that may be seen as utopian but are simply
tomorrow's realities. Thus, last year, at the Eleventh Special
Session of the United Nations, the view of the World Bank was

Translated by Eric McMillan.

that economic problems cannot be solved without considering their human aspects. This attitude implies great generosity: a faith deeply rooted in religion. These are all qualities that we find in the President of the World Bank Group. Consequently, it is not surprising that his life's work, in the end, is what we know it to be: a work of peace and brotherhood, both economic and cultural, and indeed spiritual in nature.

INTRODUCTION

The Executive Directors of the World Bank commissioned this publication to mark the retirement of Robert S. McNamara after thirteen years of outstanding service as President of this institution. By gathering together all his major addresses in one volume, it is our intention both to honor Mr. McNamara and to make more accessible a record of his thinking on development policy issues. He devoted much time and thought to these addresses because he viewed them as important instruments to promote international understanding of, and support for, economic development in the Third World. We hope that this volume will enhance public knowledge of his remarkable contribution to the evolving international development process.

The Executive Directors, World Bank

ONE

To the
BOARD OF GOVERNORS

WASHINGTON, D.C.
SEPTEMBER 30, 1968

This is my first public speech as President of the World Bank, and I speak to you with some diffidence as a newcomer with only half a year's experience in this post—but perhaps the half year in my whole life in which I have felt myself most challenged by the prospect before me.

I have always regarded the World Bank as something more than a Bank, as a Development Agency, and when I came here six months ago I was not entirely a stranger to the problems of World Development. As American Secretary of Defense I had observed, and spoken publicly about, the connection between world poverty and unstable relations among nations; as a citizen of the world I had begun to sense the truth in Pope Paul's dictum that "Development is Peace." Yet I was uneasily aware that as the peoples of the world looked at the sixties—the United Nations' Development Decade—they felt a deep sense of frustration and failure. The rich countries felt that they had given billions of dollars without achieving much in the way of Development; the poor countries felt that too little of the enormous increases in the wealth of the developed world had been diverted to help them rise out of the pit of poverty in which they have been engulfed for centuries past.

How far is this mood of frustration and failure justified by the events of the past decade? I have sought to find out the truth about this, but, though there have been many voices only too anxious to answer my question, each with a panoply of statistics to prove its point, there is no agreed situation report, nor any clear joint strategy for the future.

There have been successes: many billions in aid have been forthcoming from the developed world, and as a result of that aid and of their own increased capacity to manage their affairs, the economic growth of the poorer countries has been stimulated.

Let us make no mistake. Aid does work, it is not money wasted, it is a sound investment. Even the ultimate goal of the Development Decade, an annual rise in national incomes in the

3

poorer countries of 5% by 1970 is likely to be achieved: the average annual growth thus far has been 4.8%.

And yet . . . you know and I know that these cheerful statistics are cosmetics which conceal a far less cheerful picture in many countries. The oil-rich nations of the Middle East have prospered economically; so have some small states in East Asia. But for the nations of Africa and South Asia—nations with a population of over one billion—the average increase in national income is, at most, 3.5%, and much of the growth is concentrated in the industrial areas, while the peasant remains stuck in his immemorial poverty, living on the bare margin of subsistence.

Casting its shadow over all this scene is the mushrooming cloud of the population explosion. If we take this into account, and look at the progress for human beings rather than nations, the growth figures appear even less acceptable.

The annual growth of per capita income in Latin America is less than 2%, in East Asia only about 2%, in Africa only 1%, and in South Asia only about 0.5%. At these rates, a doubling of per capita income in East Asia would take nearly 35 years, in Latin America more than 40 years, in Africa almost 70 years and in South Asia nearly a century and a half. Even in the most progressive of these areas, the amount of improvement would be imperceptible to the average citizen from year to year.

Such a situation cries out for a greater and more urgent effort by the richer countries to assist economic growth in these poorer countries. It is clear they are financially capable of such action. During the Development Decade so far, they have added to their annual real incomes a sum of about $400 billion, an addition itself far greater than the total annual incomes of the underdeveloped countries of Asia, Africa and Latin America.

But I found, and I need hardly tell you this, that while the requirement for assistance was never higher, the will to provide it was never lower in many, though not all, of the countries which provide the bulk of economic aid.

And the disenchantment of the rich with the future of development aid was fed by performance deficiencies of many of the poorer nations. Blatant mismanagement of economies; diversion of scarce resources to wars of nationalism; perpetuation of discriminatory systems of social organization and income distribution have been all too common in these countries.

This then was the picture of the development world which I found in my first weeks at the World Bank. A confused but sharply disappointing picture, in which it was difficult to see what had gone wrong in the past (though something clearly had), or what was the right path ahead for us.

In these circumstances, I turned to a suggestion which had been put forward by my predecessor, Mr. George Woods—one of his many bits of wise advice from which we all, and I especially, have benefited. This was that we should establish a commission of men well versed in world affairs, and accustomed to influencing them, who would survey the past aid effort; seek out the lessons it can teach for the future; and then examine that future to see what needs to be done by rich and poor, developed and underdeveloped alike to promote the economic well-being of the great majority of mankind. As you know, Mr. Lester Pearson, formerly Prime Minister of Canada, has agreed to lead such a survey, which will now proceed independently of the Bank.

The Pearson Commission will be turning our eyes to the long future, marking out guidelines not just for a decade but for a whole generation of development that will carry us to the end of this century. But here are we now, living in 1968, with much that we can and must do today and tomorrow. It is already clear beyond contradiction that during the first four-fifths of the Development Decade the income gap between the developed and the less developed countries has increased, is increasing and ought to be diminished. But it is equally clear that the political will to foster development has weakened, is weakening further, and needs desperately to be strengthened.

What can the Bank do in this situation? I have been determined on one thing: that the Bank can and will act; it will not share in the general paralysis which is afflicting aid efforts in so many parts of the world. I do not believe that the Bank can go it alone and do the job of development that needs to be done around the world by itself; but I do believe that it can provide leadership in that effort, and can show that it is not resources which are lacking—for the richer countries amongst them have resources in plenty—but what is lacking, is the will to employ those resources on the development of the poorer nations.

We in the Bank, therefore, set out to survey the next five years, to formulate a "development plan" for each developing nation, and to see what the Bank Group could invest if there were no shortage of funds, and the only limit on our activities was the capacity of our member countries to use our assistance effectively and to repay our loans on the terms on which they were lent.

As a result of this survey, we have concluded that a very substantial increase in Bank Group activities is desirable and possible.

It is toward this objective that I shall attempt to guide the Bank's activities in the next few years. In doing so I shall need the advice and support of you gentlemen, our Governors, expressed through the Board of Executive Directors. Therefore I think it prudent and fitting that I should now present to you an outline of my thinking.

Let me begin by giving you some orders of magnitude: I believe that globally the Bank Group should during the next five years lend twice as much as during the past five years. This means that between now and 1973 the Bank Group would lend in total nearly as much as it has lent since it began operations 22 years ago.

This is a change of such a degree that I feel it necessary to emphasize that it is not a change of kind. We believe that we can carry out these operations within the high standards of careful evaluation and sound financing that my predecessors have made synonymous with the name of the World Bank.

Our loans will be for projects as soundly based and appraised as ever in our history. However, more and more, in looking for projects to support we shall look for those which contribute most fundamentally to the development of the total national economy, seeking to break strangleholds on development; to find those growth opportunities that stimulate further growth. And our help will be directed to those poor nations which need it most.

This, I believe, to be sound development financing, but it is not riskproof; nor do I believe that the utter avoidance of risks is the path of prudence or wisdom. For instance, I recently visited Indonesia where, for good reasons, the Bank has never made a loan of any sort in the past. What I found was the sixth largest nation in the world, rich in natural resources, striving in the wake of the most terrible disasters, both economic and political, to set itself straight on the path to development. Without external help Indonesia faces certain disasters; by giving help (as we have begun to do through the International Development Association and through the establishment of a permanent mission) we are running some risks. I do not believe you would wish it otherwise.

The parable of the talents is a parable about power—about financial power—and it illuminates the great truth that all power is given us to be used, not to be wrapped in a napkin against risk.

But if we are to lend at double the level of the past, can we raise the money? I will not speak now about the soft loan money which is raised by Government contributions—you all know how essential these funds are—but about the money we raise by bond issues in the capital markets of the world. I am confident that the money is there, because I have confidence in the immense capacity of the economies of the developed world; no country need fear bankrupting itself because it plays its full part in development.

There are, of course, certain constraints resulting from balance of payments difficulties, but I am fully aware that the balance of payments difficulty is a problem of balance among the rich economies and not of balance between those countries as a group and the rest of the world—very little of the money lent in aid stays in the developing countries, almost all of it returns quickly in payment for the goods purchased in the richer countries. It is our job in the World Bank to look at the world money markets as a whole, and see where there are surpluses, where there are reserves that can be tapped. Following this line we have gone to the Middle East, and successfully raised funds there, as well as in the more conventional markets of the world —in particular Germany and America.

As a result, in the past 90 days the World Bank has raised more funds by borrowing than in the whole of any single calendar year in its history.

I would stress that in doubling the Bank Group's lending activities we shall not depart from our high standards of investment policy. But I would not want you to think that our policy is simply "more of the same."

Our five year prospect calls for considerable changes in the allocation of our resources, both to geographic areas and to economic sectors, to suit the considerably changed circumstances of today and tomorrow.

First as to area: in the past the Bank Group has tended to concentrate its effort on the South Asian subcontinent. Much has been achieved—the harnessing of the waters of the Indus River system for power and irrigation for instance—and much remains to be achieved. I believe World Bank lending to Asia should rise substantially over the next five years. But it is not to Asia alone that our new effort will be directed. It is to Latin America and Africa as well, where in the past our activities have been less concentrated, and to some countries in great need of our help, such as Indonesia and the United Arab Republic, where our past activities have been negligible.

In Latin America, I foresee our investment rate more than doubling in the next five years. But it is in Africa, just coming to the threshold of major investment for development, where the greatest expansion of our activities should take place. There, over the next five years, with effective collaboration from the

African countries, we should increase our rate of investment threefold.

Further changes will flow from our shift to a greater emphasis on Africa and Latin America. The states of these two continents are smaller than the giants of Asia. There will be many more but smaller projects, demanding much more staff work per million dollars lent than in the past.

The work of the Bank will also be increased because in many of the countries in which we will now be investing, there is no well established Development Plan or Planning Organization. We shall try, in conjunction with other sources of funds, to help these countries to develop plans and to adopt wise and appropriate policies for development—in some cases by establishing resident missions as we have done in Indonesia—but always remembering that it is their country, their economy, their culture and their aspirations which we seek to assist.

In particular, we will exert special efforts to right one upside-down aspect of Bank Group operations: the fact that many of our poorest members, despite their greater need, have had the least technical and financial assistance from the Bank Group. About ten of these have had no loans or credits at all. This is largely because of their inability to prepare projects for consideration. In these cases we will provide special assistance to improve economic performance and to identify and prepare projects acceptable for Bank Group financing.

With the doubling of Bank Group lending and with the increase in the complexity of our operations, there will clearly be need for an increase in the total professional staff of the Bank, as well as for some streamlining of our procedures. We are now engaged in a worldwide recruiting drive to find people with the high standards of expertise and dedication that have always been the attributes of its staff. I am anxious that this should really be an International Bank, in fact as well as in name, and I intend to ensure that we move steadily in the direction of the widest possible distribution in the nationalities of our staff.

Not only should our lending double in volume and shift geographically, but we can foresee, as well, dramatic changes among sectors of investment. Great increases will occur in the sectors of Education and Agriculture.

Education is a relatively new field for the Bank on which my predecessor George Woods, with his wise sense of priorities, began to place increased emphasis. In recent years the Bank has been seeking, hesitantly but with a growing sense of urgency, to find its optimum role in this field.

We are aware of the immense numbers of illiterates in the developing world: about 30% in Latin America, 60% in Asia, 80% in tropical Africa. We know too that education is relevant to all aspects of development: it makes a more effective worker, a more creative manager, a better farmer, a more efficient administrator, a human being closer to self-fulfillment.

The need is clear, but it has been less clear how the Bank's resources can be brought to bear on this labyrinthine problem. Now, after some years of collaboration with Unesco, we believe we see a way ahead for increasing Bank investment in education —investment which we hope will call forth further investment by the government of the developing countries themselves.

Our aims here will be to provide assistance where it will contribute most to economic development. This will mean emphasis on educational planning—the starting point for the whole process of educational improvement. It will mean assistance, particularly in teacher training, at *all* levels, from primary to university. It will mean expansion of our support for a variety of other educational activities, including the training of managers, entrepreneurs and, of course, of agriculturalists.

It is important to emphasize that education, normally one of the largest employers in any country, is one of the few industries which has not undergone a technological revolution. We must help to move it out of the handicraft stage. With the terrible and growing shortage of qualified teachers all over the developing world we must find ways to make good teachers more productive. This will involve investment in textbooks, in audio-visual materials, and above all in the use of modern communications techniques (radio, film and television) for teaching purposes.

To carry out this program we would hope over the next five years to increase our lending for educational development at least threefold.

But the sector of greatest expansion in our five-year program is agriculture, which has for so long been the stepchild of development. Here again there has never been any doubt about its importance. About two-thirds of the people of the developing world live on the soil, yet these countries have to import annually $4 billion of food from the industrialized nations. Even then their diet is so inadequate, in many cases, that they cannot do an effective day's work and, more ominous still, there is growing scientific evidence that the dietary deficiencies of the parent are passed on as mental deficiencies to the children.

The need has stared us in the face for decades past. But how to help?

In the past, investment in agricultural improvement produced but a modest yield; the traditional seeds and plants did better with irrigation and fertilizer but the increase in yield was not dramatic. Now, as you know, research in the past 20 years has resulted in a breakthrough in the production of new strains of wheat and rice and other plants which can improve yields by three to five times. What is more, these new strains are particularly sensitive to the input of water and fertilizer; badly managed they will produce little more than the traditional plants, but with correct management they will give the peasant an unprecedented crop.

Here is an opportunity where irrigation, fertilizer and peasant education can produce miracles in the sight of the beholder. The farmer himself in one short season can see the beneficial results of that scientific agriculture which has seemed so often in the past to be a will-o'-the-wisp tempting him to innovation without benefit.

Our task now is to enable the peasant to make the most of this opportunity and we, with the continuing assistance of FAO, intend to do so at once and in good measure. Irrigation schemes, fertilizer plants, agricultural research and extension, the production of pesticides, agricultural machinery, storage facilities—with all of these we will press ahead in the immediate future. Indeed in the coming year we plan to process more than twice the value of agricultural loans as in the last, and our agricultural dollar loan volume over the next five years should quadruple.

There is an element of risk in all this, of course. The seeds were issued before all the tests had been completed; the resistance of the crops to local diseases or pests cannot yet be assured; the splendid harvests in India and Pakistan this year cannot all be attributed to the new seeds. But I have no doubt, though setbacks may lie ahead, that we are now on the brink of an agricultural revolution as significant as any development since the industrial revolution. It is one that gives us a breathing spell in the race between man and his resources.

This leads me to yet another area where the Bank needs to take new initiatives—the control of population growth. This is a thorny subject which it would be very much more convenient to leave alone. But I cannot, because the World Bank is concerned above all with economic development, and the rapid growth of population is one of the greatest barriers to the economic growth and social well-being of our member states.

This is the aspect of the population problem with which I shall deal, because it is this aspect which most closely concerns the World Bank and its members. It makes it impossible for any of us to brush the subject aside, however strong our inclinations to do so may be.

I do not need before this audience to deal with the terrifying statistics of population growth as a whole, which can best be appreciated in the context of a long perspective. Some 2 million years were required for the population of the world to reach 3 billion. At current growth rates, only 35 years will be required to add another 3 billion and, then, one billion will be added each eight years. Nor do I need to deal with the personal tragedies and dangers to health of unwanted births, though these were suddenly illuminated for me by an item in a newspaper last month which recorded that in the two largest cities of one European country live births were outnumbered by illegal abortions which imperiled the life of each unhappy mother.

As a development planner, I wish to deal only with the hard facts of population impact on economic growth. Recent studies show the crippling effect of a high rate of population increase on economic growth in any developing country. For example, take two typical developing countries with similar standards of living, each with a birth rate of 40 per thousand (this is the actual rate in India and Mexico) and estimate what would happen if the birth rate in one of those countries, in a period of 25 years, were to be halved to 20 per thousand, a rate still well above that in most developed countries. The country which lowered its population growth would raise its standard of living 40% above the other country in a single generation.

In terms of the gap between rich countries and poor, these studies show that more than anything else it is the population explosion which, by holding back the advancement of the poor, is blowing apart the rich and the poor and widening the already dangerous gap between them.

Furthermore these economic studies show that this drag of excessive population growth is quite independent of the density of population. This is something that needs emphasizing in view of the fact that many policy makers in the developing countries attach only minor importance to reducing population growth. It is a false claim that some countries need more population to fill their land or accelerate their economic growth. There are no vacant lands equipped with roads, schools, houses, and the tools of agricultural or industrial employment. Therefore, the people who are to fill those lands, before they can live at even the current low standard of living, must first eat up a portion of the present scarce supply of capital—it is this burden which defeats a nation's efforts to raise its standard of living by increasing its population.

No one can doubt then that very serious problems of population growth face most of the developing nations today; what are the chances of their being mastered by natural causes? The answer lies in understanding the nature of the population explosion. It is not caused by an increase in the birth rate, but by a dramatic drop in the death rate due mainly to medical advances. It is this death control which has created the present emergency, and I do not believe that anyone would wish to reintroduce pestilence—or any other of the four horsemen of the apocalypse—as a "natural" solution to the population problem.

We are, therefore, faced with the question of what action we at the Bank, as a Development Agency, should take to lift this burden from the backs of many of our members. I propose the following three courses:

First: to let the developing nations know the extent to which rapid population growth slows down their potential development, and that, in consequence, the optimum employment of the world's scarce development funds requires attention to this problem.

Second: to seek opportunities to finance facilities required by our member countries to carry out family planning programs.

Third: to join with others in programs of research to determine the most effective methods of family planning and of national administration of population control programs.

With these three proposals for immediate action, I hope we may contribute to the success of the U.N. system which is already working in this field, and to the well-being of the developing nations.

Gentlemen, I have spoken long enough. Let me conclude by saying that in the next few days, while we examine the innumerable and daunting problems which face you who exercise control over so much of the world's financial and economic power, I hope that none of us will yield to despair as we see how much there is to do, how little time in which to do it.

There is no cause for despair. There is every reason for hope. In the past few generations the world has created a productive machine which could abolish poverty from the face of the earth. As we lift up our eyes from contemplating our troubles, who can fail to see the immense prospects that lie ahead for all mankind, if we have but the wit and the will to use our capacity fully.

I am not despondent about the difficulties that lie ahead because I have faith in our ability to overcome them. That is why I have proposed a program of greatly increased activity by the World Bank Group, so that by taking a lead in development assistance we may encourage all those, rich and poor alike, who have begun to lose heart and slacken their pace.

If we in the Bank are able to double our effort, this could be the signal for others to rally again to the struggle, determined to use our overwhelming strength for the betterment of all mankind, and the fulfillment of the human spirit.

I am honored to be here tonight and delighted to have the opportunity to talk to the Inter-American Press Association which has done so much to preserve the freedom of the Press throughout the Americas.

This is my first speech away from Washington, and my first visit as President of the World Bank to Latin America. But the Bank is no stranger here.

- Twenty years ago it made its first loan ever for development in a less developed country. That loan was made in Chile to help finance electric power plants.

- Eleven years ago our newborn subsidiary, the International Finance Corporation, made its first investment in private industry. That was in an electrical equipment plant in Brazil.

- Seven years ago, just as the Alliance for Progress was beginning, the International Development Association—our concessionary loan affiliate—made its first credit to help build a road that would open for the first time almost one third of a nation. That was in Honduras.

The Bank, then, is not a newcomer here. It is a partner of long standing in the development efforts of this continent. But I am a newcomer. I have been at the Bank barely half a year, during which time I have tried to learn as much as I could about the 110 nations I serve as an international official.

I am responsible to them, and this responsibility requires me to study the development progress of our members and to comment frankly and objectively on it. This seems to me to be the first obligation of a good public servant.

On the one hand I must try to interpret our members' problems and prospects to those who provide the funds which we, in turn, re-lend. On the other hand, I am obliged to speak clearly about those courses of action which we believe best serve to promote economic and social development, and to speak frankly about our concern as to their progress.

Before coming on this trip I talked to many people about the prospects and problems, the hopes and fears, the achievements and failures of this area, the southern part of the Western Hemisphere. I found much solid achievement, many sound reasons for hope, and several causes for concern.

All over the hemisphere, the winds of social, political and economic change are blowing.

The past two decades have witnessed the laying down of impressive economic infrastructure. Throughout the region, new electric power plants, new roads and railroads, modern ports, improved systems of telecommunications, more productive farmlands, new industries large and small—testify to national resolve, to international cooperation, and to the resourcefulness of the entrepreneur. We at the World Bank are proud to have been associated with many of these achievements of your peoples.

All over Latin America there are signs too of a real public determination to improve the lot of the common man. In some countries land reform is gathering momentum; in many, education is being modernized and extended. In almost all nations, real efforts are being made for the first time to insure that all segments of the population contribute their fair share in taxes to the Government's need for development funds.

At the same time, those countries which still have open frontiers are pushing them back, settling new lands, using heretofore untapped resources. And in the great cities, there are bold experiments designed to make urban life more satisfying, more fulfilling, and more beautiful.

All this is of course only a beginning. There remains a very full agenda for action by our generation, and by generations yet to come. But there can be no denying the tremendous progress of the two decades past.

But I have seen also the dark side of the picture: the failures as well as the achievements, the unfinished business that still faces us and causes us concern.

- I am concerned that in recent decades Latin America has not fulfilled the promise of growth and modernization that prevailed at the beginning of this century.

- I am concerned that Latin American economies continue to be dependent on exports of raw materials, highly vulnerable to price and volume changes, while the world community has yet to devise a workable system for stabilizing commodity earnings.

- I am concerned that persistent destructive inflation continues to afflict several of Latin America's largest countries.

- I am concerned that Latin American industry has been confined to small national markets and that progress toward economic integration is slow.

- I am concerned by the rigidity of social systems in which the mass of the people is poor, few are rich, and there is little chance for the many to move upward from poverty.

- I am concerned about explosive population growth in most Latin American countries, growth which tends to drag down increases in per capita income, and to inhibit improvement in the lot of the individual.

- I am concerned that some countries whose development has lagged tend to blame external factors for their lack of progress. I do not underestimate the importance of these difficulties, but I do believe that the will to develop, and with it the adoption of sound domestic policies, can move mountains even in the face of difficult external conditions.

- I am concerned, deeply concerned, both as your servant and as a United States citizen, at the failure of the U.S. Congress to replenish the funds of the International Development Association, the source of low-interest, long-term loans so desperately needed by the poorest countries.

I cannot stress too strongly that my concerns as President of a World Development organization—for the Bank is more than a Bank, it is a Development Agency —include the shortcomings of the nations who are rich as well as the failings of those who are poor. But I do not despair. There are grounds for hope, solid grounds on which we can build together. We at the World Bank do not intend to sit back and lament. We intend to act, and act in partnership with you.

Last April when I came to the World Bank we began to study where we could and should direct our energies during the next five years. It is clear from that study that we can do far more, and with the help of our members we intend to do it.

In Latin America, I believe we should during the next five years lend at least twice as much as during the past five years—to go from about $350 million a year in loans in the past two years to between $700 and $800 million a year by 1972.

You well may ask: Can we obtain the funds to support such an increase? The answer is: Yes, I believe we can. In the past ninety days alone, the Bank has raised more funds by borrowing than in the whole of any single calendar year in its history.

When I stress that we plan to more than double our lending in Latin America, I do not want you to think our policy is simply more of the same. The change in quantity of loans will be accompanied by a change in emphasis as well.

We will continue and even accelerate the financing of basic infrastructure—roads, dams, power plants, etc. But we hope to do considerably more to promote efficient and diversified industrialization, to help bring Latin America forward to the stage where it can apply modern science and technology efficiently to every segment of its economic life.

And we intend to devote particular attention to two critically important sectors: to agriculture, long a neglected step-child of development, and to education which holds the keys to man's self-fulfillment.

The educational field is a relatively new one for the Bank in which we have slowly been feeling our way. We are concerned with the problem of illiteracy, but it is more than illiteracy that we seek to attack. Education is relevant to all aspects of development: it makes a more effective worker, a more creative manager, a better farmer, a more efficient administrator, a more complete human being.

Our purpose will be to provide educational assistance where it will contribute most directly to the development process. This will in some cases mean helping to plan the renovation of entire school systems, from primary to post-graduate levels. It will mean assistance in teacher training. It will mean expansion of our support for schools to train managers, entrepreneurs, technicians and agriculturalists. It will mean experimenting with different kinds of schools.

I hope that in our lending we can improve the efficiency of education, helping to alleviate the endemic shortage of qualified teachers by making good teachers more productive. This will involve investment in text books, in audiovisual materials and in the use of modern communications techniques (radio, film and television) for teaching purposes.

So far we have done very little lending for education in Latin America—only slightly more than $20 million during the last five years. In the next five, I believe we should increase this tenfold.

But the sector which will have an even greater dollar expansion during the next five years will be agriculture, on which so many Latin Americans depend for their livelihood. Some Latin American countries have long been famous for their leadership in various agricultural activities but many others lag behind, particularly in the production of foodstuffs for domestic consumption.

Our challenge is to help the campesino in the fields as well as the worker in the city and we intend to meet that challenge. Our objective is simple: to assist farmers, both large and small, to increase their production substantially. We will lend for irrigation systems, fertilizer plants, agricultural extension services, banks to provide farm credit, the improvement of livestock and of seed strains, pesticide production, agricultural machinery, and food processing and storage facilities.

Over the next two years we plan to more than double our agricultural lending in Latin America, and over the next five years to quadruple it.

This then is our resolve: to contribute in every way we can to the healthy growth of the nations of this hemisphere. At the same time, we ask you for renewed resolve to face your problems with realism, and to optimize the use of your own resources and those that come to you from outside.

- We ask for economic and social policies which will permit a more equitable distribution of the benefits from increases in production and productivity.

- We ask for effective measures to bring balanced growth without the risk of destructive inflation and repeated balance of payments crises.

- We ask for measures to promote stronger and more diversified export industries and to take advantage of large and expanding markets overseas.

- We ask restraint in expenditures for sophisticated military equipment which responds neither to internal nor external threats to national security.

- We ask a strengthening of regional ties that will encourage rational industrial growth, stimulate exports and promote co-operation in programs of education and regional development of physical facilities.

- We ask for a realistic appraisal of the effect of population growth in those countries where that growth is clearly holding back progress, and for an earnest effort to cope with this most difficult and complex problem of our times.

I fully appreciate that here I am entering on what Mr. Krieger Vasena, the Argentinian Minister of Economy and Labor, called at the recent meeting in Washington "highly controversial ground." I shall never fail to bear in mind his warning that we must act always for "the dignity of man."

I assure you that I tread this thorny path only because I am convinced that unrestrained population growth cripples economic growth, and thus in fact degrades the dignity of man by depriving him of the elementary essentials for a fuller, happier life.

The fact must be faced that rapid population growth is the greatest barrier to the economic progress and social well-being of the citizens of our member nations. And nowhere is population growing more rapidly than in Latin America. Between the Rio Grande and Cape Horn, a population of over 250 million is today experiencing the most explosive increase of any continental area in the world.

In 1900, Latin America had a population of 63 million people. It required 50 years to add the first 100 million; only 17 years to add the next 100 million. And by the end of the century, the population of Latin America will be increased by almost 400 million more to a total of nearly 650 million. It will be growing then at a rate of 100 million every 5 years.

It is not, at this stage, the absolute numbers that are most disturbing. The world can still carry a larger population. In this hemisphere it can be argued that some countries—including our host—have too few people. The deep trouble that we are in comes from the speed of growth. If population grows by 3 per cent a year, even an increase in gross national product of 4.7 per cent a year—the average for Latin American countries—leaves far too little for expanding a nation's capital structure, including that critical element in all development—the education of the young. The tidal wave of children swamps the school system, literally eats away the margin of saving, and inundates the labor market. No power on earth can ensure that there will be such rapid economic progress that all these children will grow up healthy, well educated and capable of taking their rightful place in a competitive world.

It is perhaps the most tragic irony of our time that better programs of public health, undertaken from wholly laudable and humanitarian motives, have unleashed the population explosion on the developing world. The spurt of population through the reduction of death rates has preceded modernization, and now obstructs it. If development efforts are to succeed—not development of such abstractions as "the economy" or "the state," but development of human beings, of individuals and families —we must put population policy at the center of our future strategy.

The emphasis to be placed in national policy on varying methods of population control is the responsibility of governments. The choice of methods is the inviolable right of parents. The World Bank is not attempting to dictate detailed policies.

But as a development agency, we must give priority to this problem, and we must ask that governments which seek our assistance do so too, and that they evolve a serious strategy for stabilizing the rate of population growth.

I see no alternative to our direct involvement in this crisis. Therefore:

- We will point out to our member countries the extent to which rapid population growth in itself slows down their development, and that this factor must be taken into account in the optimum employment of the world's development funds.

- We will join with others in assisting programs of research to determine the most effective methods of family planning and of national administration of population control programs.

- And we will seek opportunities to lend for population control programs to those of our member countries who seek such help.

Ladies and Gentlemen, I have spoken long enough. I have come before you not only to express concern but also to outline a basis of hope.

I have spoken not as a critic, looking at Latin America from a comfortable outside vantage point, but as a friend sharing your hopes and aspirations; and as your servant in helping to achieve them.

Eight years ago a man who profoundly influenced my own life had a vision. It came to be called the Alliance for Progress. It has faltered, perhaps, but it still exists. In his inaugural address President Kennedy spoke to the citizens of his own country about the world around them, saying, "If a free society cannot help the many who are poor, it cannot save the few who are rich."

I suggest that his words have equal meaning to you and to others who lead this hemisphere in thought and action.

Let us remember those words as we contemplate the future. Let us resolve to rekindle the flame of the Alli-

ance and make of it a burning torch for all the world
to see.

Let us take pride in the past; let us learn from our
mistakes; and let us join together for the great adventure that lies ahead.

THREE

To the
UNIVERSITY OF NOTRE DAME
NOTRE DAME, INDIANA
MAY 1,1969

I am grateful for this award, and pleased to become an honorary alumnus of Notre Dame.

This university, over the years, has become a catalytic center of creative thought. It does what universities do best: it probes. It probes the past for what is most relevant to the present. It probes the present for what is most formative of the future. And it probes the future for what will most enlarge man's freedom and fulfillment.

I want to discuss with you this afternoon a problem that arose out of that recent past; that already plagues man in the present; and that will diminish, if not destroy, much of his future—should he fail to face up to it, and solve it.

It is, by half a dozen criteria, the most delicate and difficult issue of our era—perhaps of any era in history. It is overlaid with emotion. It is controversial. It is subtle. Above all, it is immeasurably complex.

It is the tangled problem of excessive population growth.

It is not merely a problem, it is a paradox.

It is at one and the same time an issue that is intimately private —and yet inescapably public.

It is an issue characterized by reticence and circumspection— and yet in desperate need of realism and candor.

33

It is an issue intolerant of government pressure—and yet endangered by government procrastination.

It is an issue, finally, that is so hypersensitive—giving rise to such diverse opinion—that there is an understandable tendency simply to avoid argument, turn one's attention to less complicated matters, and hope that the problem will somehow disappear.

But the problem will not disappear.

What may disappear is the opportunity to find a solution that is rational and humane.

If we wait too long, that option will be overtaken by events.

We cannot afford that. For if there is anything certain about the population explosion, it is that if it is not dealt with reasonably, it will in fact explode: explode in suffering, explode in violence, explode in inhumanity.

All of us are, of course, concerned about this.

You, here at Notre Dame, have been giving constructive attention to this concern for several years. And yet it may seem strange that I should speak at a center of Catholic thought on this awkward issue which might so conveniently be ignored, or left to demographers to argue.

I have chosen to discuss the problem because my responsibilities as President of the World Bank compel me to be candid about the blunt facts affecting the prospects for global development.

The bluntest fact of all is that the need for development is desperate.

One-third of mankind today lives in an environment of relative abundance.

But two-thirds of mankind—more than two billion individuals—remain entrapped in a cruel web of circumstances that severely limits their right to the necessities of life. They have not yet been able to achieve the transition to self-sustaining economic growth. They are caught in the grip of hunger and malnutrition; high illiteracy; inadequate education; shrinking opportunity; and corrosive poverty.

The gap between the rich and poor nations is no longer merely a gap. It is a chasm. On one side are nations of the West that enjoy per capita incomes in the $3,000 range. On the other are nations in Asia and Africa that struggle to survive on per capita incomes of less than $100.

What is important to understand is that this is not a static situation. The misery of the underdeveloped world is today a dynamic misery, continuously broadened and deepened by a population growth that is totally unprecedented in history.

This is why the problem of population is an inseparable part of the larger, overall problem of development.

There are some who speak as if simply having fewer people in the world is some sort of intrinsic value in and of itself. Clearly, it is not.

But when human life is degraded by the plague of poverty, and that poverty is transmitted to future generations by too rapid a growth in population, then one with responsibilities in the field of development has no alternative but to deal with that issue.

To put it simply: the greatest single obstacle to the economic and social advancement of the majority of the peoples in the underdeveloped world is rampant population growth.

Having said that, let me make one point unmistakably clear: the solution of the population problem is in no way a substitute for the more traditional forms of developmental assistance: aid for economic infrastructure; aid for agriculture; aid for indus-trialization; aid for education; aid for technological advance.

The underdeveloped world needs investment capital for a whole gamut of productive projects. But nothing would be more unwise than to allow these projects to fail because they are finally overwhelmed by a tidal wave of population.

Surely, then, it is appropriate that we should attempt to un-ravel the complexities that so confuse this critical issue.

II

One can begin with the stark demographic dimensions. The dynamics are deceivingly simple. Population increase is simply the excess of births over deaths. For most of man's history the two have been in relative equilibrium. Only in the last century have they become seriously unbalanced.

Though the figures are well known, they are worth repeating —if for no other reason than to forestall the familiarity with unpleasant facts from cloaking itself with complacency. It required sixteen hundred years to double the world population of 250 million, as it stood in the first century A.D. Today, the more than three billion on earth will double in 35 years time, and the world's population will then be increasing at the rate of an additional billion every eight years.

To project the totals beyond the year 2000 becomes so demanding on the imagination as to make the statistics almost incomprehensible.

A child born today, living on into his seventies, would know a world of 15 billion. His grandson would share the planet with 60 billion.

In six and a half centuries from now—the same insignificant period of time separating us from the poet Dante—there would be one human being standing on every square yard of land on earth: a fantasy of horror that even the *Inferno* could not match.

Such projections are, of course, unreal. They will not come to pass because events will not permit them to come to pass.

Of that we can be certain.

What is not so certain is precisely what those events will be. They can only be: mass starvation; political chaos; or population planning.

Whatever may happen after the year 2000, what is occurring right now is enough to jolt one into action.

India, for example, is adding a million people a month to its population—and this in spite of the oldest family-planning program in Southeast Asia.

The Philippines currently has a population of 37 million. There is no authorized government family-planning program. At the present rate of growth, these limited islands—in a brief 35 years—would have to support over one hundred million human beings.

The average population growth of the world at large is 2%. Many underdeveloped countries are burdened with a rate of 3½% or more. A population growing at 1% doubles itself in 70 years; at 2% it doubles in 35 years; at 3½% it doubles in only 20 years.

Now, if we are to reject mass starvation and political chaos as solutions to this explosive situation, then there are clearly only three conceivable ways in which a nation can deliberately *plan* to diminish its rate of population growth: to increase the death rate; to step up the migration rate; or to reduce the birth rate.

No one is in favor of the first choice. On the contrary, under the impact of public health programs, death rates are falling throughout the underdeveloped areas. Even simple medical improvements—better sanitation, malaria suppression, widespread vaccination—bring on a rapid and welcome decline in mortality. The low-level death rates which Europe required a century and a half to achieve are now being accomplished in the emerging areas in a fifth of that time.

The second choice is wholly inadequate. Increased migration, on any scale significant enough to be decisive, is simply not practical. Countries concerned about their own future crowding are understandably disinclined to add to it by accepting more than a limited number of foreigners. But the more important point is that the continually expanding increment, on a global basis, is already so massive that migration as a solution to population pressure is manifestly unrealistic. We can put a man on the moon. But we cannot migrate by the millions off our own planet.

That leaves the third choice: a humane and rational reduction of the birth rate.

Is it feasible? It is.

Is it simple? It is not.

Is it necessary? Without question.

It is necessary because the consequences of continuing the present population growth rates are unacceptable.

III

Let us examine those consequences.

One cannot sense the inner significance of the cold, remote, impersonal demographic data by merely tracing a line upward on a graph, or by scanning the print-out from a computer.

The consequences of rapid population growth—piled on top of an already oppressive poverty—must be grasped in all their concrete, painful reality.

The first consequence can be seen in the gaunt faces of hungry men.

One half of humanity is hungering at this very moment. There is less food per person on the planet today than there was 30 years ago in the midst of a worldwide depression.

Thousands of human beings will die today—as they die every day—of that hunger. They will either simply starve to death, or they will die because their diet is so inadequate that it cannot protect them from some easily preventable disease.

Most of those thousands of individuals—individuals whose intrinsic right to a decent life is as great as yours or mine—are children. They are not mere statistics. They are human beings. And they are dying; now; at this very moment; while we are speaking.

They are not your children. Or my children. But they are someone's children. And they are dying needlessly.

And yet the thousands who die are perhaps the more fortunate ones. For millions of other children, suffering the same malnutrition, do not die. They live languidly on—stunted in their bodies, and crippled in their minds.

The human brain reaches 90% of its normal structural development in the first four years of life. We now know that during that critical period of growth, the brain is highly vulnerable to nutritional deficiencies: deficiencies that can cause as much as 25% impairment of normal mental ability. Even a deterioration of 10% is sufficient to cause a serious handicap to productive life.

This is irreversible brain damage.

What is particularly tragic in all of this is that when such mentally deprived children reach adulthood, they are likely to repeat the whole depressing sequence in their own families. They perpetuate mental deficiency, not through genetic inheritance; but simply because as parents they are ill-equipped mentally to understand, and hence to avoid the very nutritional deprivations in their own children that they themselves suffered.

Thus hunger and malnutrition forge a chain of conditions that only spiral the total human performance dismally downward. Alertness, vitality, energy, the ability to learn, the desire to succeed, the will to exert an effort—all these inestimable human qualities drain away.

How many children today are caught up in this crisis? How many of them subsist at levels of hunger and malnutrition that risk their being irreversibly mentally retarded for the rest of their lives? Some three hundred million.

But the population explosion's corrosive effects on the quality of life do not end with hunger. They range through the whole spectrum of human deprivation. With entire national populations, already caught up in the dilemmas of development, now doubling in as short a time as 20 years, there is a chronic insufficiency of virtually every necessity.

Current birth rates throughout the emerging world are seriously crippling developmental efforts. It is imperative to understand why. The intractable reason is that these governments must divert an inordinately high proportion of their limited national savings away from productive investment simply in order to maintain the current low level of existence.

Each additional child brought into the world must not only be fed, but clothed, housed, medically cared for, and supported by at least minimal educational services. All of this requires new capital—new capital that cannot be invested in other desperately needed sectors of the economy. For approximately the first 15 years of their lives, children cannot contribute economically to the nation: simply because they are young they are consumers rather than producers.

If the number of children in the total population—as a result of high birth rates— is very large, a nation is under the compelling necessity to expend ever greater resources simply to keep its people from slipping beneath minimum subsistence levels. A treadmill economy tends to emerge in which the total national effort will exhaust itself in running faster and faster merely to stand still.

More and more classrooms must be built; more and more teachers must be provided; more and more vocational training facilities must be established. But despite all this effort both the quantity and quality of education will inevitably decline. It simply cannot keep pace with the mounting waves of children. Thus, one of the prime movers of all human development—education—is sacrificed.

Further, as ill-educated, perhaps wholly illiterate, children reach the age when they ought to become producers in the economy, they are engulfed by the hopelessness of underemployment. In many of the world's shanty towns 50 to 60% of the adolescents are out of work.

Not only are these youngsters unequipped for the jobs that might have been available, but the total number of meaningful jobs itself tends to decline in proportion to the population simply because the government has been unable to invest adequately in job-producing enterprises. The capital that ought to have been invested was simply not available. It was dissipated by the ever rising tide of additional children.

This, then, is the cruel and self-perpetuating dilemma that governments face in underdeveloped countries overburdened for long periods with high birth rates.

Their plans for progress evaporate into massive efforts merely to maintain the status quo.

But what is true at the national level is repeated with even greater poignancy on the personal family level. Millions of individual families wish to avoid unwanted pregnancies.

And when these families cannot find legal and compassionate assistance in this matter, they often turn to desperate and illegal measures.

Statistics suggest that abortion is one of the world's most commonly chosen methods to limit fertility—despite the fact that in most societies it is ethically offensive, illegal, expensive, and medically hazardous.

In five countries of western Europe, it is estimated that there are as many illegal abortions as live births.

In India, the estimate is that each month a quarter of a million women undergo illegal abortion.

In Latin America, illegal abortion rates are among the highest in the world. In one country, they are said to total three times the live birth rate; in another, to be the cause of two out of every five deaths of pregnant women. Further, there are indications that the illegal abortion rate in Latin America is increasing, and that multiple illegal abortions among mothers are becoming common.

The tragic truth is that illegal abortion is endemic in many parts of the world. And it is particularly prevalent in those areas where there is no adequate, organized family-planning assistance.

The conclusion is clear: where the public authorities will not assist parents to avoid unwanted births, the parents will often take matters into their own hands—at whatever cost to conscience or health.

IV

Now I have noted that this entire question of population planning is incredibly complex. There are, of course, certain precise and painful moral dilemmas. But quite apart from these, there is a vague and murky mythology that befogs the issue. Not only does this collection of myths obscure the essentials of the problem, but worse still, it builds barriers to constructive action.

I should like to turn now to that mythology, and examine some of its more irrational premises.

There is, to begin with, the generalized assumption that somehow "more people means more wealth." As with all fallacies, there is a deceptive substratum of plausibility to the thesis. With the earlier rise of nationalism in the West—and the more recent emergence of newly independent countries in Asia and Africa —rapid population growth has often been regarded as a symbol of national vigor. It provided, so it was believed, the foundations of a more powerful military establishment; an economically advantageous internal market; a pool of cheap labor; and, in general, a prestigious political place in the sun.

But in the underdeveloped world, nearly every one of these assumptions is false. Because rapid population growth tends seriously to retard growth in per capita income, the developing nation soon discovers that its economic vigor is diminished rather than enhanced by the phenomenon of high fertility. The hoped-for internal market becomes a mere mass of discontented indigents, without purchasing power but with all the frustrations of potential consumers whose expectations cannot be met.

"Cheap labor" in such countries turns out not to be cheap at all. For sound economic growth requires technological improvements, and these in turn demand higher levels of training than the strained government resources can supply. Though individual workers may be paid lower salaries than their counterparts abroad, their efficiency and productiveness are so low that the nation's goods are often priced out of the competitive export market. The "cheap" labor turns out to be excessively expensive labor.

Even the argument of expanding the population in order to provide a powerful military force is suspect—not merely because the expansion of one nation's forces will, in time, lead to a reactive expansion of its neighbors' forces, but also because modern defense forces require an increasing ratio of educated recruits rather than mere masses of illiterate troops.

As for political prestige, nations caught in the catastrophe of an uncontrolled population growth do not enhance their position in the family of nations. On the contrary, they find it slipping away as their once optimistic plans for progress turn inevitably to the politics of confrontation and extremism.

Akin to the myth that "more people means more wealth" is the notion that countries with large tracts of uninhabited open land have no need to worry about birth rates, since there is ample room for expansion.

The argument is as shallow as it is misleading. For the patent fact is that mere open land does not, in and of itself, support a high rate of population growth. Such open land—if it is to become the home of large numbers of people—must be provided with a whole panoply of heavy government investments: investments in roads, housing, sanitation, agricultural and industrial development.

The sound economic argument is quite the other way round. What such raw space requires first is not surplus people, but surplus funds for investment. And it is precisely surplus people in a developing economy that make the accumulation of surplus funds so incredibly difficult.

What is equally overlooked is that a rational restraint on fertility rates in an emerging country never implies an absolute reduction of the total population. It simply hopes for a more reasonable balance between birth and death rates. And since death rates in the future are certain to drop with continued advances in medicine—and in highly underdeveloped countries the drop in the death rate is characteristically precipitous—there are no grounds whatever for fearing that a nation's population, under the influence of family planning, will dangerously ebb away. The danger is quite the opposite: that even with family planning—should it be inadequately utilized—the population will proliferate in the future to self-defeating levels.

A still more prevalent myth is the misapprehension that official programs of family planning in a developing country are wholly unnecessary since the very process of development itself automatically leads to lowered birth rates. The experience of Europe is cited as persuasive proof of this theory.

But the proof is no proof at all, for the theory is hopelessly irrelevant to today's conditions in the underdeveloped world. There are no comparable circumstances between what happened in Europe's early period of modernization, and what is happening in the emerging world today.

Aside from a lapse of logic which fails to grasp that the current population growth in these areas inhibits the very economic development which is supposed to curb that growth, the historical fact is that conditions in Europe during its initial developmental period were far more favorable to lower rates of population growth. The birth rates were much lower than they are in the underdeveloped world today, the death rates had not yet drastically fallen, and by the time public health measures had accomplished that, the infrastructure of industrialization was already in place.

Further, in nineteenth century Europe, unlike in the developing countries today, marriages were entered into later, and the level of literacy—always an important factor affecting population growth—was considerably higher.

Even in spite of all these advantages, it required some 70 years for Europe to reduce its birth rates to present levels. Today the average birth rate for developing countries is 40 to 45 per 1000 of population. To get this rate down to the 17 to 20 per 1000 that is common in contemporary Europe would require a reduction in the developing world of some 50 million births a year. To suppose that economic advancement by itself—without the assistance of well organized family planning—could accomplish this in any feasible time-frame of the future is wholly naive.

Indeed, even with family planning, no such promising results are feasible in less than two or three decades. What is feasible —indeed what is imperative—is the establishment of family planning on a scale that will stave off total economic and political disintegration in those countries where social progress is being seriously limited by the glut of unwanted births.

No government can, of course, ultimately succeed in convincing its own population to undertake family planning, if parents themselves do not really want it.

But the almost universal fact is that parents do want it. They often want it far more than their own political leaders comprehend.

People—particularly poor, ill-educated people—may not understand the techniques of family planning. Most of them have only the most tenuous understanding of human biology. Often their limited comprehension is tragically confused by gross misinformation.

But the notion that family-planning programs are sinister, coercive plots to force poor people into something they really do not want, is absurd.

The pervasive prevalence of voluntary illegal abortion should be enough to dispel that fiction.

The poor do not always know how to limit their families in less drastic and dangerous ways, but there is overwhelming evidence that they would like to know how.

Another serious misunderstanding is the fear that family planning in the developing world would inevitably lead to a breakdown of familial moral fiber—and that it would encourage parents to limit the number of their children for essentially frivolous and selfish reasons: that it would trade the responsibility of having a large number of children for the opportunity of acquiring the needless gadgetry of an advancing consumer economy.

But one stroll through the slums of any major city in the developing world is enough to dispel that concept. If anything is threatening the fiber of family life it is the degrading conditions of subsistence survival that one finds in these sprawling camps of packing crates and scrap metal. Children on the streets instead of in non-existent classrooms. Broken men—their pride shattered—without work. Despondent mothers—often unmarried—unable to cope with exhaustion because of annual pregnancies. And all of this in a frustrating environment of misery and hunger and hopelessness. These are not the conditions that promote an ethically fibered family life.

Family planning is not designed to destroy families. On the contrary, it is designed to save them.

All of us accept the principle that in a free society, the parents themselves must ultimately decide the size of their own family. We would regard it as an intolerable invasion of the family's rights for the State to use coercive measures to implement population policy. We can preserve that right best by assisting families to understand how they can make that decision for themselves.

The fact is that millions of children are born without their parents desiring that it happen. Hence, a free, rational choice for an additional child is not made in these cases. If we are to keep the right of decision in the hands of the family—where it clearly belongs—then we must give the family the knowledge and assistance it requires to exercise that right.

Nor need anyone be deterred from appropriate action by the pernicious, if pervasive, myth that the white western world's assistance in family planning efforts among the non-white nations of the developing areas is a surreptitious plot to keep the whites in a racial ascendancy. The myth is absurd on purely demographic grounds, as well as on many others. Non-white peoples on the planet massively outnumber whites. They always have and always will. No conceivable degree of family planning could possibly alter that mathematical fact.

But a more relevant answer is that if the white world actually did desire to plot against the non-white nations, one of the most effective ways possible to do so would be for the whites to deny these nations any assistance whatever in family planning. For the progressive future of the non-white world is directly related to their indigenous economic development—and that, in turn, as we have seen, is dependent upon their being able to bring birth rates down to a level that will allow a significant increase in per capita income.

V

There is one more myth that obstructs the road to action. It is the belief that the time for decisive action is past, and that sweeping famine is inevitable.

The distinguished British scientist and novelist, C. P. Snow, has recently noted that it is the view of men of sober judgment that "many millions of people in the poor countries are going to starve to death before our eyes."

"We shall see them doing so," he adds, "upon our television sets."

He stresses that when the collision between food and population takes place, "at best, this will mean local famines to begin with. At worst, the local famines will spread into a sea of hunger. The usual date predicted for the beginning of the local famines is 1975-80."

In summing up his own view, he suggests that "The major catastrophe will happen before the end of the century. We shall, in the rich countries, be surrounded by a sea of famine, involving hundreds of millions of human beings."

"The increase of population," he predicts, "all over the rich world may get a little less. In the poor world it won't, except in one or two pockets. Despite local successes, as in India, the food-population collision will duly occur. The attempts to prevent it, or meliorate it, will be too feeble. Famine will take charge in many countries. It may become, by the end of the period, endemic famine. There will be suffering and desperation on a scale as yet unknown."

Now, though Lord Snow is a brilliant and perceptive man of good will, I simply do not believe that one need feel quite so near despair—even in the face of a situation as ominous as this one.

Wholesale famine is not inevitable. I am convinced that there is time to reverse the situation, if we will but use it. Only barely sufficient time. But time nevertheless.

It is the time which has been given us by those who have created the revolution in agricultural technology: a revolution based on new seeds, hybrid strains, fertilizers, and the intensified use of natural resources.

It is a revolution which already has increased the yields of food grains by more than 100% in parts of Southeast Asia, and which promises to boost yields by one-half ton per acre throughout Asia. It is a revolution which has expanded the number of acres sown with the new seeds from 200 in 1965 to 20,000,000 in 1968—and an estimated 34,000,000 in 1969—but which has yet to touch more than a small percentage of the rice and wheat-producing acreage of the world.

If we will but speed the spread of this agricultural revolution —by adequate and properly administered technical and financial assistance to the developing countries—we can expect that for the next two decades the world's food supply will grow at a faster rate than its population.

The predicted spectre of famine can be averted.

It will take immense energy and organizing skill, and significant infusions of new capital investment—but it is possible to stave off disaster.

What is required to accomplish this is not so much a psychologically comforting optimism, as an energetic, creative realism.

I believe enough of that realism exists among men of good will—both in the developed and in the emerging world—to do the job.

This is the fundamental reason I do not share Lord Snow's degree of discouragement.

There is no point whatever in being naively over-optimistic about a situation as full of peril as the population problem.

But I am confident that application of the new technology will dramatically expand the rate of agricultural growth and will buy two decades of time—admittedly the barest minimum of time—required to cope with the population explosion, and reduce it to manageable proportions.

VI

How can this best be done?

To begin with, the developed nations must give every measure of support they possibly can to those countries which have already established family-planning programs. Many have. The governments of India, Pakistan, Korea, Taiwan, Hong Kong, and Singapore have established both policies and specific targets for reducing population growth rates and have shown some measurable progress.

Ceylon, Malaysia, Turkey, Tunisia, the United Arab Republic, Morocco, Kenya, Mauritius, Chile, Honduras, Barbados, and Jamaica are giving government support to family-planning programs, but need substantial technical or financial assistance before any significant reduction in birth rates can occur.

Some 20 other governments are considering family-planning programs.

In other countries, where governments are only dimly aware of the dangers of the population problem—but would like, nevertheless, to ponder the matter—the developed nations can quietly assist by helping with the demographic and social studies that will reveal the facts and thus point up the urgency of the issue, and the disadvantages of delay.

It is essential, of course, to recognize the right of a given country to handle its population problem in its own way. But handle it, it must.

The developed nations can point out the demographic facts; can explain the economic realities; can warn of the consequences of procrastination. They can—and should—inform. They should not—and cannot—pressure.

Technologically advanced countries can make one of their greatest contributions by initiating a new order of intensity in research into reproductive biology. They have starved their research facilities of funds in this field. The result is that we are still only on the threshold of understanding the complexities of conception, and therefore only at the outer edge of the necessary knowledge to help make family planning in the developing countries beneficial on a meaningful scale.

Annual worldwide expenditures for research in reproductive biology now total roughly 50 million dollars. The hardheaded estimate is that the sum should treble to 150 million dollars annually—for the next ten years—if we are to develop the knowledge necessary for the most effective and acceptable kinds of family planning.

Our parsimony in this matter in the United States is illustrated by the discouraging fact that out of a total budget of nearly one billion dollars, the National Institutes of Health this year are spending less than ten million dollars for research in population-related phenomena. Hundreds of millions of dollars for death control. Scarcely 1% of that amount for fertility control.

And research efforts should range far beyond biology.

Demography, as a fully developed science, remains in its infancy. It is likely that fewer than half the world's births are even registered. And while the crude estimates of birth rates almost inevitably turn out to be too low, it is essential that more precise data be developed in those areas where the population problem is the most acute.

Similarly, there is a pressing need for far more research in the socio-cultural aspects of family planning. There is manifestly a great deal more to population planning than merely birth control. Attitudes, motivation, preferences differ from country to country, and this essential research can clearly best be conducted locally. The developed nations should be generous in their financial support for such studies and surveys.

Above all else, there is a need to develop a realistic sense of urgency in all countries over the population problem.

Programs are beginning to show progress in limited areas. But no reduction in birth rates has yet been achieved anywhere in the underdeveloped areas which can significantly affect overall world population totals.

This means that family planning is going to have to be undertaken on a humane but massive scale. Other massive efforts in our century—for example, in the field of public health—have been mounted and have been successful. And granted all the difficulties, there is no insuperable reason this one cannot be.

The threat of unmanageable population pressures is very much like the threat of nuclear war.

Both threats are undervalued. Both threats are misunderstood.

Both threats can—and will—have catastrophic consequences unless they are dealt with rapidly and rationally.

The threat of violence is intertwined with the threat of undue population growth. It is clear that population pressures in the underdeveloped societies can lead to economic tensions, and political turbulence: stresses in the body politic which in the end can bring on conflicts among nations.

Such violence must not be allowed to happen.

You and I—and all of us—share the responsibility of taking those actions necessary to assure that it will not happen.

There is no point in despair.

There is every point simply in getting busy with the job. That is surely what God gave us our reason and our will for: to get on with the tasks which must be done.

I do not have to convince you of that here at Notre Dame.

You, and the Roman Catholic Church at large, are completely dedicated to the goal of development. One has only to read the Second Vatican Council's *Pastoral Constitution on the Church in the Modern World,* and Pope Paul's *Populorum Progressio* to understand that. Both these impressive documents call for a solution to the population problem as it relates to development. Such controversy as remains in this matter is merely about the means, not at all about the end.

I am confident that you in this university, and those in the Catholic community that reaches out around the globe, and the fatherly and compassionate Pontiff who stands at your helm —as well as men everywhere of whatever religious allegiance— I am confident that all of us are dedicated to that end however much we may disagree on the specifics of the means.

The end desired by the Church—and by all men of good will —is the enhancement of human dignity. That, after all, is what development is all about.

And human dignity is severely threatened by the population explosion—more severely, more completely, more certainly threatened than it has been by any catastrophe the world has yet endured.

There is time—just barely time—to escape that threat.

We can, and we must, act.

What we must comprehend is this: the population problem *will* be solved one way or the other. Our only fundamental option is whether it is to be solved rationally and humanely—or irrationally and inhumanely. Are we to solve it by famine? Are we to solve it by riot, by insurrection, by the violence that desperately starving men can be driven to? Are we to solve it by wars of expansion and aggression? Or are we to solve it rationally, humanely—in accord with man's dignity?

There is so little time left to make the decision. To make no decision would be to make the worst decision of all. For to ignore this problem is only to make certain that nature will take catastrophic revenge on our indecisiveness.

Providence has placed you and me—and all of us—at that fulcrum-point in history where a rational, responsible, moral solution to the population problem must be found.

You and I—and all of us—share the responsibility, to find and apply that solution.

If we shirk that responsibility, we will have committed the crime.

But it will be those who come after us who will pay the undeserved . . . and the unspeakable . . . penalties.

FOUR

To
THE BOND CLUB
OF
NEW YORK
NEW YORK, NEW YORK
MAY 14, 1969

Because this is the center of the financial community of a nation which holds nearly 50% of the funded debt of the World Bank, I am delighted to have this opportunity to discuss with you our plans for the future lending operations of the Bank, and the relationship between those plans and our borrowing program.

I want to begin by emphasizing a point that my predecessors Eugene Black and George Woods made over and over again: the World Bank is not only a financial institution—it is a development agency. I accepted my present position with the Bank because I believe that the development of the emerging world is one of the biggest and the most important tasks confronting mankind in this century.

But having said that, I must make equally clear that the World Bank is a development *investment* institution, not a philanthropic organization and not a social welfare agency.

Our lending policy is founded on two basic principles: the project must be sound; and the borrower must be creditworthy.

We simply will not make a loan unless both these criteria can be met—and met completely.

We insist that the investment project itself have a demon-strably high economic return and be directly related to the de-velopment of the country in which it is located. And we insist further that the total economy of the borrowing nation be capa-ble of repaying our loan, and meeting the interest and other charges—on schedule, and in full.

These have been the World Bank's criteria from the very beginning. They are its criteria today. They are going to remain its criteria in the future.

The fact is that with more than twenty years of accumulated experience, the Bank's appraisal of the technological feasibility and the economic value of new investment projects is today more sound, more searching, and more sophisticated than it has ever been.

As for the creditworthiness of our clients, I am fully aware that certain countries face mounting problems of debt manage-ment. Past burdens can tend to depress future ability to meet new obligations. We have initiated, therefore, a special study of this problem to ensure that we lend only where there is a firm basis for repayment.

Our studies of creditworthiness are not just passive examina-tions of how a country is managing its economic affairs. They are increasingly designed to make specific suggestions on how policies and programs can be improved. As you well know, changes in economic policies—once accomplished—can work near miracles in improving the creditworthiness of a country.

But although the World Bank will continue to lend only on the financial principles of sound projects and creditworthy cli-ents, I am convinced that within the limits of those principles we can and should greatly expand our lending program, if we are to fulfill our obligations to our member states.

Let me explain why.

First, I want to emphasize that what I am discussing here is the IBRD arm of the World Bank Group. It is essentially a "hard lender." There are, of course, countries that are in desperate need of development capital, but which simply cannot qualify for "hard" loans. As far as the World Bank Group is concerned, their capital requirements must be met by our International Development Association.

But that is not what I am describing here.

I am talking about our "hard-loan" operations and the issue is this: do the developing countries need more of these hard loans, and is the Bank able to make them?

Based on the most careful analysis, my colleagues and I are convinced the answer to both questions is yes.

If one looks around the globe today, it is obvious the world is characterized by an expanding economy. The industrially advanced nations are, of course, the leading edge of this surge of progress. But there are a number of developing nations as well —countries such as Malaysia and Mexico, for example—which are experiencing dramatic economic growth under the infusion of modern management, new technology, and development capital.

In the field of agriculture, we have the beginnings of a revolutionary breakthrough on our hands. The massive improvement in wheat and rice cultivation in Southeast Asia is momentous. It is no mere freak of good weather or lucky conditions. It is a carefully planned program of new seeds, intensive use of fertilizer, and modern soil and water management. The green revolution is not simply a grab bag of miscellaneous farm techniques. It is a complete and coordinated agricultural technology. If we can succeed in marrying this technology to new programs of agricultural credit and marketing, we can definitely arrest the spread of famine that threatens the world's exploding population.

Nor is it in agriculture alone that economic opportunity is strong. Both Taiwan and Korea, for example, have recently achieved annual increases in industrial production of 15%, and in industrial exports of 25%. This is economic expansion at an extraordinary rate, and suggests that the modernization of Japan over a few decades may not have been an isolated phenomenon.

These nations, and many others like them, all require development capital: capital to expand the irrigation systems, capital to build the fertilizer plants, capital to construct the storage facilities—capital to turn the immense agricultural potential into a self-sustaining reality. And they require comparable capital to stimulate and bring to the takeoff point their indigenous industrial production.

The facts, then, are clear. Capital requirements throughout the developing world have not diminished; they have expanded. The opportunities for high-return investment have mounted almost everywhere. As in the past, 85% of the new capital required will come out of the savings of the developing countries themselves. But that 85% will remain ineffectual without the other 15%, which is the irreducible foreign-exchange component these countries must borrow from abroad.

The irony is that just at the very moment when the opportunities for productive investment of external capital are expanding, the flow of that capital—particularly from the United States—has begun to shrink.

Why it is shrinking is a complicated story which we need not pursue today, beyond noting that there are two important assumptions at work here which are clearly erroneous. One is that the richer countries can no longer afford to supply capital abroad; and the second is that even if they could afford it, it would be unwise, since the overall record of developmental investment is a dismal picture of waste, incompetence, and failure.

These popular conceptions are simply not factual. But the more important point is this: how can we deal with a paradoxical situation in which significant opportunities for prudent investment in the developing world have increased, and yet in which the flow of investment funds has flagged rather than quickened.

The World Bank, just over a year ago, initiated a series of studies to determine what ought to be done about that paradox. When all the data had been sifted and thoroughly examined, the conclusion was compelling.

Our studies demonstrated beyond any question that over the next five years the demand of the developing countries for hard loans—on standards as high, or even higher than in the past—would expand substantially.

Though one could not predict with absolute precision what the new investment opportunities—when matched against the Bank's lending criteria—would justify in total lending year by year, the estimate was that it would warrant an increase, for a five-year period, of at least 100%. It seemed reasonable that the Bank could and should embark on such a course.

This is a lending program which is specifically designed to help countries improve their economic performance. Indeed, it is a program designed to improve the economic performance of the world as a whole.

But the lending program is, of course, only one side of the coin. If we were to double our lending, we clearly had to borrow more. Further, we wanted to try to improve our liquidity. In recent years the Bank's balances of cash and liquid securities had been drawn down by about $400 million, because of the difficulties of borrowing in world capital markets. To increase the flexibility of our operations, we needed to reverse that process if possible.

Was the five-year target of a 100% increase in loans, plus the desired increase in liquidity, practical in terms of our bond sales?

In broad terms, what we were proposing to do was to increase the lending of the IBRD from an annual average of some $800 million to over twice that amount, and add, in addition, a half billion dollars to our cash reserves. This would require net borrowing of about $600 million a year, which—even if it were all in long-term securities, and it is not—would amount to less than 1% of the long-term funds raised in the capital markets of the industrialized countries.

That did not seem to us then—nor does it seem to us now—an unrealistically large amount of borrowing on the worldwide capital market.

What is important to remember is that one of the principal advantages of the World Bank is that it can raise money in any member country which can provide convertible currency. This means the Bank can spread its financing throughout a large number of nations.

What we have done in recent months is to look for new sources of funds. And we have found them. We have found them, for instance, in Saudi Arabia and Kuwait. Even more importantly, we have found them in the one country with a burgeoning balance of payments surplus: The Federal Republic of Germany.

Within Germany, we have tapped a totally new source of finance for the IBRD. It is the Westdeutsche Landesbank, a clearing institution for more than 250 savings banks, with nearly 3000 branches. This is now the largest bank in the Federal Republic. It has assets of approximately $7 billion. Moreover, this institution places our bonds in other savings banks in Germany. The deposits of all these institutions total some $26 billion. During the last nine months we have placed $200 million of our bonds through the Westdeutsche Landesbank while continuing to market public issues through the syndicate managed by our long-time underwriters, the Deutsche Bank.

In the same period we have made increased use of the Central Banks of the world. Sixty-five of these institutions hold over $1 billion of our debt—approximately 25% of the total. They have increased their holdings during the current fiscal year, and there is every indication that they will continue to increase them in the future.

It should not be surprising that our securities enjoy so high a rating. The combination of assets and guarantees which provides their intrinsic strength is wholly unique:

- A portfolio of loans for projects which bring high economic returns to the borrower—returns which can run as high as 100% and which average well over 10% per year;

- A guarantee of 100% repayment of each loan by the government of the country in which the project is located;

- Cash and liquid security balances, in fully convertible currencies, equal to about 45% of the outstanding Bank debt;

- Paid-in capital and retained earnings amounting to 90% of our debt;

- All this, plus uncalled capital subscriptions backing the debt and equal to some 500% of the amount outstanding.

No other bond in the world offers that kind of security. And it is precisely because of the strength of that security—and our stated determination to maintain that strength—that we have been able to place our recent bond issues at extremely favorable rates. An issue of World Bank bonds, with 8 to 15 year maturities, was sold in Germany a few months ago at a cost to us of 6.52%. By comparison, an issue guaranteed by a major European government, of comparable maturities, was sold in the same market at a cost of 6.92%.

In essence, World Bank bonds are backed by the full faith and credit of the strongest industrial nations on earth. And yet, we have always proceeded as if this outside protection of our bonds did not in fact exist. We have sought so to conduct our business that the Bank need never call on that security—and we have succeeded.

In my view, the most persuasive guarantee of our bonds is the day-to-day prudent operation of the Bank by its experienced and expert staff. I am determined to make certain that this guarantee is the only one we will ever have to exercise.

The record of the Bank's operations under my predecessors is excellent by any standards. Profits have been good and have risen steadily in recent years. In fiscal 1969, they will approximate $170 million, compared to average annual profits during the past five years of $145 million. We fully expect them to continue to rise in the future. This is true even though Bank interest rates in the future will be set at concessionary levels as they are at present.

Today a typical 24-year Bank loan, which carries an interest rate of 6.5%, contains a grant element of approximately 20% of the face value of the loan. The combination of concessionary interest rates to our borrowers and operating profits to our stockholders is made possible by our high ratio of interest-free capital to funded debt—a ratio at present of nearly one-to-one.

Currently, the average cost to the Bank for all its funds—that is, its total funded debt, plus its paid-in capital and retained earnings—is only 3.1%. Essentially, it is the difference between this 3.1% and the Bank's lending rate, now 6.5%, which enables us to cover all our administrative costs, grant reasonable concessions to our borrowers, and continue to earn substantial profits.

But, though profits have been good, there is a far more fundamental basis on which our reputation rests. And that, of course, is the choice and supervision of our overseas investments.

I have been immensely impressed by the professional competence with which our staff analyzes both the specific project and the economy of the borrowing country, before a loan is made—and by the careful scrutiny and supervision of the project, after the loan is made.

Such deep involvement in the domestic economies of independent—often newly independent—countries is possible only because the borrowing nation understands and appreciates our genuine dedication to its development. They see us for what we in fact are: an international agency, specializing in development, with no political axe to grind. The security of our investment depends on our borrowers' development and hence their interests and ours coincide.

It is on these strict standards of appraisal and supervision that the reputation of the Bank rests. And these standards will be continued in full force during our projected expansion. That is possible simply because in twenty-two years of experience we have learned a great deal about the techniques of realistic development planning, and the successful supervision of projects in distant and often primitive surroundings.

This accumulated experience now allows us to cope efficiently with a much larger volume of work. It is, however, clear that if our work is to increase, our staff must increase. Consequently, we have set in motion a worldwide recruiting drive to find and hire economists, engineers, financial analysts, and other specialists in our field. We plan to expand our staff by about 20% this fiscal year. This will not be easy since our standards are very high. But the Bank's reputation is equally high, and this attracts the caliber of professionals we need. Our results in recruitment so far have been very promising.

As we expand, we must remain sufficiently flexible to change our emphasis as the needs of development itself change. It is no longer enough to invest in traditional infrastructure: in power, transport, and communications. Both the needs and the opportunities in the developing world now point unmistakably to such fields as agriculture, education, and population planning. But let me make it clear that in these relatively new areas we will apply the same rigorous standards of both economic profitability of the project itself, and creditworthiness of the country in question.

It is not as easy to quantify the economic benefits of a technical school as of a hydroelectric plant. Similarly, on the surface, it may appear that you have something more impressive and solid to show when you build a highway than when you simply sink a lot of tubewells. But the whole point is that a surface impression is not a sound economic analysis. A good irrigation system, for example, when combined with the use of new strains of seeds, can result in an economic return of 100% a year. That is in fact an actual case that occurred in Pakistan.

And when you reflect that the less developed countries now require $4 billion a year of food imports, it is obvious that a broad expansion of their agricultural production can have an immensely beneficial effect on their balance of payments situation—and thus enhance their overall creditworthiness.

The economists at the Bank have been working on methods for quantifying the economic returns derived from social investment—such as education. Their conclusions demonstrate that the benefits can vary enormously. A liberal arts college in a primitive underdeveloped area, can be a dead loss. But a technical high school—in an expanding economy where the available capital is not matched by the requisite skilled manpower —can pay huge dividends. One such project in Latin America brought an annual return of 50%. It is the World Bank's task to determine, in a given situation, precisely what sort of education contributes most to solid economic growth, and to invest accordingly. We have not financed in the past, and we will not finance in the future, any education project that is not directly related to that economic growth.

In developing countries with excessive birth rates, loans in the field of population planning have perhaps the highest economic benefits of all. The blunt fact is that unless the rampant rate of population growth is reasonably moderated in many of these nations, not only will their developmental projects be finally overwhelmed, but their capability of repaying foreign loans will simply be eroded within a decade or two.

Gentlemen, let me summarize the World Bank's situation.

As I have said, we conduct our affairs as though the only security behind our bonds were the technical and financial soundness of the projects themselves in our loan portfolio. But the fact remains that behind that assurance stands our very favorable ratio of equity to debt. Last month our total debt amounted to some $4 billion, compared to paid-in capital and retained earnings of roughly the same amount.

And beyond that lie two further assurances: two unique guarantees by the governments of the world. First, that each loan is the primary or guarantee obligation of the country in which the Bank's investment is made. And second, that the total of all Bank debt is backed by the uncalled capital subscriptions of the member governments—capital which can be used for no other purpose.

In the twenty-three year history of the Bank, there have been no losses on its loans—no government has failed to honor its obligations. The Bank has not been a target for debt repudiation as have bilateral aid agencies and private credit corporations. The reason is obvious. Developing nations are convinced that it is in their own best interest to keep impeccable relations with the Bank.

Even in extreme situations, such as the latter years of the Nkrumah regime in Ghana, or in the period when the U.A.R. defaulted on obligations to bilateral creditors, neither of these governments defaulted on World Bank loans. As we expand our operations and become a more and more important source of development capital, the advantage to borrowing countries of continuing to meet their obligations to us will increase.

The final security behind our bonds is represented by the uncalled subscriptions to Bank capital. These amount at present to $20.7 billion—roughly five times the total of our funded debt. That $20.7 billion includes a U.S. share of $5.7 billion and a Common Market, U.K. and Canadian share of $6.6 billion.

The guarantee represented by the uncalled subscriptions cannot be eroded. By the provisions of our charter, these uncalled subscriptions may not be drawn upon for loans or administrative expenses. They can be used solely as a protection for the obligations of the Bank.

Moreover, the uncalled subscriptions are expressed in U.S. dollars, of the weight and fineness in effect on July 1, 1944. Thus they are not subject to deterioration as a result of changes in the value of currencies.

Similarly, because the loans of the Bank, made out of borrowed funds, are disbursed and repaid in the same currencies, the Bank faces no devaluation risks on its borrowed funds: its obligations to its creditors are matched by the repayments due from the borrowers.

It is, then, not too much to say that the World Bank is an entirely unique financial institution.

It is unique in its security and strength.

And it is unique in its purpose and program.

The World Bank was founded twenty-three years ago to reconstruct and develop a smashed, war-ravaged world. The reconstruction was a success. In the years since then it has turned increasingly to the developing world. And there the task is changing. What I have described to you today is our response to that change.

Our new program has begun well. It is on schedule. To date in this fiscal year we have borrowed more than in any previous year of the Bank's history. Two-thirds of that borrowing has been outside the U.S. market. Our lending operations, both in number and in amount, are up substantially over last year. And, at the same time, our cash and liquid security balance has increased. It now stands at $1.7 billion—up $400 million over the level at the beginning of the year.

I believe you will agree these are signs of a vigorous and expanding organization—strong and secure in its financial base, prudent and precise in its decisions, and realistic in its goals.

In the business of development, hardheaded realism must be the guide. Neither a naive optimism, nor a despondent pessimism will do.

The simple fact is that in the last third of the twentieth century the underdeveloped world will either develop—or it will be caught up in catastrophe.

The one thing it will not do is stand still and wait.

You gentlemen—at the center of the most enormous and active capital market in the world—are not accustomed to standing still.

You act.

We at the World Bank propose to do the same.

FIVE

To the
BOARD OF GOVERNORS
WASHINGTON, D.C.
SEPTEMBER 29,1969

Last year, in this forum, I gave you my assessment of both the direction and pace that the World Bank ought to adopt as it neared the completion of its first quarter century of existence.

Today, I should like to:

- Report to you past progress and future plans for the expansion of the Bank's operations.

- Emphasize the increased attention we are giving to population planning, educational advance, and agricultural expansion.

- Discuss three urgent, interrelated development problems—unemployment, urbanization, and industrialization — to which the Bank and all other development institutions must direct additional effort.

- And propose an approach to the formulation of a Strategy for Development.

I. The Expansion of the Bank's Operations

Let me begin by sketching for you the broad outline of the course we set out on last year.

Our judgment was that both the urgent needs and the unique opportunities of the global development scene called for a substantially higher volume of lending—lending that was to be financed by appropriate additional borrowing, and buttressed by an increased level of liquidity. But we were determined that this expanded activity should conform to the same standards of prudence which have characterized the Bank's operations since its founding.

We moved ahead with that policy of expanded lending, and by the close of FY 1969, the World Bank Group—the International Bank for Reconstruction and Development, the International Development Association, and the International Finance Corporation—had increased their financing of development projects by 87% over the previous year. New loans, credits, and investments totalled $1,877 million, as compared with the FY 1968 total of $1,003 million.[a]

The World Bank Group, then, has accomplished in 1969 more than we had planned that it should. It has intensified its search for sound, viable, high-priority projects which will provide the maximum stimulus to development, and drawing on years of experience has immensely increased its lending activity without eroding its policy of prudence.

To finance this expanded activity, the Bank has borrowed in the world's capital markets during this same period $1¼ billion at an average cost of 6.46%. The amount borrowed—80% of which was from sources outside of the United States—represented an increase of 55% over the highest previous year of the Bank's history. Bank borrowings were increased both to support the higher level of lending and to improve liquidity: at FY 1969's close, our cash and liquid security balances had grown by over $400 million.

Our plans for FY 1970 call for continued expansion of our operations—loans, credits, and investments should approximate $2¼ billion—and we will continue to put emphasis on new areas and new sectors.

---

[a]*Included in these figures are investments by IFC totalling $93 million, which served as catalysts to seed, nurture, and bring to financial fruition aggregate investments of more than half a billion dollars in the private sectors of sixteen countries.*

In view of the current market conditions, our decision last year substantially to improve the Bank's liquidity has proven particularly advantageous. It means that, pending an improvement in the capital markets, we can borrow somewhat less than in the past twelve months and yet still maintain momentum in our lending operations. Should the markets change, and provide better opportunities for borrowing, we will take advantage of it. My view remains that our liquidity can and should remain high; it clearly helps to protect the Bank's operations from unpredictable forces beyond its control.

Despite an increase in our administrative expenses, connected with the greater workload, the Bank closed out FY 1969 with a record profit of $172 million. Administrative expenses will continue to rise as volume expands further, but we expect to end FY 1970 with a profit in excess of $200 million.[a]

But as satisfactory as fiscal 1969 has been and as bright as the outlook is for 1970, you will recall that I stressed in our last meeting that the Bank should shape its strategy to a longer time frame than mere year-to-year planning can provide.

Thus we initiated a Five-Year Program, encompassing FY 1969 through FY 1973. The overall objective of that program is that the Bank Group should lend roughly twice as much as it had in the previous five-year period; or to put it another way, that in the new Five-Year Program it should lend a total that would approach the entire amount lent in the first 22 years of its operations. I continue to believe that this program can be achieved. If it is, the World Bank Group's new financing operations will exceed $12 billion for the period.

The performance of FY 1969, and the plans for FY 1970, must be measured, then, in terms of progress toward that objective.

[a]A central key to the success of our whole Five-Year Program is, of course, the recruitment of a professional staff capable of handling the greatly increased workload. It is not merely that we need more people, but that we need the best people available on a worldwide basis. The recruitment program has been intensive this past year, and we have increased our staff by approximately 25%. We expect in the current fiscal year to expand by nearly 30% more: a total of over 60% in two years. I consider this rate of expansion to be near the practical limits of the Bank's capacity to absorb new staff effectively.

But the objective is not simply a matter of expanding the volume of lending. As I outlined to you last year, we are shifting the mix of our total operations toward new geographical areas and new sectors as well.

I indicated to you, for example, our interest in Indonesia, an immense country of 115,000,000 people with great development potential, to which—for understandable reasons—the Bank had never extended loans or credits in the past. What we have today is a clearly changing Indonesia, rising out of the turbulence and turmoil of its past. The resident mission we established there twelve months ago has explored a whole spectrum of assistance that is well within our capability to make available. In this past year alone we have extended four IDA credits totalling $51 million, and we expect to be able to do a great deal more in the years ahead.

Though the Five-Year Program aims at an increase in the level of our operations in other parts of Asia as well, particularly in the Indian subcontinent, I pointed out to you that we were convinced that more attention should be given to Latin America and Africa. That geographical shift in emphasis is well under way. We increased loans and credits to African member countries, for instance, by nearly 150% this past year. And lending operations in Latin America are rising sharply to meet our goal of more than doubling them by 1973.

But the Bank's efforts are not merely—or even mainly—quantitative in their goal. They are, above all, qualitative. We seek to provide assistance where it will contribute most to removing the roadblocks to development.

The problem is to understand precisely what these roadblocks are. It is simply not enough to propose a project here, and a project there, merely because by short-term calculation they appear profitable. This falls far short of what is required.

As a responsible, international institution, dedicated by the very title deeds of our existence to "development," it is clear that we must know—insofar as it is possible to know—what the internal dynamics of development are. We must know how its processes affect entire societies, and enlarge or diminish their chances for both economic and social growth.

Our objective is not to search for good investments in sick economies. Our objective is to try to understand what makes economies sick in the first place, and to take those remedial steps that will encourage recuperation and health. We want to seek out those projects, those procedures, those policies that will assist economies as a whole to get into the mainstream of self-generating growth and progress.

That is what I mean when I say that the efforts of the World Bank Group are "qualitative." We are trying to invest our human and material resources in a carefully integrated manner which will contribute to the vitality, diversity, and basic institutional reform of societies. We cannot be satisfied with piecemeal solutions. What we need—and what we must design—is a comprehensive strategy that will constitute an overall plan into which particular policies and individual projects can be fitted as logical, integral parts.

When I point out, then, that we have begun to put a new emphasis on population policy, and on educational reform, and agricultural expansion—and when I add that we are planning to give a new thrust to our activities related to the problems of unemployment, urbanization, and industrial growth—I am not choosing sectors or policies at random. What we are trying to do is to form a framework in which each of these vital fields can be dealt with in an interrelated and mutually reinforcing manner.

I am proposing the search for a successful overall strategy by which development in each individual sector improves and sustains it in all the others. Thus, reduced rates of population growth can take the strains off both countryside and city. Modernized agriculture can provide more job stability, income, and hope on the land. Increased yields can feed the growing cities.

It can do even more: it can reduce the present over-rapid rate of urbanization. The agricultural revolution can stimulate the growth of a new network of decentralized regional urban communities where services, processing, and light manufacture can create more jobs outside the big cities. More productive farms, and a wealthier countryside, will provide a better market for the new heavy industry in the large urban centers. And all of this can provide a larger scale of operations from which to compete in foreign markets presently dominated by experienced outside firms from the developed countries.

I do not suggest we shall get all these equations into immediate balance. But balanced development must be our objective.

If, now, I look at each of the critical sectors separately, if I take up the three sectors which last year I stated required special attention and now add three more which we need to consider more urgently, I do not wish to imply that our aim is simply to modernize separate sectors. It is rather to deal with them in such a manner that the entire society can make the transition to modern life.

It was with this in mind that last year I spoke to you of three particular sectors to which we planned to give special attention.

II. New Emphasis on Population Planning, Educational Advance and Agricultural Expansion

A. Population

The first was the area of population planning—for the simple reason that the greatest single obstacle to the economic and social advancement of the majority of peoples in the underdeveloped world is rampant population growth.

The enhancement of human dignity, and the consequent capacity to lead a fuller, freer, more thoroughly human life, is the ultimate objective of development. Economic progress is a means to that end, but no achievable rate of economic growth will be sufficient to cope with an unlimited proliferation of people on our limited planet.

I recently dealt with this matter in detail in a public statement. My purpose was to draw attention to the essential urgency of the question as it relates to the viability of all development efforts. There is clearly a growing understanding of this point and more and more governments are expressing a willingness to deal with the problem.

To assist them, we have established a Population Projects Department within the Bank. Though it is not yet fully operative, we have already found that the immediate need is less for financial assistance than for technical advice and counsel. This we are prepared to give, in concert with other elements of the UN family. Many of our member countries are asking us for this sort of help. Further, in the future, each of the Bank's Economic Reports on a country facing a population problem will discuss with candor the government's action—or lack of action—in facing up to and dealing with the issue.

B. Education

A second sector which I emphasized in my remarks last year was education. I expressed the hope that over the period of our Five-Year Program we could improve the balance between the capital available for physical development, and the trained human resources required to use that capital efficiently. To that end, we planned to increase our lending in this field at least threefold.

We are making progress. Our combined Bank and IDA lending for education in FY 1969 was more than triple what it was in the previous year, and in the current fiscal year will rise again. But while the opportunities for educational financing are almost limitless,[a] our resources clearly are not, and hence we must apply the most stringent criteria in our choice of projects.

The problem is to sort out carefully the educational priorities from country to country, and to invest as selectively as possible.

There is little dispute in the developing countries about the importance of education, but the problems of advancing it are so inextricably tangled that it is likely that many of the scarce resources devoted to it are in fact being wasted. For example:

- In many countries of Africa the dropout rate during the six years of primary school is over 70%; in large parts of Asia the rate is over 80%.

- Even among those who run the full course there is waste as an increasing number of graduates are unable to find employment. In one Asian country alone, a half million high school and college graduates—fully 10% of the total—are out of work. Many graduates who do find employment are in jobs which do not actually require the relatively costly education they have received.

These are the results of educational systems which are simply not geared to the needs or aspirations of the communities they are meant to serve. Too often antiquated systems of education are preserved because of their traditional prestige; too rarely is full attention given to modern science, useful technology or practical agriculture.

Such schools tend to prepare students for the educational ladder itself, rather than for the life they are likely to lead, and as a result there are large numbers of dropouts ill-prepared for anything. At the same time an increasingly expensive educational system puts unbearable strains on a poor country's resources.

---

[a]Four or five thousand years after the introduction of the written word, more than a third of adult mankind still remains illiterate. What is even more significant is that the absolute number of illiterates is increasing rather than diminishing. Despite all the efforts of both the UN agencies and other educational groups over the past 20 years, there are today some 800 million illiterates, 100 million more than there were in 1950.

In sum, in many countries of the developing world—countries entangled by a web of oppressive poverty which cannot be cut through until the appropriate skills of the citizenry are honed and sharpened—the educational complex is simply not relevant to the urgent needs of the society.

In this situation, the Bank intends to hold closely to its policy of providing educational assistance only where it will contribute significantly to economic development. The objective is clear. The means are less so. But, at the minimum, they will include three shifts of emphasis:

- Greater attention to functional literacy for adults in those countries where the growing pool of adult illiterates constitutes a serious obstacle to development.

- Less emphasis on physical construction—"bricks and mortar"—and more attention to assistance in curriculum design, school administration, teacher training and long-range educational planning tied directly to the developmental strategy of the economy as a whole.

- Greater commitment to educational innovation and experimentation. In collaboration with the United Nations Development Programme and Unesco, the Bank will finance a series of pilot projects designed to explore experimentally new ideas to maximize the contribution of educational systems to carefully planned economic development. We expect to participate in the financing of the first of these projects—a primary educational system in the Ivory Coast based on the use of television for instructional purposes—before the end of this year.

C. Agriculture

Still another sector to which I urged we give greater attention is agriculture, and we did. We have doubled the number of our agricultural loans this past year, and plan to expand them further in FY 1970.

We will continue to place increased emphasis on this sector, not merely because it is manifestly productive, but because whatever be the prestige or glamour of mammoth industrial projects, the fact remains that in the developing world agriculture is the indispensable foundation of a healthy economy. It is the sector that benefits the great bulk of the world's population most directly. Moreover, one of the hardest lessons for many of the developing countries to learn is that agricultural expansion fuels and accelerates industrial growth.

After years of near-stagnation, agricultural production is beginning to respond to the new agricultural technology. This year's wheat crop in Pakistan, for example, is up 60% over the average of the past four years. Recent expansion of rice production in the Philippines has ended a half-century of dependence on rice imports, and has turned these Islands into a potential rice exporter. The significant fact is that growth rates of food grain production have hitherto barely kept up with population growth. But the outlook now for the next two decades—provided there is proper financial support—is that the world's food supply will grow at a faster rate than its population.

There is a danger of looking upon this agricultural advance as merely a matter of applying the new "miracle seeds." In fact, the new hybrid strains are but a single ingredient in a total technology. Water management, land reform and development, fertilizers, pesticides, transportation, regional centers for storage, marketing facilities, and credit resources are all essential components—and must be kept in proper balance if the hopes for the Green Revolution are to remain green.

Moreover, the initial problem of achieving worldwide food sufficiency will gradually give way to second-generation problems which are even more complex. There is the innate conflict between the expansion of relatively large farming, and the survival of the small, family-oriented farm. The new technology is more readily available to richer farmers, and thus can paradoxically become punitive to poorer farmers. If the less advantaged peasants are forced to leave the countryside for the city, the

whole crisis of burgeoning urbanization is adversely accelerated, and can result in even more massive problems of welfare,
unemployment, and explosive tensions between the landed and
the landless.

In addition, food production must be economically related to
consumer demand—mass incomes must rise with the increase
in farm output. Though greater supply in most of the developing world is clearly necessary today, a sudden increase could
trigger an unexpected glut in local markets that would severely
depress prices and destroy incentives for increased production.

There is, moreover, the possibility of widespread dislocation
of international trade as the traditional food-importing nations
reach indigenous self-sufficiency. Unless food-exporting nations
can diversify as their traditional markets shrink, they can find
themselves in substantial difficulty.

The Bank stands ready to offer both technical advice and financial assistance in all these problems. But there is something
further I am convinced we ought to do. We should assume a
greater role of leadership in promoting the agricultural research
of today that will be the foundation of greater agricultural
growth tomorrow.

The economic efficacy of such research is dramatically apparent in the case of the new "miracle seeds." They are not the
result of a miracle. They are the result of a relatively modest
investment of funds, and a high degree of dedicated and creative work. The new rice strains, for example, were developed
over a period of six years with a total investment of less than
$15 million at the International Rice Research Institute in the
Philippines.

There is an urgent need for a great deal of this innovative research in fields such as the low-cost production of additional
protein; the more effective use and control of scarce water supplies; and the elimination of animal and plant diseases which in
some areas reduce livestock and crops by as much as a third.

The protein problem is particularly important, since a sufficiency of calories alone does not eliminate the ravages of malnutrition. Protein deficiency is a hidden hunger which drains
away alertness, energy, and effort in its victims, and leads to
lethargy, susceptibility to disease, high infant mortality—and
overly large families to compensate for it—poor ability to learn,
mental retardation, and overall ineffectiveness in daily tasks.

Underdeveloped areas of the world have often been unfairly
accused of being peopled with indolent, ambitionless citizens
who fail to respond to the challenges of improving their own
and their nation's lot. But it is becoming increasingly clear that
caloric and protein deficiencies result in masses of undernourished people who cannot physically and mentally function as
alert, energetic, and productive citizens.

Two-thirds of the world's children suffer from protein-defi-
cient malnutrition. Some of its more serious effects become irreversible in early childhood, and hence cripple the efficiency
of these hundreds of millions of citizens throughout their entire
adult, working lives. Were we to accomplish within the next
decade a technological breakthrough in low-cost protein production and distribution—a breakthrough on the scale of
promise of the present agricultural revolution—we could loosen
the grip of malnutrition on mankind, and trigger a massive advance in human energy and efficiency.

I hope, then, that the Bank, and organizations particularly experienced in such matters—the United Nations Development
Programme, the Food and Agriculture Organization, the aid institutions in countries such as Canada, France, Sweden, and the
United States, and the Rockefeller and Ford Foundations—can
join together with the developing nations in order to launch a
new and sustained effort in applied research in each of these
critical areas: protein production, water management, and the
reduction of animal and plant diseases.

III. The Problems of Unemployment, Urbanization
and Industrialization

I want to turn now to three other closely related problems of development which require action by the Bank: unemployment, urbanization, and industrialization.

Over the past year I have visited Latin America, Asia, and Africa. I went in order to take a realistic look at development problems at close range, and to meet with the leaders in these areas who are grappling with the issues.

These trips strengthened my view that there are immense opportunities in the developing nations for high-priority, economically sound investment. At the same time, the complexities of development are so enormous that it would be wholly naive to suppose that more money alone can solve them. There is a need—a desperate need—for additional financial support. But there is at least as great a need for more effective use of the funds presently being provided.

I can only repeat: what we need—and what we must fashion—is a more effective overall development strategy.

Everything I saw supported our decision in the Bank to give a new emphasis to population planning, educational advance, and agricultural growth. Progress in the solution of these problems is fundamental to such a strategy. But I also found that no such strategy will be complete unless it provides for an attack on the interrelated problems of unemployment, urbanization, and industrialization.

I want to discuss these issues with you for I am convinced that the Bank must play an active role in seeking new and more precise answers to these intensely complicated questions.

A. Unemployment

To begin with unemployment, the sober fact is that it is not only endemic throughout the emerging world, but is growing worse, especially in urban areas. Though the urban population in the developing countries has been increasing at an average annual rate of over 5%, industrial employment has risen much more slowly. In Latin America, the situation is particularly serious. There the urban population has grown twice as fast as the number of jobs.

As I have pointed out, the developing countries, as a group, have managed over the past decade to sustain an average annual economic growth of more than 4½%.[a] In view of the magnitude of their obstacles, this must be credited as a success. It proves that these nations can and do take advantage of technological progress, and will put to effective use the external aid that is offered them. But from another perspective, this rate of growth is grossly insufficient to cope with their burgeoning populations.[b]

It is estimated that the equivalent of 20% of the entire male labor force in the developing world is currently unemployed.

The sobering fact is that the population explosion of the fifties and sixties is only now beginning to have an impact on the size of the labor force. Fully one half of the total population in the emerging world is under 20 years of age. Population planning —even at a high degree of effectiveness—cannot make a decisive impact on the unemployment problem before the end of the century.

At the present inadequate rates of economic growth, unemployment can only grow steadily worse. In India's Fourth Five-Year Plan, for example—the Plan covering the years 1969-73— the estimate is that 19 million new jobs will be created, but that

_____
[a]*85% of the capital required for this growth was supplied by the developing nations; only 15% came from external sources.*

[b]*Not only are these countries unable to create enough jobs for the rising flood of youngsters reaching working age, but the rate of economic growth is insufficient to prevent the income disparities between rich and poor nations from increasing at an alarming pace. Today measured in terms of income per capita, that gap at its extremes is already more than $3,000. Present projections indicate that it may well widen to $9,000 by the end of the century. In the year 2000, per capita income in the United States is expected to be approximately $10,000; in Brazil, $500; and in India, $200.*

23 million new workers will come into the labor force to compete for them. The result: a 4 million increase in the millions of Indians already unemployed.

Migration from the agricultural areas into the towns, in the less developed countries, is mounting rapidly. There is virtually no chance that this surge of migrants—when added to the already rapid increase of the urban labor force from the population explosion—can be provided with jobs in an economy with a growth rate of 4½%, or even 5%.

Economists are divided on the question of precisely how high a growth rate is required in these nations to assure the absorption of even the new entrants into the labor pool, but it seems likely that in concert with whatever other actions may be required in a general strategy of modernization, an increase in the growth rate of at least one-third, to a level of at least 6% is essential. That, then, must be an objective to which the developing nations set their sights.[a]

I am confident that a 6% growth rate—while difficult to attain—can be reached and surpassed. But, by itself it will not be enough to solve the problem of unemployment in the developing world.

In the developed countries, rapid economic growth implies full employment. But, in the developing countries this is not necessarily the case. Venezuela and Jamaica, for example, both enjoyed average growth rates of 8% a year between 1950 and 1960, but at the end of the decade in Venezuela, unemployment was higher than at the beginning; and in Jamaica it was just as high, in spite of the fact that fully 11% of the labor force had emigrated from the country.

What this means is that in addition to expanding their growth rates, the developing countries must adopt national policies promoting the right balance between capital and labor-inten-

---

[a]*And little enough it is. With the Indian population expanding at 2.5% or more per year, a 6% growth rate will merely permit India's per capita income of $80 to double in twenty years.*

sive activities, and between the supply of skilled and unskilled workers so as to maximize output through full utilization of the total labor force.

Structural unemployment, in many of these nations, has been aggravated by unwise policies: policies which favor the uneconomic use of capital-intensive technology. Imported equipment is underpriced because exchange rates are overvalued. Real interest rates are-artificially low, due to inflation, and do not reflect the true value of capital. The wages of unskilled labor in the industrial sector are allowed to rise above their real value, and grow seriously out of line with those in agriculture.

In some countries, for example, the scarcity of skilled technicians contributes to the problem of unemployment among unskilled workers: for want of one skilled foreman, ten unskilled laborers may remain unemployed.

In other instances, massive urban unemployment is the result of policies which fail to stimulate labor-intensive, export-oriented industries, or reflect a lack of proper balance between rural and urban development. One of the reasons the Bank is placing such emphasis on the agricultural sector is that the new technology not only produces more food, but also provides the opportunity for greater rural employment without the massive capital investment characteristic of urban industrialization.

There is, clearly, no single all-purpose formula that will resolve the problem of unemployment. A solution must be tailored to the situation in each country. But the point I want to emphasize is that we and other institutions operating in this field must find solutions. Prolonged and mounting unemployment exacts a tremendous social cost from a nation. Let there be no doubt: social costs are real costs. And once human hopelessness and frustration have been pushed beyond the breaking point, social costs can erupt into catastrophic economic costs as well.

No one can pretend that the problem of unemployment is going to disappear in a single decade. But if we are going to avert the violence born of human desperation, we cannot risk frittering the decade away with feeble and half-hearted measures.

The bitter irony of unemployment is that there is enough unfinished business on this planet to keep everyone employed to the maximum of his ability. What we lack is not work to be done. What we lack are innovative ideas about how to get that work done—and the courage and determination to apply the lessons we have already so painfully learned.

B. Urbanization

Directly related to unemployment is the crisis of the cities. The phenomenon of urban decay is a plague creeping over every continent, but its corrosive effects are critical in the poorer nations.

The cities of the developing countries are the centers which ought to serve as the basis of both industrial growth and social change. Instead, with a growing proportion of their inhabitants living at the very margin of existence, and the quality of life deteriorating for all, the cities are spawning a culture of poverty that threatens the economic health of entire nations.

The scale of the problem is immense. During the decade of the 1950's the urban population of the developing world expanded by about 50%. Today, the major cities are doubling in size roughly every decade. By the year 2000, their total population will be some 500% higher than today. That means that from 1.2 to 1.6 billion more people will be living—if "living" is the appropriate term—in these sprawling centers of urban decay.

The resources required to provide minimal services and infrastructure for urban populations of this magnitude are staggering.

Here again, even massive family planning programs are unlikely to mitigate this situation substantially over the next 20 years. Population planning is imperative, but at best it becomes effective only gradually. Those who will seek employment in the urban environment over the next two decades have already been born.

Rural migration accounts for more than half of urban growth, and experience illustrates that as cities grow larger they attract rather than discourage movement from the countryside. The pace of migration is typically beyond any reasonable capacity to absorb it. In the richer nations, already nearly 50% of the total population lives in the city. The poorer nations are repeating this trend, and it is ominous to reflect that their already overcrowded cities currently contain only 15% of their surging populations.

If we cannot count on even highly successful population planning programs to curb urban growth before the end of the century, what can we count on? The candid answer is that we do not know.

We do not know, for example, whether it would be wiser for the developing nations to use their limited resources in an effort to motivate villagers—through intensive rural development—to remain in the countryside; or to use these funds to invest in massive urban infrastructure. And if the investment is to be in the cities, it is not clear whether it is more efficient to expand old ones, or to build entirely new ones.

Our knowledge of how best to deal with the whole issue of urbanization remains primitive. But one point is clear: the problem must be dealt with on a comprehensive, national basis. An integrated, country-wide strategy of rural-urban development is essential. It must integrate population planning, regional specialization, and industrial growth, and put far more emphasis on economic policies specifically designed to optimize and distribute with greater equity the national per capita income.

C. Industrialization

I come now to the last of these closely related issues: industrial growth.

As I have noted, there is a persistent tendency in the developing nations to neglect the causal connection between agricultural advance and industrialization. All too often they elaborate national policies that seek to protect and promote local industries at the indirect expense of agriculture. This is shortsighted, since the agricultural sector inevitably remains both a market and a source of supply for industry. To discriminate heavily in favor of the industrial sector is only to weaken the very foundation on which every developing economy must build.

It is, of course, true that industrialization in the less developed countries often requires special inducements. Normally these nations are not in a position, in the beginning, to compete in the open international market with the more technologically advanced countries. But these initial inducements are sensible only if they can return the costs they incur at a later and more efficient stage of industrialization.

Interminable inducements are self-defeating. And that is precisely what we are witnessing in far too many developing nations today. There is excessive and indiscriminate protection of import-substitution industries which has had the predictable effect of perpetuating inefficiencies, and has seriously hampered the effort to increase export earnings.

The heart of the difficulty is that the industrial sector in such countries tends to produce altogether too wide a range of items, and continues to operate at a level far below optimum economic scale. This results in a built-in incremental cost which is often two or three times the world-market cost of comparable products. Though a moderate degree of added cost may be justifiable for a reasonable period—particularly if the effect is a true saving in foreign exchange and a genuine training in new techniques—the cost can easily escalate to prohibitive and punitive levels.

A graphic instance of the indiscriminate use of this policy of protection for indigenous industry came to light in a recent Bank study which revealed that the developing nations spent an estimated $2.1 billion in domestic resources in 1965 to manufacture automotive products which had a world market value of only $800 million. It is instructive to reflect that this "loss" in a single year of $1.3 billion approximates the total amount of resources invested in industrial development by the World Bank in its entire 23 years of operation.

Local entrepreneurs and managers—nurtured in such highly protective economic environments—have little incentive to reduce costs and improve quality, and little ability to compete effectively in the world market.

What is required in these situations are renewed efforts both to rationalize the existing industrial structure, and to stimulate additional and genuinely competitive growth. The necessary reforms may be temporarily painful. I am aware that it is not easy to reduce tariff duties and import restrictions, and to adopt realistic exchange rates. Many governments are faced with the awkward problem of opposing vested economic interests, prepared to exert heavy political pressure to preserve their privileged positions.

But the lessons of history remind us that governments too timid to initiate necessary reforms often lose not only their popularity, but their mandate as well.

For us in the Bank, the relevant question is what can we do to help the developing countries constructively and impartially in this whole complicated process of rationalizing their industrial sectors. I believe the relevant answer is: much more than we have done in the past. Our record is good. But it can be better.

In the last two years our loans to Development Banks—which are themselves organized to finance local industry—have averaged about twice the level of the preceding two years. And in

FY 1969, IFC—after five years of continued growth—nearly doubled its volume of investment.

But I believe that we must do even more. As a step in that direction we are establishing an Industrial Projects Department in the World Bank. Its purpose will be both to expand our lending in the industrial sector, and to make practical recommendations to the developing countries as to how they can best accelerate their own industrial growth.

Each developing nation has, of course, its distinctive set of problems and needs. But the common tendency is to promote industrialization by looking inward. That policy must change toward a more healthy and realistic tendency of looking outward: looking outward by putting greater emphasis on production for export; looking outward by joining in cooperative efforts to create and expand regional markets.

The developed nations have a responsibility to assist in this by dismantling the discriminatory barriers erected in the past against goods manufactured in the less advantaged countries. The capital-exporting nations, after all, have invested both money and effort in making it possible for the poorer countries to come of age industrially. It is wholly absurd for the rich countries to invest billions in developing the poorer countries, and then to refuse to be repaid in those goods which are the first fruits of development.

There is no genuine economic reason for the developed nations to fear the industrial growth of the less advantaged countries and the establishment of new patterns of international trade in manufactured goods. On the contrary, the wealthier nations should target their own growth in the direction where their greatest comparative advantage already lies: the production of goods and services requiring sophisticated levels of technology. It would be to the benefit of the world economy as a whole for the technically advanced societies to concentrate more in these fields, and gradually to relinquish the simpler and less complicated manufacturing to those developing nations which can efficiently do the job.

Industrialization will need to be encouraged in different ways in each country. I attach great importance, therefore, to comprehensive industrial-sector reviews for each of the developing nations. These we will introduce in the months ahead as regular and integral parts of a new pattern of reporting.

D. An Expanded Program of Country Economic Reports

I am convinced that the Bank has both the opportunity and responsibility greatly to expand its program of Country Economic Reports. We can render a unique service in this matter by becoming a highly informed and impartial source of precise and professional development reports—reports that are both current and comprehensive. Our Country Economic Reports can and should become increasingly useful tools to all organizations working in the field of development. Beginning this year, therefore, we will organize a regular annual mission to each major developing country to report in detail on economic and social progress and on the prospects for the future. These missions will investigate all major sectors of the economy, and will seek to determine priorities for both investment and pre-investment activities. We will look to other relevant international organizations for assistance in their fields of specialization, and preliminary discussions have indicated that such cooperation will be willingly extended. We believe that the reports of these comprehensive missions, to be published on a regular twelve-month cycle, will be useful not only to the country itself and to the Bank, but to bilateral aid organizations and to the United Nations and its other agencies as well. They will provide an independent, objective, and wholly nonpartisan basis for evaluating progress in the Second Development Decade.

IV. Towards a Strategy for Development

These, then, are some of the problems which we in the World Bank—as well as other developmental organizations—will be dealing with over the next few years. They are problems of a magnitude that clearly call for the adaptation of some traditional policies, the design of some wholly new ones, and the integration of both into a "Strategy for Development."

It was with this in view that just a year ago I acted on a wise suggestion of my predecessor, Mr. George Woods, who had foreseen the need for just such an advance in global development planning. It was our good fortune that Mr. Lester Pearson, Nobel Prize winner and former Prime Minister of Canada, agreed to preside over a group of distinguished world citizens to study this problem.[a]

I am very pleased to announce that the Pearson Commission has completed its work and its report is currently being printed. It will be distributed during our meetings this week.

As you know, though the work of the Commission has been financed by the Bank, it has been from its very outset a wholly independent effort. Its findings are not a report to the Bank, but a report to the world at large. Its recommendations are addressed to every development institution, public and private; and to every government, rich and poor. As such, the Commission Report is a public document of high importance, deserving the widest possible public distribution.

Quite apart from the merits of its specific proposals, the Report is important in that it takes a detached and objective view of issues that can sometimes be clouded by narrow and partisan considerations. There are other important studies in preparation: the UN program for the Second Development

[a] *In addition to Prime Minister Pearson, the members of the Commission are:*
Sir Edward Boyle (United Kingdom), Member of Parliament
Roberto de Oliveira Campos (Brazil), former Minister of Finance
Douglas Dillon (United States), former Secretary of the Treasury
Wilfried Guth (Germany), Member, Board of Management, Deutsche Bank
Sir W. Arthur Lewis (West Indies), Professor of Public and International Affairs, Princeton University
Robert E. Marjolin (France), Professor, Faculty of Law and Economic Science, University of Paris
Saburo Okita (Japan), President, Japan Economic Research Center and Special Adviser to Minister of Economic Planning

Decade; the Jackson Report on the development capacities of the UN system; reports of national commissions, including the Peterson Committee established by President Nixon. All of these studies are related and will command our consideration.

But I want to stress the importance of immediate action on the Pearson Commission Report. It represents the mature and independent views of eight distinguished men who are notable both for the wealth of their personal experience, and the variety of their national perspectives. They, and their highly competent professional staff, have worked hard and thought deeply about the problems that most interest us all. Their research has been vigorous and thorough, has included visits to every major area of the developing world, and meetings with representatives of more than 70 governments for on-the-spot discussions and evaluations.

The World Bank commissioned the Pearson Report precisely in order to stimulate discussion and debate—and prompt action —on the issues in the widest possible forum: among governments, among international agencies, among public and private organizations of every size and description which are concerned with what I believe history will regard as the most crucial task that confronted our century: the orderly development of mankind itself in an era of revolutionary technological change.

The Report will be available, in English, in the bookstores next Monday. Translations into French, German, Italian, Japanese, Spanish, and Portuguese are under way, and editions in these languages will be published within the next few weeks. Discussion of the Report—directed toward action—in both political and academic forums is being planned throughout the world. One of the first of the conferences, to be attended by prominent international specialists in the field of development economics, will meet under the auspices of Columbia University early next year at the invitation of the President of the University and the Albert Schweitzer Professor of International Development, Barbara Ward. The ecumenical movement linking the Roman

Catholic and Protestant churches plans to take discussion of the Report to every diocese and parish in the course of 1970.

For the Bank's part, I propose to undertake a careful analysis of each of the Commission's recommendations which in any way bears upon our work, and to submit these analyses to the Bank's Directors with proposals for appropriate action.

Following the completion of the Directors' review, I will propose that a report, summarizing the conclusions and decisions on each of the Commission's recommendations relating to the Bank's field of activity, be transmitted to the Board of Governors.

I am sure you will join me in urging that other institutions affected by the Commission's recommendations—the United Nations Development Programme, the Food and Agriculture Organization, Unesco, the World Health Organization, the International Labour Organisation; the major bilateral aid-providing nations, particularly those which are studying expansion of their programs; the Organisation for Economic Co-operation and Development, and its Development Assistance Committee; the Inter-American, Asian, and African Development Banks, and other development finance agencies—will likewise move formally to consider and act upon the Report's conclusions.

*   *   *   *   *   *   *   *

By any set of quantitative standards, the World Bank has made progress this past year. The most profound significance of that progress, however, cannot be measured. The advance of the human condition—which in the ultimate analysis is what our entire efforts are directed toward—cannot be summed up in a set of statistics, no matter how precise they may be.

All reality is rich in complexity, and the realities of global development are clearly no exception.

The tasks before us, then, require comprehensive action, and comprehensive action can only have its roots in comprehensive and creative thinking.

Economic development requires financial resources. Indeed, it requires far more than have yet been made available.

But the resource it requires most is creative innovation.

The World Bank Group is—at its core—an innovative, problem-solving mechanism. Its problem is to help fashion a better life for mankind in the decades ahead.

To the degree that we are innovative and resourceful, we can succeed at that task.

I believe that you and I—and all of us in this effort—could ask for no more significant a responsibility than the one we share.

It is an endeavor demanding the very best that is in us.

Its reward is the very best, too: the satisfaction of demonstrating that though man's ancient limitations in nature may be perennial, his ancient deprivations of dignity need not be permanent.

Our disappointment is about man's past.

Our dissatisfaction is over man's present.

Our dedication is to man's future.

SIX

To the
COLUMBIA UNIVERSITY
CONFERENCE
ON
INTERNATIONAL ECONOMIC
DEVELOPMENT

NEW YORK, NEW YORK
FEBRUARY 20, 1970

I am pleased to be here, because your deliberations in this conference on the Report of the Pearson Commission are most timely. They are a preface to the Second Development Decade. They are addressing the issues on which a sound, sensible strategy for the Seventies must be fashioned. After the past quarter-century of experience, governments in the more affluent nations no longer question the general need for global development. What they do question—and what they have every right to question—is whether or not the specific programs of the past are still relevant to the problems of the present, and the imperatives of the future.

Decision makers in these governments—under the understandable pressures of competing priorities—need a clear view of development goals, and a workable set of options designed to meet those goals. They need practical, politically feasible programs that can command and sustain legislative and popular support. What is particularly valuable about the Pearson Commission Report is that it realistically addressed itself to that need, and it is clear from announcements by governments in the past several weeks that already the work of the Commission has had an impact:

- Chancellor Brandt of the Federal Republic in addressing the Bundestag has announced: "The Federal Government will endeavor to attain the aim envisaged in the

97

Report of the Pearson Commission for a public share
in development aid by an annual average increase rate
of 11 per cent. . . . The number of German development
experts and volunteers will be increased with a view
to doubling it by the mid-seventies. The Federal Government will continue to improve the quality of German aid."

- Prime Minister Wilson, calling the Report "one of the
most important documents of the twentieth century,"
announced increases in Britain's Aid Program for each
of the next three years. And Judith Hart, the Minister
for Overseas Development, stated in Parliament: "Taking a high estimate for private flows, we could expect
to reach the 1 per cent target not much after the date
of 1975 recommended by the Pearson Commission. In
any case, the Government intends, unless our balance
of payments should preclude it, to reach the target of
1 per cent total flow not later than the end of the
Second Development Decade."

- The King of Norway, in his speech from the throne,
announced: "The Government has worked out a framework plan for state aid to the developing countries,
which will involve a tripling of the amount made available between the years 1968 and 1973."

- Prime Minister Holyoake of New Zealand has pledged
that his Government will aim to meet the Pearson Commission target of 1 per cent of Gross National Product
in external aid.

- Prime Minister Sato of Japan has stated that economic
aid would double in the near future, rising from the
present level of $1 billion per year to $2 billion.

France is already providing official development assistance in
amounts exceeding the Pearson targets. And Sweden, before the
Report was published, announced it was increasing budgetary
appropriations for aid by 25 per cent per year which will permit
it to achieve the targets by 1975. Similarly, in The Netherlands,

the Government has requested Parliament to provide for fiscal year 1970 a 21 per cent increase in foreign aid, and a still further increase in 1971.

All of this lends encouragement to the view that the decline in official foreign aid is now reversing itself. The trend in the richer countries is manifestly to make more official aid available —with one overwhelming exception. And that is in the richest country of all: the United States. This is, of course, ironical in view of America's performance in the past.

In the whole of history there has probably never been a more thoroughly successful program of assistance than the Marshall Plan. The economic vitality of Western Europe today stands as a witness to its wisdom. The resources the United States committed to this effort were generous, but realistic, and the results in benefits to the entire Atlantic community, including America, have fully justified the investment.

In 1949, at the beginning of the Marshall Plan, American economic aid amounted to 2.79 per cent of its GNP, and 11.5 per cent of its federal budget. In FY 1970, the AID programs constitute less than one-fifth of 1 per cent of the GNP, and less than 1 per cent of the total federal budget. The United States now ranks ninth in the proportion of GNP devoted to aid.

But despite this present adverse trend in America towards foreign assistance, there are signs that the situation will improve. The President is firmly committed to the principle of development aid, and is supporting it. When he signed the Foreign Assistance authorization bill, he stated: "It is my personal conviction that such assistance remains vitally necessary if we are to effectively cooperate with less wealthy countries struggling to improve the lives of their citizens." In appointing the Peterson Task Force on International Development, he charged its members to come up with new and creative proposals. The President is seeking renewal, reform, and innovation in U.S. foreign aid policy, not stagnation.

No one can question that American domestic problems— particularly in the social and environmental fields—require increased attention and funding. But it is wholly unrealistic to suppose that this can only be achieved at the cost of cutting off aid to desperately poor nations abroad. The argument is sometimes made that rich countries must first take care of their own poor before worrying about the poor of other nations. Charity, after all—we are reminded—begins at home.

But I suggest that this argument, while appealing, misses the point. The President has pointed out that in the next ten years the U.S. will increase its wealth by 50 per cent and that the Gross National Product in 1979, at constant prices, will be $500 billion greater than last year. The fact is, then, that the American economy is so immense it can readily support a just and reasonable foreign aid program, within the general dimensions outlined by the Pearson Commission Report, and at the same time deal justly and effectively with domestic needs. The country is clearly wealthy enough to afford allocating a realistic percentage of its expanding resources to both tasks: to assist in alleviating underdevelopment both at home, and abroad.

There is no lack of capacity in the American economy to meet this twin set of responsibilities. What may be lacking is a broad commitment of the national will to do so. Or perhaps the deficit is not so much a lack of national will, as a lack of national understanding; not so much a case of a people indifferent to their responsibilities, as a case of understandable confusion over the competing claims on their attention and resolve.

What is certainly true is that the decision to respond both to the pressures of domestic problems, and the urgency of essential foreign assistance is, in the end, dependent on the response to a far more basic and searching question—a question that must be faced not in the United States alone, but in every wealthy, industrialized country of the world. And that question is this. Which is ultimately more in a nation's interest: to funnel national resources into an endlessly spiraling consumer economy —in effect, a pursuit of consumer gadgetry with all its senseless by-products of waste and pollution—or to dedicate a more reasonable share of those same resources to improving the fundamental quality of life both at home and abroad?

The dilemma that faces the wealthy nations of the world is not whether they should devote more of their GNP to solving domestic crises, and less of it to helping eliminate inhuman deprivations abroad; but rather whether they are going to seek a more equitable balance between private opulence and public responsibility. Private wealth cannot be preserved and public responsibility cannot be met by a heedless indifference to common crises that in the end will touch rich and poor alike.

What we must grasp is that gross measures of economic strength and gross measures of economic growth—for example, levels of GNP or rates of change of GNP—as necessary as they are, cannot measure the soundness of the social structure of a nation. The United States itself is a classic illustration of this truth. Technologically the most advanced society on earth, it produces the greatest GNP ever recorded in history, and enjoys a per capita income that is 30 times greater than that of the peoples in a quarter of the nations of the world.

But what do such figures mean when we remember that even for the affluent, life is beset by smog, pollution, noise, traffic congestion, urban violence, youthful disaffection and a terrifying increase in the drug problem? Worse still, the wealthiest society on earth has within its midst more than 20 million people so poor that their lives verge on mere subsistence. In 1967, 10 per cent of all white families and 35 per cent of all black families in America lived beneath the poverty line.

The poor in America are like the poor everywhere. Statistically their economic condition is improving, but the progress is so slow in relation to the more advantaged groups in society that they are actually growing poorer relative to the rich. The point is illustrative of a phenomenon common throughout the world. Though men have inhabited the same planet for more than a million years, they coexist today in communities that range in the extremes from stone-age simplicity to space-age sophistication.

That degree of inequality would not, perhaps, be as socially and politically explosive as it in fact is, could it remain a well kept secret. For centuries stagnating societies and deprived peoples remained content with their lot because they were unaware that life was really any better elsewhere. Their very remoteness saved them from odious comparisons. But the technological revolution has changed all that. Now, with the transistor radio and the television tube in remote corners of the world dramatizing the disparities in the quality of life, what was tolerable in the past provokes turbulence today.

And what else but turbulence could one expect on a planet linked by instantaneous communication but fragmented by conspicuous inequality. It is inconceivable that one-quarter of mankind, moving forward into a self-accelerating affluence, can succeed in walling itself off from the other three-quarters who find themselves entrapped in a self-perpetuating cycle of poverty.

It is not too much to conclude that the nature of the principal threat to the nations of the world today is internal strife rather than external aggression. In the case of the United States, that is precisely what Dr. Milton Eisenhower did conclude in his final report as Chairman of the National Commission on the Causes and Prevention of Violence. He was clear and emphatic in his analysis: "Our most serious challenges to date," he told the President, "have been external—the kind this strong and resourceful country could unite against. While serious external dangers remain, the graver threats today are internal."

The outlook for the Seventies is that the fault line along which shocks to world stability travel will shift from an East-West axis to a North-South axis, and the shocks themselves will be significantly less military and substantially more political, social, and economic in character.

In view of this, it is tragic and senseless that the world today is spending $175 billion a year on armaments—a sum so huge that it is 25 times larger than the total spent in all foreign assistance programs. What is even worse is that defense spending is increasing by some 6 per cent a year, a growth rate in destructive power that is greater than the growth rate of the world's total production of all goods and services. And the final irony in this litany of irrationalities is that arms spending in the less developed countries is rising at the rate of 7.5 per cent a year, as against the world average of 6 per cent.

Prudent military preparedness has its place. Prodigal military proliferation is human folly at its worst.

Now as I have pointed out, growth rates of GNP are entirely valid and necessary economic indicators, but they are not adequate measures of the development of a nation. Nor are they satisfactory terms in which to frame the objectives of development programs.

In the First Development Decade, the primary development objective, a 5 per cent annual growth in GNP, was achieved. This was a major accomplishment. The 5 per cent rate exceeded the average growth rates of the advanced countries during their own early stages of progress in the last century. But this relatively high rate of growth in GNP did not bring satisfactory progress in development. In the developing world, at the end of the decade:

- Malnutrition is common.

  The FAO estimates that at least a third to a half of the world's people suffer from hunger or nutritional deprivation. The average person in a high standard area consumes four pounds of food a day as compared with an average pound and a quarter in a low standard area.

- Infant mortality is high.

  Infant deaths per 1000 live births are four times as high in the developing countries as in the developed countries (110 compared with 27).

- Life expectancy is low.

  A man in the West can expect to live 40 per cent longer than the average man in the developing countries and twice as long as the average man in some of the African countries.

- Illiteracy is widespread.

  There are 100 million more illiterates today than there were 20 years ago, bringing the total number to some 800 million.

- Unemployment is endemic and growing.

  The equivalent of approximately 20 per cent of the entire male labor force is unemployed, and in many areas the urban population is growing twice as fast as the number of urban jobs.

- The distribution of income and wealth is severely skewed.

  In India, 12 per cent of the rural families control more than half of the cultivated land. And in Brazil, less than 10 per cent of the families control 75 per cent of the land.

- The gap between the per capita incomes of the rich nations and the poor nations is widening rather than narrowing, both relatively and absolutely.

  At the extremes that gap is already more than $3,000. Present projections indicate it may well widen to $9,000 by the end of the century. In the year 2000, per capita income in the United States is expected to be approximately $10,000; in Brazil, $500; in India, $200.

Just how much worse these conditions are at the end of the decade than they were at the beginning is difficult to determine. For most of them, even today, we lack satisfactory indicators and data. The result is that trying to plan to improve these conditions, in the absence of such measures and indicators, is like trying to plan price stabilization without price indices. It is an impossible task.

The lesson to be learned is that in setting the objectives, planning the programs, and measuring the progress of development in the Seventies, we must look to more than gross measures of economic growth. What we require are relevant "development indicators" that go beyond the measure of growth in total output and provide practical yardsticks of change in the other economic, social, and moral dimensions of the modernizing process. To limit our attention to expanding GNP, even though it be from 5 per cent per year to 6 or 7 per cent, can only lead to greater political, social and economic disequilibrium. However important an increase in GNP may be as a necessary condition of development, it is not a sufficient condition.

This is not to say that the Pearson Commission and Tinbergen Committee target of reaching a 6 per cent annual growth rate of GNP for the developing world in the Seventies is not both feasible and necessary.

It is feasible if those of us in the wealthier world will complement the growing savings of the developing countries by moving toward the development assistance objectives endorsed by both these distinguished groups. And it is necessary, if the broader objectives of development are to be met.

But if we achieve the "quantity" goals, and neglect the "quality" goals of development, we will have failed. It is as simple as that. We will have failed.

The Second Development Decade gives us the opportunity to establish and pursue "quality" goals of development with new insights, new strategies, and new emphases.

With that in mind, I would like to put before you one or two points on the possible role of the World Bank in this new task of seeking quality in the process of development. As a Bank we are naturally committed to the continuance and expansion of our role of mobilizing capital and using it for growth of the productive capacity of the developing nations. We plan during the five years 1969-73 to increase our lending by 100 per cent over the level of the previous five years. The very great advances in the developing countries' skills and infrastructure over the last decade have broadened the opportunities for productive investment, and we are determined at the Bank to take full advantage of them.

But—and I repeat the point—we cannot content ourselves with the mere quantity of our operations if they are not adding to the genuine quality of man's life on the planet. And if our investments are to meet this wider goal, I frankly admit that we and other investors need to add to the patterns of analysis a new dimension of social concern.

This concern must, of course, be as rigorous, factual and informed as any of our other economic analyses and forecasts.

We do not want simply to say that rising unemployment is a "bad thing" and something must be done about it. We want to know its scale, its causes, its impact and the range of policies and options which are open to governments, international agencies and the private sector to deal with it.

We do not want simply to sense that the "green revolution" requires a comparable social revolution in the organization and education of the small farmer. We want to know what evidence or working models are available on methods of cooperative enterprise, of decentralized credit systems, of smaller-scale technology, and of price and market guarantees.

We do not want simply to deplore over-rapid urbanization in the primary cities. We want the most accurate and careful studies of internal migration, town-formation, decentralized urbanism and regional balance.

These issues are fully as urgent as the proper exchange rates or optimal mixes of the factors of production. The only trouble is that we do not know enough about them. I would go further and say that, up to a point, we do not even know how to think about them. Just as the censuses of the 1950's helped to alert us to the scale of the population explosion, the urban and employment crises of the Sixties are alerting us to the scale of social displacement and general uprootedness of populations which are exploding not only in numbers but in movement as well. But we are still only picking up the distress signals. We still do not know how to act.

We should be frank about this. As we enter the Seventies, in field after field, we have more questions than answers. Our urgent need is for new instruments of research and analysis with which to dispel our ignorance of the social dimensions of economic change and help us formulate a more comprehensive strategy for the decade ahead.

We in the World Bank cannot, of course, alone and from our own resources, provide all the new information and expertise demanded by the scale of our ignorance. But we can stimulate and be part of a wider effort of research and education, and we can help draw together new resources for the formulation of wise development policies. We propose to seek the cooperation of universities, foundations, research units, other international institutions, and experienced administrators for that purpose.

Further, to provide a solid foundation for consultation and action by both developed and developing nations, in the whole field of development strategy and administration of aid, we plan a new and expanded program of Country Economic Missions. These will be regularly scheduled, thoroughly staffed, comprehensive missions whose mandate will be to assist the member government to draw up an overall development strategy which will include every major sector of the economy, and every relevant aspect of the nation's social framework.

One significant innovation in these missions is that the team itself will include representatives from the UNDP, who will play a central role in working out a pre-investment program, so that future development financing may be on a firmer foundation. Where appropriate, the team will include agricultural specialists from FAO, educational specialists from Unesco, medical officers from WHO, and employment experts from ILO, as well as other competent consultants in specialized sectors.

Our own Bank staff on the mission will be looking into not only the traditional problems of economic growth, but the other facets of development as well: questions of population increase, urbanization, land reform, income distribution, public health, environmental preservation, and all the related issues. Once the mission is completed, we will promptly produce for use by all of the parties concerned a thorough Economic Report which will serve as a profile of the country's progress, and of its overall development plan.

In our larger member countries—those containing 80 per cent of the population of the developing world—we will undertake these new Economic Missions annually; in other member countries, every two or three years. The essential point is that they will be comprehensive in scope, regular in schedule, and will form the basis for strategic rather than merely tactical development financing.

Perhaps one of the most wasteful mistakes that both developing countries and aid agencies can make is to proceed on a random project-by-project basis, rather than first to establish an overall development strategy, and then select projects that mutually support and interlock with one another within that overall plan. Our new program for Country Economic Reports is designed to provide a foundation for such a strategy.

●   ●   ●

All of us, within the worldwide community, have a mandate in common. Our ultimate goal is to help build the planet into a more habitable home for mankind, and to help create a political, social and economic environment in which individual men and women can more freely develop their own highest potential.

The funds we require to accomplish this are small compared with the funds the wealthy nations are already devoting to prodigiously disproportionate objectives.

The talents and managerial skills we require are at hand. We only need to organize them.

Finally, the most important ingredient of all—the dedication, the drive, the determination to see the task through—is, I believe, within our grasp. If development becomes a social as well as an economic objective, if it aims squarely at an end of grinding poverty and gross injustice, I believe it has a constituency waiting for it among the emerging generation of young adults. These young men and women are looking for goals beyond their own personal affluence. Human development is surely a challenge that can command their dedication, provided it is a development not simply in goods and gadgets but in the self-respect and dignity of man.

That, I believe, is the true dimension of the task that lies before all of us in the Second Decade of Development.

SEVEN

To the
BOARD OF GOVERNORS
COPENHAGEN, DENMARK
SEPTEMBER 21, 1970

The year that has passed since we last met has been a pivotal one. It marked the beginning of the second quarter-century of the Bank's existence, and prefaced the opening of the Second Development Decade. In our meeting twelve months ago I sketched out our plans for maintaining the momentum of the Bank Group's accelerated activity, stressed the need for fashioning a more comprehensive strategy for development, and welcomed the publication of the Pearson Commission Report.

Today, I would like to:

• Report to you on the Bank Group's operation in the fiscal year 1970.

• Review progress toward meeting the projected goals of our Five-Year Program.

• Discuss the responses to the key recommendations of the Pearson Commission.

• And comment upon the objectives of development in the Seventies.

I. THE BANK GROUP'S OPERATIONS IN FY70

Let me begin by touching upon our operations during the past fiscal year. For that period, new loans, credits, and investments totalled $2.3 billion. This compares with $1.88 billion in 1969 and $1.0 billion in 1968.

The Bank's cash and liquid security balances continued to rise and on June 30 of this year totalled $2.1 billion, up $250 million from June 30, 1969 and $700 million from June 30, 1968.

111

As I indicated to you at our last meeting, we believe that our plans for expanded operations—particularly at a time of uncertainty in the world's capital markets—ought to be backed by a high level of liquidity. This provides greater flexibility in our financing, and enables us to ride out market fluctuations over which we have no control. We propose to continue that policy.

The Bank's administrative expenses are, of course, rising as operations expand and as price inflation continues. But despite increases in operating costs, profits in FY 1970 amounted to $213 million: the highest in the Bank's history, and up 25% over 1969. Approximately one-half of the net income is to be retained in the Bank to support future concessionary lending and $100 million is recommended for transfer to the International Development Association.

II. THE FIVE-YEAR PROGRAM

The Bank Group's performance in 1970 was that of a vigorous and growing organization. But as I stressed last year, I believe the organization should shape its strategy to a longer time frame than year-to-year planning can provide. For that purpose, we have developed a Five-Year Program and in measuring any given year's performance, we should look to the larger framework of that Plan to assess our progress.

One objective is to double the Bank Group's operations in the five-year period 1969-1973, as compared with the period 1964-1968. Should we succeed, it will mean that we will have approved loans, credits, and investments during these five years that aggregate $12 billion for high-priority development projects —projects whose total cost will approximate $30 billion.

We have now completed the first two years of that Five-Year Program, and I can report to you that we are on schedule, and that I remain confident that we can reach our goals, formidable as they are.

They are formidable not merely, or even mainly, because of their quantitative magnitude, but because of their qualitative character. The Bank Group over the past two years has not simply been trying to do "more"—but to do more of what will best contribute to the optimal development of the developing nations.

Over the past 24 months we have made specific and significant shifts in that direction:

- We have intensified our efforts in the agricultural sector—to guarantee more food for expanding populations, to promote agricultural exports, and to provide a necessary stimulant to industrial growth. Our agricultural projects in 1969 and 1970 alone totalled half as many as in the entire previous history of the Bank.

- We have substantially increased our financing of education projects—projects designed to reduce the drag of functional illiteracy on development. Lending for education in these past two years was more than the total of all prior years put together.

- We have broadened our geographical scope considerably so that we could be of service to more developing countries and in particular to more small and very poor countries. In each of the years 1969 and 1970 we lent to a total of 60 countries, 75% more countries in each year than in the average year 1964-1968. Further, in the same two-year period, we have served 14 countries (including such very poor countries as Indonesia, Rwanda, Chad, Dahomey, Democratic Republic of the Congo, and Nepal) which had received no loans or credits in the previous five years.

- We have begun work in the field of population planning—admittedly more modestly than the urgency of the problem demands—at the specific request of countries such as India, Indonesia, Jamaica, and Tunisia.

- We have made a start at broadening the concept of development beyond the simple limits of economic growth. The emerging nations need, and are determined to achieve, greater economic advance. But as I will state more fully later, we believe economic progress remains precarious and sterile without corresponding social improvement. Fully human development demands attention to both. We intend, in the Bank, to give attention to both.

• We have initiated a new and expanded program of Country Economic Missions in order better to assist the developing nations in their formulation of overall development strategies, and at the same time to provide a foundation for the donor nations and international agencies to channel their technical and financial assistance in as productive a manner as possible. Practical planning in the development field calls for current and comprehensive socio-economic data. The World Bank Group will gather, correlate, and make available this information to the appropriate authorities. As this program gains momentum we will schedule regular annual reports on the 30 largest of our developing member countries—we recently issued the first in this new series—and biennial or triennial reports on another 60 countries.

III. THE PEARSON COMMISSION RECOMMENDATIONS

I want to turn now to the attention given to the recommendations of the Pearson Commission. As you know, the Commission's work was financed by the Bank, but with the stringent safeguard that it should be completely independent in its investigations, and that its conclusions should represent the candid consensus of the Commissioners themselves, speaking their minds frankly. The Report was addressed not to the Bank itself, but to the world at large, and its purpose was to take a fresh and impartial look at every significant factor in the global development scene.

A. Recommendations Relating Specifically to the Bank

At our last annual meeting, which coincided with the publication of the Report, I indicated that we in the Bank would undertake a thorough analysis of each of the Commission's recommendations that touched upon our own activities. There were 33 such recommendations. After giving the most careful consideration to these proposals, I have so far submitted to the Executive Directors detailed memoranda on 31 of them for discussion and review. In the great majority of instances, I expressed agreement with the Commission's recommendations.

The Commission, for example, recommended that the policies of the International Finance Corporation should be reoriented to give greater emphasis to the development implications of its investments, and should not simply stress their profitability. I fully agreed with that viewpoint, and, after review by the Executive Directors, the IFC issued in January a new Statement of Policies which reflects the recommended shift in emphasis.

The Commission was concerned, as well, over the danger of the excessive use of export credits—a practice that has led a number of countries to assume external debt of unmanageable proportions. To guard against this hazard the Commission recommended that the Organization for Economic Cooperation and Development and the Bank develop what it termed "a strong early warning system" which can help developing countries avert sudden debt crises. We agree that there is a role here for the Bank: we are working, therefore, with the OECD to improve the scope and quality of information on external debt and with the International Monetary Fund to identify debt problems and help developing countries work out solutions.

Another recommendation dealt with the issue of establishing new multilateral groupings which could provide for annual reviews of the development performance of recipients and help to assure that external aid is closely linked to their economic objectives. I concur, and with the approval of the governments concerned, we are currently organizing new groups for the Republic of the Congo, Ethiopia, and the Philippines, and reactivating the groups for Thailand and Nigeria.

The Commission felt that the Bank should participate in discussions of debt-servicing problems, with a view to searching out new solutions to that increasingly complicated question. We agree and have initiated a series of studies of the debt-servicing difficulties facing a number of our member nations. The external public debt of developing countries has increased fivefold since the mid-1950s, and debt-service payments have grown at a rate of 17% annually while foreign exchange receipts from exports have risen only 6% per year. Obviously such trends cannot be allowed to continue indefinitely.

The Commissioners, in another proposal, suggested that international centers should be established within developing countries for essential scientific and technological research that could be practically applied to urgent problems. The case of agriculture is particularly important, since the work on new wheat and rice strains, for use on irrigated land, has dramatically demonstrated what can be achieved. But as encouraging as these discoveries have been, it is clear that a food crisis in the 1980s and 1990s is unlikely to be avoided unless additional research is devoted now—in the 1970s—to the improvement of rain-fed cultivation of rice and wheat, as well as to other essential food resources, such as sorghum, maize, oilseeds, grain, legumes, and livestock.

What we require is not simply incremental improvements in agriculture, but whole new technologies adaptable to the conditions of the developing countries. The Bank is seeking to find ways in which it can assist in stimulating and supporting such a program.

Among the very few recommendations of the Commission with which I disagreed, there is one on which I should comment. This was the suggestion that the International Development Association may require reorganization. By implication, the Commission appeared to be saying the Bank would operate as a bank and not as a development agency, and therefore IDA should be set up independently to go its separate way.

Such a conclusion appears to reflect the view that because the Bank obtains its funds by borrowing in the world's capital markets whereas IDA is financed by appropriations from governments, the two will of necessity follow different lending policies. But this is not the case. Subject only to creditworthiness considerations, I believe the two organizations should lend on the basis of identical criteria. The source of the funds to be lent is irrelevant to the economic case for their investment. *What contributes most to the development of the borrowing country should be the decisive factor in both Bank and IDA operations.*

If the Bank were in fact subordinating the development interest of its borrowers to other considerations, the proper solution, in my opinion, would be to change the Bank's policies—not to reorganize IDA. Any policy which can be justified for IDA as consistent with its development function can, I believe, be equally justified for the Bank, and the Bank should adopt it.

There is occasional criticism of both our Bank loans and IDA credits because of the stringent conditions on which they are negotiated. But those very conditions are specifically designed to assist the borrowing country. Their purpose is to insure that the Bank Group's resources are used for the optimum development of our borrowers. Economic losses and financial waste are, after all, of no benefit to any country's development. Our standards of prudence and performance should be just as strict for IDA credits as they are for Bank loans. Indeed, it is the poorest countries, those who benefit most from IDA, who can least afford losses or waste.

B. Recommendations to Others

As I have noted, the Pearson Commission Report was addressed not specifically to the Bank, but to the world at large. And it is clear that three of its most far-reaching recommendations dealt with:

- Establishing and meeting a realistic target for the flow of external assistance to the developing countries.

- The design of better criteria and the creation of new machinery to measure and assess the performance of both donor and recipient nations in the development field.

- And the urgent need to find acceptable and effective measures to reduce excessive rates of population growth in those countries where the promise of a better future is being swept away by a tidal wave of unwanted births.

The first of these recommendations—the formulation and achievement of a realistic target of development assistance—is making encouraging progress. Action by the development community on the other two issues is far from satisfactory.

Let me discuss for a moment the first.

C. The Aid Target

Not only is the Pearson Commission's proposal on this matter one of its most important recommendations for the 1970s, but the whole background of the question is worth recalling.

In 1960 the UN General Assembly adopted a resolution to the effect that "the flow of international assistance and capital should be increased substantially so as to reach as soon as possible approximately 1% of the combined national incomes of the economically advanced countries." This concept was elaborated by the United Nations Conference on Trade and Development in 1964, and was endorsed as well by the Development Assistance Committee of the Organization for Economic Cooperation and Development. At the second meeting of UNCTAD in 1968 the target was reformulated to call for 1% of Gross National Product, and was adopted again by resolution.

As the Pearson Commission points out, the irony is that although the 1% target was in fact exceeded during the five years prior to its formal adoption by the DAC in 1964, it has not been fully met in any year since.

What is perhaps not fully understood by the public is that the target of 1% of GNP has not, in the strict sense, been an aid target at all. In practice, it has described the total flow of financial resources from the richer nations to the poorer nations, and has not distinguished between conventional commercial transactions, and concessional, development-oriented aid as such. Commercial transactions can contribute to the development process. But private capital flows are simply not available on the terms required for many of the priority projects—schools, for example, or roads, or irrigation — which the developing countries need so badly. The Commission concluded, therefore, that the flow of official development aid was indispensable. And yet in relation to GNP in the developed world, official development aid fell by a third during the 1960s.

It was for these reasons that the Commission strongly recommended that a separate target be established for official development assistance—a target equivalent to 0.7% of GNP—and urged that this target be reached by approximately the middle of the decade, but in no case later than 1980.

This is a target calling for a very substantial effort. Since the total official development aid of the member governments of DAC amounted in 1969 to 0.36% of their combined GNPs, the Commission was in effect recommending that government aid, in relation to GNP, be doubled in the Seventies.

What has been the response to this recommendation?

To the surprise, perhaps, of the skeptics, it has on the whole been very positive. With but a single exception, no member government of DAC has rejected the target, and several—including Belgium, the Netherlands, Norway and Sweden—have fully accepted it. Canada and the United Kingdom have agreed in principle on the size of the commitment, but have not set a firm date for its achievement. France is already meeting the target, and both the Federal Republic of Germany and Japan have stated they will move toward it.

Among the first consequences of the decisions of governments to increase their official development aid, and reflecting their concern over the growing burden of debt, was their agreement to support a Third Replenishment of IDA, for the years 1972, 1973, and 1974 at a rate of $800 million per year, as compared to $400 million per year in the previous period.

Though it is true that the United States has noted that it cannot commit itself to specific quantitative aid targets, the U.S. Administration provided strong support to the substantial increase in the replenishment of IDA and has stated it intends to propose expanding the flow of U.S. aid from the present low levels.

In 1949, at the beginning of the Marshall Plan, American economic aid amounted to 2.79% of GNP and 11.5% of its federal budget. In 1970, the AID programs constitute less than 0.3% of GNP, and less than 1% of the budget. The United States now ranks eleventh, among the 16 DAC members, in the proportion of GNP devoted to aid.

No one can question that American domestic problems—particularly in the social and economic fields — require increased attention and financial support. But it is wholly unrealistic to suppose that this can only be achieved by cutting off aid to desperately poor nations abroad. Economists have pointed out that in the next ten years the U.S. will increase its income by 50% and that the GNP in 1979, at constant prices, will be $500 billion greater than in 1969. It would appear that the country is wealthy enough to support a just and reasonable foreign aid program, and at the same time deal effectively with domestic needs. And to me it is inconceivable that the American people will accept for long a situation in which they—forming 6% of the world's population but consuming almost 40% of the world's resources—contribute less than their fair share to the development of the emerging nations.

As I have noted elsewhere, the decision to respond both to the pressure of domestic problems, and the urgency of essential foreign assistance, will in the end be dependent upon the response to a far more basic and searching question—a question that must be faced not in the U.S. alone, but in every wealthy, industrialized country of the world. And that question is this. Which is ultimately more in a nation's interest: to funnel national resources into an endlessly spiraling consumer economy—with its by-products of waste and pollution—or to dedicate a more reasonable share of these same resources to improving the fundamental quality of life both at home and abroad?

Following the end of World War II, the world witnessed a massive transfer of resources from the wealthy nations to both the war-torn and the less-developed countries. This began as an unprecedented act of statesmanship. Over the years, however, this capital flow was increasingly influenced by narrow concepts of national self-interest. Some nations saw it as a weapon in the cold war; others looked upon it mainly as a means to promote their own commercial gain.

Today these narrow views are waning. More and more, the concept of economic assistance is being accepted as a necessary consequence of a new philosophy of international responsibility. It is a philosophy which recognizes that just as within an individual nation the community has a responsibility to assist its less advantaged citizens, so within the world community as a whole the rich nations have a responsibility to assist the less advantaged nations. It is not a sentimental question of philanthropy. It is a straightforward issue of social justice.

A growing number of governments are accepting this conclusion and there are, therefore, solid grounds for concluding that the decade of the Seventies will witness a substantial increase —both in absolute amounts, and in proportion to the GNP— of the critical flow of official development aid from the wealthier nations to the poorer nations.

D. Better Coordination and Assessment of Effort

But as the Commission points out, the global development effort is currently fragmented into an almost bewildering number of overlapping and uncoordinated activities. This leads inevitably to duplication of effort, inefficient planning, and a scattering of scarce resources. What is required is organizational machinery that can effectively and authoritatively monitor and assess the performance of donor and recipient countries alike, reduce the proliferation of unstandardized reporting, and effect more coherent, cooperative and purposeful partnership throughout the entire development community.

This is particularly important if we are to rally the necessary public understanding and support in the industrialized countries for the critical tasks of global development that lie before us.

The Commission recommended that the President of the World Bank call an international conference on this matter this year. However, within the United Nations system, of which the Bank is a part, these functions are the responsibility of the Economic and Social Council. That body is presently considering proposals for new machinery for review and appraisal of development programs at the national, regional, and international levels. Under the circumstances it would be premature for the Bank to take action at this time. The problem itself, however, remains and we must find ways—and find them soon—to secure a far greater measure of coordinated management of the combined capabilities of the national and international agencies participating in the development process. Such an objective is, in itself, one of the most productive goals we could pursue as the new decade begins.

But if the issues of an official development aid target, and improved management within the development community, are among the most important recommendations of the Pearson Commission for the short-term, the most imperative issue for the long-term is population planning.

E. Population Planning

The Commission faced this problem squarely, without hedging its views. "No other phenomenon," it stated flatly, "casts a darker shadow over the prospects for international development than the staggering growth of population. . . . It is clear that there can be no serious social and economic planning unless the ominous implications of uncontrolled population growth are understood and acted upon."

Are the "ominous implications of uncontrolled population growth" being acted upon effectively? If one is to be candid, the answer would have to be *no*. With the exception of Singapore and Hong Kong, which are special cases, in only two developing countries, Taiwan[a] and Korea, is there clear evidence that the rate of population growth has been significantly reduced by family planning programs.

It is worth asking why.[b]

One prominent authority in the population field has pointed out that the prospects for the success of family planning throughout the world are at one and the same time promising, and dubious: promising if we do what in fact can be done; dubious if in fact we continue as we are.

The task is difficult for many reasons, but primarily because of its sheer overwhelming size. Consider the magnitude of the factors involved: there are dozens of countries plagued with the problem—each of them different, each of them possessing their own particular set of social and cultural traditions. There are thousands of clinical facilities to be established; hundreds of

[a]Even Taiwan, which through a most effective population planning program has reduced its growth rate from 2.8% in 1965 to 2.3% in 1969, will—if it succeeds by 1985 in reaching a point where couples only replace themselves—see its present population of 14 million rise to 35 million before it becomes stationary.

[b]I am indebted to Bernard Berelson, President of the Population Council, for a number of the points in this section.

thousands of staff workers to be recruited, trained and organized in the administration of the vast national programs; hundreds of millions of families to be informed and served; and well over one billion births to be averted in the developing world alone, if, for example, by the year 2000 the present birth rate of 40 per 1000 population were to be reduced to 20 per 1000. What we must understand is that even if an average family size of two children per couple is achieved, the population will continue to grow for an additional 65 or 70 years and the ultimate stabilized level will be far greater than at the time the two-per-couple rate is achieved.[a]

Thus, even with gigantic efforts, the problem is going to be with us for decades to come. But this fact, rather than being an excuse for delay, is all the more an imperative for action—and for action now. Every day we fail to act makes the task more formidable the following day.

What must we do?

First, we must have a feasible goal. I suggest that goal should be to gain a few decades on what would occur to fertility in the absence of population planning. The achievement of this goal would mean a substantial increase in the quality of life for both the parents and the children of the developing countries —in better health, better education, better nutrition, and in many other ways—as a direct result of populations totalling some 6 billion less than would otherwise be the case.

And what must be done to achieve this goal? Five ingredients are needed:

1. The political will to support the effort.

2. The required understanding and the willingness to act on the part of the people.

3. The availability of effective, acceptable birth control methods.

[a]If, for instance, by the year 2000, the developed countries were to reach the point at which couples only replace themselves, and the developing countries were to reach that point by the year 2050—and both these achievements appear unlikely—the world's present population of 3.5 billion would not become stationary before the year 2120, and would then stand at fifteen billion.

4. An efficient organization to administer the program.

5. Demographic data and analyses to evaluate results and point to program weaknesses requiring correction.

Where do we stand on each of these?

To begin with, there has recently been a dramatic increase in political support for population planning. The latest example is the Philippines, a country with a severe population problem, but a country in which it has been understandably difficult to take the open, public decisions that are required. President Marcos faced the delicate issue frankly in his State of the Nation message to his Congress a few months ago:

"With a soaring birth rate, the prospects for a continued economic development are considerably diminished. Indeed, there is a strong possibility that the gains which we have carefully built up over the years may be cancelled by a continuing population explosion. . . . After a careful weighing of factors, I have decided to propose legislation making family planning an official policy of my Administration."

His Minister of Foreign Affairs put the matter with equal candor:

"The control of population is essentially an economic, cultural, and political problem. One of the most hopeful means of bringing the birth rate down to near replacement level is the Department of Education's plan to introduce this entire subject into the curricula of schools and colleges. . . . Underlying this approach is a clear recognition that education has the twofold obligation to reinforce, and where necessary, to help change public mores. Educational institutions, from the elementary to the postgraduate years, can perform no more useful service in the seventies than to illuminate the principles of human survival and to dedicate themselves to preserving and enhancing the quality and diversity of life."

In 1960 only three countries had population planning policies, only one government was actually offering assistance, and no international development agency was working in the field of family planning.

In 1970 (as indicated in the attached table) 22 countries in Asia, Africa, and Latin America—countries representing 70% of the population of those continents—have official population programs. More than a dozen other countries, representing a further 10% of the population, provide some assistance to family planning, though they as yet have no officially formulated policy. And among the international agencies, the UN Population Division, UNDP, Unesco, WHO, FAO, ILO, UNICEF, OECD, and the World Bank have all stated a willingness to participate in population planning activities.

There are geographical differences (in Asia, some 87% of the people live in countries with "favorable family planning policies," while in Latin America and Africa the figure is only 20%), but political acceptance of family planning programs is widespread. Even where the political support is currently more apparent than real, it is becoming stronger with each passing year.

If, then, the first requirement for the success of family planning is political support at the top—and that is improving—where are the roadblocks?

The first is that the citizenry lacks access to the information and assistance required. Surveys indicate that the interest in family planning among people everywhere is high, but that their understanding is often tenuous at best and tragically erroneous at worst. Millions of parents, even in remote areas of the world, want fewer children, but they simply lack the knowledge to achieve this. Programs must be developed to provide them with the information they seek.[a]

But political support and widespread knowledge are still not enough. The techniques of family planning must, themselves, be adequate, appropriate, and available. The means we currently have at hand are much better than those of a decade ago, but are still imperfect. They can be used to accomplish much more than has been already achieved, but concurrently a massive program to improve them must be initiated. Our knowledge in this field is so incomplete that though we know

[a] In only a handful of developing countries is there a significant percentage of women of reproductive age following fertility control practices. The percentage of women in developed countries who are doing so is six times as great.

that certain techniques do work, we still do not completely understand how or why they work. The fact is that compared to what we need to know, our knowledge remains elementary, even primitive.

The clear consequence of this is that there must be a greatly expanded research effort in basic reproductive biology. At present, I know of only seven locations in the world in which as many as five full-time senior researchers are working in this field. Some $275 million a year is spent on cancer research. But less than $50 million a year is spent on reproductive biology research, and this includes all the funds allocated, worldwide, by public and private institutions alike. The estimate is that an optimal program of research and development in this field would require $150 million a year for a decade. That is an insignificant price to pay in the face of a problem that—if left unsolved—will in the end exact social and economic costs beyond calculation.

Finally, a population planning program to be successful requires a strong administrative organization and a comprehensive data analysis and evaluation service. With but one or two exceptions, none of the developing countries has established adequate support in either of these areas. I know, for example, of only one location in the world where as many as three senior researchers are working full-time on the evaluation aspects of population planning. A number of governments have made a start at strengthening the organizational structure of family planning, but progress is thwarted by bureaucratic difficulties, lack of technical assistance, and inadequate financial support. It is in these areas that the international institutions can be most effective. Additional effort is required from all of us, including the Bank. Many of our members are appealing for greater support. They want our advice as well as our financial help, and I propose to organize our capability to provide them with more of both.

The additional funds required to attack the population problem on all fronts—for reproductive biological research, for social science research, and for better organization and administration—are relatively small, less than 50¢ per capita per year. But the time that will be required to achieve results will be greater than many have realized. This is all the more reason for accelerating our pace. An OECD study concluded that in 1968 family planning programs in developing countries accounted for only 2½ million averted births, compared to the total of over one billion that must be averted in the next three decades if the rate of growth is to be reduced to 1% by the year 2000. If we are to achieve an average fifteenfold increase in the effectiveness of the program over the next 30 years, we must accelerate our efforts now.

The Pearson Commission emphasized that the population problem will not go away. It will be resolved in one way or another: either by sensible solutions or senseless suffering. If we want a sensible solution, with the corresponding enhancement of the quality of life for hundreds of millions of children, as well as for their parents — all of whom clearly have the intrinsic right to something more than a degrading subsistence —then we must get on with it.

IV. THE OBJECTIVES OF DEVELOPMENT IN THE SEVENTIES

I want to emphasize the last point and relate it to the objectives of development in the Seventies. The profound concern we must feel for the rapid growth of population stems precisely from the menace it brings to any morally acceptable standard of existence. We do not want fewer children born into the world because—to quote the more extreme critics of population policy—we do not like their color, or fear their future enmity, or suspect that they will in some unspecified way encroach upon the high consumption standards of already industrialized lands. This is not, as is sometimes claimed, an exercise in concealed genocide, perpetrated by the already rich on the aspiring poor. It has one source and one only—the belief that without a slowing down and control of the population explosion, the life awaiting millions upon millions of this planet's future inhabitants will be stunted, miserable, and tragic or, if you prefer the hackneyed but fitting phrase of the philosopher Hobbes, "nasty, brutish and short."

This fact takes us far beyond the population explosion. We have to see population as part—a vital, critical part but still only a part—of a much wider social and political crisis which grows deeper with each decade and threatens to round off this century with years of unrest and turbulence: a "time of troubles" during which the forces of historical change threaten to disintegrate our frail twentieth-century society.

We cannot divert these forces. They are an essential part of the process by which mankind is adapting the whole of its life to the advances in science and technology. About one-third of humanity has moved far in the transfer toward modernization and relative affluence. Now the rest of the human species jostle behind. They certainly have no intention of renouncing or missing the wealth and prosperity, above all, the power locked up in modern technology.

"Modernization" is a central thrust throughout the still-developing lands, but they are seeking to modernize under quite unprecedented conditions. Technological and scientific modernization is now more complicated, more hazardous than it was for the industrial nations a century ago. This is in fact the real root of the crisis.

Mr. Lester Pearson in a speech at the Columbia University Conference in February this year, gave a cogent and relevant resume of the historical differences between nineteenth- and twentieth-century development. He emphasized the contrast between the balanced and fundamentally progressive character of economic, social, and technological change in the nineteenth century, and the growing evidence of fundamental imbalance and hence regressive forces at work in the unfolding of the same processes of modernization today.

In the nineteenth century, population—held down by epidemics and poor public health—caused the work force to grow by less than 1% per year. This was just about the amount which the technology of the times could usefully absorb and employ. Agricultural productivity rose and temperate land was opened up for European use all around the globe. The cities grew as centers of manufacturing, and by the time technology demanded fewer and more sophisticated workers, and public health had lowered the death rate, education and city-living had produced a more stable population. In addition, the vast migration of Europeans to new lands was a further safety valve.

Today, every one of the nineteenth-century conditions is reversed.

Just as the censuses of the 1950s first alerted the world to the scale of the population explosion, so today surveys made in the 1960s of unemployment, of internal migration, of city growth, begin to lay bare for us a new world topography of vast social imbalance and deepening misery.

Advances in public health have resulted in a growth of population which increases the work force by at least 2% per year. At the same time technology becomes steadily more capital-intensive and absorbs steadily fewer men. Although agricultural productivity is now on the rise, the new techniques are destabilizing in the sense that they widen income inequities and release still more workers from the overcrowded land. And where today can the rural migrants go? The world is already allotted, the land occupied by the nineteenth-century modernizers.

So the cities fill up and urban unemployment steadily grows. Very probably there is an equal measure of worklessness in the countryside. The poorest quarter of the population in developing lands risks being left almost entirely behind in the vast transformation of the modern technological society. The "marginal" men, the wretched strugglers for survival on the fringes of farm and city, may already number more than half a billion. By 1980 they will surpass a billion, by 1990 two billion. Can we imagine any human order surviving with so gross a mass of misery piling up at its base?

Let us for a moment look at this misery in the developing world in the realities of human suffering and deprivation:

- Malnutrition is common.
  The FAO estimates that at least a third to a half of the world's people suffer from hunger or nutritional deprivation. The average person in a high-standard area consumes four pounds of food a day as compared with an average pound and a quarter in a low-standard area.

- Infant mortality is high.
  Infant deaths per 1000 live births are four times as high in the developing countries as in the developed countries (110 compared with 27).

- Life expectancy is low.
  A man in the West can expect to live 40% longer than the average man in the developing countries and twice as long as the average man in some of the African countries.

- Illiteracy is widespread.
  There are 100 million more illiterates today than there were 20 years ago, bringing the total number to some 800 million.

- Unemployment is endemic and growing.
  The equivalent of approximately 20% of the entire male labor force is unemployed, and in many areas the urban population is growing twice as fast as the number of urban jobs.

- The distribution of income and wealth is severely skewed, and in some countries becoming more so.
  In India, 12% of the rural families control more than half of the cultivated land. In Brazil, less than 10% of the families control 75% of the land. In Pakistan, the disparity in per capita income between East and West, which amounted to 18% in 1950, became 25% in 1960, 31% in 1965, and 38% in 1970.

- The gap between the per capita incomes of the rich nations and the poor nations is widening rather than narrowing, both relatively and absolutely.
  At the extremes that gap is already more than $3,000. Present projections indicate it may well widen to $9,000 by the end of the century. In the year 2000, per capita income in the United States in terms of today's prices is expected to be approximately $10,000; in Brazil, $500; and in India, $200.

At least a quarter of the human race faces the prospect of entering the twenty-first century in poverty more unacceptable by contrast than that of any previous epoch. Frankly I do not see this as a situation in which any of our shared hopes for a long peace and steady material progress are likely to be achieved. On the contrary, I agree with Lester Pearson's somber belief that "a planet cannot, any more than a country, survive, half-slave, half-free, half-engulfed in misery, half-careening along towards the supposed joys of almost unlimited consumption." In that direction lies disaster, yet that is our direction today unless we are prepared to change course—and to do so in time.

How then should we react to these deepening risks? I must assume that we will react, for to carry on any of our activities as political leaders, government officials, business and labor leaders or responsible citizens, we must take for granted a certain minimum rationality in human affairs. And it is not rational to confront historical pressures on a far greater scale than those of the revolutionary periods of the eighteenth and nineteenth centuries without accepting the consequences.

So I would like to end my report to you with four possible points for your agenda.

The first is that we accept the full scale of the world crisis. Over the last decade the developing nations have achieved the historically unprecedented rate of growth of 5% a year. This has been made possible in part by a reasonably sustained level of external assistance. Yet as the 1970s open, the evidence accumulates that economic growth alone cannot bring about that steady social transformation of a people without which further advances cannot occur. In short, we have to admit that economic growth—even if pushed to the 6% annual rate proposed as a target for the '70s both by the Pearson Commission and by the United Nations Committee on the Second Development Decade—will not, of itself, be enough to accomplish our development objectives. Growth is a necessary but not a sufficient cause of successful modernization. We must secure a 6% growth rate. We must deploy the resources necessary for it. But we must do more. We must ensure that in such critical fields as population planning, rural renewal, fuller employment, and decent urbanism, positive policies support and hasten the social transformation without which economic growth itself becomes obstructed and its results impaired.

This brings me to my second point. I have already discussed at some length the difficulties attendant upon any strategy for family planning. I think we have to admit that in other equally critical fields as well we still lack the necessary understanding and expertise. It must be our prime purpose in research and analysis to close these gaps.

We do not want simply to say that rising unemployment is a "bad thing" and something must be done about it. We want to know its scale, its causes, its impact and the range of policies and options which are open to governments, international agencies and the private sector to deal with it.

We do not want simply to sense that the "green revolution" requires a comparable social revolution in the organization and education of the small farmer. We want to know what evidence or working models are available on methods of cooperative enterprise, of decentralized credit systems, of smaller-scale technology, and of price and market guarantees.

We do not want simply to deplore over-rapid urbanization in the primary cities. We want the most accurate and careful studies of internal migration, town-formation, decentralized urbanism and regional balance.

These issues are fully as urgent as the proper exchange rates or optimal mixes of the factors of production. The trouble is that we do not know enough about them. As we enter the '70s we have in field after field more questions than answers. But this only adds to the urgency and determination with which we must intensify our intellectual attack.

This urgency in turn is related to my third point. I need not belabor it. It is simply that we cannot allow the fundamental task of developing the undeveloped nations of this planet to fail for lack of resources—both the resources needed for research and experiment, and the much larger resources needed to back the policies which we already feel to be successful.

Let us look for a moment at this question of resources. For the so-called security of an ever spiraling arms race, the world is spending $180 billion annually and the figure steadily goes up.

Four years ago in a speech in Montreal, I tried to point out that more and more military hardware does not provide more and more security. There is a point of diminishing returns beyond which further financial expenditure on military power does not yield increased returns and does not provide greater strength. I believed then, and I believe today, that most of the nations of both the developed and the developing world are beyond that point of diminishing returns.

If that is true, it is tragic that for the fundamental security of societies progressive enough not to explode into lethal revolution, the developed nations hesitate to maintain even the present $7 billion of public aid expenditure. That twenty times more should be spent on military power than on constructive progress appears to me to be the mark of an ultimate, and I sometimes fear, incurable folly. If there were only a 5% shift from arms to development we would be within sight of the Pearson target for official development assistance. And who among us, familiar with the methods and audits of arms planning, would not admit that such a margin could be provided from convertible waste alone?

This brings me to my last point. There are really no material obstacles to a sane, manageable, and progressive response to the world's development needs. The obstacles lie in the minds of men. We have simply not thought long enough and hard enough about the fundamental problems of the planet. Too many millennia of tribal suspicion and hostility are still at work in our subconscious minds. But what human society can ultimately survive without a sense of community? Today we are in fact an inescapable community, united by the forces of communication and interdependence in our new technological order. The conclusion is inevitable: we must apply at the world level that same moral responsibility, that same sharing of wealth, that same standard of justice and compassion, without which our own national societies would surely fall apart.

Thus the challenge of the scientific revolution is not a tremendous technological conundrum like putting a man on the moon. It is much more a straightforward moral obligation, like getting him out of a ghetto, out of a favella, out of illiteracy and hunger and despair. We can meet this challenge if we have the wisdom and moral energy to do so. But if we lack these qualities, then I fear, we lack the means of survival on this planet.

CLASSIFICATION OF DEVELOPING COUNTRIES IN RELATION TO GOVERNMENTAL POPULATION PLANNING POLICIES[a]

Population size (millions)	Governments With Official Population Policy	Governments Providing Assistance to Family Planning but Without An Official Population Policy	Governments With No Population Planning Policy and No Assistance to Family Planning	
400 and more	India (27) Mainland China (35)			
100-400	Pakistan (21) Indonesia (24)			
50-100		Nigeria (27)	Brazil (25)	
25-50	Philippines (21) Thailand (21) Iran (24) UAR (25) Turkey (26) South Korea (28)		Mexico (21) Burma (31)	
15-25	Morocco (21)	Colombia (21)	Sudan (22) Afghan.(28) Congo (DR) (32)	Ethiopia (33) N. Viet-Nam (33) S. Viet-Nam (33)
10-15	Kenya (23) Malaysia (25) Ceylon (29) Rep. of China (31) Nepal (32)	Venezuela (21)	Algeria (22) Peru (23)	N. Korea (25) Tanzania (27)
Less than 10	Dom. Rep. (21) Ghana (24) Tunisia (24) Mauritius (28) Singapore (29) Jamaica (33)	Costa Rica (19) Ecuador (21) El Salvador (21) Honduras (21) Panama (21) Nicaragua (24) Dahomey (27) Hong Kong (28) Chile (31) Botswana (32)	Kuwait (9) Iraq (21) Jordan (21) Paraguay (21) Syria (21) Libya (23) Cambodia (24) Guatemala (24) Guyana (24) Lebanon (24) Niger (24) Rwanda (24) Zambia (24) Saudi Ar. (25) Yemen (25) Madagascar (26) Togo (27) Uganda (27)	Haiti (28) Laos (28) Malawi (28) Bolivia (29) Chad (29) Ivory Coast (29) Mali (29) Senegal (29) Somalia (29) Burundi (31) Guinea (31) Sierra Le. (31) Cameroon (32) CAR (32) Congo (B) (32) Mauritania (32) Upper Volta (33)

[a]Only developing countries with population growth rates in excess of 2.0% are listed on this table. The number of years in which their population will double, at current growth rates, is indicated in parentheses after each country. Since the growth rates for most of these countries are not known with great precision, the ''doubling times'' are necessarily approximations.

EIGHT

To the
BOARD OF GOVERNORS
WASHINGTON, D.C.
SEPTEMBER 27, 1971

I. INTRODUCTION

Today I want to talk with you mainly about basic problems of development: nutrition, employment, income distribution, and trade. However, before doing so, let me comment briefly on the events of the past few weeks and their relation to the developing world.

It is clear that we are in for a difficult period of basic readjustments in international monetary and trade arrangements and that the repercussions may continue for some time. Although the solution of these problems is not the responsibility of the World Bank, we are deeply concerned with the manner of their resolution because of the impact it may have on the external trade of the developing countries, and on the resource flows to them.

The transfer of public and private capital to the developing countries—to which all the advanced countries are committed—is critically dependent on the operation of an exchange system that does not interfere with their continued flow. Foreign exchange difficulties have at various times induced donor countries to tie their aid to domestic procurement, to inhibit the outflow of private capital, and sometimes to limit their appropriations for public development loans and grants. In recent years a serious obstacle to the achievement of the United Nations target of a transfer of public and private capital equal to 1% of the GNP of the developed countries has been the preoccupation of some of the donor countries with the effect of such transfers on their balance of payments. Whatever steps are taken to improve the operation of the international monetary system must be such as to permit a continuing increase in capital flows to meet the targets to which the developed countries have subscribed: an increase in public development assistance from $8 billion per year in 1970 to $12.5 billion per year in 1975.

The developing countries are just as dependent for their continued growth on a rapid expansion of trade with advanced countries. Developing and developed countries alike will benefit from an international financial framework which permits smooth and rapid growth of production and trade. I will develop this subject at greater length further on.

137

In our previous meetings in this forum I have stressed the view that our era is characterized by a basic demographic shift whose consequences reach to the very heart of the development problem. Progress in both the qualitative and quantitative aspects of life of the vast majority of developing countries is severely threatened by the gross imbalance between birth and death rates.

Since we met together a year ago the world's population has grown by more than 70 million people. For every two deaths there have been five births. Between 85 and 90% of this population growth has occurred in the poorer countries.

Development has brought death rates down in those countries, but a corresponding adjustment in the birth rate is not automatic, and to date has been negligible.

The profound implications of the resulting population explosion on development policy are not yet fully understood. I should like to explore some of those implications with you today.

Before turning to those issues, however, I want to report to you on the operations of the World Bank Group during the past year, and on our plans for the remaining period of our first Five-Year Program.

II. THE BANK GROUP'S OPERATIONS IN FISCAL YEAR 1971

During the past fiscal year our new loans, credits, and investments totalled $2.6 billion. This compares with $2.3 billion in 1970, $1.9 billion in 1969, and $1.0 billion in 1968. The total cost of these development projects, which have been financed in part by the Bank Group during the past year, amounted to $7.0 billion. For 90% of the projects, it was possible to prepare estimates of the annual rates of return to the developing countries: they average 18%.

To finance a rise in disbursements, and to increase liquid reserves, the Bank borrowed $1.37 billion during the year. This brought its level of liquidity to $2.6 billion—up $500 million from June 30, 1970. Disbursements will continue to rise in the coming years as the increase in commitments translates into expenditures. The net flow of funds from the Bank Group to the developing countries now represents about 10% of the total received from public external sources, up from 4 or 5% a few years ago.

Our operations in 1971, as was the case in 1970, benefited from the unusually high rate of earnings on the investment of our liquid reserves with the result that the year's net income totalled $212 million.

III. THE BANK GROUP'S FIVE-YEAR PROGRAM

You will recall that in my initial address to you three years ago, I outlined a Five-Year Program for the Bank Group. Our overall objective was to double the level of investments for development in the period FY 1969-1973 as compared with the previous five years when investments had totalled $5.8 billion.

In FY 1971, the midpoint of the five-year target period was reached. What have been the results? New commitments for the first three years have totalled $6.8 billion. Taking account of the operating program for the current year, FY 1972, and the prospects for the following year, it seems probable that the final total of new investments in the five-year period will in fact exceed the initial objective of $11.6 billion, and the total cost of Bank-supported projects for the period should exceed $30 billion.

As you remember, our goals also included trebling lending in the field of education, and quadrupling it in the agricultural sector. At midpoint in the Five-Year Program, those goals are on schedule and are being met.

Another objective we have sought is to give greater emphasis to assisting the very poorest among our member countries—countries with per capita incomes of $100 or less. Our current estimate is that during the five-year period from 1969 to 1973 we will have assisted the poorest countries with a total of 215 separate projects. The comparable figure for the first 23 years of the Bank's activities—from 1946 to 1968—was 158.

The twelve months since we last met have, then, been vigorous and productive in the pursuit of our first Five-Year Program's objectives. Those objectives appeared arduous when we set out in 1968, and despite the encouraging results thus far, they remain so. But already we are planning in a preliminary way what the Bank might do in a second Five-Year Program from FY 1974 to 1978. These plans will become clearer over the next 12 months, and we will want to discuss them with the Governors at next year's meeting.

It is becoming increasingly apparent that such future plans of the World Bank Group, as well as of other bilateral and multilateral development finance agencies and, most importantly, of the developing countries themselves, must give far greater attention to the basic problems affecting the lives of the developing peoples. These problems—which stem largely from the unanticipated growth of population—include severe malnutrition, rising unemployment, and the growing inequality in the distribution of income.

Unless we deal with these fundamental issues, development will fail. The best appraised project, with the highest rate of financial return, will be of no avail if the community as a whole dissolves into bankruptcy or civil chaos.

It is to these problems and their implications for all who are engaged in development that I turn now.

IV. THE CURRENT STATUS OF POPULATION PLANNING

Events of the past year have reinforced the thoughts I expressed at our meeting in Copenhagen. You will recall that I stressed then my belief that population planning must have high priority in most of the developing countries—even in those countries where the symptoms of overpopulation are not yet fully evident. The reason is clear: much more time is required than is generally imagined in order to translate population-planning programs into reductions in the birth rate sufficiently large to result in reasonable rates of growth.

Last year I noted that 22 developing countries had adopted official population-planning policies. In launching Ghana's National Family-Planning Program in 1970—the first such national program in West Africa—the Minister of Finance stated:

"The present rate of growth increases our population by 5,000 people every week . . . In simple terms, it means that as a Nation we are increasing in number faster than we can build schools to educate our youth, faster than we can construct hospitals to cater for the health needs of the people, and faster than we can develop our economy to provide jobs for the more than 140,000 new workers who enter our labour force each year. Our rate of population growth thus poses a serious threat to our ability both as individuals and as a Government to provide the reasonable needs of our people. . . . Thus we see that our population growth and our reproductive habits pose very serious problems which must be tackled realistically and effectively NOW if we are to avoid the justifiable curse of our children and those who come after them.

"We are aware that there will be some in our midst to whom these dangers are more imaginary than real. There are those in the grip of the dangerous illusion that the vast expanses of underdeveloped land invalidate the argument for the regulation of population growth in Ghana. They fail to realize that invariably the land remains undeveloped because of the lack of capital and technical skills required for its development. There are also those who still cling to the equally dangerous misconception of the prestige value of large populations in a technological age when the quality of our people is more important than their numbers."

In the past 12 months several more governments have moved in this direction. But though this trend is encouraging, one must admit that only in a handful of developing countries is the population problem perceived by the top political leadership as a matter of high priority.

It is in part due to the absence of strong political support that the measurable effect to date of population-planning programs on fertility rates is insignificant. But it is becoming increasingly evident that even with the requisite political support, even with expected advances in contraceptive technology, even with major improvements in the administration of the programs—and to all of these critical elements we must give much greater emphasis—decades will pass before the rate of growth declines to acceptable levels. In the meantime, the world is going to get immensely more populous than it already is.

The latest demographic studies, completed within this past year, indicate that if a net reproduction rate of one (an average of two children per couple) is reached in the developing countries by the year 2040—a possible but by no means certain achievement—their present population of 2.6 billion will increase more than fivefold to nearly 14 billion. If the net reproduction rate of one could be reached two decades sooner, the ultimate size of the population of the developing countries alone would be reduced by over 4 billion, a figure substantially in excess of the planet's total population today.

	Billions of People		
	Developed Countries	Developing Countries	World
Present Population	1.1	2.6	3.7
Ultimate Population:			
• If replacement rate is reached by developing countries in 2040 and developed countries in 2020	1.8	13.9	15.7
• If replacement rate is reached two decades earlier	1.6	9.6	11.2

Two important conclusions can be drawn from these projections:

- Each decade of delay in addressing the population problem in developing countries will lead to an ultimate population in those nations approximately 20% larger than would otherwise be the case.

- Even on very favorable assumptions, the populations of the developing countries will continue to grow rapidly for several decades, expanding perhaps fourfold from present levels and reaching a total of nearly 10 billion.

The implications of these facts for all of us engaged in development are clear:

- We must intensify our efforts in population planning, seeking to shorten the time required to reduce the rate of growth.

- We must reshape development programs for the next

decade or two to take account of what is certain to be a continuing rapid growth of total population.

Development programs have not as yet faced up to the adjustments that the consequences of continuing population growth require. Two of these consequences—widespread malnutrition and chronic and growing unemployment—require particular attention. It is to them that I turn now.

V. MALNUTRITION AND DEVELOPMENT[a]

Much of the most significant knowledge dealing with nutritional deficiencies—and most particularly the implications for development—has been discovered only recently. Even now the full extent of these deficiencies in the less-advantaged countries and the degree to which they seriously limit economic and social progress is only beginning to become apparent. And we have hardly even begun to develop plans to deal with the problem.

The argument I shall make is that:

- Malnutrition is widespread.

- It is a major cause of high mortality among young children.

- It limits the physical—and often the mental—growth of hundreds of millions of those who survive.

- It reduces their productivity as adults.

- It is therefore a major barrier to human development.

And yet, despite the evidence that with a relatively small per capita expenditure of resources major gains can be achieved,

---

[a]I am indebted to Nevin Scrimshaw, Chairman of MIT's Department of Nutrition and Chairman of the FAO/WHO/UNICEF Protein Advisory Group; and to Alan Berg, Senior Fellow, The Brookings Institution, for many of the points in this section.

there is scarcely a country in the developing world where a concerted attack on the problem is under way.

The number of childhood deaths is enormous in the poorer countries. Malnourishment severely lowers immunity to infection, and tens of millions of children succumb each year to preventable fatalities simply because they have no reserves of resistance. The Food and Agricultural Organization states that "malnutrition is the biggest single contributor to child mortality in the developing countries." And that contention is borne out by the Pan American Health Organization's reports of studies in Latin America which show malnutrition to be either the primary cause, or a major contributing factor, in 50 to 75% of the deaths of one- to four-year-olds.

How great is child mortality in the developing world?

- In India, there are large areas where deaths in the first year of life number as many as 150 to 200 per 1000 live births.

- In the United Arab Republic, the proportion of children between the ages of one and two who die is more than 100 times higher than in Sweden.

- In Cameroon, children under five, although only one-sixth of the population, account for one-half of the deaths.

- In Pakistan, the percentage of children between the ages of one and four who die is 40 times higher than in Japan.

Clearly, the first result of widespread malnutrition is high child mortality.[a] But not all malnourished children die. Hundreds of millions of those who live—and the FAO and WHO estimate that as many as two-thirds of all surviving children in the less-developed countries have been malnourished—suffer serious deprivation of the opportunity to realize their full human potential.

---

[a]It is becoming clear that the population problem and the nutrition problem are closely intertwined. In the end better nutrition will have a beneficial effect on reducing fertility, despite the short-run reduction in infant mortality. Indeed, many authorities believe that reduced infant and child mortality are preconditions for successful population control.

The deprivation often begins before the child is born. In the last three months of pregnancy, and the first two years after birth, a child's brain reaches nearly 90% of its structural development. During this critical period, a deficit of protein can impair the brain's growth. Autopsies have revealed that young children who die of protein-calorie malnutrition may have less than half the number of brain cells of adequately nourished children in the same age group.

While it is difficult to distinguish the effects of protein deficiency on child development from other aspects of poverty in the child's environment, there can be no serious doubt that there is a relationship between severe malnutrition in infancy and mental retardation—mental retardation which more and more scientists are concluding is irreversible.

But malnutrition attacks not only the mind but the body as well. Protein deficiency seriously limits physical growth. The Director of the National Institute of Nutrition in India reports that 80% of the nation's children suffer from "malnutrition dwarfism." Low-income populations almost universally have a smaller body size. The FAO estimates that more than 300 million children from these groups suffer "grossly retarded physical growth."

Prolonged into adulthood, the poor mental and physical growth characteristics of the early years can greatly impair the range of human capacities. Add to that the current low standards of nutrition for grown adults in much of the developing world, and it is clear why there are adverse effects on the ability to work. Workers who are easily fatigued and have low resistance to chronic illness not only are inefficient, but add substantially to the accident rate, absenteeism, and unnecessary medical expenditure. More serious still, to the extent that their mental capacity has been impaired by malnutrition in childhood, their ability to perform technical tasks is reduced. Dexterity, alertness, initiative: these are the qualities that malnutrition attacks and diminishes.

We are not speaking here of dietetic nuances, or the fancies of food faddists. We are speaking, instead, of basic nutritional deficiencies which affect the minds and bodies of human beings. But the problem is so dimly perceived, so readily dismissed under the pressure of other priorities that we have neither applied the knowledge now at hand, nor mobilized the resources required to broaden that knowledge further.

In one sense, of course, the ultimate cause of malnutrition is poverty. But this does not mean that we either must, or can even afford, to wait for full economic development to take place before we begin to attack the problem. On the contrary, reducing the ravages of serious malnutrition will itself accelerate economic development and thus contribute to the amelioration of poverty. And there are a number of practical steps which can be taken even within the limitations of our current knowledge and economic priorities.

As in the case of the population problem, the nutrition problem represents less a need for new and immense amounts of development capital, than a need for realistic understanding of the situation. What we already know suggests that to meet basic nutritional deficiencies of hundreds of millions of the developing peoples will not entail unacceptable costs. It has been estimated, for example, that at a cost of $8 per child per year one could make up the deficiencies of a diet that now deprives him of one-fourth of his protein need and one-third of his caloric need.

There are, in fact, many promising possibilities for increasing the nutritional value of food through low-cost agricultural and industrial solutions:

- Crop shifts—through appropriate pricing policies—from low-protein cereals to high-protein pulses.

- The introduction of higher nutritive strains of conventional cereals, such as the new high-lysine corn which doubles protein value.

- The fortification of existing basic foods to improve their nutritional value, such as the protein fortification of cereals, and the vitamin and iron fortification of wheat flour.

- The development and distribution of wholly new low-cost processed foods, particularly for the feeding of young children, using available oilseed protein.

There are, of course, many other solutions—some already available, some near at hand on the research horizon—which deserve support. But the central conclusion I wish to propose to you is that the international development community and the individual governments of the countries concerned must face up to the importance and implications of the nutrition problem.

I turn now to another serious consequence of the population explosion: unemployment.

VI. THE UNEMPLOYMENT PROBLEM

The fall in the death rates, which caused the population explosion in developing countries, disproportionately affected the youngest age groups, with the result that the major increase in population occurred initially among children under the age of 15. The growth in the labor force (i.e., in the age group 15 and over) has been slower, but is now accelerating. Between 1950 and 1960, it rose at 1.6% compared with the population growth rates of 2.3%; and in the period 1960-70 at roughly 1.9% compared with 2.6%.

Throughout the developing world the labor force will grow at an even faster rate in the 1970s than it did in the 1960s. On average it will rise by 2.3% per year. And when one reflects on the expected 2.8% growth in population for the next decade, it is clear that labor-force growth rates for the developing world as a whole will inevitably accelerate in the two or three decades immediately ahead. In Latin America these rates are already over 3%.

What these figures mean for some of the principal countries is staggering. It is estimated, for example, that the Indian labor force will grow by over 50 million in the next 10 years. This is equivalent to the combined labor force of Great Britain and the Federal Republic of Germany.

These rates of growth are far higher than the 1-1.5% per year faced by the developing countries of Western Europe a century ago—growth rates which could readily be relieved by massive emigration to the then underpopulated New World with its abundant natural resources. No such large-scale relief is available for today's developing countries.

Available statistics and concepts of employment and unemployment are both inadequate and ambiguous in less-developed countries. However, there is ample evidence that although growth rates of national product have increased substantially over the past decade, very few developing economies have expanded fast enough to absorb the growth in their labor force. Today I believe most economists would agree that:

- Unemployment and underemployment are extremely serious in the developing countries, much more so than in the developed countries.

- On reasonable definitions—including allowances for underemployment—unemployment approximates 20-25% in most countries.

- If past patterns continue, unemployment is bound to become worse.[a]

It can be misleading to speak of *the* employment problem. There are in fact two distinct employment problems: one urban, and one rural. Of the two, the urban problem is usually the more dramatic. Estimates of total open unemployment in most developing countries are in the range of 5 to 10% of the total labor force. But as this unemployment is very heavily concentrated in cities, the proportion of the urban labor force that is unemployed is much greater.

Urban surveys in the Sixties showed unemployment to be widespread in many developing countries. In the urban areas

---

[a] The following table (prepared by the International Labour Organisation), while suffering from the weaknesses affecting all such estimates, illustrates the magnitude of the problem. It projects an increase of 170 million in the labor force during the next decade, with only half as great an increase in the number of full-time jobs.

Level of Unemployment and Underemployment in Developing Countries, excluding mainland China (in millions and percent)

	1970	1980	1970		1980	
Fully employed	504	592	75.3%		70.5%	
Underemployed	130	200	19.4		23.8	
Employed	634	792	94.7%	24.7%	94.3%	29.5%
Unemployed	36	48	5.3		5.7	
Total Labor Force	670	840	100.0%		100.0%	

of Algeria it was 27% and in the Philippines 13%; in Kaduna it was 31%; in Abidjan 20%; in Kingston 19% and in Bogota 16%. The age group most adversely affected is the 15- to 24-year-olds. Nearly 40% of this age group in Ceylon's urban labor force was unemployed in 1968. Such massive unemployment among youth carries with it a very heavy social cost: there is the lost opportunity to acquire productive skills and steady work habits at the most receptive age, plus a corrosive social frustration that can ultimately erupt into open and irrational violence.

Underemployment is also common in urban areas. Far more people eke out a meager living in unproductive and excessively duplicated service activities than are actually required by the volume of work performed. It is impossible to measure precisely the extent of this phenomenon. But, for example, the proportion of the non-agricultural labor force engaged in services in most Latin American countries is between 60 to 70% and tending to rise, whereas in the developed countries of Europe it has been generally constant for several decades at between 40 to 50%.

As bad as the urban situation is, almost everywhere the rural underemployment problem is numerically worse; and since it involves the poorest people of a developing society, it is even more tragic. Typically it results from large families sharing the little work provided by tiny farms, or landless laborers who can find jobs only at peak seasons of the year. The result is an immense waste of potentially productive resources. It has been estimated that in Latin America in 1960 rural underemployment already amounted to the equivalent of one-third of the agricultural labor force. This is likely to have risen since then.

Even more important than this waste of resources is the cost of underemployment in terms of human misery. The problem is not only that people are unoccupied for so much of the year, but that the employment which they can find yields them so little income. In Brazil the poorest 20%, who are predominantly rural, had in 1960 an average income only one-sixth of the national average. Recent studies indicate that between 40 and 50% of the population of India currently have incomes below a poverty line nationally established in terms of basic nutritional needs. And these studies suggest that the situation has worsened rather than improved in recent years.

Rural underemployment is a major cause of the large and often widening gap between urban and rural incomes. In most developing countries average incomes in the urban areas are far higher than in the rural areas. In metropolitan Manila, for example, the average income is almost four times that of rural areas in the Philippines. These inequalities are reflected in statistics on national income distribution, which often suggest less equality in developing than in developed countries. In most developed countries the share of the richest 5% is about two-thirds that of the poorest 60%. In many of the developing countries, the share of total income going to the richest 5% of families is larger than the share of the poorest 60%, and in one of the largest Latin American countries, it is almost twice as great.

Rural and urban unemployment are clearly related: that in urban areas results from the growing inequality between the incomes of those fortunate enough to obtain urban employment, and the mass of the rural poor. To many in the countryside it appears more attractive to migrate to the cities and wait there—even without work—in the hope of eventual employment, rather than to endure the poverty of underemployment in agriculture.

Although there is a good deal that can and must be done to increase the rate of growth in productive jobs in the urban areas—as I will discuss later—so long as rural underemployment exists, the income gap will exist, and migration to cities will tend to exceed the number of new jobs there. So, solving the urban problem depends on solving the rural problem. And the solution to the rural problem must be found mainly in the rural areas. There simply is no hope, in most countries, that urban job creation will be fast enough to absorb all the underemployed from the countryside.

For employment to grow at 4.5% per year in the urban areas of the developing world would be a tremendous achievement, and beyond what has been achieved in the past. Growth of manufacturing employment in developing countries between 1955 and 1965 approximated 4%, with growth of manufacturing output of over 7%; and in all regions of the world the gap between these rates was tending to widen. The bulk of the population of the developing world is in countries with at least 70% of the people now living in rural areas. In such countries a 4.5% growth in urban jobs would provide work for an increase to the total labor force of 1.3%—approximately one-half of the increase anticipated. The remainder must be accommodated in the rural sector, already characterized by heavy underemployment.

One of the more disturbing facts about the mounting under-employment of labor and the increase in rural poverty is that they have taken place during a period when total income was growing at an unprecedented rate. In aggregate terms, the First Development Decade (1960-1970) appears very success-ful: the average annual growth in GNP of the developing countries more than met the target of 5% per year. But the distribution of this GNP increase has been so unequal—as be-tween countries, regions, and socio-economic groups—that it has finally created a reaction against growth as the primary development objective, and a demand for greater attention to employment and income distribution.[a]

As I have already stressed, my view is that development policies must explicitly aim at greater employment and greater equality of income distribution. The lesson of the last decade has been that we cannot simply depend on economic growth alone to solve the problems of employment and income dis-tribution. Fiscal systems cannot be counted upon to redistribute the fruits of that growth in a socially equitable way: tax collection practices are too inadequate, and political pressures are too severe. The only effective solution is to raise the in-comes of the poorest groups by increasing the number of pro-ductive jobs available to them.

But it is equally true that to frame the issue as a mutually exclusive choice between economic growth and employment is to oversimplify a very complex matter. What is required is a

---

[a]A measure of the lack of concern over the problem of income distribution is the fact that virtually no data has been gathered on it. For only 20 de-veloping countries is there any data whatever; in only 7 of these are there even rudimentary time-series; and for none of them is the data comprehen-sive.

realistic search for measures which will provide satisfactory rates of both job creation and economic growth. We believe that such measures are within reach.

Let me turn now to a consideration of such actions, first in the field of agriculture and then in industry. Later, I shall discuss the requirement for an expansion of exports to provide the foreign exchange necessary to support the advances in agriculture and industry.

VII. AGRICULTURE AND RURAL DEVELOPMENT

Development programs that place the relief of poverty, the elimination of malnutrition, and the provision of employment high among their goals must give prime attention to agriculture. In the great majority of developing nations over half the labor force is engaged in that field. In the poorest countries of the world the proportion is over 80%. As we have seen, this labor force is already disproportionately poor and underemployed, but is nevertheless certain to continue to grow.

It is in the nature of the growth process that the relative importance of agriculture in every economy declines as economic development proceeds. As people grow richer they spend diminishing proportions of their incomes on food, and more on manufactured goods and services. As technology advances, proportionately fewer resources go into producing raw materials, and proportionately more into processing these materials into increasingly sophisticated manufactured goods.

The realization that at a later stage in a given society agriculture will gradually lose its primacy to other sectors does not justify neglecting it at an earlier stage. But this is just what is happening in many cases today. Public investment often favors urban areas; trade, exchange-rate and price policies often discriminate against agriculture. Excessive export taxes and rigid price controls restrict farm earnings, and squeeze the farmer who has to buy manufactured inputs and consumer goods from protected high-cost domestic industries.

Five years ago drought on the Indian subcontinent awakened the world to the precariousness of its food supply. Asian prospects appeared particularly grim. Since then progress in Asian cereal production has been dramatic enough to justify the term revolution. But this revolution has been primarily in the production of wheat, rice, and maize, and it has been largely confined to irrigated agriculture. So far its impact has been massively felt in only a few countries: principally India, Pakistan, and the Philippines.

The Green Revolution has not solved the long-term world food problems, but it has given us confidence that they can be solved. It has reminded us that once persuaded of the urgency of the task, man's ability to solve technological problems is immense. In the same spirit, we have to see the social and economic problems of development—where mankind's record so far has been less impressive—as challenges rather than as a cause for discouragement.

The need to sustain the momentum of the Green Revolution continues to provide such challenges, both technological and socio-economic. At present, the new technology requires irrigation. But over 75% of India's arable land, and about 50% of Pakistan's are without irrigation. To benefit the majority of farmers, technological research on new varieties suitable for non-irrigated agriculture is essential.

Further agricultural research is needed in all parts of the developing world. Little research is going on for certain important crops—tubers, for example, and high-yielding pulses. Little research is going on for certain important regions—the deep-water rice areas, for example, of the Ganges and Mekong Delta. Developed countries normally spend very much more on agricultural research in relation to the size of the sector than do the developing countries. The United States, Israel, and Australia spend on agricultural research the equivalent of between 2 and 3% of the contribution that agriculture makes to the GNP; Japan and Western Europe spend about 1%. But the developing countries of Asia and Latin America spend only about one-tenth to one-fifth of 1% of agriculture's contribution to the GNP.

Because of the immense importance of this type of research, the Bank has taken a new step, and has joined with FAO and the United Nations Development Program to sponsor a consultative group to mobilize finance in order to continue and expand the work of existing international research centers, and to establish new ones.

The social and economic challenge is to prevent the benefits of the Green Revolution from being monopolized only by wealthier farmers. So far, the more-advantaged farmers have obtained disproportionate shares of irrigation water, fertilizers, seeds, and credit. Unwise financial policies have sometimes encouraged these farmers to carry out excessive mechanization. Farm machinery has been made available at too cheap a price by allowing equipment to be imported at over-valued exchange rates, and purchased with loans bearing unrealistically low interest rates.

This is not to argue that farm mechanization in countries with rural employment problems is always unwise. Sometimes it may increase employment by multiplying the crop cycles during the year. In itself the Green Revolution should lead to an increase in employment per acre by increasing output, by encouraging double-cropping, and by stimulating the development of ancillary agricultural activities. But this can be offset by excessive mechanization.

The benefits of agricultural progress may also be limited if its effect is that the already more-advantaged large farmers expand at the expense of sharecroppers and small farmers. In India and Pakistan, agricultural incomes are largely exempt from direct taxation, and large farmers have used their windfall profits to enlarge their farms even further. In contrast, the Republic of China imposes a seven-acre limit on farm size in Taiwan, and agricultural development has in consequence been relatively labor-intensive.

What is frequently forgotten is that small farmers often work their holdings more intensively than large farmers, and often achieve a higher output per acre. Research in Colombia has shown that if land, labor, and capital are given prices appropriate to their relative scarcities, farms of less than 25 acres can be economically more efficient than substantially larger farms. Studies in India and Brazil have indicated similar findings.

All this suggests that there are many communities in which the reasonable redistribution of land, currently held in excessively large blocks, to the landless or to small farmers would be desirable not only on grounds of equity, but on grounds of efficiency as well. Mere land redistribution by itself, however, is not likely to lead to more output unless those who receive it are also given the necessary assistance to finance and improve farming techniques. This will require a change in the structure of credit institutions and extension services, which typically serve large farmers.

If the poorer farmers do not benefit from the Green Revolution's increase in output, they cannot increase their own food consumption, and the whole drive towards greater productivity will be diminished by a sluggish market. Conversely, an increased availability of food and income to large segments of the rural population could well be self-reinforcing in boosting labor productivity. It would also provide an opportunity for countries to utilize their unemployed on rural investment in transport, schools, clinics, and irrigation—and without the costs of food imports or inflation. Experience with such programs in the Asian subcontinent and in Tunisia during the 1960s were encouraging, and India has recently begun to blueprint a new program of rural works.

The measures I have outlined here suggest that there need be no necessary economic conflict between the goal of helping the mass of the rural population and other goals of economic development. Land reform and practical assistance for the small farmer will benefit those who can get the highest output from the scarcest factor—land. Realistic prices for productive factors, and for output, will not only help to maximize total output, but will tend to increase employment as well. Rural works will serve both to build up rural infrastructure, and to raise incomes.

Recent projects financed by the Bank have been directed expressly to small farmers and to an integrated approach to rural development. But we have to admit that in this whole area we are still feeling our way. None of us in the Bank or in the development community at large can yet presume that we are experts at designing the most effective institutions for helping small farmers, or that we know enough about the use of labor-intensive methods of construction, or how best to launch large-scale rural works programs. All these matters manifestly need further study and experimentation.

But the evidence now available does not indicate that greater attention to the poorer agricultural groups must inevitably entail sacrifice of economic growth. Quite the contrary, we are confident that formulas can be found for furthering at one and the same time both healthy rural growth and much more equitable income distribution.

I have argued that the solution to the worst problems of poverty and unemployment must be sought in the countryside. But under the best of circumstances, agricultural employment will not be able to grow fast enough fully to absorb the growing rural labor force. Therefore, a rapid expansion of industrial production will be required.

VIII. A STRATEGY FOR INDUSTRIALIZATION

Postwar industrial expansion in the developing world has been very impressive. In most developing countries manufacturing has been the fastest growing sector, although starting from a very small base.

Manufacturing in the developing world increased at an average rate of 6 to 7% between 1950 and 1970, exceeding the rate of increase in most of the industrial nations of today at a comparable stage of their development. Manufacturing now accounts for 17% of the combined gross domestic product of developing countries, as compared to 12% two decades earlier. Its contribution to employment creation, however, was limited. With annual increases of about 4%, manufacturing employment absorbed less than one-fifth of the approximately 200 million increase in the labor force between 1950 and 1970.

In a very real sense the contribution that manufacturing makes to economic development is understated by a simple calculation of the value of its output, or of the number of jobs it provides. For countries whose economies are dependent on the export of a few primary products, perhaps with poor long-run prospects or fluctuating prices, it contributes an important degree of diversification. Industrialization furthers the training of a skilled labor force; it encourages the emergence of managers and indigenous entrepreneurs; it expands the development of a local capital market; and it tends to promote investment in infrastructure and technical facilities which might not otherwise be economically feasible. In other words, it contributes to modernization in general.

The desirability of expanding the industrial sector has therefore been obvious for many years to the governments of most developing nations. And when starting the process, those with sizable internal markets have naturally begun by producing at home items which they have had to import in the past.[a] Usually these are simple consumer goods. In order to encourage domestic production, some sort of protective policies against imports—high import duties or quota restrictions— have often been applied.

It is hard to think of any other way in which the industrialization process could get started. But once the process is under way, developing countries are confronted with an important choice which substantially affects the benefits which they can derive from industrialization. This choice is whether to continue to rely on the domestic market as the basis for industrial expansion, or to attempt to break out into foreign markets. And at this point many, if not most, of the developing countries have made the wrong choice: they have continued too far along the path of import substitution.

Experience has shown that though this pattern of industrialization may for some years be conducive to high growth rates of manufacturing output, sooner or later it faces increasing difficulties. In the first place, once imports of any product have been replaced, that industry's growth is limited to the growth of the domestic market. To maintain industrial momentum requires import substitution in continually new products. Frequently this means moving into products less and less suited to the size of the market and the nature of the economy. Many developing countries—already short of capital, and burdened with high unemployment—have found themselves in the un-

[a]Small countries, and most of the developing countries are small, have restricted possibilities for pursuing an import substitution strategy because of the extremely limited size of domestic markets.

economic position of providing high levels of protection to capital-intensive industries.

There are other difficulties as well. High levels of protection have often made it possible to maintain over-valued exchange rates. This has penalized exports, and, since most capital goods are imported, has kept the price of capital equipment low thereby encouraging the uneconomical use of labor-saving techniques.

These problems can be overcome by an alternative strategy of development which gives greater emphasis to manufacture for export. The industries stimulated by such a program will be those most suited to conditions in developing countries. Many are likely to be relatively labor-intensive, thus contributing to the solution of the employment problem, and production for foreign as well as domestic markets should help insure the benefits of large-scale production.

These advantages are not merely hypothetical. The results in countries which have oriented their manufacturing sectors towards exporting have been more promising than those relying entirely on import substitution. Their industrial growth rates— often as great as 10 to 15%—have been higher, and the expansion of employment has been substantially faster.

Among the most notable successes have been those in Korea and the Republic of China, which switched to exporting early in the industrialization process.

Undoubtedly it is easier to shift to greater exporting before the structure of manufacturing becomes fixed in a distorted high-cost pattern. Recent achievements in Mexico, Brazil,[a] and Yugoslavia, however, suggest that it is possible for countries which have long emphasized import substitution to adjust export incentives to offset protection, and as a result to enjoy a marked increase in manufactured exports.

Policies outside the foreign trade field also are important in determining the pattern of manufacturing development and labor absorption. All too often investment in capital goods in

---

[a] By reorienting its industrial sector from import substitution to exports, Brazil increased its export earnings from manufactured goods from $144 million to $412 million in only four years' time (1966 to 1970).

the developing countries has been encouraged by tax concessions and subsidized interest rates, while use of labor has been
discouraged by revenue systems based primarily on payroll
taxes. Such taxes are extraordinarily high in many countries of
Latin America: in one, for example, they amount to 28% of
the wage paid. There is no reason why education, pensions,
insurance, housing, and the many other public expenditures
for which these taxes are used, should not be financed in a way
that has a less harmful effect on the volume of employment.

There is no conflict here between employment creation and
economic growth. Industrial policies which cause prices to reflect more accurately the scarcity of capital, and the abundance
of labor, will lead not only to greater output and a healthier
balance of payments, but to increased employment as well.

The suggestion that developing countries base their trade
and industrial policies on a clearer recognition of international
opportunities and of the relative scarcities of productive factors
has been made many times. I myself emphasized it in my
address at this meeting two years ago. Yet the subject is often
received with a good deal of scepticism. It is worth discussing
why.

In the first place, it is sometimes doubted whether an appropriate labor-intensive technology exists in most branches of
manufacturing industry. I agree that the choice of technology
is often limited, and certainly a good many of the apparently
more labor-intensive methods of production are inefficient and
obsolete. Nevertheless, there is evidence that in the production
of many products there is a genuine prospect for substituting
labor for capital. This is particularly true in the transport, handling, and packaging of materials. There are also possibilities
for more widespread use of multiple-shift operations.

There are a number of examples where differences in the
relative costs of labor and capital have led to new techniques
of production. In the case, for instance, of the production of
plywood in Korea, what at first appears to be a manufacturing
process very similar to that carried out in the United States,
turns out, on inspection, to be full of innovative and indigenous variations. In America, mechanical sensors are used to
detect defective pieces of timber, and the entire slab is then

discarded. In Japan, defective pieces of timber are located and cut out by hand. In Korea, the defective area—a knothole, for example—is located and patched up by hand.

Admittedly, the empirical knowledge in all these matters is incomplete. That is why the Bank is at present exploring whether there are ways in which it might encourage the development of more labor-intensive technologies. And it is why our research program is examining the possibilities of labor/capital substitution, in order to provide both ourselves and our member countries with a more complete picture of how these issues work out in practice.

An even more critical question to this general line of reasoning is whether if developing countries produce manufactured goods at competitive prices, the tendency of advanced nations to protect their existing industries will block their export. I shall turn to this issue next, both because of its effect on employment and because of its relationship to the availability of the foreign exchange required for the financing of a nation's total development program.

IX. THE NEED FOR FOREIGN EXCHANGE

The target for the Second Development Decade, adopted by the United Nations General Assembly following our meeting in Copenhagen, calls for an average GNP growth rate of 6% during the 1970s. This acceleration of economic growth, from the 5% rate achieved in the 1960s, will require that imports grow more rapidly than national income. This explains why the U.N. General Assembly calls for an annual increase of approximately 7% in the imports of the developing countries during the Seventies, a rate confirmed by the Bank's own projections.

Foreign exchange requirements will grow faster than this. Developing countries have had to borrow an increasing proportion of such requirements. The result has been a rapid rise in obligations for the servicing of this debt in the form of amortization and interest. The Bank's projections indicate that these borrowings will lead to an increase in debt service substantially exceeding the rate of increase of national income. In other words, in order to attain a rate of import growth close to 7%, and meet their debt obligations, developing countries will require foreign exchange resources to grow by over 7% a year.

Foreign exchange is available from three sources: export earnings, foreign aid, and private capital. Export earnings provide about 75% of the total; foreign aid, 15%; and foreign private capital, 10%. These are averages. Private capital, other than for investment in extractive industries, tends to go disproportionately to the somewhat more-advanced developing countries, and foreign aid is of special importance to the less-advantaged countries.

I have repeatedly stressed the need for increasing foreign aid, and in particular the aid available on concessionary terms. This is essential for the developing countries so that they can both service their debt and supplement their domestic savings. Yet even if the developed nations which have subscribed to the 1% of GNP aid target do meet their goal in full, the fact remains that the major portion of the increase in foreign exchange needed by the developing countries will have to come from increased export earnings and these must grow at a rate in excess of 7% per year, doubling in the present decade.

Let us examine the prospects for accomplishing this formidable task.

X. TRADE OBJECTIVES FOR THE 1970s

The developing world as a whole can achieve this large export expansion only by a very rapid growth in its manufactured exports. There are, of course, some exceptions. Fuel exports are growing at an average rate of 10% a year, and already account for one-third of export earnings. But three-quarters of these earnings go to six countries, containing only about one-fortieth of the population of the developing world.[a]

The other developing countries obtain about two-thirds of their export earnings from primary commodities, and one-third from manufactures. Most of the primary exports are foodstuffs and agricultural raw materials. These are growing very slowly. For some items the market in the richer countries is not expanding very quickly, and for others, especially foodstuffs, the

---

[a]Excluding mainland China.

problem is aggravated by protectionist policies. Non-fuel mineral and metal exports are growing somewhat faster than agricultural products, but even so the average annual growth in the value of non-fuel primary exports probably will not exceed 3 to 4%.

If the industrialized countries would reduce tariffs and other obstacles to primary imports, this rate of growth could certainly be increased, but not enough to provide the foreign exchange that the developing countries need for rapid economic growth.

The conclusion is clear. If the developing countries are to secure the foreign exchange they need, and achieve fuller employment, they must substantially increase their manufactured exports. It is here that world demand grows most rapidly. And there is a variety of products which these countries can produce at competitive cost: products that generally have either a high labor content, or that utilize domestic materials. The major groups of manufactures which are particularly profitable for the developing countries are listed in the Appendix.

Growth in exports of manufactured goods from the developing countries has already been rapid. They have increased at an annual rate of about 15% during the period 1962-69. They started, however, from such a small base that the share of the manufactured exports of the developing countries remains only 5% of the manufactured imports of the developed nations, and one-third of 1% of their GNP.

If manufactured imports from the less-advantaged nations could continue to grow at 15% until 1980, this would be enough—if aid targets are met—to offset the slow growth of primary exports and to satisfy projected import requirements.

But a 15% rate of growth in manufactured exports will be harder to achieve in the Seventies than it was in the Sixties. To do so, annual exports, which rose from less than $2 billion in 1960 to $7 billion in 1970, will have to quadruple to $28 billion in 1980. Even if this level were to be reached by 1980, the total volume of such exports would still remain a very small part— approximately 7%—of the expected manufactured imports of the advanced countries, and only 1% of their projected GNP.

Although these exports need not all be aimed exclusively at the markets of the richer countries, the principal markets must be provided in the developed nations. The developing countries have justifiable grounds for complaint that they are being treated unfairly in their attempts to expand their manufactured exports to those markets. On the average, tariffs are higher on the kinds of manufactured goods imported from poor countries as compared to imports from rich countries. According to a recent study, tariffs on the two groups of imports average 7 and 12% in the United States, 9 and 14% in the United Kingdom, and 7 and 9% in the European Community.

Even worse than the absolute level of tariffs is their structure. Tariffs rise with the degree of fabrication. Thus, in the European Community cocoa beans imported from non-associated countries bear a 3% duty, while the tariff on processed cocoa products is 18%. In the United States, hides and skins enter duty free, but tariffs of 4 to 5% apply on leather and 8 to 10% on shoes. This margin could well offset the comparative advantages in processing found in many developing countries.

Finally, and perhaps worst of all, non-tariff barriers to trade have proliferated throughout the rich countries in recent years. Restrictions on market access exist in a variety of administrative and fiscal measures, including quotas, subsidies, valuation techniques, and preferential buying arrangements under government procurement. They too are more severe for developing countries.

An important element of the U.N. development strategy for the Seventies is the proposal that the more-developed countries grant preferential treatment to the manufactured exports of developing countries. Representatives of 18 industrialized countries have undertaken to try to implement this proposal. The European Community, the Nordic countries, and Japan have already adopted the plan, with various limitations. However, even if all 18 countries carry out their part, these measures will enable the developing nations to increase their trade by only $1 billion a year.[a] If the remaining $20 billion of additional

---

[a]Over a three- to five-year-period, approximately $400 million annually would be represented by additional imports into the European Economic Community; $400 million by additional imports into the United States; and $200 million by additional imports into other developed countries.

exports per year is to be achieved during the Seventies, the developing countries must radically change their industrial policy from import substitution to export-oriented manufacturing, and the developed countries must provide the necessary markets by greater efforts to remove discriminatory trade restrictions.

We must face the fact that expanding the volume of manufactured imports from the poor countries into the rich countries, while benefiting the majority of the citizens of the rich countries, will involve injuries to certain sectors of their economies. These injuries will be strongly—and rightly—resisted by the individuals and firms affected unless appropriate adjustment assistance policies and procedures are introduced which keep fully in step with the reduction of tariff and non-tariff barriers. Few, if any, developed countries now possess such policies and procedures.

To urge both the more-advanced countries and the less-developed countries to expand their trade with one another— the former by more freely admitting labor-intensive imports, and the latter by not resorting to excessive import substitution—is not to urge that one set of countries do the other set of countries a favor. I am simply recommending that each recognize where their true mutual interests lie.

XI. SUMMARY AND CONCLUSIONS

Let me now summarize and conclude the central case I have put before you:

- Economic development in the second half of this century is increasingly dominated by the consequences of rapid population growth. Mortality has fallen faster than fertility, and the effects of this disequilibrium require major changes in development policy if we are to achieve significant improvements in human welfare.

- In the longer run, the most important issue is effective population planning. Its goal must be to stabilize the planet's population several decades earlier—and several billions lower—than would otherwise occur.

- Since reducing birth rates to replacement levels will

necessarily require decades, we must reshape development programs now in order to take account of what is certain to be a continuing rapid growth of population to levels heretofore considered unlikely. Two of the consequences of such growth—widespread malnutrition and chronic and growing unemployment—require particular attention.

- It is clear that malnutrition prevents realization of the full genetic potential of hundreds of millions of persons in the developing world and retards both economic and social development. But research has pointed to feasible means to make immediate progress on this neglected problem.

- The problems of unemployment and underemployment are already severe and will become worse as the rate of growth of the labor force accelerates in the two or three decades ahead.

- More equitable income distribution is absolutely imperative if the development process is to proceed in any meaningful manner. Policies whose effect is to favor the rich at the expense of the poor are not only manifestly unjust, but in the end are economically self-defeating. They push frustrations to the point of violence, and turn economic advance into a costly collapse of social stability.

- Poverty, inequality, and unemployment cannot be effectively dealt with by expanding the urban sector alone, but must be attacked directly in the rural areas through measures which will raise the incomes of the poorer farmers and the landless.

- To achieve accelerated economic growth, an expanding flow of foreign aid remains critically important. At best, however, it will be insufficient to meet the total foreign exchange requirements of the developing countries. Hence there must be a dramatic increase in their manufactured exports. This requires policy changes in the rich and poor countries alike: changes which will necessitate difficult economic adjustments and require astute political leadership.

The Bank Group's role in all of this is clear. Our mandate is to assist. That assistance must be both in the form of the policy advice leading to sound social and economic development programs—advice conforming to the principles I have outlined this morning—and an augmented capacity to provide financial support for those programs.

In the end, development is like life itself: complex. The danger is to oversimplify. Development has for too long been expressed simply in terms of growth of output. There is now emerging the awareness that the availability of work, the distribution of income, and the quality of life are equally important measures of development.

Although this is gradually being accepted in theory, it has yet to be translated into practice by either the developing countries or the suppliers of external capital.

It is toward this broader concept of the entire development process that the World Bank is moving. If we are to meet our mandate to our member countries—and indeed to man himself—I believe we must move even faster.

With your support, that is precisely what we propose to do.

APPENDIX

Major Groups of Manufactured Goods Particularly Profitable for
Developing Countries

(a) *Processed primary products:* These involve items such as
vegetable oils, foodstuffs, plywood and veneer, pulp and
paper products, and fabricated metal. As these products are
cheaper to transport in a processed form, rather than in
raw, unprocessed bulk, the countries processing them enjoy an additional advantage vis-à-vis the user markets.
These goods presently account for roughly two-fifths of the
manufactured exports of the developing countries.

(b) *Traditional labor-intensive goods:* These comprise garments, textiles, footwear, and simple engineering products.
Their low labor costs make the developing countries competitive in these commodities, which currently account for
another two-fifths of their manufactured exports.

(c) *Newer labor-intensive industrial products:* Goods such as
plastic and wooden items, rattan furniture, glassware, pot-
tery, and wigs have made their appearance in recent years.
While it is difficult to distinguish them from other categories, they appear to account for about one-tenth of the
total of manufactured exports.

(d) *Electronic and mechanical items:* A few developing countries are beginning to export a wide range of more complex
products of labor-intensive manufactures, chiefly parts and
components for assembly elsewhere. Exports of radios,
other electrical equipment, and machine tools have also
been rising. These products may have reached approximately one-tenth of the manufactured exports of developing countries, and their share is likely to increase.

NINE

To the
UNITED NATIONS CONFERENCE ON TRADE AND DEVELOPMENT

SANTIAGO, CHILE
APRIL 14, 1972

I. INTRODUCTION

This is the first opportunity I have had since becoming President of the World Bank to attend a session of the United Nations Conference on Trade and Development, and I am very pleased to be here.

What I have to say will be brief and candid.

My view is this:

- The state of development in most of the developing world today is unacceptable—and growing more so.

- It is unacceptable, not because there hasn't been progress in the past 20 years—and particularly in the decade of the sixties—but because development programs have been directed largely at gross economic goals, and have failed to insure that all nations, and all groups within nations, have shared equitably in the economic advance.

- As the Second Development Decade unfolds, the mistakes of the past have begun to be perceived, but neither the developing nor the developed nations have moved to deal with them effectively.

- Finally, if the state of development today is unacceptable—and it is—we must not waste time looking for villains in the piece, or even worse, waste energy in fruitless confrontation between rich nations and poor nations. Rather, the entire international development community—all of us—must promptly move forward with practical measures which are conceptually sound, financially feasible, and which can command the requisite public support. I hope to suggest some of these today.

171

II. THE UNEVEN AND UNACCEPTABLE STATE
OF DEVELOPMENT

I have said that I believe the state of development in most of the developing world today is unacceptable.

It is unacceptable, but not because there has not been progress. There has been. The total economic growth, measured in GNP terms, for the developing countries during the First Development Decade was impressive. For some of these countries it was the most successful decade—measured in these gross economic terms—in their history.

But such economic measurements, useful as they are, can be seriously inadequate.

What is inadequate about them is that they do not, in themselves, tell us much about what is happening to the individual lives of great masses of people in the developing countries.

But the improvement of the individual lives of the great masses of people is, in the end, what development is all about.

What are we to say of a world in which hundreds of millions of people are not only poor in statistical terms, but are faced with day-to-day deprivations that degrade human dignity to levels which no statistics can adequately describe?

- A developing world in which children under age five account for only 20% of the population, but for more than 60% of the deaths.

- A developing world in which two-thirds of the children who have escaped death will live on, restricted in their growth by malnutrition—a malnutrition that can stunt both bodies and minds alike.

- A developing world in which there are 100 million more adult illiterates than there were 20 years ago.

- A developing world, in short, in which death and disease are rampant, education and employment scarce, squalor and stagnation common, and opportunity and the realization of personal potential drastically limited.

This is the world of today for the two billion human beings who live in the more than 95 developing countries which are members of the World Bank. The personal catastrophe that affects the individual lives of hundreds of millions of these individuals is such that we can no longer take much satisfaction in the simple statistical achievement of the overall GNP growth goal of 5% by the close of the First Development Decade.

To begin with, that average figure conceals the fact that the growth rate was very uneven among the developing countries; and that income grew the least where it was needed the most—in the poorest countries, with the largest aggregate population.

Based on a study of the individual countries, the picture that emerges demonstrates just how uneven that growth has been.

- The major oil-exporting countries, with less than 4% of the population, enjoyed a GNP growth rate not of 5%, but of 8.4%.

- The developing countries with a per capita GNP exceeding $500, with 9% of the population, had a growth rate of 6.2%.

- The countries with a per capita GNP between $200 and $500, with 20% of the population, had a growth rate of 5.4%.

- And the poorest countries—those with a per capita GNP of less than $200—with an overwhelming 67% of the population, had a growth rate of only 3.9%.

So the first obvious conclusion is that by lumping all developing countries together, and measuring progress by an average GNP growth rate for the entire group, we obscure the significant differences between these countries.

What is more, we obscure the even larger differences in their per capita income growth.

- In the poorest countries, with 67% of the population, per capita income during the First Development Decade grew at only 1.5% annually.

- In the two middle categories of countries, per capita income grew far faster than that—2.4% and 4.2% respectively.

- In the oil-exporting countries, it grew more than three times as fast: 5.2%.

But what is most misleading of all is to assume that once we have calculated the GNP growth rate of a particular developing country, and then expressed it in per capita terms, we have arrived at a sound picture of the level of economic development in the country.

We have not.

For rates of growth of GNP, and of GNP per capita, tell us nothing about how income is actually distributed within a country.

III. THE MALDISTRIBUTION OF INCOME WITHIN DEVELOPING COUNTRIES

Such evidence as is available suggests that even the developing countries which have registered significant gains in GNP growth rates are plagued with severely skewed income distribution patterns.

In the last decade Brazil's GNP per capita, in real terms, grew by 2.5% per year, and yet the share of the national income received by the poorest 40% of the population declined from 10% in 1960 to 8% in 1970, whereas the share of the richest 5% grew from 29% to 38% during the same period. In GNP terms, the country did well. The very rich did very well. But throughout the decade the poorest 40% of the population benefited only marginally.

In Mexico the picture is similar. Over roughly the past 20 years, the average income per capita grew, in real terms, at 3% per year. The richest 10% of the population received about half the total national income at the beginning of the period and an even larger share at the end of the period (49% in 1950 and 51% in 1969). But the share of the poorest 40% of the people was only 14% in 1950, and declined to 11% in 1969. The share of the poorest 20% during the same period sank from 6% to 4%.

In India, there has been progress in overall GNP growth during the past decade. But, today, some 40% of the entire population—200 million people—live beneath a poverty line: a line defined as the point at which serious malnutrition begins. And the evidence is that the poorest 10% of the nation—50 million people—have not only not shared in the progress of the decade, but may even have grown poorer.

These examples are not atypical. A recent study of income distribution patterns in more than 40 developing countries estimates that at the beginning of the First Development Decade the average share in the national income of the richest 20% of the people was 56%—but the share of the poorest 60% of the people was only 26%. Although comparable data for the beginning of the Second Development Decade are as yet too sketchy to draw detailed conclusions, preliminary indications are that this severely distorted income distribution is not only continuing, but in many countries may be growing worse. The poor are sharing only to a very limited extent in the benefits of growth.

Why is this the case?

The reasons, of course, are complex. We still have far more questions than answers, but I believe that certain points are clear.

To begin with, economic growth is a necessary condition of development in any poor country—but it is far from being a sufficient condition.

Without a climate of growth, the domestic savings and export earnings crucial for internal investment simply cannot be mobilized. That is obvious enough.

What is less obvious is that economic growth in a poor country, in its early stages, is likely to penalize the poorest segment of the society relative to the more affluent sectors unless specific action is taken to prevent such an effect.

This is particularly true of those subsistence agrarian economies in which economic growth began with a narrow but intense exploitation of rich natural resources. The historical experience of these situations is that unless the government takes steps to broaden the base of development by rapid reinvestment of the export revenues from such resources, the income share of the poorest 60% of the population declines, and the income share of the richest 5% increases.

Even the small middle-income group in such societies—the approximately 20% of the population whose average share of the national income clusters near the median point—even this incipient middle class receives a declining share of the national income when growth is sudden and too confined to enclave types of activity.

As development in a poor country broadens its base, the middle-income group begins to benefit. This group prospers, largely as a function of its education and employment opportunities. But the 30 to 40% of the total population, who range from the poor to the very poor, continue to receive a disproportionately small and frequently declining share of national income. Typically, it is these poorest 40% who are most vulnerable to the economic hardships associated with high birth rates, poor educational opportunities, mounting inflation, the difficulty of obtaining credit for family farming or small-scale local enterprises, and the migration from a stagnant countryside to a jobless urban slum.

What this amounts to in most developing countries is a desperate and seemingly self-perpetuating situation.

What can be done about it?

What must be done about it is to reduce the crushing disparities of opportunity.

To begin with, there must be more equitable and comprehensive tax measures; land reform laws; tenancy security policies; and, above all, concrete programs to increase the productivity of small farmers. And not just programs and measures languishing in legislative debate and delay, or lost in legal complexities so hedged about with exceptions that they end by being more rhetoric than reality. What are required are feasible fiscal, agrarian, and educational reform measures that can be fully and fairly enforced. What is needed most of all is a determination to move against the inequities of income distribution.

There is no need to point out that this is politically difficult. Without question it is. But when the distribution of land, income, and opportunity becomes distorted to the point of desperation, what political leaders must often weigh is the risk of unpopular but necessary social reform—against the risk of social rebellion.

"Too little too late" is history's most universal epitaph for political regimes which have lost their mandate to the demands of landless, jobless, disenfranchised and desperate men.

What I am suggesting is that we should stop thinking of massive poverty in a developing country as simply a symptom of underdevelopment—and begin, rather, to think of it as a condition that must be attacked within the framework of the nation's overall development program.

If developing countries themselves do not adopt the policies to deal with this problem, there is little that international institutions and other external sources of aid can do to help the poorest 40% of their peoples—those 40% who suffer the greatest deprivations, and who are in the most desperate need.

But if the developing countries do adopt policies to insure that the benefits of growth will be more equitably distributed among their own peoples, then these countries both need and deserve the assistance necessary to insure that a reasonable rate of overall growth can be achieved. That is why the Second Development Decade's goal of 6% growth in GNP per year was established. It is, in my view, a necessary and an attainable target. But it cannot be met unless external assistance, in the form of both aid and trade, is made available in amounts larger than those which now appear likely.

IV. THE NEED FOR OFFICIAL DEVELOPMENT ASSISTANCE

The developed countries in adopting the strategy for the Second Development Decade, and in support of the growth target, stated that the level of external aid to be provided in the form of Official Development Assistance should reach .7% of their GNPs by 1975.

Where do we stand today in that effort?

A number of the developed countries have made significant progress towards the objective, as the attached table indicates. However, on the basis of present indications, only two (Norway and Sweden) will reach or exceed the target. Six more (Australia, Belgium, Canada, Denmark, France, and the Netherlands) will come close. Four others will substantially increase their percentage but still fall well below the target (Austria, Japan,

Switzerland, and the United Kingdom). And the contribution from the United States, which accounts for roughly half of the total GNP of such countries, continues to decline. It has already fallen from above .5% of GNP in the early years of the last decade to .31% in 1970. It is likely to fall further to around .24% by 1975.

I feel obliged, therefore, to conclude that the total flows of ODA for the first half of the decade are likely to average out at approximately .35% of GNP, only half of the Second Development Decade target.

This is a most unwelcome conclusion. But we must face facts. Not only is there no evidence that ODA as a percentage of GNP will rise above one-half of the target rate by 1975, but unless there are prompt and marked changes in attitudes, it is difficult to foresee any great improvement in the second half of the decade.

Was the .7% target too ambitious? Are the difficulties within the domestic economies of the developed countries such that it is unrealistic to assume they can afford this degree of assistance to international development?

Certainly not.

I have pointed out the severe maldistribution of income and wealth which exists within the developing countries, and I have stressed that these nations must act to shape future economic growth in such a way as to redress that imbalance. But an analogous situation exists in the distribution of the *world's* wealth and income—there is severe maldistribution between the rich nations and the poor nations—and given that fact, one must face up to analogous conclusions.

During the First Development Decade, the total GNP of the world increased by $1100 billion. That is an increase in income almost beyond comprehension.

But how was that growth in income distributed throughout the world?

Eighty percent of the increase went to countries where per capita incomes already average over $1000—and they contain only one-quarter of the world's population.

Only 6% of the increase went to countries where per capita incomes average $200 or less—but they contain 60% of the world's people.

Today the average per capita income in the developed countries is approximately $2400. The comparable figure for the developing countries is $180. By 1980, after the 25% of the world's people who live in the developed countries once again receive 80% of the total increase in the world's income, their per capita income will have risen by some $1200. The comparable increase in the per capita income of the 75% of the world's people who live in the developing countries—even if the Second Development Decade growth objective is achieved — will be less than $100.

The collective GNP of the developed countries in 1970 totalled roughly $2000 billion. In constant prices, it is projected to grow to at least $3000 billion by 1980.

What this means is that in order to raise the current ODA flows of .35% to the targeted .7%, the developed countries would need to devote only about 1.5% of the amount by which they themselves will grow richer during the decade.

The remaining 98.5% of their incremental income will provide them with sufficient funds to meet their domestic priorities.

Granted these facts, are we to say seriously that these wealthy countries cannot reach the ODA target of .7% of their combined GNPs?

It is manifestly not a case of their being unable to afford it.

Nor, in my view, are the reasons for the serious shortfall in ODA the lack of generosity of the peoples of the developed world, or their indifference to justice.

It is much more a matter of ignorance: a failure to comprehend the inhuman conditions which characterize the lives of hundreds of millions of people in the developing countries; a failure to grasp how severe the maldistribution of income actually is between rich nations and poor nations; and a failure to understand how modest are the amounts of the wealthy nations' incremental income which, if made available to the developing countries, would make so great a difference in their ability to meet minimal growth objectives.

It is said that in wealthy countries the case for foreign assist-ance has no constituency. I do not believe that is true. What I do believe is that the constituency in most of the countries must be better informed, better mobilized, and better motivated. In the end, that is a matter of leadership.

But if that constituency in important parts of the developed world remains at its present level of concern—and governments continue to reflect this—then one is compelled to conclude that the flow of ODA will remain at its present wholly inadequate level throughout the decade.

In view of the degree of poverty that oppresses the human spirit in so much of the world, that would be tragic. Let me, for a moment, analyze what in fact that failure would mean.

The ODA deficit will penalize the poorest countries the most. It is unlikely that they will be able to reach the growth target. Their need for ODA is the greatest, and if it stagnates at its present level, they will feel the effects the most severely.

But for even those developing countries which are somewhat better off, a deficiency in ODA will force them to seek external finance from less desirable sources—particularly sources de-manding high rates of interest or early repayment. The danger of overreliance on such sources is well known: it adds signifi-cantly to short- and medium-term debt burdens by mortgaging larger proportions of export earnings, and, in the event of an unexpected decline in those earnings, it can cause severe strains on the whole of the economy.

V. THE DEBT PROBLEM

The truth is: *if ODA flows level off at substantially less than the target for the decade, mounting debt problems for the de-veloping world are inevitable.*

Achievement of the 6% GNP growth objective would require an increase in the volume of imports by over 7% a year. This increase would, in the main, have to be financed by a rapid growth in export earnings, as I will note in a moment. But even if these earnings increase at a rate greater than imports, the trade deficit, which would have to be financed by grants and external borrowings, would grow by approximately 7.5% a year in current prices. In these circumstances, in the face of an ODA deficit, the developing countries would either have to reduce their rates of growth, or increase their debts above reasonable levels. Both are likely.

Since the mid-1950's, publicly guaranteed debt has been growing at about 14% a year. At the end of 1971 it stood at over $60 billion and annual debt service exceeded $5 billion. Servicing of debt since the mid-1950's, has been growing at the same average annual rate of about 14%. This is about twice the rate at which the export earnings, from which the debt must be serviced, have been growing. Such a relationship cannot continue indefinitely.

With the prospect of a leveling off of ODA at far less than the targeted amount, and its partial replacement with financial assistance on harder terms, debt service ratios will inevitably rise. Debt financing has a continuing role in development. But it has its outer limits of prudence and these must be recognized by debtors and creditors alike.

VI. THE EXPANSION OF TRADE

If they are to offset shortfalls in ODA, and keep debt burdens within manageable proportions, it is clear that the developing countries' most imperative need is greatly to expand their export earnings.

How can this be done? Can it be done at all?

It can. But only by difficult economic adjustments, broad policy changes, and astute political leadership in the rich and poor countries alike.

The general outline of the problem is clear enough. From an export point of view, there are three broad categories of developing countries:

- Those countries which export fuel. Fuel exports account for a third of all export earnings in the developing world, and are growing at an average rate of 10% a year. But three-quarters of these substantial earnings go to only six countries, containing less than 3% of the world's population.

- Those countries, many of them with very low income, which remain highly dependent on exports of agricultural products.

- Those countries, many of them in the middle-income group, which have the possibility of increasing their earnings through exports of manufactures.

The relative inelasticity of demand for agricultural raw materials means that the growth of exports of primary commodities, excluding fuel and minerals, is not likely to exceed 3 or 4% a year. However, even for countries dependent on the exports of such products, the developed countries can provide assistance.

They can negotiate stabilization agreements—on the international coffee agreement model—for cocoa and other commodities. Such agreements might provide for multilateral financial assistance.

And the wealthier nations could well afford to leave more of their markets open to agricultural imports from developing countries. Agricultural protectionism, particularly in the current climate of inflationary food prices in wealthy nations, makes neither domestic nor international sense. The sugar-beet growers of the temperate countries, for example, have other ways of earning their living; the sugarcane growers of the Caribbean, Mauritius, and Fiji do not—and the same could be said for many other commodities.

For the countries with greater capabilities for the export of manufactures—countries whose populations total over one billion—we have estimated that achievement of the 6% growth target will require an increase in their export earnings, in current prices, of nearly 10% a year. This, in turn, necessitates an annual increase of their manufactured exports of 15%.

Can this rate of growth be achieved?

It is in the manufactured-products sector that world demand grows fastest, and the record of the developing countries in this sector during the sixties was impressive. Their manufactured exports did in fact grow at the rate of about 15% a year.

What is needed in the seventies is that the momentum be maintained. The natural comparative advantage for developing countries lies clearly in those manufactured products which have a high labor input, or which utilize abundant domestic materials. These include items such as textiles, garments, footwear; vegetable oils, processed foodstuffs; plywood, furniture, glassware, plastic and wooden products; and electronic and engineering sub-assemblies.

But though demand exists for these manufactures in the developed countries, the developing nations have in some cases clung too long to inward-looking, import-substitution policies —policies which may have been appropriate at earlier stages of their industrial growth, but which now unnecessarily hobble export promotion efforts.

There are a number of specific actions which governments in these situations can take. They can reduce the heavy protectionist tariffs on necessary inputs; supply local credit on more reasonable terms for small, labor-intensive, export-oriented enterprises; and adopt and maintain realistic exchange rates.

But if the developing countries must realign their industrial policies to move from reliance on import substitution to greater efforts at export promotion, the developed countries must make just as great a shift from excessive protectionism to more equitable and less restricted import policies.

It is, for example, wholly illogical, after 20 years of development assistance to poorer countries, for the wealthy nations to negate that effort by maintaining higher tariffs on the manufactured goods these poorer countries export than on manufactures from their affluent counterparts. But that is precisely what the wealthy countries are doing. The levels of tariffs on imports of manufactured goods from rich and poor trading partners respectively average out in the United States to 7 and 12%, in the United Kingdom to 9 and 14%, and in the European Community to 7 and 9%.

But it is not only the level of tariffs that is discriminatory against the developing countries. It is their structure. For tariffs rise with the degree of fabrication. In the United States, there is no customs duty on hides and skins, but tariffs on leather are 5%, and on shoes 10%. Similarly, in the European Community cocoa beans from non-associated countries carry a 3% duty, while processed cocoa products must bear an 18% tariff. This manifestly means that processing—even simple processing—can by such tariffs be priced out of the developing country's most appropriate markets.

Even more repressive of the developing countries' export opportunities is the whole series of restrictive non-tariff barriers which rich countries have erected over the years. These take the form of quotas, subsidies, and various preferential purchasing arrangements.

One of the most important elements in the strategy of the Second Development Decade is that the wealthier countries should grant preferential treatment to the manufactured exports of the developing countries. Japan, the Nordic countries, and the European Community have adopted this proposal, with various limitations, and other developed countries are considering it.

It is essential that this plan be carried out in full, but much more is required. The proposed preference agreement would increase the developing countries' exports of manufactures by only about $1 billion a year. And if these countries are to maintain the necessary momentum of a 15% growth in manufactured exports, their annual volume—which rose from less than $2 billion in 1960 to $7 billion in 1970—will have to quadruple to $28 billion by 1980.

That is clearly going to be an enormous task. But one must not dismiss its feasibility, and certainly not on the grounds that it would impose an intolerable import burden on the wealthy countries. Should the $28 billion in exports from developing countries be achieved, it would amount to only about 7% of the expected manufactured imports of the affluent countries, and would represent less than 1% of their GNP.

The volume of trade in manufactured goods among the developed countries themselves is massive, and mutually beneficial. The rich nations accept huge quantities of manufactures from one another. There is no logical reason to suppose that it would not be equally beneficial—indeed, in terms of true comparative advantage, even more beneficial—for these highly industrialized nations to open a greater share of their expanding market for manufactured goods to the developing nations.

The rich nations' absorptive capacity for such goods is immense, and by accepting the more labor-intensive manufactured items from the developing countries, they can turn their attention to where their own true comparative advantage lies: to the production of more sophisticated items, and those employing capital-intensive technology.

It is precisely these goods that the developing countries will increasingly require, and a vast potential market exists among them for such imports provided they can secure, in return, an adequate share of the market for their own manufactured goods.

But even those who accept the probability of long-term gains to the developed countries from opening their markets to the imports from the developing nations may point to the short-term pains of adjustment. Much of the rising tide of protectionism springs from the fears of those whose jobs and investments will be displaced.

It is a political fact of life that the developed countries must adopt realistic adjustment policies to cushion the impact of import competition by retraining, relocation, and refinancing. Few have done so to date. Until they do, labor and management opposition to trade liberalization will be great—and justly so.

In sum, what we should all be seeking in development trade policies—both agricultural and industrial—is closer approximation to the principle of true comparative advantage. The basis for it exists in both the developed and the developing countries, but both must be prepared to modify inward-looking policies in order to achieve it. Only in an environment of more liberal international trade can the efforts of international and national aid agencies to improve the conditions of life in the developing world be fully effective.

VII. THE WORLD BANK

It is in this context that I would like to add a word about the World Bank.

Some four years ago, we set out in the Bank on a Five-Year Program. Our overall objective was that the Bank Group should lend roughly twice as much in the five years ending June 30, 1973, as it had in the previous five-year period; or to put it another way, that in the Five-Year Program period it should lend a total that would approach the entire amount lent in the first 23 years of the Bank's operations.

Taking into account the operating program for the current fiscal year, and the prospects for the following and final year of the Five-Year Program, it now appears probable, assuming ratification of the Third Replenishment of IDA, that the total of new investments in the five-year period will in fact surpass the initial objective of $11.6 billion, and the total cost of Bank-supported projects should exceed $30 billion.

Our goals also included trebling lending in the field of education, and quadrupling it in the agricultural sector. These goals, too, are being met.

Still another objective we have pursued is to give greater emphasis to assisting the very poorest among our member countries—countries with per capita incomes of $100 or less. Our estimate is that during the five-year period from 1969 to 1973 we will have assisted the poorest countries with a total of 215 separate projects. The comparable figure for the first 23 years of the Bank's activities—from 1946 to 1968—was 158.

Now that we are approaching the end of our Five-Year Program, we are giving concerted attention within the Bank to what we can most usefully do to assist our developing member countries in a second Five-Year Program from FY 1974 to 1978. These will be crucial years for the success of the Second Development Decade, and we intend to play as productive a role as possible.

It is already clear that there will be a pressing need for an expansion of IBRD lending, and for a substantial increase in IDA assistance during the Fourth Replenishment Period. We are confident that the necessary increases in IDA assistance, and in other forms of ODA as well, can be achieved. These achievements would be facilitated if plans were made to link the financing of such aid, either directly or indirectly, to future issues of Special Drawing Rights.

VIII. SUMMARY

I want to conclude by summarizing the chief points I have put before you today:

- There is an urgent need to relate the goals of national growth to realistic targets of more equitable income distribution. A climate of economic growth is necessary for the advancement of the developing peoples, but it does not in itself assure equitable participation in the fruits of that growth.

- Unless this is done by the developing countries themselves, no amount of external assistance, whether in the form of aid or trade, will do much to improve the welfare of the lower 40% of their populations which are living in conditions of the most abject poverty.

- The 6% growth goal established for the Second Development Decade cannot be met without substantial flows of Official Development Assistance. But current and projected flows of ODA—at less than half their stated target—are wholly inadequate. Unless ODA expands, the poorest countries will simply be unable to reach their objectives, and many of the others will face increasingly serious problems of debt.

- Even with ODA flows at the targeted level of .7% of GNP, achievement of the Second Development Decade's growth goal would require substantial trade assistance to the developing countries by the wealthy nations. Action must be taken to help stabilize and expand the agricultural exports of those developing nations which are dependent on them. And for those countries with the potential for exports of manufactured goods, discriminatory barriers to markets must be removed and preferences made available.

- Just as we must conclude that it is the responsibility of the political leaders of the developing nations to recognize the inequities that exist within their nations and to move to correct them, so we must likewise conclude that the wealthy nations of the world—possessing 25% of its people, but 80% of its wealth—should move now to provide the additional assistance, in the form of aid and trade, which the developing nations need to meet minimum national goals. That additional assistance can be financed by diverting but a tiny percentage of the incremental income which will accrue to the developed countries during the 1970's.

Our clear duty for the remainder of this decade is to face up to mass poverty for what it really is, determine its dimensions, locate its whereabouts, set a limit beneath which we will not accept its continuance, and make our first priority a threshold of human dignity and decency which is achievable within a generation.

That, ladies and gentlemen, is how I—for one—view the development task.

What we need most to do is to get on with it.

Projected Flow of Official Development Assistance Measured as a Percent of Gross National Product[a]

	1970	1971	1972	1973	1974	1975
Australia:	.59	.58	.59	.59	.59	.60
Austria:	.13	.16	.17	.19	.22	.25
Belgium:	.48	.51	.54	.58	.62	.66
Canada:	.43	.45	.48	.51	.55	.59
Denmark:	.38	.43	.48	.53	.58	.64
France:	.65	.65	.65	.65	.65	.65
Germany:	.32	.31	.32	.33	.33	.34
Italy:	.16	.16	.16	.16	.16	.16
Japan:	.23	.24	.29	.31	.33	.35
Netherlands:	.63	.64	.64	.64	.65	.68
Norway:	.33	.36	.47	.56	.66	.72
Portugal:	.45	.41	.45	.45	.45	.45
Sweden:	.37	.49	.52	.60	.74	.88
Switzerland:	.14	.16	.22	.26	.30	.32
United Kingdom:	.37	.38	.38	.38	.41	.43
United States:	.31	.31	.30	.28	.26	.24
Total DAC:	.34	.35	.35	.35	.35	.35

[a]Countries included are members of OECD Development Assistance Committee, accounting for more than 95% of total Official Development Assistance. Projections are based on World Bank estimates of growth of GNP, on information on budget appropriations for aid, and on aid policy statements made by governments. Because of the relatively long period of time required to change legislatively authorized levels of aid, and then to translate legislative authorizations first into commitments and later into disbursements, it is possible to project today, with reasonable accuracy, ODA flows (which by definition represent disbursements) for 1975.

TEN

To the
UNITED NATIONS CONFERENCE ON THE HUMAN ENVIRONMENT

STOCKHOLM, SWEDEN
JUNE 8, 1972

I. INTRODUCTION

I am pleased to have the opportunity to participate in these deliberations. This conference, and the concern that has brought it into being, are of immense moment. But while the issues before us are serious, they are not beyond solution. Intensified research, precise analysis, and decisive day-to-day action are what they most require.

What they least require are anxious speculation and alarmist accusation.

In my view, what clearly needs to be done is to examine the relationship between two fundamental requirements: the necessity for economic development, and the preservation of the environment.

I would like to comment briefly on that relationship this morning. When I have done so, I would like to outline the steps we are taking in the World Bank to deal with the ramifications of that relationship, and illustrate practical measures which are proving to be both feasible and effective. Finally, I would hope to suggest the general direction all of us in the international development community might most usefully pursue in integrating our mandate to assist in the economic advance of the developing countries with our responsibility to preserve and enhance the environment.

II. THE STATE OF DEVELOPMENT

One must begin with a candid appraisal of the state of development throughout most of the developing world.

It is—as I have noted recently in another United Nations forum—unacceptable.

It is unacceptable because hundreds of millions of people are living at levels of deprivation that simply cannot be reconciled with any rational definition of human decency.

Throughout the developing nations:

- Hunger and malnutrition are sapping energy, stunting bodies, and slowing minds.

- Illiteracy is locking out learning, and paralyzing opportunity.

- Unemployment is not only robbing men of the minimal means to make their way, but leaving their pride broken and their ambition atrophied.

- Wholly preventable diseases are injuring infants, killing children, and aging adults long before their time.

- In sum, hundreds of millions of individual human lives—with all their inherent potential—are being threatened, narrowed, eroded, shortened, and finally terminated by a pervasive poverty that degrades and destroys all that it touches.

The picture is not exaggerated. Throughout the developing world the estimates are that well over a billion human beings are hungry or malnourished. There are a 100 million more adult illiterates than there were two decades ago. Underemployment and unemployment entrap roughly one out of every five in the labor force. Infant and child mortality is four times greater than it is in the affluent world, and life expectancy is 40% shorter. To alleviate pain and arrest disease, there are in some developing countries fewer than one doctor for every 50,000 people—compared to one per 700 in the United States.

These facts are neither pleasant nor comfortable. But they are facts. They symbolize the lives of three-quarters of the human race.

III. THE DILEMMA OF DEVELOPMENT VERSUS GROWTH

Current development programs are seriously inadequate because they are not significantly reducing the poverty which shapes and limits these lives. And though the matter is complex, basically we know why.

There are two overriding reasons: the developing countries are not moving decisively enough to reduce the severe social and economic inequities among their own peoples; and the developed countries are not moving decisively enough to reduce the gross imbalance between their own opulence and the penury of the less-privileged nations.

As I pointed out at the United Nations Conference on Trade and Development in Santiago, the broad statistical evidence is clear that there is dangerously skewed distribution of income both within developing nations, and between the collectively affluent and the collectively indigent nations.

I will not recount that evidence here, but I would reemphasize the conclusion: development simply cannot succeed unless that massively distorted distribution of income —both at the national and international levels—is brought into a more just and reasonable balance.

If it is not, the penalties of prolonged injustice are likely to be unavoidable. Restlessness will edge toward rebellion, and reason will give way to violence. Not only would that fail to assure development. It would prove to be catastrophically costly to rich and poor alike.

If development is to succeed, action is required by rich nations and poor nations alike—and that action can only proceed in a climate of growth.

It is here that the complexity of the problem becomes apparent.

For a poor country to operate an economy which distributes income among the people more justly, there manifestly must be economic growth. Without economic growth a poor country can only remain poor. There is little point in trying to redistribute indigence.

But economic growth means manipulating the traditional environment.

As we now know well enough, it is at this point that injury to the environment can take place. If nature is abused beyond limits, its revenge is inevitable.

If poor nations are faced with the problem of growth within acceptable environmental limits, the rich nations are clearly caught up in it even more seriously. We are meeting in this worldwide conference largely because the evidence is now overwhelming that roughly a century of rapid economic expansion has gradually contributed to a cumulatively monstrous assault on the quality of life in the developed countries.

There is no need to chronicle that evidence to this gathering.

But there is a need to ponder the dilemma it poses.

And that dilemma is this: the achievement of a level of life in accord with fundamental human dignity for the world's two and three-quarter billion poor is simply not possible without the continued economic growth of the developing nations, and the developed nations as well.

But economic growth on the pattern of the past—and most particularly that in the already highly industrialized wealthy nations—poses an undeniable threat to the environment and to the health of man.

There is nothing artificial or contrived about the dilemma. It is very real.

Both elements of the dilemma demand the most deliberate attention.

The question is not whether there should be continued economic growth. There must be. Nor is the question whether the impact on the environment must be respected. It has to be. Nor—least of all—is it a question of whether these two considerations are interlocked. They are.

The solution of the dilemma revolves clearly not about whether, but about how.

At its macro level, this dilemma demands a great deal more research than it has yet received. The preparations for this conference have made an impressive beginning. And the conference's great value will be the impetus to expand and broaden that research.

Such research is necessary, not merely to provide us with a better understanding of the overall resolution of the dilemma, but to amend in a more scholarly manner the alarmist views of some who are deeply persuaded of the problem, but unaware of the full complexity of its elements. Mathematical modeling is useful. But it is only as useful as the validity of its assumptions and the comprehensiveness of its inputs.

What is needed in this issue—and what has not yet been achieved—is the close cooperation of economists and ecologists, of social and physical scientists, of experienced political leaders and development project specialists. The manifest danger in the solution of this dilemma at the macro level is to oversimplify.

When that oversimplification suggests the imminent risk of overloading the planet's life-support systems, or exhausting its essential resources, the developing peoples of the world are suddenly faced with a fearsome prospect. On top of all their present disadvantages, are they now going to be asked to forego their efforts at development in the name of preserving the already disproportionate (and still rising) patterns of consumption of the rich?

The poor are right to be indignant over such a prospect.

But in my view that issue need never arise.

It need never arise because there is no evidence that the economic growth—which the developing countries so desperately require—will necessarily involve an unacceptable burden either on their own or on anybody else's environment.

IV. THE WORLD BANK AND ENVIRONMENTAL CONCERN

Let me illustrate this view by a brief account of what we in the World Bank are doing to deal with the environmental issue in our day-to-day operations.

In 1970, we established the post of Environmental Advisor with a strong mandate to review and evaluate every investment project from the standpoint of its potential effects on the environment.

Our subsequent experience has been that the most careful review of environmental issues need not handicap our fundamental task to get on with the progress of development. On the contrary, it can enhance and accelerate that progress.

In cooperation with other development agencies, we have designed a careful set of guidelines, and have built into our whole economic assistance strategy a feasible method for correlating ecological protection with effective and cost-conscious development.

What we have discovered is significant.

By careful analysis, we have found, in every instance to date, that we can reduce the danger of environmental hazards either at no cost to the project, or at a cost so moderate that the borrower has been fully agreeable to accepting the necessary safeguards.

Central to the success of this approach is the principle that in the issue of environmental damage, prevention is infinitely to be preferred to cure. Not only is it more effective, but it is clearly less expensive.

Responsible officials in the developing countries are aware of this. We in the Bank have found no evidence that they are unresponsive to what can be demonstrated to be a serious ecological hazard or a threat to health and social well-being. It is unfair to suggest that the poor countries are indifferent to the environmental issue, and simply dismiss it out of hand as a rich nation's problem. They do not.

What they are concerned about, and justly so, is that some of the rich—under the influence of doomsday alarmism—may be tempted to impose unilateral and unreasonable roadblocks on the poor countries' desperate need to develop.

The poor nations, after all, have no desire to see their own environment contaminated or wantonly abused. But they also have no desire to remain caught in the permanent contamination of poverty.

Our experience is that environmental protection can be built into development projects as competently and success-fully as any other requisite element. Our project officers are thoroughly briefed in our environmental criteria, and in their early discussions with potential borrowers draw these considerations to their attention. Far from being resented, the considerations are welcomed.

Each project processed in the Bank is now reviewed by the Environmental Office, and a careful in-house study is made of the ecological components. If the project warrants it, an on-site "ecological reconnaissance" study is commissioned by the Bank with the use of qualified consultants. If more serious problems are uncovered, a still more intensive on-site evaluation is undertaken in order to determine what specialized solutions should be incorporated into the project's specifications.

While in principle the Bank could refuse a loan on environmental grounds—in a situation, for example, in which the problems are of such severity that adequate safeguards cannot be applied, or in which the borrower is wholly unwilling to take reasonable measures in his own interest—the fact is that no such case has yet arisen. Since initiating our environmental review, we have found that in every instance the recommended safeguards can and have been successfully negotiated and implemented.

We have been careful to include in our environmental guidelines not merely physical and health-related factors, but cultural considerations as well. We are concerned in the Bank that a development project does not adversely affect the indigenous culture that the country wishes to preserve.

When a project may require the relocation of people, we assure that plans are adequate for their successful resettlement, and that injurious disruptions of their socio-economic opportunities are avoided.

Health factors are, of course, often involved in environmental considerations. In those instances where a development project may threaten to create a new or intensify an existing disease problem, the Bank incorporates in the loan agreement appropriate arrangements for the requisite preventative health-care measures.

Nor does the Bank limit its operations simply to the environmental side effects of development projects. It finances many

projects that are directed specifically at environmental goals—
urban water supply and sewage treatment, for example, as well
as soil erosion control, and water resources management.

The fact is that the environmental criteria we have established in the Bank encompass the entire spectrum of development. They consist of a comprehensive checklist of questions
designed to insure that foreseeable and injurious environmental consequences are carefully considered from the initial
concept of a project, through its design stage, its actual construction, and into its ongoing operations.

The range of the checklist includes sectors as diverse as
textiles and tourism, power stations and paper plants, steel-
making and irrigation systems, fertilizer factories and harbor
facilities—and many, many more.

Sample questions in some of these sectors illustrate their
scope:

- **Irrigation Systems:** Will the changes in water patterns
  introduce disease-bearing organisms into previously unaffected areas? Will runoff water contain residues—such
  as pesticides and fertilizers—that contaminate down-
  stream waters? Will there be sedimentation and erosion
  problems? What will be the ecological consequences of
  changes in land patterns and population distribution?

- **Ports and Harbor Development:** Will topographical
  changes adversely affect marine life? How will wave and
  current action be modified? Will ships create unhealthy
  air pollution from stacks in view of prevailing winds? Will
  the development create waterfront slum areas?

- **Fertilizer Plants:** What types and quantities of gaseous,
  liquid, and solid effluents will be discharged into the air,
  soil and water? Will nitrogen and phosphorous entering
  surface water bodies stimulate the growth of algae and
  aquatic weeds? How will raw materials be handled and
  stored?

- **Petrochemical Complexes:** Have hydrologic, geologic,
  seismologic, and meteorologic studies of the site been
  made to anticipate and minimize damage to human

populations and the environment if accidents occur? Will effluents contain toxic materials? How will they be controlled? What are the dangers of oil or chemical spills? What clean-up contingency plans are available?

- **Highway Construction:** Do plans include provisions for preventing unnecessary despoilment of the landscape and vegetation during construction? Will top soil be stored for respreading? Can temporary drainage systems, barriers, and sedimentation basins be used to prevent eroding materials from reaching waterways? Have provisions been made for adequate living conditions for people displaced by construction activities or for those attracted to newly-opened areas?

These are merely examples of the kinds of issues raised. The full checklist is far more comprehensive, and it provides borrowers with precisely the questions they themselves should analyze in their planning for pragmatic environmental protection.

The projects which pass for review through our Environmental Office include every major region of the developing world.

- In its funding of the expansion of a steel plant in Turkey, on the Black Sea, the Bank cooperated with the borrower in building into the specifications—as a result of thorough on-site study—provisions to control within acceptable levels the flow of liquid wastes into the sea, and gaseous effluents into the air. Originally no such controls had been contemplated. The study convinced the borrower that this would result in unacceptable damage to both off-shore waters and the surrounding terrain, and the recommended pollution-control technology was adopted. The cost for providing this important protection for the environment, as well as for the health of the local population, was only 2% of the overall project costs.

- In the Yagoua district of Cameroon, the rice farmers are poor. The Bank's estimate was that their cash income could increase five-fold in a decade if only irrigation facilities could be improved. But a serious environmental hazard had to be reckoned with: bilharzia. This water-borne disease is carried by the Bulinas snail, and is endemic to the area. Though the proposed irrigation network would serve 3000 hectares of land and 2800 farm families, it was feared that the project might significantly increase the incidence of illness. To assess the problem, the Bank sent a highly qualified expert in the control of the snail vector to Cameroon. After on-site research, his report recommended changes in the engineering design of the canals, provisions for periodic surveys of the snail population, and appropriate molluscicide application as required. The borrower welcomed these recommendations, adopted them, and during the loan negotiations further agreed that public health officials would carefully monitor the region. Thus, an urgent development project was protected from potential ecological risk by inexpensive and practical preventative measures.

• In its financing of a marine terminal at Sepetiba Bay in Brazil—as part of an iron ore mining project near Belo Horizonte, and its attendant rail transportation to the sea —the Bank commissioned an ecological team to study in depth what was required to keep this unspoiled estuary free from pollution. The bay supported an important fishing industry, and possessed tourist and recreational potential. The Bank's team included a marine biologist, a shellfish expert, and an oceanographer. Their recommendations have been built into the loan agreement, and provide for protection against ore and oil carriers flushing their huge holds in the bay, contingency equipment for accidental oil spills, solid waste handling and terminal sewage treatment facilities, and landscaping to preserve the aesthetic values of the area. All of these measures— which will insure that the fishing industry can survive and the bay remain a tourist and recreational attraction— represent less than 3% of the total project cost.

These case histories could be multiplied. But what is common to them all is that they illustrate a critical truth: valid environmental considerations need not deny the advance in economic development the less-privileged countries so gravely require.

V. WHAT MUST BE DONE

How then can the international community—rich and poor nations alike—best proceed?

It is clear that in environmental matters the developing countries enjoy one of the very few advantages of being late-comers in the development process: they are in a position to avoid some of the more costly and needless mistakes the developed countries made in the past.

Now what does that imply?

To begin with, what it does not imply is that late-comers to the development process must forego industrialization and technological advance.

That would simply mean stagnation. It is easy enough for the wealthy to romanticize about the supposed charm of pre-technological society. But the plain fact is that there was nothing pretty at all about the squalid poverty which the common man—in what are now the affluent nations—had to endure in the pre-technological period. For the vast majority it was a life of destitution and disease. No one wants to go back to that.

Anyone in doubt has only to examine poverty in the developing countries today. The deprivation is appalling by any acceptable standards of human decency.

It is not surprising, then, that those who call for a slowing down or a complete halt to economic growth tend to be those who are already amply provided with the advantages which that very growth has made possible.

What I mean by the environmental advantage of the late-comers to the development process is that they can far more easily and inexpensively build into their industrial infrastructure the practical preventative measures necessary to avoid the ecological damage the developed world has already suffered.

Our experience in the Bank confirms this. There is an increasingly broad variety of anti-pollution technologies available to the poorer countries—technologies the affluent countries have had to develop at a far later and more difficult stage of their industrial expansion.

Those technologies can work, and work well.

The air over London, for example, is substantially cleaner today than it was 15 years ago. There has been an 80% reduction in smoke emission, a 40% reduction in sulphur dioxide, and a consequent near doubling in the average hours of winter sunshine. It is estimated that this dramatic improvement—largely the result of the enlightened Clean Air Act of 1956—has cost Londoners only about 35 cents per annum. What it has saved them in discomfort and illness is beyond calculation, but one need only recall the disastrous and fatal smog of 1952—a smog that killed an estimated 4000 people—to reflect on the importance of the improvement.

There has been a corresponding improvement in the environmental conditions of many of the rivers in Britain through intensified sewage management. Ten years ago there were no fish at all in the Thames in a 30-mile stretch above and below the city of London. Three years ago more than 40 species were observed.

As the affluent nations continue to take their environmental problems more seriously, they are going to discover a whole new range of technology to abate and avoid ecological dangers. The less-privileged countries can adapt these technical advances to their own local conditions.

The danger that we will fail to achieve our twin objectives of advancing the development of the less-privileged nations while preserving the environment stems not from technological weaknesses but from potential failures of political will and social responsibility.

Ecological considerations have made us all more aware of the interdependencies of our world. We have come to see our planet as "spaceship earth." But what we must not forget is that one-quarter of the passengers on that ship have luxurious first-class accommodations and the remaining three-quarters are traveling in steerage. That does not make for a happy ship —in space or anywhere else. All the less so when the steerage passengers realize that there are at hand the means to make the accommodations more reasonable for everyone.

Have we the political and social awareness to give more attention to the present living conditions of the overwhelming majority of the travelers? It means, in practice, making available more development assistance, and removing inequitable trade, tariff, and other discriminatory barriers. Those barriers are blocking the mutual benefits that can flow from application of the principle of comparative advantage. Justice and intelligent self-interest both suggest that it is wiser to open a vital bulkhead on increased opportunity than to keep it senselessly sealed in the name of some narrow and parochial protectionism.

There should be no question about whether the wealthy countries can afford to combine rising domestic environmental protection costs with increased development assistance for the developing countries.

It is clear that they can.

The continued growth of their gross national product will provide them by the end of the decade with an additional one thousand billion dollars per annum.

The suggestion that the rich countries cannot spare for the poor countries the miniscule percentage of that incremental income necessary to raise concessionary aid from its present level of .35% of GNP to the United Nations target of .7% is simply beyond credence.

The wealthy nations may not in fact meet that target. And they may delay dismantling the discriminatory barriers to a more just and mutually advantageous flow of trade. But if the rich do refuse greater trade and aid to the poor, it will have nothing to do with a disinterested and universal reverence for the environment. It will be because of a provincial response to the pressures of special interests.

What, then, must be done to reconcile our mandate to assist in the economic advance of the developing countries with our responsibility to preserve and enhance the environment?

In my view there are five essential requirements. We must:

- Recognize that economic growth in the developing countries is essential if they are to deal with their human problems.

- Act on the evidence that such growth, if properly planned, need not cause unacceptable ecological penalties.

- Assist the developing countries in their choice of a pattern of growth which will yield a combination of high economic gain with low environmental risk.

- Provide the external support required for that economic advance by moving more rapidly toward meeting the United Nations concessionary aid target of .7% of GNP, and by dismantling and discarding inequitable trade barriers which restrict exports from poorer countries.

- And, above all, realize that human degradation is the most dangerous pollutant there is.

In the end, it is respect for man—and his home—that has brought us to this conference.

When we leave, let us go with the conviction that that respect can and must be translated into practical action. The leading edge of that action must be to protect man from the one hazard which can injure not only his habitat and his health—but his spirit as well. Poverty. Cruel, senseless, curable poverty.

Our task is not to create an idyllic environment peopled by the poor.

Our task is to create a decent environment peopled by the proud.

ELEVEN

To the
BOARD OF GOVERNORS
WASHINGTON, D.C.
SEPTEMBER 25, 1972

I. INTRODUCTION

L ast year, in this forum, I discussed a number of problems which were of serious concern as the Second Development Decade got under way. Now that the trend of the decade is becoming more clearly predictable, I want to explore with you today an issue that is central not only to its success, but to the efficacy of the entire development process.

That issue is the critical relationship of social equity to economic growth.

But before turning to that, I should like to:

• Report on the Bank Group's operations in Fiscal 1972.
• Review the progress of our Five-Year Program for the fiscal years 1969-73.
• Assess the current state of development throughout our developing member countries.
• And, based on that assessment, sketch the outline of a program for the Bank for the five years 1974-78.

II. THE BANK GROUP'S OPERATIONS IN FISCAL YEAR 1972

Let me begin by touching upon our operations during the past fiscal year. For that period, new loans, credits and investments totalled $3.1 billion. This compares with $2.6 billion in 1971, $2.3 billion in 1970, $1.9 billion in 1969, and $1.0 billion in 1968.

To finance growing disbursements, and to increase the level of liquidity, the Bank borrowed, net of retirements, $1.1 billion during the year. This brought our liquid reserves to $3.2 billion —up $700 million from June 30, 1971. Net income for the year was $183 million, excluding a gain on revaluation of $51 million.

The year, then, was a productive one operationally. But as I have indicated to you before, the development task before us requires that we plan on a broader scale than year-to-year operations make possible. That is why in the fall of 1968, when I first met with you, I proposed a Five-Year Program. That Program will be completed next June 30th, and I want to report to you now on its progress.

III. THE BANK GROUP'S FIVE-YEAR PROGRAM

You will recall what we set out to accomplish. Our analysis of the overall requirements for economic progress in our developing member countries convinced us that we should greatly broaden and expand the Bank Group's operations both in scope and in size.

We proposed as our overall lending objective that we should double the Bank Group's operations in the period 1969-73, as compared with the period 1964-68. Were we to achieve this goal, it would mean that during the five years the volume of lending would approach the total amount lent during the previous 23 years of the Bank's operations.

I can report to you today that we will not only meet that goal, but will surpass it.

But it was not principally the size of our operations which concerned us when we launched the Five-Year Program. We did not merely want to do more. We wanted to do more of what would contribute most to development.

Thus, within the overall lending program, we were resolved to shift our emphasis both into different sectors and into different geographical areas.

What does that mean in practice?
- In a developing world in which hunger is chronic, it means intensifying our efforts in agriculture. We have quadrupled our operations in that sector.
- In a developing world darkened by functional illiteracy, it means expanding our efforts in education. We have tripled our operations in that sector.
- In a developing world caught up in the threat of unmanageable population pressures, it means facing up to that complex and controversial problem. We have established a Population Projects Department, and we have launched important initiatives in that sector.

In our previous meetings, I have stressed the damaging effect of runaway population growth on a developing economy. I have pointed out the strains this creates both at the family and the national level for any country struggling to improve the quality of life for its people.

Overly rapid population growth simply erodes and dissipates development gains in every sector: savings evaporate, scarcities multiply, resources are stretched so thin that in the end they cannot cover the most essential needs.

While the population problem is clearly one which cannot be solved within the confines of a five-year plan, or a development decade, or indeed even during what is left of our century, it is by its very nature a problem that can grow only worse with procrastination and delay. That is why we believe the entire international community must assign it the highest priority.

The Bank's initial work in the population field consisted of sector missions to a dozen different countries and projects deliberately initiated in smaller member countries in order to provide us with working experience on a scale commensurate with our new capabilities.

But in the early summer of this year we approved far-reaching projects in two of our largest member nations: India and Indonesia.

The project in India—a joint effort with the Government of Sweden—will develop what promises to be the most advanced systems approach to the population problem in any developing country. It will provide the essential information and analysis required to shape the overall massive effort India is making to reduce its current population growth.

Both the size of India's problem, and the magnitude of its effort to solve it, can be grasped in the statistics. The nation's total population now stands at over half a billion. It is growing by an additional million each month. The government has set up an organization of 80,000 persons to administer a family planning program to serve one hundred million couples. The Bank project is designed to help support that program with the experimentation and the systems analyses required to make it effective.

Like India, Indonesia is serious in its determination to provide its people with effective family planning assistance. With a population of more than 120 million, currently growing at an annual rate of 2.5%, it ranks fifth among the world's most heavily populated countries. Some two-thirds of its people live in Java and Bali, where the average density is nearly 1600 persons per square mile.

With the participation of the United Nations Fund for Population Activities, WHO, UNESCO and UNICEF, the Bank project provides $13 million for a greatly expanded family planning program. In addition to the construction of 300 health centers and the provision of the required vehicles and equipment, the project will help finance the training of several thousand field workers, the preparation of public school curricula, and a program of research and evaluation.

Should the overall objectives of the project be reached—and both the government and we are confident that they can—Indonesia's population by the end of the century, even though it will be twice as large as it is today, will be 50 million less than it would otherwise be.

What all this demonstrates is that our Five-Year Program has shifted the Bank's emphasis toward those sectors which in today's conditions require intensified effort: agriculture, education, and population, among a number of others.

But as I have indicated, our shifts in emphasis have been geographical as well as sectoral. In Africa, we expect to more than treble our lending over the previous five-year period.

And for the group of our poorest member countries—those whose per capita incomes average less than $100—we will quadruple our lending.

To achieve these goals has, of course, required a substantial strengthening of the Bank Group both organizationally and financially. The professional staff, for example, by the end of the five-year period will have increased by 125%.

Recruitment of highly qualified staff, representing the broadest possible geographical experience, has been facilitated by a worldwide interest in the work of the Bank. In the past year, more than 2400 candidates, from 98 countries, applied for 52 available openings in our Young Professionals Program.

Doubling the volume of our lending operations has meant, of course, that we had greatly to expand our borrowing capacity. This in turn depends on governments granting us access to their countries' capital markets. Despite recurrent and unsettling readjustments in the international monetary system, they have continued to do so.

Not only have we continued to borrow in our more traditional markets, but we have entered new markets as well, and have utilized new borrowing instruments, and new channels of distribution. Net borrowing for the five-year period will approximate three and three-quarter times that of the earlier period and liquid reserves will increase by about 125%.

Neither the expansion of operations nor the shift into less traditional sectors of lending has adversely affected net income. On the contrary, total net income during the five-year period will be approximately 30% higher than that of the previous period, and this despite a significant increase in the subsidy to the developing countries implicit in the Bank's lending rate.

Organizationally, then, and financially, the Bank Group will complete the first Five-Year Program in a position of strength.

But while encouragement over the Bank's operations is one thing, complacency with the state of development is quite another. And there is little danger of confusing the two if we take an objective look at the current prospects of the developing nations.

IV. THE STATE OF THE DEVELOPING WORLD AND THE BANK'S PROGRAM FOR FY74-78

In its strategy for the Second Development Decade, the United Nations set as a target that the average annual rate of growth in Gross National Product for the developing countries should be at least 6%. To make that possible, the developed countries were to increase their concessionary aid—known as Official Development Assistance—to .7% of their GNPs by 1975.

As I pointed out earlier this year at the United Nations Conference on Trade and Development in Santiago, it is now clear that the objective of .7% will not be reached. There seems little likelihood that during the first half of the decade Official Development Assistance will exceed .37% of GNP—only half of the Second Development Decade target (see attached table).

That is regrettable in the extreme, but we must be realistic. And realism dictates that we try to assess the effects of this massive shortfall in concessionary aid.

The first, and least tolerable, of the effects is that the poorer of our member countries—those with per capita GNPs of less than $200—will be penalized the most. Their needs for Official Development Assistance are the greatest, and their chances for finding feasible alternatives are the least.

What is more, these countries collectively contain 1.1 billion people, 64% of the aggregate population of our entire developing country membership. They are the very countries which have suffered the greatest burdens of poverty during the past decade. Their GNPs grew annually at an average rate of only 4.1% and their per capita incomes at a miniscule 1.7%.

With the ODA objective only half achieved, these poorer nations have almost no hope of attaining the 6% growth target. That will condemn them to so slow an economic advance over the decade that hundreds of millions of individuals within these countries will be able to detect virtually no improvement whatever in their desperately low standards of living. Their per capita incomes will rise by no more than two dollars a year.

Projected to the end of the century—only a generation away —that means the people of the developed countries will be enjoying per capita incomes, in 1972 prices, of over $8000 a year, while these masses of the poor (who by that time will total over two and one-quarter billion) will on average receive less than $200 per capita, and some 800 million of these will receive less than $100.

The deficit in development assistance will penalize the poorest countries the most. But even for those developing countries which are somewhat better off, a deficiency in ODA will cause serious economic and financial problems.

Publicly guaranteed debt in the developing world currently stands at about $75 billion, with annual debt service of approximately $7 billion. Debt service payments rose by 18% in 1970, and by 20% in 1971, representing twice the average rate of increase over the 1960s, and reflecting a hardening of the terms of debt as the proportion of concessionary aid in the total flow of external assistance to developing countries declined.

Given the shortfall in ODA, and the growing debt problem, it seems clear that the World Bank Group should try to continue to expand its operations. If we were to fail to make this effort, our developing member countries would be driven to an even greater dependence on higher-cost, shorter-maturity sources of external capital with the inevitable exacerbation of their debt-servicing burdens. They would have little choice, for without a reasonable flow of external finance they simply cannot meet even minimal development requirements.

For the Bank Group to relax in its resolve to do everything it feasibly can to assist in this situation would be to shirk our central responsibility: to recommend those policies, provide that technical assistance, and help finance those projects which will most effectively support our developing member countries' own struggle to advance the welfare of their people.

With careful planning and your support, we are convinced that the Bank Group can obtain the necessary funds to continue to expand its operations during a Second Five-Year Program. And that is what we propose to do.

As an overall goal, for the period FY 1974-1978, we propose to increase our financial commitments to our developing member countries by an average of 11% a year, and to shift an increasing percentage of these commitments to International Development Association credits.

If we can achieve this expanded level of operations—and I am confident that it is possible—it would mean that the World Bank Group would help finance, and provide technical assistance for some $50 billion of capital improvements in our developing member countries during the Second Five-Year Program period. This would be in contrast to $30 billion of such projects from 1969 to 1973, and $13 billion from 1964 to 1968.

V. SOCIAL EQUITY AND ECONOMIC GROWTH

Given the unfortunate shortfall in ODA, the consequent aggravation of the debt problem, and the procrastination of the developed countries in dismantling discriminatory barriers to trade from the developing countries, the Second Development Decade's 6% growth target is not going to be met by many nations and is going to be an exceptionally arduous task for many others.

But let us suppose that it were in fact to be accomplished by 1980.

Would that achievement, in itself, guarantee a significant advance in the quality of life for the majority of the two billion people who live in our developing member countries?

The frank answer is no.

The answer is no because increases in national income—as essential as they are—will not benefit the poor unless they reach the poor.

They have not reached the poor to any significant degree in most developing countries in the past, and this in spite of historically unprecedented average rates of growth throughout the sixties.

To understand this, it is useful to distinguish between three broad categories of poverty in the developing world.

First, there is great poverty in those countries, generally rather small, which simply have very few resources—natural, financial, or skilled—with which to promote growth. There is so little wealth in these nations that even if it were more equitably distributed, virtually everyone would still be very poor. These are the countries (there are 25, with populations totalling 140 million) which the United Nations has designated as the least developed and for which special measures of assistance have been·approved.

Second, there are particularly impoverished regions in most of the larger developing countries—for example, the southern republics of Yugoslavia, the North East of Brazil, or the North East of Thailand. The integration of these regions into the more rapidly growing parts of the economy often poses difficult cultural as well as economic problems. These areas are, however, readily identifiable geographically, and it is possible to devise and implement programs specifically aimed at increasing the productive capacities and incomes of their populations.

But it is the third category that is the largest, the most pervasive, and the most persistent poverty of all. It is the poverty of the low-income strata—roughly the poorest 40%—of the total population in all developing countries. It is they who—despite their country's gross economic growth—remain entrapped in conditions of deprivation which fall below any rational definition of human decency.

This is not simply the poverty of a highly disadvantaged country, nor of a particularly backward geographical region in an otherwise rapidly advancing country. Rather, it is the poverty of those people widely dispersed throughout every developing country who, for whatever reason, lie beyond the reach of traditional market forces and present public services. It is the poverty of those masses of the population which current government policies do not adequately encompass, and which external assistance cannot directly reach.

This poverty of the poorest 40% of the citizenry is of immense urgency since their condition is in fact far worse than national averages suggest. Our studies, for example, indicate that:

- In 10 countries, with per capita incomes averaging $145, the poorest 40% of the population receive a per capita income of only $50.
- In another 10 countries with per capita incomes averaging $275, the poorest 40% of the population receive a per capita income of only $80.

What we are dealing with here are problems that are difficult to grasp in their concrete, day-to-day realities.

When we reflect that of the more than half a billion persons living on the Indian subcontinent, some 200 million subsist on incomes that average less than $40 a year, how are we to comprehend what that really implies? The estimate is that if India were to depend exclusively on the growth of national income to solve its massive nutrition problems, it would require more than 30 years before the poorest third of the country could afford an adequate diet.

When we reflect that of the two billion persons living in our developing member countries, nearly two-thirds—some 1.3 billion—are members of farm families, and that of these there are some 900 million whose annual incomes average less than $100, what frame of reference are we to call on to make that fact meaningful?

To many in the affluent world, to be a farmer suggests a life of dignity and decency, free of the irritation and pollution of modern existence: a life close to nature and rich in satisfactions.

That may be what life on the land ought to be. But for hundreds of millions of these subsistence farmers, life is neither satisfying nor decent. Hunger and malnutrition menace their families. Illiteracy forecloses their futures. Disease and death visit their villages too often, stay too long, and return too soon.

Their nation may be developing, but their lives are not. The miracle of the Green Revolution may have arrived, but for the most part, the poor farmer has not been able to participate in it. He simply cannot afford to pay for the irrigation, the pesticide, the fertilizer—or perhaps even for the land itself on which his title may be vulnerable and his tenancy uncertain.

His nation may have doubled or tripled its educational budget, and in the capital city there may be an impressive university. But for 300 million children of poor farmers like himself there are still no schools—and for hundreds of millions of others if a school, no qualified teacher—and if a qualified teacher, no adequate books.

His nation may be improving its communications, and jet aircraft may be landing at its international airport in increasing numbers. But for the poor farmer who has seldom seen an airplane, and never an airport, what communications really means —and what he all too often does not have—is a simple all-weather road that would allow him to get his meager harvest to market when the time is right and the prices are good.

Let us be candid.

What these men want are jobs for their survival, food for their families, and a future for their children. They want the simple satisfaction of working toward something better: toward an end to misery, and a beginning of hope.

We are not talking here about a few maladjusted discontents.

We are talking about hundreds of millions of desperately poor people throughout the whole of the developing world. We are talking about 40% of entire populations. Development is simply not reaching them in any decisive degree. Their countries are growing in gross economic terms. But their individual lives are stagnating in human terms.

What can be done?

That is the question I want to explore with you now.

VI. A PLAN OF ACTION

One must begin by analyzing the policy options which are generally proposed. They present clearly conflicting schools of thought.

One view is that governments in developing countries should make rapid economic growth the first objective, and that income redistribution and increased employment can be achieved later through fiscal and institutional changes.

Others argue that the growing pressures of poverty are so overwhelming that their widespread relief should be the central objective of development strategy, even if that entails major sacrifice in the pace of overall growth.

Of course it would be comforting to continue to believe that there is no conflict between rapid overall growth and comparable improvement in the incomes of the poor. But, unfortunately, in the real world in which we live, the evidence suggests that there is.

There is a natural tendency for growth to be concentrated in the modern sectors of the economy with little current benefit to the lowest income groups. What data there are—while admittedly incomplete—indicate that this pattern of growth has developed in many countries.

But if few dispute the fact that there exists some conflict between maximization of growth and the rapid reduction of poverty, many argue that in the long term the conflict is irrelevant since it can—given sufficient time—be resolved. In the long term, rapid growth will increase productivity, and furnish the resources which can be redistributed to those who cannot yet be accommodated in the high-productivity, high-wage, modern sector.

The same view holds that even in the shorter term—in a decade, say—it is possible at least to reduce the conflict between rapid growth and more equitable income for the poor by shaping an economy which provides the proper incentives, which prices labor and capital correctly, which strengthens the fiscal system, and which emphasizes the right adaptive technologies.

But although this argument is correct as far as it goes, it doesn't go far enough. A decade may be the short term for a development planner. But a decade is the long term for a subsistence tenant farmer whose children are most likely to die before the age of five, whose diet is already so inadequate that he cannot stave off chronic ill health, whose illiteracy limits his future ability to learn new skills, and whose perpetual indebtedness to the money lender and dependence on the land owner leave him neither options nor hope.

On the other hand, one must recognize that if a government were to initiate policies to increase the income growth of the lowest 40% of the population—with a view to assuring that, at a minimum, their share of the nation's overall economic growth does not decline as it has in the past—there are legitimate questions as to what the impact of such policies would be on the rate of overall national growth. Would it seriously hamper it? Would it prevent it altogether? What precisely would happen?

There are at least three possible consequences of economic policies directed to more equitable income distribution which are thought to hamper growth. They are: reduced entrepreneurial incentives; lower savings rates; and the choice of obsolete technology.

Let us consider these for a moment.

It is often suggested that wide disparities in income are necessary in order to provide entrepreneurial incentives. Without arguing whether such incentives are important stimuli to productivity, one can question the amount of incentive that is required to motivate the desired degree of effort.

In a study of the income disparities of 39 developing countries, in which the income of the wealthiest 5% is measured as a multiple of the bottom 40%, there is a wide range of differences among countries. There are eight countries in which the per capita income of the top 5% is more than 30 times greater than that of the lowest 40%. There are 16 countries in which the ratio is less than 15 to one.[a]

But the significant point is that when one compares these two sets of countries on their per capita growth performance during the 1960s, there is no discernible relationship between the size of the incentives and the rapidity of the growth. The average rate of growth of the group of countries with the greatest disparities was not significantly different from the group with the least. This indicates that there may well be substantial scope in the developing countries for moderating the highly skewed disparities in income without crippling the incentives to greater productivity.

Similarly, flexibility in the relationship between income distribution and the volume of savings available for socially productive investment may, in fact, be far greater than is generally assumed. While it is true that higher incomes permit a higher rate of savings, the real question is what becomes of those savings. If they are used for production of luxury goods to meet a demand pattern distorted by a skewed income distribution, it is questionable whether the high savings rate is, in fact, promoting any crucial national interest. If, on the other hand, a more equitable distribution of income results in a somewhat lower gross rate of savings, but more investment in the production of essential commodities, the lower rate of growth in national income may be accompanied by an increase in the incomes of the bulk of the population.

Finally, there is the question of the choice of technology. It is often asserted that rapid economic growth demands adoption of technologies which, by their very nature, penalize employment and perpetuate poverty. The argument is that unless the modern sector is so equipped, its inefficiencies will restrict the country's capacity to export and perpetuate a costly dependence on imports for even the most basic requirements.

---

[a] In the United States, the ratio is 5 to 1.

But here again, the argument is oversimplified. The issue is not so much modern technology versus traditional technology. The real issue is efficient technology versus inefficient technology, and the essential question is how ought one to measure that efficiency. Efficiency as such is a relative term. A technology is efficient or inefficient relative to the resources one has available. In a labor-scarce, affluent, developed economy, the most efficient technology is capital-intensive and highly automated—it produces at the lowest cost per unit in terms of the scarce resource: labor.

But in a developing economy, where labor is abundant, and sophisticated skills are scarce, it is clearly inefficient to emulate technologies which lead to high costs per unit measured in terms of the scarce resource: capital. And yet that is the result when, in the rush to industrialize, developing countries subsidize capital by creating a structure in which foreign exchange is undervalued, credit is underpriced, and tax incentives misdirected.

If government policy were directed towards promoting a price structure which reflected the scarcity values of labor and capital more realistically, the technological choice would be different. The result would be greater employment, broader income distribution, and more competitive patterns of production of precisely those labor-intensive goods which labor-scarce affluent countries need, but cannot themselves produce inexpensively.

What, then, are we to conclude from this analysis?

The answer is that while we obviously do not know as much as we want to know about the relationship of more equitable income distribution to overall economic growth, we know enough to conclude that:

- It is possible to design policies with the explicit goal of improving the conditions of life of the poorest 40% of the populations in the developing countries—and that this can be done without unacceptable penalties to the concomitant goal of national growth.
- Without specific emphasis on such programs, there will not be significant progress in reducing poverty within acceptable time periods.

We know, in effect, that there is no rational alternative to moving toward policies of greater social equity.

When the highly privileged are few and the desperately poor are many—and when the gap between them is worsening rather than improving—it is only a question of time before a decisive choice must be made between the political costs of reform and the political risks of rebellion.

That is why policies specifically designed to reduce the deprivation among the poorest 40% in developing countries are prescriptions not only of principle but of prudence. Social justice is not merely a moral imperative. It is a political imperative as well.

What, then, can be done to attack the problem of massive poverty within the developing world?

The first and obvious step is the political resolve to make the effort.

It is clear that in the end each country must make its own decision as to how and when to deal with its internal inequities. The problems of poverty are rooted deeply in the institutional frameworks, particularly in the distribution of economic and political power within the system. Outside agencies can assist but cannot solve such problems. It is governments that have the responsibility of essential domestic reform, and there is no way they can escape that responsibility. To postpone reform on the grounds of political expediency is to invite political extremism. To remain indifferent to social frustration is to foster its growth.

Political will, then, is the first requisite.

Public understanding is the second. The fact is that all of us need a clearer perception of the problem. We need both more and better quantitative data on past and current trends in employment and in income distribution. And we need them urgently. I propose that the developing countries address this task of gathering income data, and that as a practical matter they set a target date of 1975 for a greatly expanded program of censuses, sample surveys, and specific studies. The international agencies—our own included—can assist technically and financially, and provide a multilateral forum for this effort.

Third, all of us need to identify concrete policies and actions which can reduce the skewness of the income distribution. Admittedly, we are on the frontier of a new field of knowledge here, and we have far more questions than we have answers. But the urgency of the situation is such that we simply cannot wait until all the answers are in. We must begin now with what we know now. And we clearly know enough to at least make a beginning. If we make mistakes we will simply have to learn from them. But the greatest mistake of all would be for the international development community to sit back and continue to do in the future what it has done in the past: to ignore the problem. It is the time for new approaches.

What ought they to be?
- The first step should be to establish specific targets, within the development plans of individual countries, for income growth among the poorest 40% of the population. I suggest that our goal should be to increase the income of the poorest sections of society in the short run—in five years—at least as fast as the national average. In the longer run—ten years —the goal should be to increase this growth significantly faster than the national average.
- Given the intimate link between poverty and massive unemployment, unemployment and underemployment must be attacked head-on. With 20% or more of entire populations already jobless or virtually idle—and with the population explosion pouring a growing stream of new entrants into the labor pool each year—unless policies and programs are devised to absorb surplus labor into productive jobs, little can be done to improve the lot of the desperately poor. Job creation must therefore become a direct objective in itself. It will be necessary to organize rural and urban public works—the building of market roads; construction of low-cost simple housing; reforestation programs; expansion of irrigation and drainage facilities; highway maintenance, and similar low-skill, labor-intensive, and economically useful projects. The Bank will assist in financing such projects.
- Institutional reforms to redistribute economic power are critically required in many developing countries: land reform, corporate reform, tax reform, credit and banking reform, and many others. Continuation of the existing land

tenure patterns, tax laws, and banking regulations will simply assure that the present distribution of assets and income will be perpetuated. The Bank will support reforms in these areas with technical and financial assistance.

• Shifts in the patterns of public expenditure represent one of the most effective techniques a government possesses to improve the conditions of the poor. Too often these expenditures—on health, on transport, on water supply, on education, and on many other sectors—end by benefiting the already privileged far more than the mass of the disadvantaged.[a] This, in part, is because these services are more concentrated in the urban areas and better neighborhoods. But it is also a function of the greater participation of the highly privileged in the political process. Governments can best begin to shift public expenditure towards those who need it the most by initiating surveys on the effects of their current patterns of disbursement: where do the funds really go, and who benefits the most? The Bank will assist in such surveys and, based on them, will help design programs, to be financed by it and others, which will improve the distribution of public services.

• Finally, policies should be undertaken to eliminate distortions in the prices of land, labor, and capital. To underprice capital for the wealthy and make credit expensive for the poor; to allow liberal access to scarce resources for the privileged, and price them out of reach of the deprived; to provide subsidies for the powerful, and deny them to the powerless—these are wholly self-defeating approaches to development. Such policies lead a nation inevitably toward economic imbalance and social instability.

These, then, are the general measures which all of us in the international development community should move toward with all the urgency that we can command. We in the World Bank Group can assist our developing member countries in this effort, and we fully intend to do so.

---

[a]This is strikingly illustrated in the access to public services. School enrollment ratios and the quality of education, for instance, are almost uniformly higher in the higher income groups. And, in a sample of 20 developing countries, the allocation of scarce foreign exchange was ten times greater for the importation of private cars than for public buses.

VII. SUMMARY AND CONCLUSIONS

Let me summarize and conclude the argument I have put before you this morning.

Current development programs are seriously inadequate. They are inadequate because they are failing to achieve development's most fundamental goal: ending the inhuman deprivation in hundreds of millions of individual lives throughout the developing world.

Why are these programs failing?

There are two overriding reasons: the affluent nations are not moving effectively enough to assist the indigent nations; and the indigent nations are not moving effectively enough to assist the poorest 40% of their own populations.

The affluent nations have, of course, their own domestic priorities. But their growing incremental income is so immense, their technological capacity so powerful, and their whole range of advantages so disproportionately gigantic, that no rational argument can be made for their refusal to do more to assist the disadvantaged nations.

Collectively, the affluent nations are currently providing only half the targeted .7% of their GNPs in the Official Development Assistance which will make so decisive a difference to the development efforts of the poor countries. These amounts of money are miniscule in light of the fact that the collective gross national products of the developed nations, which totalled $2000 billion in 1970, are expected to grow to more than $3000 billion in 1980.

The rich nations are not being asked to diminish their riches in order to help the poor nations. They are only being asked to share a tiny percentage of their continually increasing wealth.

Further, the rich nations are failing the poor nations—and themselves—in another critical respect. They are refusing to give the poor nations a more reasonable opportunity to trade fairly with them. Discriminatory trade restrictions on the part of wealthy countries are indefensible on two counts: they penalize the people of the poor countries, and they penalize their own domestic consumers. The trade problem is admittedly complex, but the essence of it is simple enough. The political pressures of special-interest groups in affluent nations are prevailing over the interests of the majority of ordinary citizens in rich and poor countries alike.

If the rich nations do not act—through both aid and trade—to diminish the widening imbalance between their own collective wealth and the aggregate poverty of the poor nations, development simply cannot succeed within any acceptable time frame. The community of nations will only become more dangerously fragmented into the privileged and the deprived, the self-satisfied and the frustrated, the complacent and the bitter. It will not be an international atmosphere conducive to tranquility.

The developed nations, then, must do more to promote at least minimal equity in the distribution of wealth among nations.

But the developing nations must do more as well.

Their internal equity problems are no less important than those of the international community at large. In the developing nations' pursuit of rapid economic growth, the poorest 40% of their populations are being largely left behind.

It is becoming increasingly clear that the critical issue within developing economies is not simply the pace of growth, but the nature of growth. The developing nations achieved an overall average annual GNP growth rate of more than the targeted 5% by the end of the sixties. But the social impact of that growth was so severely skewed, and the numbers of individuals all but passed by so absolutely immense, that the simple statistical achievement of that target was misleading.

Governments exist to promote the welfare of all of their citizens—not just that of a privileged few. Absolute egalitarianism is as chimerical as absolute laissez-faire, but what is certain is that absolute human degradation—when it reaches the proportions of 30 to 40% of an entire citizenry—cannot be ignored, cannot be suppressed, and cannot be tolerated for too long a time by any government hoping to preserve civil order.

It would be naive not to recognize that that time in many quarters of the world is running out.

The task, then, for the governments of the developing countries is to reorient their development policies in order to attack directly the personal poverty of the most deprived 40% of their populations. This the governments can do without abandoning their goals of vigorous overall economic growth. But they must be prepared to give greater priority to establishing growth targets in terms of essential human needs: in terms of nutrition, housing, health, literacy, and employment—even if it be at the cost of some reduction in the pace of advance in certain narrow and highly privileged sectors whose benefits accrue to the few.

Such a reorientation of social and economic policy is primarily a political task, and the developing countries must decide for themselves if they wish to undertake it. It will manifestly require immense resolve and courage.

The task of political leadership in the wealthy world is to match that resolve and courage with a greater commitment to equity between their own affluent nations and the grossly disadvantaged developing nations.

I believe that no one within this forum would deny that the time for significantly greater social and economic equity both among nations and within nations has indeed come.

Given more than a million years of man's life on earth, it has been long in arriving.

Now that it is here we cannot escape asking ourselves where our responsibilities lie.

It seems to me that the character of our entire era will be defined by the shape of our response.

Projected Flow of Official Development Assistance
Measured as a Percent of Gross National Product[a]

	1970	1971	1972	1973	1974	1975
Australia	.59	.52	.59	.59	.59	.60
Austria	.13	.06	.17	.19	.22	.25
Belgium	.48	.49	.54	.58	.62	.66
Canada	.42	.37	.48	.51	.55	.59
Denmark	.38	.43	.48	.53	.58	.64
France	.68	.68	.65	.65	.65	.65
Germany	.32	.34	.33	.36	.36	.38
Italy	.16	.17	.16	.16	.16	.16
Japan	.23	.23	.28	.32	.36	.40
Netherlands	.63	.60	.70	.74	.76	.78
Norway	.32	.33	.47	.56	.67	.75
Portugal	.61	.75	.45	.45	.45	.45
Sweden	.36	.45	.50	.56	.65	.71
Switzerland	.15	.12	.22	.26	.30	.32
United Kingdom	.37	.41	.41	.41	.45	.46
United States	.31	.32	.30	.28	.26	.24
Total	.34	.35	.36	.36	.36	.37

[a]Countries included are members of OECD Development Assistance Committee, accounting for more than 95% of total Official Development Assistance. Figures for 1970 and 1971 are actual data. The projections for later years are based on World Bank estimates of growth of GNP, on information on budget appropriations for aid, and on aid policy statements made by governments. Because of the relatively long period of time required to translate legislative authorizations first into commitments and later into disbursements, it is possible to project today, with reasonable accuracy, ODA flows (which by definition represent disbursements) for 1975.

TWELVE

To the
BOARD OF GOVERNORS
NAIROBI, KENYA
SEPTEMBER 24, 1973

I. INTRODUCTION

Last year I began a discussion with you of the critical relationship of social equity to economic growth. I emphasized the need to design development strategies that would bring greater benefits to the poorest groups in the developing countries—particularly to the approximately 40% of their populations who are neither contributing significantly to economic growth nor sharing equitably in economic progress.

In the twelve months since our last meeting, we in the Bank have given high priority to further analysis of the problems of poverty in the developing countries and to an evaluation of the policies available for dealing with them. On the basis of these studies, I should like this morning to:

- Discuss the nature of the poverty problem, particularly as it affects the rural areas.
- Suggest some of the essential elements of a strategy for dealing with it.
- And outline a plan for World Bank operations in support of this new strategy.

But before turning to these matters, I want to report to you on the results of the Bank's Five-Year Program for the fiscal years 1969-73—a program that concluded on June 30th of this year; and then to suggest the financial objectives for a second five-year plan for the years 1974-78.

233

II. THE BANK'S FIVE-YEAR PROGRAM FOR
FISCAL YEARS 1969-73

It was in September of 1968 that I first met with you in this forum and outlined the goals of a Five-Year Program for the World Bank Group. You will recall what our objectives were. We stated that we were "formulating a 'development plan' for each developing country to see what the Bank Group could invest if there were no shortage of funds, and if the only limit on our activities were the capacity of our member countries to use our assistance effectively and to repay our loans on the terms on which they were lent."

Based on these analyses, we proposed to double the Bank's operations in the fiscal period 1969-73 as compared with the previous five-year period 1964-1968. That objective has been met: total financial commitments of the IBRD, IDA, and IFC, in current prices, in the 1964-1968 period, were $5.8 billion; in the 1969-1973 period, $13.4 billion. In real terms, the increase was 100%.

As indicated in the table below, in the five years we achieved a level of operations that exceeded the total of all the operations that the Bank had undertaken in the developing world in the 23 years from 1946 through 1968.

**Bank Group Financial Commitments to Developing
Countries by Region**
(dollars in millions)

Region	Numbers of Projects		Amount of Commitments (current prices)	
	1946-68	1969-73	1946-68	1969-73
East Africa	78	104	$ 834	$ 1,099
West Africa	35	102	522	891
Europe, Middle East, N. Africa	113	168	1,785	3,198
Latin America and Caribbean	281	176	3,554	3,734
Asia	201	210	3,927	4,496
Total	708	760	$10,622	$13,418

But it was not just quantity that we were seeking. We did not simply want to do more than had been done in the past, but to do more of what was best suited to the rapidly changing needs of the developing countries. That meant that within our overall objective we had to shift our emphasis both geographically and sectorally.

While continuing to serve the regions where we had been particularly active, we decided to expand substantially in other areas.

In Africa, for example, we set out to triple our lending—and we have done so.

We undertook operations, for the first time, in Indonesia— and in the five years have committed $523 million there.

For the poorest and least developed of our member countries, those with average per capita incomes of $120 or less, we have nearly tripled our lending. During the Five-Year Program period we have initiated 217 separate projects in these countries. The comparable figure for the whole of the previous 23 years of the Bank's operations is 167.

Geographically, then, our planned shifts in emphasis have been carried out, and carried out concomitantly with an increased level of lending in our more traditional regions.

But it was clear to us in 1968 that the Five-Year Program must shift emphasis sectorally as well. Accordingly, we proposed to triple lending in education and quadruple lending in agriculture. We have done so.

Perhaps the most significant shift was into a sector in which the Bank had previously had no operations at all: the sensitive and difficult, but clearly critical, sector of population.

We established a Population Projects Department, and from the very beginning received more requests for technical and financial assistance from our member countries than we could immediately provide. We deliberately began our project work in a number of smaller countries in order to work effectively within our limited staff resources. But by the end of the Five-Year Program period agreements had been signed for projects in seven countries, including two of the largest and most heavily populated nations: India and Indonesia.

In addition to the Population Projects Department—to which has now been added the responsibility for nutritional projects—we launched other initiatives within the Bank. Among them are new departments for Industrial Projects, Urban Projects, and Tourism Projects; an Office of Environmental Affairs; an Operations Evaluation Unit; and a new program of comprehensive country economic reporting.

To achieve the doubled level of our operations, it was necessary, of course, to strengthen the Bank both organizationally and financially. Worldwide recruitment was increased and the staff was expanded by 120% during the period. We were determined in this effort to broaden its international character to the maximum degree feasible. In 1968 the staff represented 52 nationalities. It now represents 92. In 1968 the proportion of staff from our developing member countries was 19%. The proportion is now 29%, and continues to grow.

Lending more has of course meant borrowing more, and that in turn has depended on governments granting us access to their capital markets. This they have continued to do, despite unsettled conditions and monetary fluctuations. It is a mark of confidence in the Bank's financial structure that we have been able to borrow not only in our more traditional markets, but in altogether new ones, and to utilize new borrowing instruments and new channels of distribution.

Net borrowing for the five-year period has been approximately four times that of the earlier period, and our liquid reserves have risen to $3.8 billion, an increase of 170%.

Neither the increase in operations, nor the shift in emphasis toward more socially oriented sectors, has adversely affected net income. On the contrary, total net income for the five-year period was $965 million, 28% more than in the previous period, and this despite the fact that the Bank's lending rate was held down to levels resulting in a substantially greater subsidy to the developing countries than in earlier years.

We have completed the Five-Year Program, then, by meeting the quantitative goals we had set for ourselves in 1968, and by making a sustained effort to improve the overall quality of our work.

But our task now is to move forward with a second Five-Year Program. Like the first, its goals and shifts in emphasis must be shaped by the evolving development situation itself.

I should like to give you my assessment of that situation.

III. THE BANK'S SECOND FIVE-YEAR PROGRAM: FY1974-78

Most of our developing member countries are faced with three interrelated difficulties:

- An insufficiency of foreign exchange earnings from trade.
- An inadequate flow of Official Development Assistance.
- And an increasingly severe burden of external debt.

Each of these problems is serious in itself. But together they threaten the outcome of the entire development effort.

Let me examine each of them briefly.

The Trade Problem

The core of the trade problem for the bulk of the developing countries is that they cannot expand their exports rapidly enough to pay for their essential imports. These imports are themselves often the key to greater export capability—and higher foreign exchange earnings—and thus the dilemma of trade imbalances in these countries tends to become self-perpetuating.

The problem is compounded by the delay of the wealthy nations in dismantling discriminatory trade barriers against the poor countries. Our studies indicate, for example, that if the affluent nations were gradually to reduce their present protectionist trade restrictions against agricultural imports from the developing world, the poorer nations could, by 1980, increase their annual export earnings by at least $4 billion.

An Acute Shortage of Development Assistance

Secondly, the current flow of Official Development Assistance (ODA)—financial aid on concessionary terms—is acutely inadequate. Not only is it far below what the developing nations need and what the affluent nations can readily afford, but, as the attached table indicates, it is only half the modest target prescribed by the internationally accepted United Nations Strategy for the Second Development Decade.

That target called for reaching ODA levels of .7% of gross national product (GNP) by 1975. In fact, by 1975 ODA will not exceed .35%. And yet achievement of the target neither requires the people of the developed nations to reduce their already high standards of living, nor to neglect their domestic priorities. It asks them only to dedicate a tiny fraction of the *incremental* income—income over and above that which they already enjoy— that will accrue to them in the decade of the 70s.

During the decade, the annual GNP of these affluent nations will grow, in constant prices, from $2 trillion in 1970 to approximately $3.5 trillion in 1980: an increase in output virtually beyond one's capacity to comprehend.

In order to double the ODA flows, and thereby raise them to the targeted .7%, the developed countries would need to devote to that end less than 2% of the amount by which they themselves will grow richer during the period. The remaining 98% of their incremental income would provide them with more than sufficient funds to meet their domestic priorities.

I have heard it said in the developed countries—in the United States and elsewhere — that their domestic problems are so pressing that they require an exclusive claim on the immense incremental wealth which will accrue to their societies in future years, and that not even the 2% of this additional income, which we suggest should be diverted to the developing countries, can be spared. But I believe that such critics of additional assistance to the poorer nations, when citing the needs of their own cities and countryside, fail to distinguish between two kinds of poverty: what might be termed relative poverty and absolute poverty.

Relative poverty means simply that some countries are less affluent than other countries, or that some citizens of a given country have less personal abundance than their neighbors. That has always been the case, and granted the realities of differences between regions and between individuals, will continue to be the case for decades to come.

But absolute poverty is a condition of life so degraded by

disease, illiteracy, malnutrition, and squalor as to deny its victims basic human necessities.

It is a condition of life suffered by relatively few in the developed nations but by hundreds of millions of the citizens of the developing countries represented in this room. Many of you have cause to know far better than I that:

- One-third to one-half of the two billion human beings in those countries suffer from hunger or malnutrition.
- 20% to 25% of their children die before their fifth birthdays. And millions of those who do not die lead impeded lives because their brains have been damaged, their bodies stunted, and their vitality sapped by nutritional deficiencies.
- The life expectancy of the average person is 20 years less than in the affluent world. They are denied 30% of the lives those of us from the developed nations enjoy. In effect, they are condemned at birth to an early death.
- 800 million of them are illiterate and, despite the continuing expansion of education in the years ahead, even more of their children are likely to be so.

This is absolute poverty: a condition of life so limited as to prevent realization of the potential of the genes with which one is born; a condition of life so degrading as to insult human dignity—and yet a condition of life so common as to be the lot of some 40% of the peoples of the developing countries. And are not we who tolerate such poverty, when it is within our power to reduce the number afflicted by it, failing to fulfill the fundamental obligations accepted by civilized men since the beginning of time?

I do not wish you to interpret my remarks as those of a zealot. But you have hired me to examine the problems of the developing world and to report to you the facts. These are the facts.

It is true that some citizens of the developed countries protest against increasing their assistance to the developing countries because of poverty in their own societies. They do so either because they are unacquainted with these facts; or because they fail to distinguish between relative and absolute poverty; or perhaps because they are obscuring the truth even from themselves —unwilling to admit that the principal pressure on the incremental incomes of their economies comes not from a legitimate concern for the less fortunate in their societies, but from the endless spiral of their own demands for additional consumer goods.

There are, of course, many grounds for development assistance: among others, the expansion of trade, the strengthening of international stability, and the reduction of social tensions.

But in my view the fundamental case for development assistance is the moral one. The whole of human history has recognized the principle—at least in the abstract—that the rich and the powerful have a moral obligation to assist the poor and the weak. That is what the sense of community is all about—any community: the community of the family, the community of the village, the community of the nation, the community of nations itself.

I, for one, cannot believe that once the gross deficiency in the flow of Official Development Assistance is better understood; that once the degree of deprivation in the developing nations is more fully grasped; that once the true dimensions of poverty in the less privileged world are more realistically compared with the vast abundance in the affluent world (that once the people of the United States, for example, understand that they, with 6% of the world's population, consume about 35% of the world's total resources and yet, in terms of economic assistance as a percent of GNP, rank fourteenth among the sixteen developed nations)—I cannot believe that in the face of all this the people and governments of the rich nations will turn away in cynicism and indifference.

The Growing Burden of Debt

Finally, there is the growing burden of external debt in the developing world. Publicly guaranteed debt currently stands at about $80 billion, with annual debt service of approximately $7 billion.

It is important to understand what the essence of the debt problem is. It is not the fact that there is debt, nor even the size of the debt. It is, rather, the composition and dynamics of the debt; the fact that debt, and debt payments, are growing faster than the revenues required to service them.

Restricted trading opportunities, exacerbated by inadequate flows of ODA, tend to drive developing countries to over-reliance on export credits and other short-term, high-cost loans. It is these factors that threaten to increase the debt burden beyond reasonable limits. Already, since 1970, the situation in several countries — Ghana, Chile, Pakistan, India, Indonesia, and Sri Lanka among others—has led either to debt rescheduling or to unilateral defaults.

The Bank's Program for FY74-78

Given the nature of this interrelated set of problems in our developing member countries—an insufficiency in foreign exchange due to trade difficulties, the inadequate flow of ODA, and the growing debt burden—the Bank, far from relaxing the momentum of our operations over the next five years, must increase it. And that is what we intend to do.

We plan to expand both our IBRD and IDA lending at a cumulative annual rate, in real terms, of 8%.[a]

For the five-year period FY1974-78, our lending — in 1973 dollars—should total $22 billion for almost 1000 projects.

The total cost of these projects will approach $55 billion.

Our $22 billion in new commitments will constitute, in real terms, a 40% increase over the 1969-1973 period, and a 175% increase over the 1964-1968 period.

This, then, in financial terms is our plan for the Second Five-Year Program. It will represent the largest program of technical and financial assistance to developing countries ever undertaken by a single agency.

But the qualitative changes in the program will be of even greater significance than the increase in its size. We plan to place far greater emphasis on policies and projects which will begin to attack the problems of absolute poverty to which I referred

---

[a]In last year's address, I stated that our plan, in terms of current prices, was to increase financial commitments 11% per year. The "real terms" equivalent was 8%. Today, because of changes in exchange rates and accelerated price increases, a growth rate of 8% per annum in real terms, for the period FY74-78 vs. FY69-73, will probably require an increase in financial commitments of approximately 14% per year in current prices.

earlier—far greater emphasis on assistance designed to increase the productivity of that approximately 40% of the population of our developing member countries who have neither been able to contribute significantly to national economic growth, nor to share equitably in economic progress.

In the remaining sections of this statement I would like to discuss the nature of this poverty problem, consider what means are at hand to alleviate it, and indicate what part the Bank can play.

IV. POVERTY IN THE DEVELOPING WORLD

Poverty and Growth

The basic problem of poverty and growth in the developing world can be stated very simply. The growth is not equitably reaching the poor. And the poor are not significantly contributing to growth.

Despite a decade of unprecedented increase in the gross national product of the developing countries, the poorest segments of their population have received relatively little benefit. Nearly 800 million individuals—40% out of a total of two billion —survive on incomes estimated (in U.S. purchasing power) at 30 cents per day in conditions of malnutrition, illiteracy, and squalor. They are suffering poverty in the absolute sense.

Although the collection of statistics on income distribution in the developing world is a relatively recent effort, and is still quite incomplete, the data point to what is happening. Among 40 developing countries for which data are available, the upper 20% of the population receives 55% of national income in the typical country, while the lowest 20% of the population receives 5%. That is a very severe degree of inequality—considerably greater than in most of the advanced countries.

The data suggest that the decade of rapid growth has been accompanied by greater maldistribution of income in many developing countries, and that the problem is most severe in the countryside. There has been an increase in the output of mining, industry, and government — and in the incomes of the people dependent on these sectors—but the productivity and income of the small farmer have stagnated.

One can conclude that policies aimed primarily at accelerating economic growth, in most developing countries, have benefited mainly the upper 40% of the population and the allocation of public services and investment funds has tended to strengthen rather than to offset this trend.

Reorienting Development Policy

The need to reorient development policies in order to provide a more equitable distribution of the benefits of economic growth is beginning to be widely discussed. But very few countries have actually made serious moves in this direction. And I should stress that unless national governments redirect their policies toward better distribution, there is very little that international agencies such as the World Bank can do to accomplish this objective.

Without intruding into matters that are the proper concern of individual governments, I would like to discuss an important first step that could lead to a more rapid acceptance of the required policy changes. This step would be to redefine the objectives and measurement of development in more operational terms. While most countries have broadened the statements of their development goals to include references to reducing unemployment and increasing the income of the poor —as well as emphasizing traditional growth in output—they still measure progress toward these complex objectives with a single measuring rod: the growth of GNP.

But the fact is that we can no more measure the achievement of multiple development objectives by the GNP alone than we can describe the quality of life in a city exclusively by its size. The Gross National Product is an index of the total value of goods and services produced by an economy; it was never intended to be a measure of their distribution.

It is important to remember that indices of the increase in gross national product implicitly weight the growth of each income group according to its existing share of total national income. Since in the developing countries the upper 40% of the population typically receive 75% of all income, the growth of GNP is essentially an index of the welfare of these upper income groups. It is quite insensitive to what happens to the poorest 40%, who collectively receive only 10-15% of the total national income.

Were we to fashion a new index which gave at least the same weight to a 1% increase in the incomes of the poorest groups in society as it gave to a 1% increase in the incomes of the well-to-do, we would get a much different picture of development in the past decade. The growth of total income in several of the largest countries in Latin America and Asia, for example, would be significantly lower than the growth as measured by the GNP.

But, in a number of cases—including for instance, Sri Lanka and Colombia—the opposite would be true. In these countries, giving equal weight to the growth of income of each citizen, regardless of his income level, would result in a more accurate assessment of development performance than does GNP because it would give credit for some redistribution of the benefits of growth toward the lower income groups.

Adopting this kind of a socially oriented measure of economic performance would be an important step in the redesign of development policies. It would require governments, and their planning and finance ministries, to look at the allocation of resources in a much more comprehensive way. For they would have to consider not only the total output of an investment but also how the benefits would be distributed. This would give practical, operational significance to the rhetorical statements of social objectives now embodied in most development plans. And it would insure that important questions of equity became an integral part of project evaluation procedures both within the developing countries and the lending agencies. We are, in fact, beginning to develop this approach in the World Bank.

Identifying the Concentrations of Poverty

This proposed reorientation of development strategy would require far greater precision in identifying the main concentrations of the poorest people in a given society and examining much more intensively the policies and investments through which they can be reached.

Clearly, the bulk of the poor today are in the rural areas. All of our analysis indicates that this is likely to continue to be the case during the next two or three decades[a]:

- At present, 70% of the population of our developing member countries and an equivalent percentage of the poor live in the countryside.
- Although demographic projections indicate that 60% of the population increase in these countries (an increase of two billion people by the end of the century) is expected to take place in the urban areas—largely through internal migration —in the year 2000 more than half of the people in the developing world will still reside in the countryside.
- Rapid urbanization is already creating very serious problems. Under present policies, per capita public expenditures in urban areas are typically three to four times as great as they are in rural areas. Thus, efforts to relieve rural poverty by still greater migration to the cities will result in an even more inequitable division of public expenditures and only exacerbate the existing inequalities of income.
- Within the rural areas the poverty problem revolves primarily around the low productivity of the millions of small subsistence farms. The truth is that despite all the growth of the GNP, the increase in the productivity of these small family farms in the past decade has been so small as to be virtually imperceptible.

But despite the magnitude of the problem in the countryside, focusing on rural poverty raises a very fundamental question: is it a really sound strategy to devote a significant part of the world's resources to increasing the productivity of small-scale subsistence agriculture? Would it not be wiser to concentrate on the modern sector in the hope that its high rate of growth would filter down to the rural poor?

The answer, I believe, is no.

Experience demonstrates that in the short run there is only a limited transfer of benefits from the modern to the traditional

---

[a] It is true, of course, that millions of the victims of poverty in the developing world live in the slums of the urban areas and that their social and economic advance depends on an acceleration of the pace of industrialization. I have discussed this subject with you before and will do so again, but today I want to concentrate on the problem of poverty in the countryside where the overwhelming majority of the people live.

sector. Disparities in income will simply widen unless action is taken which will directly benefit the poorest. In my view, therefore, there is no viable alternative to increasing the productivity of small-scale agriculture if any significant advance is to be made in solving the problems of absolute poverty in the rural areas.

But that does not mean there need be an irreconcilable conflict between that objective and the growth of the rest of the economy. On the contrary, it is obvious that no attempt to increase the productivity of subsistence agriculture can succeed in an environment of overall economic stagnation. The small farmers cannot prosper unless there is significant growth in other sectors, both to provide the development resources they will require, and to create the demand for their additional output.

The point is that the reverse is also true—and it is time we recognized it. Without rapid progress in smallholder agriculture throughout the developing world, there is little hope either of achieving long-term stable economic growth or of significantly reducing the levels of absolute poverty.[a]

The fact is that very little has been done over the past two decades specifically designed to increase the productivity of subsistence agriculture. Neither political programs, nor economic plans, nor international assistance—bilateral or multilateral—have given the problem serious and sustained attention. The World Bank is no exception. In our more than a quarter century of operations, less than $1 billion out of our $25 billion of lending has been devoted directly to this problem.

It is time for all of us to confront this issue head-on.

V. A STRATEGY FOR RURAL DEVELOPMENT

In presenting a strategy for rural development I should like: first, to analyze the scope of the problem; second, to set a

---

[a] It is not my purpose today to discuss the food crisis presently affecting wide areas of the globe. However, any long-term solution of the food shortage, in a world in which population will increase for at least a century to come, clearly requires substantial increases in smallholder productivity. In addition, to provide insurance against the vagaries of the weather, some coordinated system of national food reserves must be established. I strongly support the efforts of the Director-General of the FAO to organize such a program, and I am fully prepared to recommend that the World Bank participate in its financing.

feasible goal in order to deal with it; and third, to identify the measures required to meet that goal.

The Scope of the Problem

Let me begin by outlining the scope of the problem in the developing countries which are members of the Bank. It is immense:

- There are well over 100 million families involved—more than 700 million individuals.
- The size of the average holding is small and often fragmented: more than 100 million farms are less than 5 hectares; of these, more than 50 million are less than 1 hectare.
- The possession of land, and hence of political and economic power in the rural areas, is concentrated in the hands of a small minority. According to a recent FAO survey, the wealthiest 20% of the landowners in most developing countries own between 50 and 60% of the cropland. In Venezuela they own 82%; in Colombia 56%; in Brazil 53%; in the Philippines, India, and Pakistan about 50%. Conversely, the 100 million holdings of less than 5 hectares are concentrated on only 20% of the cropland.
- Even the use of the land which the small farmer does have is uncertain. Tenancy arrangements are generally insecure and often extortionate. In many countries tenants have to hand over to the landlord 50-60% of their crop as rent, and yet in spite of this are faced with the constant threat of eviction. The result is that their incentive to become more productive is severely eroded.

It has often been suggested that the productivity of small-scale holdings is inherently low. But that is simply not true. Not only do we have the overwhelming evidence of Japan to disprove that proposition, but a number of recent studies on developing countries also demonstrate that, given the proper conditions, small farms can be as productive as large farms. For example, output per hectare in Guatemala, the Republic of China, India, and Brazil was substantially greater on smaller farms than on larger ones. And it is, of course, output per hectare which is the relevant measure of agricultural productivity in land-scarce, labor-surplus economies; not output per worker.

There is ample evidence that modern agricultural technology is divisible, and that small-scale operations need be no barrier to raising agricultural yields.

The question, then, is what can the developing countries do to increase the productivity of the small farmer. How can they duplicate the conditions which have led to very rapid agricultural growth in a few experimental areas and in a few countries so as to stimulate agricultural growth and combat rural poverty on a broad scale?

The first step is to set a goal. A goal is necessary both so that we can better estimate the amount of financial resources required, and so that we can have a firm basis for measuring progress.

Setting the Goal

I suggest that the goal be to increase production on small farms so that by 1985 their output will be growing at the rate of 5% per year. If the goal is met, and smallholders maintain that momentum, they can double their annual output between 1985 and the end of the century.

Clearly this is an ambitious objective. A 5% rate of growth has never been achieved on a sustained basis among smallholders in any extensive areas of the developing world. Smallholder production has risen on average only about 2.5% per year in the past decade.

But if Japan in 1970 could produce 6720 kg. of grain per ha. on very small farms, then Africa with its 1270 kg. per ha., Asia with 1750 kg., and Latin America with 2060 kg. have an enormous potential for expanding productivity.

Thus, I believe the goal is feasible. It recognizes that progress will be slow during the next five to ten years while new institutions evolve, new policies take hold, and new investments are implemented. But after this initial period, the average pace of growth in smallholder agricultural productivity can be more than double today's rate and thereby benefit the lives of hundreds of millions of people.

Now, what are the means necessary to accomplish this goal?

Neither we at the Bank, nor anyone else, have very clear answers on how to bring the improved technology and other inputs to over 100 million small farmers—especially to those in dry-land areas. Nor can we be fully precise about the costs. But we do understand enough to get started. Admittedly, we will have to take some risks. We will have to improvise and experiment. And if some of the experiments fail, we will have to learn from them and start anew.

What, then, can we begin to do now?

Measures Necessary to Meet the Goal

Though the strategy for increasing the productivity of small-holder agriculture is necessarily tentative, the following are essential elements of any comprehensive program:
- Acceleration in the rate of land and tenancy reform.
- Better access to credit.
- Assured availability of water.
- Expanded extension facilities backed by intensified agricultural research.
- Greater access to public services.
- And most critical of all: new forms of rural institutions and organizations that will give as much attention to promoting the inherent potential and productivity of the poor as is generally given to protecting the power of the privileged.

These elements are not new. The need for them has been recognized before. But they will continue to remain little more than pious hopes unless we develop a framework of implementation, and agree to a commitment of resources commensurate with their necessity. That is what I propose.

Organizational Changes

The organizational structure for supporting smallholder agriculture is without doubt the most difficult problem. Let me examine this subject first and then turn to the others in sequence.

Obviously, it is not possible for governments to deal directly with over 100 million small farm families. What is required is the organization of local farm groups, which will service millions of farmers at low cost, and the creation of intermediate institutions through which governments and commercial institutions can provide the necessary technical assistance and financial resources for them.

Such institutions and organizations can take any number of forms: smallholder associations, county or district level cooperatives, various types of communes. There are, of course, many experiments already going on in different parts of the world. What is imperative is that at each organizational level financial discipline be rigorously required, and that the entire structure be oriented toward initiative and self-reliance. Experience shows that there is a greater chance of success if the institutions provide for popular participation, local leadership, and decentralization of authority.

The reorganization of government services and institutions is equally important. No program will help small farmers if it is designed by those who have no knowledge of their problems and operated by those who have no interest in their future.

The sad truth is that in most countries, the centralized administration of scarce resources—both money and skills—has usually resulted in most of them being allocated to a small group of the rich and powerful. This is not surprising since economic rationalizing, political pressure, and selfish interest often conspire to the detriment of the poor. It will clearly require courageous political leadership to make the bureaucracy more responsive to the needs of the subsistence farmers.

The ablest administrators, for example, should no longer be reserved exclusively for the urban sectors. Top engineering talent must be devoted to designing low-cost solutions to the problems of small-farm irrigation. Young graduates can be motivated to take on the problems of the rural poor, and be adequately rewarded for solving them. Educational institutions should recognize that the training in practical skills is as important as the accumulation of theoretical knowledge. In short, national managerial and intellectual resources must be redirected to serve the many instead of the few, the deprived instead of the privileged.

Acceleration of Land and Tenancy Reform

But there are other structural changes necessary as well. And the most urgent among these is land and tenancy reform. Legislation dealing with such reform has been passed—or at least been promised—in virtually every developing country. But the rhetoric of these laws has far outdistanced their results. They have produced little redistribution of land, little improvement in the security of the tenant, and little consolidation of small holdings.

That is extremely regrettable. No one can pretend that genuine land and tenancy reform is easy. It is hardly surprising that members of the political power structure, who own large holdings, should resist reform. But the real issue is not whether land reform is politically easy. The real issue is whether indefinite procrastination is politically prudent. An increasingly inequitable situation will pose a growing threat to political stability.

But land and tenancy reform programs—involving reasonable land ceilings, just compensation, sensible tenancy security, and adequate incentives for land consolidation—are possible. What they require are sound policies, translated into strong laws which are neither enervated by exceptions nor riddled by loopholes. And most important of all, the laws have to incorporate effective sanctions, and be vigorously and impartially enforced.

What we must recognize is that land reform is not exclusively about land. It is about the uses—and abuses—of power, and the social structure through which it is exercised.

Better Access to Credit

But realistic land and tenancy reform—as essential as it is—is not enough. It is one thing to own land; it is another to make it productive. For the smallholder, operating with virtually no capital, access to credit is crucial. No matter how knowledgeable or well motivated he may be, without such credit he cannot buy improved seeds, apply the necessary fertilizer and pesticides, rent equipment, or develop his water resources. Small farmers, generally, spend less than 20% of what is required on such inputs because they simply do not have the resources.

In Asia, for example, the cost of fertilizer and pesticides required to make optimum use of the new high-yielding varieties of wheat and rice ranges from $20 to $80 per hectare. But the small farmer there is spending only $6 per hectare because that is all he can finance. And most of that $6 does not come from government or institutional sources, but from local landlords or village money lenders at usurious rates of interest.

The present institutions in the rural areas are simply not geared to meeting the needs of smallholder agriculture. In countries as disparate as Bangladesh and Iran, less than 10% of institutional credit is available to rural areas; in Thailand, the Philippines, and Mexico less than 15%; in India less than 25%. And only a fraction of this is available to the small farmer. Even then it is accompanied by stringent tests of creditworthiness, complicated application procedures, and lengthy waiting periods.

Existing commercial institutions are reluctant to make credit available to the small farmers because the administrative and supervisory costs of small loans are high. Further, the subsistence farmer is operating so close to the margin of survival that he is simply not as creditworthy as his more wealthy neighbors.

Nor do governmental credit policies always help the small farmer, even though the intention may have been to shape them for that purpose. The fact is that concern over the usurious rates the farmer pays the money lender has led to unrealistically low rates for institutional credit. The smallholder does not need credit subsidized at an annual interest rate of 6% for projects which will yield 20% or more per year. He would be much better off if he had to pay a realistic rate of interest but could actually get the money.

In reviewing their financial policies for agriculture, governments should take care that good intentions do not have self-defeating consequences. In many of our member countries, radical restructuring of interest rates is long overdue.

Assured Availability of Water

No less essential than credit—indeed even more so—is an assured supply of water for the smallholder. Without it, seeds, fertilizer, and pesticides are useless. This means continued research into the most productive uses of water, as well as substantial investment in irrigation and increased attention to on-farm irrigation methods.

It is estimated that the presently irrigated area in the developing world of 85 million hectares can be expanded by another 90 million hectares, but the additional cost would be high: over $130 billion. And not only is expansion of irrigated land expensive, it is a slow process. No major irrigation dam which is not already in the active design stage is likely to yield significant on-farm benefits before the mid-1980s. Although investments in major irrigation projects will continue to be an important part of national investment plans, and of Bank financing, they must be supplemented by more quick-yielding programs designed to benefit the small farmer.

This calls for much greater emphasis in on-farm investment which can take advantage of existing large irrigation projects. There are too many cases—in our experience and that of others —in which it has taken ten years or more after the dam was completed for the water actually to reach the farmers. Major irrigation schemes often preempt necessary resources for on-farm improvement. The drama of harnessing a major river may be more exciting than the prosaic task of getting a steady trickle of water to a parched hectare, but to millions of smallholders that is what is going to make the difference between success and failure. The allocation of scarce budgetary resources should reflect this reality.

Thus, development of major irrigation works, though necessary, is not enough. Too many small farmers would be left unaffected. These programs need to be supplemented by others which can bring water to farms outside major irrigation projects —and do so cheaply. Tubewells, low-lift pumps, and small dams can make major contributions to productivity. Moreover, these investments—while not always within the reach of individual poor farmers—can often be afforded by organized smallholders.

Expansion of Extension Services and Applied Research

The small farmer needs credit and water, but he needs technical information as well. And he is not getting nearly enough of it. The projected number of trained personnel who will graduate annually from existing agricultural educational institutions can at best satisfy less than half the total needs of the developing world. In the developed countries, the ratio of government agricultural agents to farm families is about 1 to 400. In developing countries, it is on average 1 to 8000. And only a small fraction of even these limited services is available to the small farmer.

It is not primarily the deficiency of funds that is delaying the necessary expansion of extension services. It is the deficiency of resolve to do more for the small farmer who desperately requires them. There is scarcely a single developing country which does not produce too many lawyers, but there is no developing country which produces enough extension agents. Governments cannot control personal career objectives, but they can offer appropriate incentives, and promote vocational choices which will contribute more directly to economic development and social modernization.

Thus the annual cost of training the required extension personnel would be modest as a percentage of GNP or budgetary resources. The net cost—after deducting savings from changed allocations—would be even less. As long as the supply of extension workers is grossly inadequate, only the large farmers will benefit and the needs of the poor will be ignored.

Behind extension services, of course, lies applied research. In a sample of five major developed countries, the governments are allocating annually from $20 to $50 per farm family for such research. The comparable figures for five major developing countries are only 50 cents to $2 per farm family.

The international network of agricultural research has grown impressively. The Bank, for example, chairs the Consultative Group on International Agricultural Research and contributes to the financing of the research institutes, including the financing of the new institute for the semi-arid tropics. But very much more needs to be done at the national level to explore the special-equipment needs of the small operator, to develop new technologies for the non-cereal crops, and to help the farmer in non-irrigated areas.

General expenditures on research and development in the developing countries are notoriously low and must be increased substantially. In doing this, governments should give very high priority to strengthening that type of research which will benefit the small farmer—research to produce low-risk, inexpensive technology that he can put to immediate use.

Greater Access to Public Services

In other areas too, public services are grossly inadequate. The income of the small farmer could be substantially increased if he were supported by better physical infrastructure. Because of the costs involved, it is not within the power of the developing countries to provide all of this infrastructure quickly to the millions who need it. But governments can provide much of it by organizing rural works programs to construct small feeder roads, small-scale irrigation and drainage systems, storage and market facilities, community schools and health centers, and other facilities which make extensive use of local labor and relatively simple skills.

There is no mystery about designing these programs. They have worked successfully at various times in experimental projects in Bangladesh, Tunisia, Indonesia, and other countries. The major handicap has been their limited scale and inadequate management. The task for governments is gradually to extend these projects to a national scale.

Basic changes are also necessary in the distribution of other public services. In the rural areas these services are not only deplorably deficient, they are often not geared to the needs of the people they are supposed to serve.

Educational systems should stress practical information in agriculture, nutrition, and family planning for those both within and outside of the formal school program. Health services should be developed which can assist in eradicating the common enervating diseases that afflict the rural poor. Electricity for rural areas should not be considered a luxury, nor should its purpose be merely to place a lightbulb in every dwelling. One of its most important uses is to supply power for production appliances, such as water pumps. Power is admittedly almost always in short supply, but urban lighting and air conditioning should no longer be given such a disproportionate priority in the national systems.

Every country must examine why it can afford to invest in higher education, but fails to offer incentives to attract teachers to rural areas; why it can staff urban medical centers and export its doctors abroad, but fails to provide doctors for the countryside; why it can build urban roads for the private automobile, but cannot build feeder roads to bring produce to market.

Resources are scarce in the developing countries, and their redistribution cannot provide enough for everyone's needs. But a major redistribution of public services is required if the small farmer is to have at least the necessary minimum of economic and social infrastructure.

The programs I have discussed above can all be initiated quickly by governments, and will make a major contribution to the goal of a 5% growth rate in the output of small-scale agriculture by 1985. And all of these programs deserve, and will have, the full support of the Bank Group.

But the fact remains that the measures I have outlined are primarily the responsibility of the developing countries. It would be a great disservice if the aid agencies were to try to convince either these countries or themselves that policies for alleviating rural poverty can be fashioned and delivered from abroad. The problem must be perceived and dealt with by the countries themselves.

But the international community can, and must, help. The resources required to achieve a 5% growth rate in the yields on small farms by 1985 are very large. One estimate would place the annual cost of on-farm investment, land and water resource development, additional training facilities, and minimum working capital requirements for smallholder agriculture at $20-25 billion by 1985. This would be about 3.5% of the combined annual GNP of the developing countries.

Part of these resources must come from additional savings generated by the farmers themselves, and part must come from redirecting resources from other sectors in the developing countries.

But some of these resources must come from the international community—in the form of services and financing which the small farmer needs.

An Action Program in the Bank

What can the Bank do to assist in this effort?

First of all, we expect to lend $4.4 billion in agriculture during our next five-year program (1974-78), as compared to $3.1 billion in the first five-year program (1969-73), and $872 million in the 1964-68 period.[a]

This in itself is a formidable target, but more importantly we intend to direct an increasing share of our lending to programs which directly assist the small farmer to become more productive. In the next five years we expect that about 70% of our agricultural loans will contain a component for the smallholder. We are now preparing these programs in consultation with member governments.

But we recognize that at best our lending can finance only a small portion of the total credit and investment needs of smallholder agriculture. That is why we intend to give particular attention in our economic advice to governments to those sectoral and financial policies which most affect the rural poor so that the resources to be invested by governments will have a maximum impact.

And though experimentation and innovation will remain essential, the broad policies governing the Bank's program are clear:

- We are prepared to do much more to assist governments in the reform of their agricultural financial structure, and to support institutions designed to bring credit to the small farmer.

- We intend to continue to invest in large irrigation projects and in the recovery of saline lands, but we will emphasize on-farm development incorporating a maximum of self-financing so that the benefits of irrigation can reach small farmers more quickly.

- We will support non-irrigated agriculture, including the financing of livestock production, and in particular small-scale dairy farming in milk-deficient areas.

---

[a] Figures for all three periods are in 1973 dollars.

- We are prepared to finance the expansion of training facilities for extension agents who can help raise the productivity of the rural poor.

- We are prepared to finance rural works programs as well as multi-purpose rural development projects.

- We are ready to assist land and tenancy reform programs by providing the follow-up logistical support required by the small farmer, and to help in the technical and financial aspects of land purchase and consolidation.

- We have financed agricultural research institutions in the past and are fully prepared to do more in the future, particularly in the development of an appropriate technology for semi-arid agriculture. We propose to support investigation into the most effective uses of water at the farm level, especially in water-deficient areas. We are already assisting one such investigation in Mexico.

- We will, in our lending for infrastructure, strongly urge that account be taken of the pressing needs of the rural areas.

VI. SUMMARY AND CONCLUSIONS

Let me now summarize and conclude the central points I have made this morning.

If we look objectively at the world today, we must agree that it is characterized by a massive degree of inequality.

The difference in living standards between the rich nations and the poor nations is a gap of gigantic proportions.

The industrial base of the wealthy nations is so great, their technological capacity so advanced, and their consequent advantages so immense that it is unrealistic to expect that the gap will narrow by the end of the century. Every indication is that it will continue to grow.

Nothing we can do is likely to prevent this. But what we can do is begin to move now to insure that absolute poverty—utter degradation—is ended.

We can contribute to this by expanding the wholly inadequate flow of Official Development Assistance.

The flow of ODA can be increased, by 1980, to the target of .7% of GNP—a target originally accepted within the United Nations for completion by 1975.

This is feasible, but it will require renewed efforts by many nations, particularly the very richest.

Further, we must recognize that a high degree of inequality exists not only between developed and developing nations but within the developing nations themselves. Studies in the Bank during this past year reinforce the preliminary conclusions I indicated to you last year: income distribution patterns are severely skewed within developing countries—more so than within developed countries—and the problem requires accelerated action by the governments of virtually all developing nations.

A minimum objective should be that the distortion in income distribution within these nations should at least stop increasing by 1975, and begin to narrow within the last half of the decade.

A major part of the program to accomplish this objective must be designed to attack the absolute poverty which exists to a totally unacceptable degree in almost all of our developing member countries: a poverty so extreme that it degrades the lives of individuals below the minimal norms of human decency. The absolute poor are not merely a tiny minority of unfortunates—a miscellaneous collection of the losers in life—a regrettable but insignificant exception to the rule. On the contrary, they constitute roughly 40% of the nearly two billion individuals living in the developing nations.

Some of the absolute poor are in urban slums, but the vast bulk of them are in the rural areas. And it is there—in the countryside—that we must confront their poverty.

We should strive to eradicate absolute poverty by the end of this century. That means in practice the elimination of malnutrition and illiteracy, the reduction of infant mortality, and the raising of life-expectancy standards to those of the developed nations.

Essential to the accomplishment of this objective is an increase in the productivity of small-scale agriculture.

Is it a realistic goal?

The answer is yes, *if* governments in the developing countries are prepared to exercise the requisite political will to make it realistic.

It is they who must decide.

As for the Bank, increased productivity of the small, subsistence farmer will be a major goal of our program of expanded activity in the FY1974-78 period.

But no amount of outside assistance can substitute for the developing member governments' resolve to take on the task.

It will call for immense courage, for political risk is involved. The politically privileged among the landed elite are rarely enthusiastic over the steps necessary to advance rural development. This is shortsighted, of course, for in the long term they, as well as the poor, can benefit.

But if the governments of the developing world—who must measure the risks of reform against the risks of revolution—are prepared to exercise the requisite political will to assault the problem of poverty in the countryside, then the governments of the wealthy nations must display equal courage. They must be prepared to help them by removing discriminatory trade barriers and by substantially expanding Official Development Assistance.

What is at stake in these decisions is the fundamental decency of the lives of 40% of the people in the 100 developing nations which are members of this institution.

We must hope that the decisions will be the courageous ones.

If they are not, the outlook is dark.

But if the courageous decisions are made, then the pace of development can accelerate.

I believe it will. I believe it will because I believe that during the remainder of this century people everywhere will become increasingly intolerant of the inhuman inequalities which exist today.

All of the great religions teach the value of each human life. In a way that was never true in the past, we now have the power to create a decent life for all men and women. Should we not make the moral precept our guide to action? The extremes of privilege and deprivation are simply no longer acceptable.

It is development's task to deal with them.

You and I—and all of us in the international community—share that responsibility.

INSERT FOR PAGE 240, PREPARED AFTER THE TEXT WAS PRINTED IN SEPTEMBER 1973

I should digress at this point to report briefly on progress in the negotiation of the 4th Replenishment of IDA. You are all aware that the funds of the 3rd Replenishment will be fully committed next July 1. In anticipation of that, at the last annual meeting of the Governors, it was proposed that the 4th Replenishment negotiations begin in the fall of 1972 and be completed by mid-year 1973, leaving 12 months for the necessary legislative action.

All donor governments but one have adhered to this schedule and all governments but one have agreed to an acceptable level of replenishment. It had been hoped that final agreement of all governments would be reached on Saturday last here in Nairobi. Agreement was not reached.

As a result, there is now danger of a complete termination of IDA activities next June 30.

The effect of such a breakdown would be devastating for the nations that depend on IDA for major support of their development programs: the countries of the Sahelian zone now suffering from the worst drought in their history; the other "least-developed" nations, designated by the United Nations as deserving of increased levels of support; Pakistan, which requires huge sums of external aid for its recovery from massive flood damage; the heavily populated nations of India, Indonesia, and Bangladesh, a total of 750 million people with incomes averaging less than $100 per capita per year; and a score of other nations.

I cannot believe that governments will permit IDA's operations to terminate. If that disaster is to be avoided, agreement on the 4th Replenishment must be reached before Governors leave Nairobi.

Projected Flow of Official Development Assistance Measured as a Percent of Gross National Product[a]

	1960	1965	1970	1971	1972	1973	1974	1975	1976
Australia	.38	.53	.59	.53	.61	.58	.59	.60	.62
Austria	—	.11	.07	.07	.09	.19	.22	.25	.26
Belgium	.88	.60	.46	.50	.55	.58	.65	.70	.70
Canada	.19	.19	.42	.42	.47	.49	.50	.52	.53
Denmark	.09	.13	.38	.43	.45	.52	.56	.61	.63
France	1.38	.76	.66	.66	.67	.65	.65	.65	.65
Germany	.31	.40	.32	.34	.31	.32	.34	.36	.38
Italy	.22	.10	.16	.18	.09	.16	.16	.16	.17
Japan	.24	.27	.23	.23	.21	.28	.34	.40	.40
Netherlands	.31	.36	.61	.58	.67	.66	.70	.72	.76
Norway	.11	.16	.32	.33	.41	.56	.67	.75	.82
Portugal	1.45	.59	.67	1.42	1.51	.45	.45	.45	.45
Sweden	.05	.19	.38	.44	.48	.56	.65	.71	.75
Switzerland	.04	.09	.15	.11	.21	.26	.30	.32	.34
United Kingdom	.56	.47	.37	.41	.40	.37	.40	.40	.40
United States[b]	.53	.49	.31	.32	.29	.25	.22	.22	.21
Total	.52	.44	.34	.35	.34	.34	.34	.35	.36

[a]Countries included are members of OECD Development Assistance Committee, accounting for more than 95% of total Official Development Assistance. Figures for 1972 and earlier years are actual data. The projections for later years are based on World Bank estimates of growth of GNP, on information on budget appropriations for aid, and on aid policy statements made by governments. Because of the relatively long period of time required to translate legislative authorizations first into commitments and later into disbursements, it is possible to project today, with reasonable accuracy, ODA flows (which by definition represent disbursements) through 1976.

[b]In 1949, at the beginning of the Marshall Plan, U.S. Official Development Assistance amounted to 2.79% of GNP.

THIRTEEN

To the
BOARD OF GOVERNORS

WASHINGTON, D.C.
SEPTEMBER 30, 1974

I. INTRODUCTION

In the twelve months since our meeting in Nairobi the world economic scene has grown increasingly turbulent. The series of changes which have occurred have been of a magnitude previously associated only with major wars and depressions. New problems have arisen, older problems have become more acute, and the cumulative impact of events has touched every nation represented in this room.

What I propose, then, to do this morning is to review with you:

- The scope and interrelated nature of these events;
- Their implications for development on various groups of our member countries;
- The general measures which might be taken to assist those developing countries most seriously affected by the current problems;
- And what I believe the World Bank can and should do in its Fiscal Year 1975-1979 Program to help meet this new situation.

I want to emphasize at the outset one fundamental point which will underlie the whole of my subsequent argument. It is this. Though all of us have been affected in varying degrees by these complex events, by far the most adverse effects have fallen on those countries least able to cope with them: our poorest developing member nations.

These low-income countries—relatively disadvantaged in natural resources, without significant foreign exchange reserves, and already suffering from serious internal deprivations—now find themselves caught in a web of external economic forces largely beyond their control. They can do little to influence the current disequilibrium, nor did they precipitate its underlying causes. And yet they have become the principal victims, and are faced with the severest penalties.

These countries contain a billion individuals.

Whatever the problems and preoccupations of the rest of us

267

may be, we simply cannot turn our backs on half the total population this institution serves.

The real issue, then, is whether we, in this forum, fully understand what is happening to the poorest countries—and having understood it, are ready to do what is necessary to assist them.

That is the essence of what I want to talk to you about this morning.

But before I turn to that in detail, I want to refer back to our last two meetings.

II. SOCIAL EQUITY AND ECONOMIC GROWTH

Two years ago I began a discussion with you of the critical relationship of social equity to economic growth. I emphasized then the wide disparity in income that exists among the peoples of the developing countries, and the need to design development strategies that would bring greater benefits to the poorest among those peoples: the roughly 4⌣% of the population in every developing country who are neither contributing significantly to their nation's economic growth nor sharing equitably in its economic progress.

Last year in Nairobi I explored this problem further, pointing out that among the 2 billion people living in the more than 100 developing countries the Bank serves, there are hundreds of millions of individuals barely surviving on the margin of life, living under conditions so degraded by disease, illiteracy, malnutrition, and squalor as to deny them the basic human necessities. These are the "marginal men," men and women living in "absolute poverty"; trapped in a condition of life so limited as to prevent realization of the potential of the genes with which they are born; a condition of life so degrading as to insult human dignity—and yet a condition of life so common as to be the lot of 40%, some 800 million, of the peoples of the developing countries.

At Nairobi I outlined a program for the Bank which would begin to deal with these issues. That program will put primary emphasis not on the redistribution of income and wealth—as justified as that may be in many of our member countries—but rather on increasing the productivity of the poor, thereby providing for a more equitable sharing of the benefits of growth. I want to report on the steps we have taken to initiate that program and something of what we see ahead.

The first step in reaching the poorest 40% is to identify them—where they are, what they earn, and what public services reach them. With 70% of the population in the developing countries living in the rural areas, the center of the problem is there. And within the rural areas, we can usefully distinguish the following poverty groups:

1. Small farmers whose land holdings are of a size and quality which should enable them to sustain themselves and their families, as well as to produce a marketable surplus, but who now do not do so;
2. Small farmers who cannot sustain the farm family without additional land or without supplementary income from non-agricultural activities;
3. The landless, some of whom migrate to larger towns and cities for off-season temporary employment.

Altogether, these categories contain some 700 million individuals. We do not now have all the information we need to identify the different groups in individual countries. We are, therefore, collaborating with the Food and Agriculture Organization on the development of a better data base and on obtaining a better understanding of the present and potential levels of productivity of individuals in each category.

You will recall that we stated that a reasonable overall productivity improvement objective was to increase production on the 100 million farms, with areas of less than 5 hectares, so that by 1985 their output would be growing by 5% per year, a rate more than double that of the 1960s. It is clearly an ambitious goal, but one whose achievement is made more urgent by the continuing food shortage in the developing world.

The Bank is determined to pursue this goal. But I should stress that what the Bank does is much less important than what governments do to deal with these issues. Progress will only be possible if the countries themselves are willing to make strong commitments to pursue agricultural strategies directed toward the promotion of new income and employment opportunities for the poorest groups. This will involve commitment to effective land reform, assurance of adequate credit at reasonable cost, and reassessment of pricing, taxation, and subsidy policies which discriminate against the rural areas. We are prepared to work closely with governments that wish to take such actions.

Already we see evidence that the objective of a 5% per annum increase in production can be realized. In the past year, we assisted in financing 51 rural development projects in 42 countries involving a total investment of almost $2 billion. These projects are expected to benefit directly at least 12 million individuals. They should generate increases in production of more than 5% per annum for the beneficiaries whose present incomes average less than $75 per capita.

During the next five years our lending to agriculture should double, supporting projects whose total costs will approximate $15 billion and whose direct benefits should extend to 100 million rural poor.

We expect the economic returns on these investments to exceed 15%. They would be similar to the following five projects which were approved by the Bank's Board of Directors in a single two-week period this summer.

- A $10.7 million credit for agricultural development in the southern region of the Sudan which will provide a higher standard of nutrition for some 50,000 farm families through expanded food crops; will assist an additional 13,000 farm families through new cash crops; and will benefit roughly half the region's total population of three million people through improved, disease-free livestock.
- An $8 million credit for a comprehensive rural development project in Upper Volta, covering extension services, small-farmer credit, improved water resources, and greater access to health facilities; a project calculated, in all, to benefit some 360,000 individuals, 7% of the country's total population in over 10% of the country's cultivated land area.
- A $21.5 million credit for a broadly based livestock development program in Kenya, including provisions designed to

assist traditional nomadic herders; to improve 10 million acres of communal rangeland; and to expand wildlife areas in order to lessen the conflict for food and water between wildlife and cattle. The program will enhance the incomes of 140,000 rural inhabitants.

• An $8 million credit for an integrated rural development project in Mali providing farm inputs and equipment; an expanded functional literacy program; improved medical and veterinary facilities; and an agricultural research program. The program will reach over 100,000 farm families— some one million individuals—with agricultural services that are projected to triple their per capita incomes.

• A $30 million credit for a comprehensive dairy development project in India, providing for an increase in production of a million tons of milk a year, as well as for 100,000 heifers; and organizing small cattle owners into 1800 dairy cooperatives which will directly benefit some 450,000 farm families —2½ million individuals—the majority of whom own holdings less than two hectares in size, or are landless. The economic return of the project is estimated at more than 30% on the capital invested.

Last month the Board approved:

• A $10 million credit for a rural development project in one of the poorest regions in Tanzania to enhance the productivity, incomes and living standards of some 250,000 people —roughly half the entire rural population of the area— through improvements in agricultural practices and infrastructure investments for 135 newly established villages. The project aims at doubling the per capita incomes of the villagers over a twelve-year period.

Many more similar projects are under preparation. For example:

• A project in the three northern states of Nigeria providing for the construction of 3500 kilometers of low-cost farm-to-market roads, 250 earth dams, 480 rural water supply ponds, and new marketing and credit services. It is designed to benefit 226,000 rural families—over one and one-half million

people—by raising incomes substantially above their present
level of $40 per capita per year.

- A project in one of the poorest regions of Northeastern
  Brazil to raise the productivity of 33,000 farms (which support 200,000 people) by increasing the number of extension agents; establishing demonstration farm plots; and
  introducing improved credit, marketing, health, and education facilities.

- A project in India's drought-prone areas which cover 250,000
  square miles, and in which 66 million people live. It aims to
  diversify their production into activities less dependent on
  rainfall. The project includes minor irrigation works, water-
  shed management, improved crop production methods,
  sheep and dairy development, credit facilities (especially to
  smallholders), applied research, and farmer training programs. A population of over one million will have their
  incomes increased as a direct result of the project. One
  hundred thousand man-years of additional employment will
  be generated.

Perhaps the most comprehensive project we are working on
is an effort to assist the Government of Mexico in its nationwide
program of rural development. It is designed to reach the lowest
income groups, and would involve a total investment of $1.2
billion over a four-year period. The program grew out of the
Government's realization that although the nation had achieved,
over the last three decades, the highest sustained growth in agricultural production in Latin America, rural poverty appeared to
have worsened in many regions throughout the country, especially in semi-arid zones. The economy had been unable to provide the growing rural population with productive employment.

The thrust of the new program is to provide productive investments in low-income rural areas through small-scale irrigation,
rainfed crop production, fruit and vegetable growing, and rural
industries. These will be supported by associated investments
in labor-intensive feeder road construction, water and soil conservation projects, and support services for the implementation
of the Mexican land reform program. There will be provision,
too, for social infrastructure, such as rural schools, water supply,

health facilities, and electrification. This is, in fact, the most complex program with which the Bank has ever been associated.

It is true that the risks of failure are greater in rural development projects than in some of our more traditional investments. Complicated problems of technology, organization, land tenure, and human motivation remain to be resolved. And yet for the first time we are beginning to see substantial income and employment benefits within the reach of very large numbers of the rural poor, along with high economic returns to the national economy.

What is common to all these efforts within the Bank is an increased emphasis on innovative project design directed toward raising the productivity of the absolute poor, and toward helping them become greater participants in their country's progress. It is clear that development efforts of the past, both by governments and by the Bank, have simply not made an adequate contribution to the welfare of this huge and growing group. We must make sure that the unprecedented combination of events which is presently disturbing the world's economy—to which I now want to turn—does not distract our attention from this fundamental task.

III. RECENT ECONOMIC EVENTS

While the economic changes of the past year have been massive, the fact is that no one can see clearly yet either their extent or their duration. In such circumstances, projections of the future are bound to be uncertain. But they must be made if we are to initiate the long lead-time actions required to minimize the adverse effects of the changes, particularly those which are so seriously affecting many of the developing nations.

In this section I want to review the scope and interrelated nature of these events, with particular emphasis on worldwide inflation; changes in the prices of petroleum and other commodities; and the impact of these changes on the outlook for economic growth in the developed nations (which constitute the principal export markets of the developing countries). This discussion will be followed by a review of the effects of these events on the growth prospects and capital requirements of the developing countries through the remaining years of this decade.

Inflation in the Developed Nations

There has, of course, been a significant acceleration in the rate of inflation in the developed nations. It began before the rise in the prices of petroleum and other primary commodities, and it is only partially explained by them.

Index of International Prices[a]

	1956	1968	1972	1973	1974	1975	1980
Index (1967-69 = 100)	94	98	128	154	175	194	278
Percent change over previous year	2.3	−1.4	10.1	20.5	14.0	10.9	7.5

International prices, which had risen only 6% in the decade prior to 1968—less than 1% per year—have risen at an annual rate of nearly 10% in the five years since. The annual rate of inflation will surely decline from the 1974 level of 14% but could well average more than 7% for the period 1976-80.

Inflation benefits virtually all of the developing countries by reducing the burden of their debt service in relation to the value of their exports. However, for many of them—and especially the poorest—this benefit will be more than offset by the deterioration in their terms of trade.

Furthermore, inflation has already eroded the value of the concessionary aid which they receive. Most governments have not increased the amounts appropriated for Official Development Assistance (ODA) to offset inflation. ODA has declined, therefore, from 0.34% of the GNP of OECD countries[b] in 1972 to 0.30% in 1973 and is likely to fall further in the years ahead.

Petroleum Price Increase

Contributing to world inflation during the past twelve months has been the increase in the price of petroleum. Relative to export prices of manufactured goods, it has risen by four hundred percent. Although there had previously been a slow, long-term decline in petroleum prices which called for correction, the

---

[a] An index of capital goods and manufactured exports prices of major developed countries. The index also reflects changes in exchange rates.

[b] Twenty-four developed countries which are members of the Organisation for Economic Co-operation and Development.

recent action has resulted in a price that is more than twice as high as it has been in the postwar period in relation to other commodities.

Since imported oil has provided the principal increase in world energy supplies in recent years and cannot rapidly be replaced by other sources, the effect of the price rise is a global imbalance of payments of unprecedented magnitude. Although the export surplus of the members of the Organization of Petroleum Exporting Countries (OPEC) will be offset in part by rapidly rising imports and perhaps by a reduction in oil prices, a substantial trade imbalance is likely to persist at least through the end of the decade.

I am concerned here not with the decision to increase the price of oil, but rather with its consequences for the less developed countries. There are two:

- The cost of their current volume of oil imports has been increased by some $10 billion, which is 15% of their total import bill, and equal to 40% of the entire net inflow of external capital last year. As a result the countries least able to finance this cost increase have already had to curtail their development programs.

- By the end of the decade some of the OPEC countries are likely to have a continuing balance of payments surplus totalling some $30-60 billion per year (in 1974 prices), the amount depending on their absorptive capacity and price policies as well as the success achieved by oil-importing countries in developing other sources of energy. Of this surplus, roughly a quarter—$8-15 billion in 1974 prices—would be directly with the other developing countries. The remaining $22-45 billion of the surplus would be with the developed countries. Such an imbalance would be so large as to exert a cumulative strain on the economies of the developed nations and on international financial markets, making it more difficult for developing countries to expand export earnings and to finance their balance of payments deficits.

Other Commodity Price Changes

Prices of other primary products—prices which had remained

fairly stable from the 1960s to mid-1972—have been increasing very rapidly since then. The high prices of commodities exported by developing countries in 1973 reflected the high level of demand prevailing in a period of exceptionally rapid growth in almost all industrial nations. The failure of wheat and rice crops in widespread areas of the world in 1972 and 1973 also had far-reaching effects on prices of cereal grains. Although some developing countries have benefitted from the recent commodity boom, only a small number of them—principally mineral producers—is likely to continue to do so for the remainder of the decade.

Beyond 1974, price projections for primary commodities depend on the assumptions made about growth in the industrial countries, the major markets for such products. Since, as will be discussed below, the growth prospects in these markets for the remainder of the decade are less than they were in the 1960s and the early 1970s, the prices of most primary commodities are not likely to be very buoyant in the years ahead.

Effect of Price Changes on the Terms of Trade

The net effect of the increase in the prices of petroleum and other primary commodities, together with widespread inflation in the industrialized nations, will be a substantial change in the terms of trade of the developing countries—that is, in the relationship between the prices of their exports and imports.

Terms of Trade: 1973 vs 1980
(1967-69 = 100)

	Population (in millions)	Terms of Trade 1973	Terms of Trade 1980
Developing Countries:			
1. Major Oil Producers	300	140	350
2. Mineral Producers	100	102	102
3. Other Developing Countries			
A. With per capita incomes over $200	600	104	95
B. With per capita incomes under $200	1,000	95	77
Total	2,000		
OECD Countries	600	99	89

For the average of all primary commodity exports, 1973 represented a return to the peak price levels of the Korean War.

However, this commodity boom has benefited mainly the richer primary producers, while the poorest suffered both in terms of trade and in their export volumes. By the end of the decade, as indicated in the table above, there is likely to be a decline in the terms of trade of virtually all of the developing countries, with the exception of the petroleum and mineral producers. The poorest countries will in general be the most severely affected. They are likely to suffer a decline of over 20%. As a result, even with expanding export volumes, there will be little increase in the purchasing power of their exports in the face of rapidly increasing import requirements.

The Outlook for Economic Growth in the Developed Countries

The industrialized nations have reacted to the rise of petroleum prices and other commodity prices, and to the worldwide inflation, in ways which have reduced their growth rates. Although they have been pursuing policies designed to adjust to the higher costs of energy and to the other inflationary forces, with minimum impact on production and employment, some slowdown of their economies following a period of very high growth was inevitable.

The sharp increase in the cost of petroleum was bound to lead to basic shifts in the structure of their economies, while the sharp rise in balance of payments deficits and the higher levels of inflation have exacerbated the already complex problems of managing the international financial system. All of these factors will continue to have an impact on the growth rates of the OECD countries. The effect to date is shown by the table below.

Rates of Real Growth of OECD Countries
(Gross National Product)

1960-70 (average annual)	4.9%
1972	5.8
1973	6.7
1974	1.3

In comparison to growth rates of 5 and 6% in past years, present indications are that the GNP of the OECD countries in 1974 is growing at only 1.3%.

As for the future, a return to the 5% rate of growth realized in the 1960s would require both effective measures to reduce inflation without reducing production, and, equally important, the orderly recycling of the surpluses of the OPEC countries to finance the structural deficits of the industrial countries. Given the difficulties of achieving these objectives, it is only prudent to consider the effects on the developing countries of a drop in GNP growth in the OECD countries to, say, 3.5% or 4.0% for the remainder of the decade.

The adverse effect on the developing countries of such a reduction in economic growth in their major markets would be great. There is a strong relationship—almost 1 to 1—between changes in the growth rate of the OECD countries and that of the oil-importing developing nations. This is not surprising. Exports to OECD countries constitute 75% of the total exports of those nations. A diminished growth rate in the OECD countries translates very quickly into reduced demand for these developing nations' exports, leading in turn to a reduced capacity to import, and hence to lower rates of growth.

IV. CONSEQUENCES OF RECENT EVENTS FOR THE DEVELOPING COUNTRIES

Any one of the events described above—the deterioration in the terms of trade, worldwide inflation, the increase in the price of oil, the slowdown in the rate of growth of the OECD countries—would have had a serious impact on the developing nations. In combination, the effect on some nations has been near disaster. The trade deficit of all the oil-importing developing nations will more than double this year to approximately $20 billion, and, if they are to maintain even minimum economic growth, it will continue to rise for the remainder of the decade.

Moreover, if present trends continue, Official Development Assistance, as a percentage of GNP, will continue to decline, and may not even increase sufficiently to offset the effects of inflation. Furthermore, unless steps are taken to expand the supply of capital on intermediate and market terms to the more creditworthy developing countries, they will have difficulty competing with the OECD countries in international markets for the funds necessary to finance their increased trade deficits.

If we were to assume that capital flows to the developing nations, with some adjustments for inflation, would rise from

$20 billion to as much as $33 billion between 1973 and 1980, including an increase in Official Development Assistance from $10 billion to as much as $17 billion—assumptions which are probably optimistic and which I will examine in greater detail in a moment—it is estimated that the growth rates for the developing nations would be as shown in the table below:

Developing Country Rates of Growth Per Capita

Developing Countries by Group	Population (in millions)	GNP Growth Per Capita Average 1965-73	GNP Growth Per Capita Average 1974-80
1. Major Oil Producers	300	5.4%	8.4%
2. Mineral Exporters	100	1.2	3.8
3. Other Developing Countries:			
A. With per capita incomes over $200	600	4.3	3.4
B. With per capita incomes under $200	1,000	1.1	−0.4
Total	2,000		

As is apparent, the growth rates projected for all of the developing nations, other than the petroleum and mineral exporters, are substantially below the levels which were thought likely only a few months ago.

Some countries—for example, Thailand and the Philippines whose reserves have benefitted from buoyant export prices, or Turkey and Yugoslavia which have received substantial remittances from their workers abroad—can partially finance the heavy 1974 trade account deficits and can avoid severe deterioration of their growth rates. The prospects of other countries such as Korea and Brazil, which have been steadily expanding their export of industrial goods, are much better than those of countries dependent on agricultural exports.

The major impact is on the poorest nations. The rising prices of imported petroleum, fertilizer, and cereals; the slack demand for their exports to developed countries; and the erosion by inflation of the real value of development assistance, all have dealt severe blows to the growth aspirations of the poorest members of the Bank. These nations, with a population of one billion, and incomes averaging less than $200 per capita, on the most likely set of assumptions regarding commodity prices, capital flows, and growth rates in the OECD countries, would suffer an actual decline in their per capita incomes. The effect of this on the already marginal condition of life of the poorest 40% within these countries is an appalling prospect.

The countries thus affected are mostly in South Asia and Africa. Consider the following cases:

- INDIA: Higher oil prices will add $800 million to India's import bill this year—an amount equivalent to roughly two-thirds of her entire foreign exchange reserves, over 25% of her total exports, and far in excess of the previously projected net resource transfer. Price increases for nitrogenous fertilizer—and India is the world's largest importer of this essential ingredient of increased agricultural production—will add another $500 million; and higher prices for essential foodgrain imports still another $100 million.

- SRI LANKA: Despite large cuts in food rations, in 1974 cereal grain import costs will rise by $100 million, fertilizer by $40 million, and petroleum by $100 million. And stagnating world prices of tea—Sri Lanka's major export—have in effect locked the country into a long-term deterioration in its terms of trade.

- BANGLADESH: Devastated by both flood and war, the country has had to devote most of its imports to essential reconstruction and minimum food requirements. It has been unable as yet to mount a sustained development program which its more than 75 million people desperately require. To do so it would have to increase its imports substantially, and yet this year alone the new oil prices will add $70 million to its costs, and food and fertilizer price increases an additional $100 million.

- The SAHELIAN COUNTRIES OF AFRICA: Due to the most devastating drought in their history, Mali, Niger, Upper Volta, Mauritania, Senegal, and Chad have been unable to take advantage of the favorable world prices of their chief exports: groundnuts, cotton, and livestock. The surge in petroleum prices has driven the cost of their essential fuel imports from 10% of their export earnings to 30 or 40%, at the same time that their food import requirements—literally to stave off mass starvation—have risen drastically.

The East African countries of Tanzania, Somalia, and Kenya are also facing severe balance of payments pressure.

V. MEASURES TO SPEED THE ADJUSTMENT PROCESS

To assist the developing countries in meeting the cumulative impact of these problems, the Bank has examined the internal and external adjustments which might be undertaken to minimize the setback to development summarized in the tables above.

Much must be done by the developing countries themselves, particularly in restructuring their patterns of use and procurement of energy and even more in expanding their production of cereal grains.

Restructuring Patterns of Use and Production of Energy

The impact of the petroleum price increases on the balance of payments of the developing nations could be diminished, of course, if they could reduce their consumption of imported petroleum. This could result either from a reduction in their consumption of energy in general, or through a shift from imported petroleum to domestic sources of energy supply.

While greater efficiency and conservation in energy use may be feasible in some cases, the amounts involved will be small. On average, the one billion people in the countries with per capita incomes below $200 consume only about 1% as much energy per capita as the citizens of the United States. Reduction of energy consumption in those countries in any significant degree can only lead to reductions in industrial and agricultural production, and a lowering of the standards of living for the masses of the population.

The outlook for substituting other forms of energy for petroleum is brighter. It will be possible in many countries, for example, India, Pakistan, Brazil, and Turkey, to generate power using alternative energy sources. Petroleum-based plants can be replaced with hydropower, geothermal power, or with coal, lignite or nuclear fuel plants. But even in countries where these alternative energy sources are available (and in some, such as Kenya and Upper Volta, this is a very uncertain prospect), exploiting these sources will require time-consuming geological or hydrological surveys and very large additional capital investments.

Moreover, the resources to be used for these investments must be drawn away from other projects, thereby reducing the countries' development programs. And in any event, it will be from 5 to 7 years before such facilities for energy production can become operational and begin to offset the increased foreign exchange costs of petroleum imports.

Expanding the Production of Food Grains

Although there has been a reasonable long-run balance between supply and demand of food grains for the world as a whole, there has been a serious and growing shortage of food production in the developing countries. Unless remedial action is taken, the situation will become much worse. The principal reasons for the shortage have been the rapidly expanding population in these countries and their failure to achieve satisfactory levels of agricultural productivity.

Were present trends to continue, it is estimated that the cereal grain import requirements of the developing nations could double between 1970 and the middle of the next decade. By that time those countries would be seeking to import 70 to 80 million tons per year, and the foreign exchange required each year could reach $20 billion. This additional requirement could not be met from any reasonable projection of export earnings or capital inflows. There is only one answer to this problem: the 2.9% rate at which the developing countries have increased their output of food grains over the past two decades must be increased substantially.

This can be done. Grain yields in the developing countries are no more than 40% of the yields in the developed countries. The developing countries do have the potential to increase their agricultural productivity. But that potential cannot be realized unless the developing countries themselves initiate action on a wide front, including measures to expand the cultivated areas under irrigation, promote the availability and use of fertilizer, and maintain a price structure which provides farmers with adequate incentive to grow more food. These are the prerequisites to increasing productivity, and they will require substantial sums of capital.

Investments in world fertilizer capacity have been inadequate to cope with the sharp increase in the demand for fertilizers in the major grain-exporting countries of the OECD, and in the developing countries which have been modernizing their agriculture. The developing countries' share in total world consumption of fertilizers has increased from 10% in 1961 to about 17% today, and it is projected to increase further to 25% by the end of the decade.

We estimate that by 1980 the demand for nitrogenous and phosphatic fertilizers in the developing countries will exceed 22 million metric tons annually, only half of which can be produced with their existing capacity and its currently planned expansion. To add 11 million tons of additional production capacity would require an investment of some $6 to $10 billion.

Many developing nations have already initiated action to conserve energy and to explore alternatives to continuing increases in petroleum imports. Some have started to reduce their dependence on imported foodgrains. But years will pass before these efforts bear fruit. In the meantime, the higher import costs of petroleum, food grains, fertilizer, and manufactured goods will place a heavy burden on their balance of payments and reduce their savings available to finance investment. Unless these requirements are met by additional capital flows, the result will be further declines in their rates of growth.

This brings us to a discussion of the volume of capital required, in particular by the poorest developing countries, to prevent this outcome.

VI. CAPITAL REQUIREMENTS

Earlier I stated that were we to assume that capital flows to the developing nations would increase from $20 billion to $33 billion between 1973 and 1980, with Official Development Assistance rising from $10 billion to $17 billion, growth rates during these years for the developing nations (excluding the petroleum and mineral exporters) would average 3.4% per capita for the countries with individual incomes over $200 and would actually decline for those with incomes below $200. It is time to examine that assumption (shown as Case I in the following tables) and to consider alternatives.

The 3.4% per capita rate of growth projected for the middle and high income countries is far from satisfactory, and the decrease of .4% projected for the poorer countries is totally unacceptable. Were we to raise these rates by planning on a 4% per capita growth for the countries with incomes over $200 and a rate one-half of that for those with incomes of $200 or less, we estimate that the capital requirements by 1980 would rise by 60%. Total capital required would increase from $33 billion to $53 billion. ODA would have to rise to $24 billion, a huge sum, but a sum which would still be no larger than its present share of the donors' projected GNP. These data are shown in Case II.

Table I
Developing Country Rates of Growth Per Capita

Developing Countries by Group	Population (in millions)	Average 1965-73	GNP Growth Per Capita Average 1974-80 Case I	GNP Growth Per Capita Average 1974-80 Case II
1. Major Oil Producers	300	5.4%	8.4%	8.4%
2. Mineral Exporters	100	1.2	3.8	3.8
3. Other Developing Countries:				
A. With per capita incomes over $200	600	4.3	3.4	4.0
B. With per capita incomes under $200	1,000	1.1	−0.4	2.1
Total	2,000			

Table II
**Net External Capital Flow Required
to Achieve Growth Rates in Table I**
(Amounts in billions of dollars)

	1973	1980 Case I	1980 Case II
ODA—Amount	$ 9.4	$16.7	$24.4
% of Donor GNP	.30%	.20%	.30%
Other Concessional Aid	$ 1.9	$ 5.5	$ 5.5
Market Terms Borrowing	$ 8.8	$10.8	$23.6
Total Net External Capital Flow	$20.1	$33.0	$53.5

Two-thirds of the increase in the capital required from 1973 to 1980 is needed simply to compensate for the higher prices of commodities and services imported by the developing countries.

Are such capital flows attainable?

In considering the question, I want to emphasize two points:

- First, the substantial increase in market terms borrowing that the middle and higher income developing countries must undertake—efforts which can succeed only if the recycling mechanisms make special provision for the very large capital requirements of these countries as well as for those of the developed nations.
- And second, the alarming rate at which inflation is eroding ODA flows and the failure to compensate for this because of what might be termed the "money illusion"—that is, failing to recognize that in periods of rapid inflation the same number of dollars, at different moments of time, do not represent the same real values.

While the rapid growth of the Eurocredits extended to the developing countries in the recent past is striking, the total market borrowing by these countries was heavily influenced by the amounts lent to a few of the nations with a high credit standing. More than $3.3 billion out of the total of $8.8 billion raised in 1973 by the developing countries went to just three nations—Mexico, Brazil, and Peru—and an additional $2.1 billion went to the oil- and mineral-exporting countries. Very little was loaned to Turkey, Korea, the Philippines, Thailand, and other middle income countries which will need large amounts of such capital in the future.

To support Case II, the amount of $8.8 billion raised in 1973 would have to increase to $15 billion within the next two years and to some $24 billion in 1980; and the number of borrowers would have to increase significantly.

It is to be hoped that the international banking community will recognize that many of the developing nations, if assisted to make the structural adjustment necessary to realize their long-term growth potential, represent excellent opportunities for profitable placement of surpluses, particularly those generated initially in the OPEC countries. But, as I suggested before, one cannot be sanguine about the prospects of increased borrowing by the developing countries from the Eurocredit markets unless the developed countries provide some support to those markets. The developing countries will face heavy competition from the developed countries seeking to draw on OPEC surpluses to finance their own balance of payments deficits.

Market borrowing has not been a source of funds open to the lower income countries. These nations must depend mainly on concessionary flows, principally ODA. And it is in relation to ODA that the effects of the "money illusion" become most apparent.

Actual and Projected Flows of
Official Development Assistance
(Amounts in billions of dollars)

Total	1960	1965	1970	1971	1972	1973	1974	1975	1980 Case I	1980 Case II
In Current Prices	4.7	5.9	6.8	7.8	8.7	9.4	10.7	11.9	16.8	24.4
In 1973 Prices	7.7	9.0	9.3	10.0	10.0	9.4	9.4	9.5	9.3	13.5
As % of GNP	.52	.44	.34	.35	.34	.30	.30	.29	.20	.30
ODA Deflator	61	65	73	78	86	100	114	126	181	181

In the past ten years, ODA in relation to GNP has decreased by one-third. Today it is running at scarcely 40% of the .7% target. Since that objective was established by the United Nations General Assembly in 1970, there has been no increase, in real terms, in the concessionary flow despite a 12% increase of GNP in the donor nations. The reason, I believe, is clear: legislatures fail to recognize that the 62% increase between 1970 and 1974 in the money value of the ODA which they have appropriated not only contributes nothing toward attaining the .7% objective, but just barely maintains the real value of the 1970 level of assistance.

The most important single step the developed nations could take to assist the one billion people of the poorest countries would be to recognize that the effects of inflation alone require —and will continue to require—major increases in the appropriated money values of Official Development Assistance.

The OPEC countries are beginning to help meet the capital requirements of the developing nations, including making contributions to ODA which are larger in proportion to gross national product than those of the OECD nations.

Excluding Indonesia and Nigeria which are not in a position to export long-term capital, the projected change in the financial position of the OPEC countries, between the years 1973 and 1980 is shown in the following table:

Projected Change in the Financial Position of the OPEC Countries
(Excluding Indonesia and Nigeria)

	1973	1980
OPEC GNP—Amount	$76 billion	$411 billion
% of OECD GNP[a]	2.5%	5.0%
GNP per capita—OPEC	$ 951	$ 4240
OECD[a]	$4735	$11980
OPEC Foreign Exchange Reserves and External Investments	$24 billion	$624 billion
OPEC Income on External Investments	$ 2 billion	$ 40 billion

The data show that the OPEC countries will be highly liquid in 1980, although their GNP will be but a small fraction of that of OECD countries, and their per capita incomes, on average, substantially less. In these circumstances, it can be expected that they will divert a portion of their liquid funds to the financing of the ODA increases required by the poorest countries. But a far larger portion of the OPEC surpluses will no doubt be used to finance the very large capital requirements of the middle- and higher-income nations.

The OPEC countries have already taken a number of initiatives which may lead to an increase in the flow of their development aid. These range from Iran's and Iraq's agreements to supply India with specified quantities of oil on deferred payment terms, to the creation of the Saudi Arabian Development Fund, and the very substantial expansion of the Kuwait and Abu Dhabi Devel-

---

[a]The OPEC GNP figures are not strictly comparable with those of the OECD countries. The former include a high proportion of income from the production of non-replaceable assets for which no depreciation allowance has been provided. Were this factor to be taken into account, OPEC per capita GNP in 1980 would probably be 30% less than shown.

opment Funds. But many of these initiatives will take time to organize and to staff. Disbursements are, therefore, likely to be slow. The World Bank has offered its assistance to these institutions to accelerate the flow of funds.

VII. THE CONTRIBUTION OF THE WORLD BANK GROUP FOR FISCAL YEARS 1975-79

The net effect of the events we have discussed is a dramatic increase in the capital required by the developing nations for the achievement of even modest rates of growth during the remaining years of the decade. The present plans of the OECD and OPEC countries do not indicate that sufficient capital will be available. Under these circumstances I believe the World Bank Group must expand its lending to the maximum permitted by prudent financial management and the availability of funds. The program which I have presented to our Board of Directors for their consideration is a first step in that direction.

It provides for total lending in the five fiscal years 1975-79 of $36 billion. The program which the Board has approved for FY75 contemplates commitments totalling $5.5 billion, compared to $4.5 billion in the fiscal year just ended, and $3.5 billion in the year before that.

The total of $36 billion for the five years compares with $16 billion for the previous period (FY1970-74). However, the increase of $20 billion—125% in money terms—provides for an increase of only 40% in real terms (7% per annum).

At Nairobi, the negotiators of the countries contributing to the International Development Association (IDA) believed that their pledges of $4.5 billion for the 4th Replenishment period would provide an increase of 55% over the level of the 3rd Replenishment. Already that expected increase has been more than offset by actual or projected inflation. It now appears that the 4th Replenishment, in real terms, will be slightly smaller than the 3rd. To minimize the impact of this loss of value, we propose to shift the allocation of scarce IDA resources in such a way as to concentrate them on the countries most seriously affected by the recent economic developments. We intend to give priority in these countries to raising agricultural production in general and the productivity of the rural poor in particular.

The proposed Bank Group program is large. It will require net borrowing during the five years of over $13 billion. Much of that amount can, I believe, be borrowed from OPEC countries. They have been most cooperative with the Bank and in recent months we have received loan commitments from them totalling $2 billion. But as large as the Bank program is, in combination with the other funds which the OECD and OPEC countries indicate they plan to make available to the developing countries, it is totally inadequate to meet minimum development objectives.

I strongly recommend that the proposed Joint Ministerial Committee, as its first item of business, appraise the needs of the developing nations for additional capital and examine possible sources of funds to meet those needs. The formation of the Committee offers a new and welcome opportunity to focus the attention of the world's governments on the progress, or lack of progress of the developing nations, as well as the progress, or lack of progress of the richer countries in meeting their responsibility to support development in those nations.

VIII. SUMMARY AND CONCLUSIONS

Let me now conclude by summarizing the central points I have made this morning.

Although there are many ingredients that have contributed to the current economic turbulence, there are at least three principal and interrelated factors which are of major significance for the development scene.

One, of course, is inflation. Itself the troublesome child of many forces, inflation not only penalizes the poor proportionately more than the rich, and severely erodes the value of Official Development Assistance, but in leading to lower growth rates in the developed nations it threatens to reduce demand for the developing countries' exports, as well as to trigger protectionist tendencies.

The second factor is the sudden surge in the price of petroleum. Though it has contributed to balance of payments problems in many nations, it has fallen with the greatest severity on the poorest countries. They possess neither the flexibility of the developed nations to readjust trade and investment, nor the margin to reduce consumption.

And the third factor is the general boom in most other primary commodities. This has clearly benefited some developing countries. But it has also created further difficulties for the poorest nations whose exports simply cannot offset the price increases for fertilizer and food, which, in combination with the increases in oil and manufactured goods, have substantially reduced their terms of trade.

If, then, we survey the development scene as a whole, it is evident that countries with some 20% of the population of the nations we serve have registered a net gain: the oil-exporting countries and some of the mineral producers.

For certain other developing countries, representing about 30% of the total population, the long-run outlook is good although they face serious problems of adjustment to the new conditions. Most of them are in the middle and upper income categories of developing nations. They should be able to borrow much of what they need on the world capital markets if the recycling mechanism is designed and managed with their needs in mind. In addition, they will need large sums on intermediate terms and the Bank must expand its program to help meet this requirement.

But for the poorest of our member countries—countries that represent fully half of the total population of all the nations we serve, countries containing one billion human beings—the situation is desperate.

Almost every element in the current economic situation has worked to their disadvantage, and has been compounded even further for many of them by the natural disasters of flood, drought, and crop failures.

These countries, then, need additional assistance on concessionary terms, and they need it promptly: $3 to $4 billion more per year in the remaining years of the decade.

Can such assistance be mobilized in the current economic environment—an environment in which the real per capita incomes of many of the largest donors have decreased in the past twelve months and in which all traditional donors face severe inflation, unacceptable unemployment, and uncertain growth prospects?

I believe it can—and I believe it must.

The world has not suddenly lost its wealth. The OPEC countries have gained huge amounts, and the traditionally wealthy nations continue to be wealthy. They are less wealthy than they hoped to be at this time, but they are more wealthy than they were as recently as twenty-four months ago, and immeasurably more wealthy than the nations of the developing world.

What, after all, really constitutes wealth? And what more fundamental measures of wealth are there than the levels of nutrition, literacy, and health? It is in these terms that the average citizen of a developed nation enjoys wealth beyond the wildest dreams of the one billion people in the countries with per capita incomes under $200: his caloric intake is 40% greater; his literacy rate is four times higher; the mortality rate of his children is 90% lower; and his own life expectancy 50% more. Are there any more basic terms in which to compare the wealth of the developed and developing nations?

The developed nations, understandably preoccupied with controlling inflation, and searching for structural solutions to their liquidity imbalances, will be tempted to conclude that until these problems are resolved, aid considerations must simply be put aside.

But aid is not a luxury — something affordable when times are easy, and superfluous when times become temporarily troublesome.

It is precisely the opposite. Aid is a continuing social and moral responsibility, and its need now is greater than ever.

It is true that the affluent nations in the face of shortages and inflation, and in order to continue to expand aid, may have to accept for the time being some selective reduction in their already immensely high standard of living. If they have to, they can absorb such inconveniences.

But for the poorest countries such a downward adjustment is a very different matter. For them downward does not mean inconvenience, but appalling deprivation. And for millions of individuals in these countries downward means simply the risk of death.

The problem, then, is not that the developed nations have suddenly lost their capacity to assist those countries most in need. They have not. The amounts of additional financial assistance that would mean the difference between decency and utter degradation for hundreds of millions of the absolute poor are, in relative terms, minute—perhaps 2% of the increase in real income the developed world can look forward to in the remaining years of the decade.

The basic problem, then, is a philosophical one—a problem of values.

Will 1974 be best remembered as the year prices exploded? Or will it, perhaps, be better remembered in the longer perspective of history as the year when the word interdependence stopped being rhetoric, and started being reality?

One thing is certain: the development task has not diminished. It has only become more urgent. The responsibility of us all is to get on with it.

Flow of Official Development Assistance
Measured as a Percent of Gross National Product[a]

	1960	1965	1970	1971	1972	1973	1974	1975	1980[d] Required for Case I	Case II
Australia	.38	.53	.59	.53	.59	.44	.53	.54		
Austria		.11	.07	.07	.08	.13	.13	.13		
Belgium	.88	.60	.46	.50	.55	.51	.56	.62		
Canada	.19	.19	.42	.42	.47	.43	.51	.51		
Denmark	.09	.13	.38	.43	.45	.47	.49	.50		
France	1.38	.76	.66	.66	.67	.58	.55	.51		
Germany	.31	.40	.32	.34	.31	.32	.30	.28		
Italy	.22	.10	.16	.18	.09	.14	.10	.08		
Japan	.24	.27	.23	.23	.21	.25	.24	.24		
Netherlands	.31	.36	.61	.58	.67	.54	.61	.65		
New Zealand[b]					.23	.27	.36	.47		
Norway	.11	.16	.32	.33	.41	.45	.63	.65		
Portugal	1.45	.59	.67	1.42	1.79	.71	.47	.42		
Sweden	.05	.19	.38	.44	.48	.56	.69	.70		
Switzerland	.04	.09	.15	.11	.21	.15	.15	.15		
United Kingdom	.56	.47	.37	.41	.39	.35	.34	.32		
United States[c]	.53	.49	.31	.32	.29	.23	.21	.20		
GRAND TOTAL										
—ODA $ millions (current prices)	4665	5895	6832	7762	8671	9415	10706	11948	16760	24400
—ODA 1973 prices	7660	9069	9346	9976	10059	9415	9391	9452	9259	13480
—GNP $ billions (current prices)	898	1340	2010	2218	2550	3100	3530	4100	8200	8200
—ODA as % GNP	.52	.44	.34	.35	.34	.30	.30	.29	.20	.30
—ODA Deflator	60.9	65.0	73.1	77.8	86.2	100.0	114.0	126.4	181.0	181.0

[a]Countries included are members of OECD Development Assistance Committee, accounting for more than 95% of total Official Development Assistance. Figures for 1973 and earlier years are actual data. The projections for 1974 and 1975 are based on World Bank estimates of growth of GNP, on information on budget appropriations for aid, and on aid policy statements made by governments. Because of the relatively long period of time required to translate legislative authorizations first into commitments and later into disbursements, it is possible to project today, with reasonable accuracy, ODA flows (which by definition represent disbursements) through 1975.

[b]New Zealand became a member of the DAC only in 1973. ODA figures for New Zealand are not available for 1960-71.

[c]In 1949, at the beginning of the Marshall Plan, U.S. Official Development Assistance amounted to 2.79% of GNP.

[d]Case I leading to a −0.4% change in GNP per capita per annum in countries with incomes of under $200 per capita would require ODA of $16.7 billion (.20% of DAC GNP) in 1980; Case II with 2.1% growth in GNP per capita would require $24.4 billion (.30% of DAC GNP) in that year.

FOURTEEN

To the
BOARD OF GOVERNORS
WASHINGTON, D.C.
SEPTEMBER 1, 1975

I. INTRODUCTION

Last year within this forum I outlined the problems imposed upon the developing countries by worldwide inflation, deterioration in their terms of trade, and stagnation in their export markets. In the intervening months these threats to development have not abated. They have grown more ominous.

I would like, then, today to explore with you the developing countries' urgent need for increased flows of foreign exchange—both from exports and from external capital—to help offset these adverse forces.

The one billion people of the low-income nations have become the principal victims of the current economic turbulence. They did not cause it. By themselves they cannot change it. And they have little margin to adjust to it. Granted all they can and must do to work out their own problems, they desperately need additional external assistance.

Many of the middle-income countries as well are facing a foreign exchange crisis. In the long run this can be met only by more exports. In the short run, they too need greater access to external capital.

This, then, is the most immediate and pressing problem in the global development scene.

But underlying this emergency situation—and partially obscured by it—lies the more fundamental problem of poverty itself, and the need to shape an effective strategy to deal with it. That is the second issue I want to discuss with you today.

What is required is a strategy that will attack absolute poverty and substantially reduce income inequities, not merely through programs of welfare, or simply through redistribution of already inadequate national wealth, but rather through measures designed specifically to increase the productivity of the poor.

Two years ago in Nairobi I outlined the elements of such an attack on poverty as it exists in the countryside. We chose the rural areas as the initial target for an intensified World Bank

297

effort because it is there that the vast concentrations of the absolute poor—some 700 million individuals—in fact live.

But poverty degrades life for hundreds of millions in the slums of the cities as well. Though their total numbers are smaller than those in the countryside, their rate of increase—through migration—is greater. In certain areas of the developing world their deteriorating conditions have already begun seriously to strain the fabric of their societies. The Bank is giving increased attention to this issue, and we believe we are ready now to undertake a far more comprehensive effort to help governments deal with it.

In summary, then, what I propose to do this morning is this:

- Analyze the immediate problem of increased foreign exchange requirements in the developing world, and indicate what the OECD nations, the capital-surplus OPEC countries, and the World Bank itself can do to help meet this need;

- Report on the progress the Bank is making in its implementation of a strategy to reduce poverty in the rural areas;

- And outline a program for an integrated approach to attack poverty in the cities.

Let me begin with the problem of foreign exchange requirements.

II. FOREIGN EXCHANGE REQUIREMENTS IN THE DEVELOPING COUNTRIES

For most of the developing countries the past year has been a period of painful accommodation to a global economic disequilibrium.

At least four principal factors—all of them interrelated—have combined to threaten their future growth prospects:

- Persistent worldwide inflation;

- The surge in the cost of petroleum;

- The deterioration in their terms of trade;

- And the prolonged recession in the OECD countries.

Inflation always exacts greater penalties from the poor than from the rich, and most of the developing countries have been faced with major increases in the prices of critical imports, particularly manufactured goods, foodgrains, and fertilizer.

The unprecedented rise in the cost of oil has been especially difficult for them to deal with since they have relatively little capability for a rapid conversion to other sources of energy, and only an insignificant margin for consumer conservation.

But though inflation has raised the cost of most of what the developing countries must import, it has failed to sustain the high prices of many of their exports. Last year the prices of their imports rose by 40%, but their export prices increased only 27%. This year inflation will add at least another 6% to the cost of their imports, but very little to the price of their exports. The result has been a substantial deterioration in their terms of trade, making it increasingly more difficult for them to pay for what they need.

Finally, not only have their export prices failed to keep pace with import costs, but in many cases their export volume has stagnated or even declined as the recession has grown more serious in the industrialized countries. The OECD nations are the chief markets of the developing countries, and normally absorb 75% of their total exports. As the recession has deepened, demand for these exports has declined.

Given these four factors—persistent inflation, the high cost of petroleum, deterioration in their terms of trade, and prolonged recession in the developed nations—the oil-importing developing countries find themselves confronted with an array of unanticipated obstacles to achieving even minimal development objectives in the remaining years of the decade. Indeed, in many respects, the outlook now appears worse than it did twelve months ago.

For the poorest countries—those with per capita incomes of less than $200—the situation is particularly grave.

In 1974, per capita incomes of the one billion people living in these nations declined an average .5%. For the hundreds of millions of them already severely deprived, it meant hunger, illness, and an erosion of hope.

This year the outlook is for a further weakening of these economies, and the per capita incomes of the one billion people are likely to fall again.

The middle-income developing countries—those with per capita incomes of $200 and above—have not felt the full impact of the deterioration of the world economy until this year. Last year, due to a series of emergency measures—including the drawing down of reserves, the expansion of short-term debt, and the postponement of long-term development programs— they managed to maintain average GDP growth per capita of 3.9%. This year, however, the growth of GDP is expected to be less than the growth of population and their per capita incomes are projected to decline by more than 1%. Moreover, their trade deficit will exceed 3% of their gross national product—twice as large as it had been in the late 1960s.

The events of the past two years have in effect swept away the progress these countries had made in reducing their dependence on external capital.

The 1976-1980 foreign exchange requirements of the oil-importing developing countries ought, then, to be viewed as composed of two principal elements: a declining transitional component, needed until export earnings can grow to offset higher import costs, and the more traditional external capital supplement to domestic savings, equivalent to about 1.5 to 2% of their GNP.

Growth Rates and Related Capital Flows

To better grasp the capital requirements of the developing countries over the next five years, it is useful to examine alternative levels of capital flows and resulting rates of growth of per capita income. Two such projections are set out below.[a]

In each of these examples, growth rates are linked to "capital flows." The flows represent the amounts of foreign exchange

[a]The projections simply illustrate rough orders of magnitude. They serve as a guide to appropriate policy decisions. No claim is made for the precision of the forecasts themselves. But we believe they indicate the severity of the economic problems confronting the developing countries, and they point to ways in which the rest of the world can assist their efforts to cope with them.

required in the short run, over and above currently projected export earnings. In the longer run, of course, most of these foreign exchange needs, if they are to be met at all, must come from higher export earnings.

There is much the developing countries themselves can do to create a more favorable climate for export expansion. All too often their policies of subsidized capital, overvalued exchange rates, and excessive regulation discourage entrepreneurial incentive to sell abroad. Their own efforts to remove these self-imposed roadblocks to greater export earnings are essential if their full trade potential is to be realized.

But it will take time for these fundamental policy changes to become fully effective, and that is why in the short run the "capital flows" in the projections are representative of the amounts of external capital required to support the alternative growth rates.

The first set of data, labeled Case I, assumes substantial growth in capital flows in nominal terms between 1975 and 1980, but no increase in real terms. It assumes also that the industrialized countries will make a relatively rapid recovery from the current recession. Should that turnaround be delayed, the projected rates of growth of per capita income in the developing countries would of course be lower, or the external capital requirements higher.

These Case I growth rates—especially for the low-income countries—are far below the targets of the Second Development Decade, and, on average, provide barely perceptible increases in per capita incomes for the poorer countries. As this is a wholly unacceptable prospect, we have estimated—in Case II—what the additional capital requirements would be to raise income growth for the oil-importing developing countries to the Second Development Decade targets, at least for the remaining years of the decade. These requirements are substantial, even though the growth rate for the decade as a whole would still be far below the target level.

In both Case I and Case II, the principal increases in capital would have to be supplied on concessional terms, and the bulk of this assistance would have to come from the OECD countries. It is not difficult to understand why.

Annual GDP Growth Rates, Per Capita, In Oil-Importing Developing Countries and Related Capital Flows in Billions of Current Dollars

	Average '69-'73	1974	1975	Average '76-'80 Case I	Case II
Growth Rates					
Low-Income Countries[a]	.5%	−.5%	−.7%	1.2%	3.2%
Middle-Income Countries[a]	4.5%	3.9%	−1.2%	2.8%	3.8%
Capital Flows					
Net Official Capital	$7.9	$15.0	$19.8	$24.0	$35.2
Private Capital	7.5	19.4	22.9	25.4	26.5
Total	15.4	34.4	42.7	49.4	61.7
ODA as % Donor GNP					
OECD	.34%	.33%	.32%	.29%	.48%[b]
OPEC	.00%	1.41%	2.57%	1.56%	1.56%

[a]The population of the Low-Income developing countries totals 1 billion and of the Middle-Income developing countries, 725 million. Here, as throughout these remarks, the statistics do not include those nations which are not members of the Bank.

[b]For ODA to average .48% of GNP during the five years 1976-80 would require that it reach at least .70% in 1980.

Even to achieve the wholly inadequate levels of economic activity of 1975, the developing countries have had to borrow large sums from the private capital markets. They will have to continue to do so in the future. But there are limits to creditworthiness and these make it unlikely that they will be able to borrow significantly more in real terms, over the next five years, than they are doing now.

That is the reason many of the developing countries, and particularly the poorer ones, will have to depend so heavily on concessional aid for the additional capital. And if these Official Flows are to grow, it is likely that most of the growth must come from the OECD nations.

In 1974, the capital-surplus OPEC countries supplied about one-sixth of the concessional assistance (ODA) made available to the developing countries. This year their disbursements for ODA have been rising further and could reach an estimated $4.5 billion. This would represent about 3% of their GNP, and 10% of their current balance of payments surplus.

But it is unlikely that the OPEC countries can maintain this level of aid throughout the decade. They are themselves developing countries and the source of their capacity to make aid available is not the size and strength of their combined GNP—which is only a small fraction of that of the OECD countries—nor even of their GNP per capita, which on average is also substantially less, but rather the levels of their surplus trade balances.

By 1980, it is estimated that only a few of the OPEC countries will have current accounts still in substantial surplus. The others, which have provided about half the group's aid commitments over the past two years, are likely to reduce their level of aid as their imports rise and their trade surpluses diminish.

The OECD nations will be in the strongest position to assist the developing countries, and particularly the poorest among them, to achieve at least minimally acceptable rates of per capita income growth in the years immediately ahead.

To illustrate the problems of the developing countries in another way, consider the decade of the 1970s as a whole, and compare the economic progress—actual and projected—of three groups of people: the one billion people of the poorest developing countries; the 725 million people of the middle-income developing countries; and the 675 million people of the developed nations.

Income and Investment Levels 1970-1980 for Developed and Developing Countries[a]
(In 1970$s)

Country Group	1975 Population (in millions)	GNP Per Capita 1970	GNP Per Capita 1980	GNP Growth Rate Per Capita p.a.	Estimated Investment Per Capita p.a. Dom. Svg.	Ext. Cap. Inflow	Total
I. Low-Income Countries (Under $200 per capita p.a.)	1,000	$ 105	$ 108	.2%	$ 14	$ 2	$ 16
II. Middle-Income Countries (over $200 per capita p.a.)	725	$ 410	$ 540	2.8%	$ 75	$ 10	$ 85
III. OECD Countries	675	$3,100	$4,000	2.6%	$850	$−15	$835

[a]Excludes Centrally Planned Economies and OPEC. Assumes Case I rates of growth for the developing countries 1976-80.

As the table makes clear, the Second Development Decade would result in virtually no progress at all for the one billion people in the low-income countries and would mean that both they and the 725 million in the other developing nations would be growing relatively poorer when compared to the people of the developed countries.

To raise the growth rates of the developing nations to the level of Case II for the remainder of the decade would not require Official Development Assistance in 1980 to exceed the United Nations target of .7% of GNP. And that target could be reached were the developed countries willing to dedicate to ODA a minor fraction—no more than 2%—of the incremental wealth which they can expect to receive in the second half of the decade as their economies recover from the recession.

In contrast, as the table on page 334 shows, today the developed nations are contributing less than half of that goal—only .33% of GNP. Moreover, many of these nations, under present policies, are failing to increase their concessionary aid commitments by amounts sufficient both to offset inflation and to reflect their rising real incomes. Unless such policies are changed, ODA during the remainder of the decade, relative to GNP, will continue to fall, declining to perhaps .28% by 1980. It is essential, therefore, that the developed nations reexamine their concessionary aid programs. As government revenues and national incomes rise in the years ahead, ODA in relation to GNP should first be returned to former levels, and then later move toward the .7% target.

In view of the critical need of the developing countries for additional capital, I want to turn now to what the World Bank itself can do.

The World Bank Program

As events have unfolded this past year and the capital crisis engulfing our developing member countries became more apparent, we resolved that the Bank must take a number of steps to help meet that crisis.

The first step was to expand the overall level of our lending program.

We propose to expand it both in nominal and in real terms to the maximum level consistent with our capital structure, the availability of funds, and the creditworthiness of our borrowers.

As inflation has persisted, the dollar volume of our loan commitments has necessarily increased. The average dollar amount of each loan has gone up in order to insure that our borrowers will in fact be receiving over the years of the loan's disbursement amounts sufficient to meet the rising costs of the project.

The following table illustrates how inflation has affected the real value of our lending operations.

Amount Required to Finance Equivalent of $100 Million Commitment in FY65[a]

	US$ Million
FY65	100
FY70	141
FY75	228
FY80	300

[a]Allowing for price changes during the disbursement period.

By 1980, it will require $3 of commitments to accomplish what $1 did in FY65, and more than $2 to equal $1 in FY70.

But in addition to expanding our lending program in nominal terms by an amount that will fully offset the effects of inflation, we propose also to expand the real transfer of resources represented by that program in order to meet as far as we can the critical capital shortage which has such corrosive effects on the growth rates of our developing member countries.

To meet both objectives, we increased in FY75 the Bank Group's new financial commitments to $6 billion, compared to $4.5 billion in FY74. I have proposed $7 billion for FY76 and the total for the five-year period FY76-80 should approximate $40 billion. Such a level of new commitments would constitute, in real terms, a 58% increase over the previous five years, FY71-75, and a 153% increase over the preceding period, FY66-70.

Though this represents the largest program of financial and technical assistance to developing countries ever undertaken by a single agency, it of course still falls far short of meeting the full scope of the capital needs of those countries.

World Bank Group Lending: Actual and Proposed,
In Current and Constant Dollars
(in billions of dollars)

Fiscal Years	Current $s	In FY75$s
1966-70	$ 7.5	$14.2
1971-75	$19.9	$22.8
1976-80	$42.0	$35.6

As an interim measure, therefore, to help our lower-income member countries in their efforts to obtain additional resources for development, we have proposed, and the Executive Directors have approved, the formation of a new lending facility within the Bank—the so-called Third Window—which will provide funds at a concessional interest rate midway between that of Bank loans and IDA credits.

The purpose of the Third Window is to make available additional development assistance on terms suited to the limited ability of the developing countries to service additional debt, and with longer maturities than that currently being provided by emergency mechanisms such as the IMF Oil Facility.

We plan to begin this intermediate-term lending within a few weeks, with an initial level of operations of $500 million—which we hope to expand to $1 billion. To subsidize the interest rate of these new funds, we have been seeking contributions from a number of our OECD and OPEC member governments. Twelve have already indicated they intend to support the plan.

The Third Window facility is at best only an emergency measure. It can supplement, but in no way substitute for our IDA operations.

And because the capital requirements of our poorer member countries have now reached such a critical degree of urgency, it is imperative that we begin before the end of this year serious negotiations for a substantially increased IDA Replenishment.

IDA IV funds will be fully committed by June 30, 1977. In order to provide our member governments with adequate time to secure legislative approval—and to avoid the procedural delays which in the end penalize not the Association, but the poor countries all of us are trying to help—it is essential that our

member governments move decisively and generously to negotiate, approve, and bring into being an IDA V Replenishment appropriate to the unprecedented needs it is designed to serve.

The new replenishment must be established at a level sufficient both to fully offset the effects of inflation, and to provide
an appropriate measure of real growth. It should be supported
by its traditional donors, and by those additional countries
which, since the last replenishment, have benefited from major
increases in their national incomes and foreign exchange
reserves.

Finally, within the next few years, the need will arise to review
the capital structure of the Bank and the International Finance
Corporation.

I have presented to the Executive Directors a proposal for a
Selective Increase in the Bank's subscribed capital and in paid-in
capital. The proposal, which parallels the proposed increases in
IMF quotas—and which should be acted upon as soon as the
Fund takes a decision—makes provision for additional increases
in the capital subscription of OPEC countries to reflect their increased economic and financial strength and their growing importance as a source of loan capital to the Bank.

The catalytic role of IFC in mobilizing additional private investment in the developing countries takes on even greater
importance in a period of capital shortage, and we are exploring
ways to increase its resources as well.

Although the Selective Increase for the Bank will significantly
strengthen its ability to continue its role as a major source of
development finance, the impact of inflation on the nominal
amounts of our operations will make it mandatory to consider
a General Increase in IBRD subscribed capital in the course of
the next few years. The Articles of Agreement of the Bank provide that loans outstanding and disbursed shall not exceed the
equivalent of unimpaired subscribed capital, reserves, and surplus. This provision would force us, at the proposed level of
lending, to cease making loans in the early 1980s. To permit
adequate time for the necessary legislative action, we must start
soon to discuss an appropriate solution to this situation.

The Bank's entire lending program, and its future plans, clearly must be derived from the nature and scale of the problem that confronts the developing countries.

A major element of that problem consists of a desperate need for external capital for high-priority development investment that can enhance the living standards of nearly two billion people.

Let me summarize, then, the nature of that problem as I have outlined it thus far. Essentially it is this:

The developing nations are confronting a foreign exchange crisis. It is a crisis compounded of all the turbulent economic events of the past two or three years, and the cumulative effect will be to bring the economic progress of many of these nations virtually to a halt unless corrective action is taken. It is clear that at such a time additional efforts to mobilize internal resources and greater efficiency in the use of these resources become critically important and the governments of the developing countries must give high priority to these actions. The fact remains, however, that they desperately need additional imports to get their economies moving again. And the foreign exchange to finance those imports can only come from greater official and private external flows, and increased export earnings. The Bank itself must contribute to the expansion of the external capital flows and we intend to do so.

But despite all of this—despite the urgency for all of us to focus our attention on this emergency, and to take every step we can to try to deal with it—we cannot allow this to diminish our concern with the central issue of development which underlies the present situation: the necessity of creating an effective strategy to deal with the fundamental problem of poverty itself.

Let me turn to that consideration now.

III. ABSOLUTE POVERTY AND THE REDUCTION OF INEQUALITY

Three years ago I began a discussion with you of the critical relationship of poverty and economic growth. I pointed out that this problem in the developing world can be summed up very succinctly: roughly half the population are neither contributing significantly to economic growth nor sharing equitably in its benefits. These are the poor. Within most developing societies they form a huge group at the lower end of the income spectrum, receiving only a fraction of what the middle and upper-income groups do.

Some 900 million of these individuals subsist on incomes of less than $75 a year in an environment of squalor, hunger, and hopelessness. They are the absolute poor, living in situations so deprived as to be below any rational definition of human decency. Absolute poverty is a condition of life so limited by illiteracy, malnutrition, disease, high infant-mortality, and low life-expectancy as to deny its victims the very potential of the genes with which they are born. In effect, it is life at the margin of existence.

In addition to the absolute poor there are what I have termed the relative poor. These are individuals with incomes somewhat above the absolute poverty level, but still far below their national average. Because of the distortion in income distribution —a distortion which in most developing countries far exceeds that of the industrialized nations—they too have been bypassed by economic progress.

The heaviest concentration of absolute poverty is in Asia. India, Pakistan, Bangladesh, and Indonesia are particularly afflicted. One out of every two individuals there is enmeshed in it.

In Africa, most countries are plagued with both absolute and relative poverty. Not only are per capita incomes meager on average, but often highly skewed as well.

In Latin America, many countries enjoy higher per capita incomes, with only about one individual in six at Asian or African levels of absolute poverty. But income distribution throughout the region is marred by serious inequality, and relative poverty is widespread and severe.

Analysis of income data makes it clear that policies aimed at diminishing income inequalities through direct redistribution of wealth will not be sufficient to end indigence. That is not to say that adjustments in this direction are not desirable on the grounds of equity, but no degree of egalitarianism alone will solve the root problem of poverty. What is required are policies that will enhance the productivity of the poor.

The truth is that throughout the developing world—in the countryside and cities alike—there is a huge and largely untapped potential to reduce absolute and relative poverty, and to increase economic growth, by directly assisting the poor to become more productive.

Two years ago in Nairobi I outlined a strategy for moving against poverty in the countryside. In the interim we have accelerated our efforts to implement that strategy, and I would like to report to you on that now.

IV. REDUCING POVERTY IN THE RURAL AREAS

We chose the rural areas to begin an assault on poverty because the overwhelming majority of the absolute poor are there. As I pointed out, the poverty problem in the countryside revolves primarily around the low productivity of the millions of small subsistence farms. Despite the growth of the GNP in most developing countries, the increase in output of these small family holdings over the past decade has been so low as to be virtually imperceptible.

The scale of the problem is immense. More than 100 million families—some 700 million individuals—are involved. The size of the average holding is not only small, but often fragmented. More than 50 million of these families are farming less than one hectare.

You will recall the objective we recommended that the international development community adopt: to take the steps necessary to increase production on these farms so that by 1985 their output will be growing at an average rate of 5% per year.[a]

---

[a] Such an increase in productivity is necessary not only to advance the well-being of the 100 million small farmers, but also to help assure that global food requirements will be met. Though I will not deal specifically with the food problem in my remarks today, I do want to emphasize the Bank's concern with this issue. Following the World Food Conference last year in Rome, the Bank, in association with the FAO and the UNDP, established the Consultative Group on Food Production and Investment in Developing Countries.

Clearly no simple formula exists to move forward so complex an objective as rural development. It is the interplay and mutual reinforcement of a coordinated array of national policies that is required. To help shape effective action, the Bank over the past two years has researched and published a series of policy papers that range over a broad spectrum of issues. These include major statements on Rural Development, Agricultural Credit, Land Reform, Education, and Health.

But we have not merely elaborated policy. We have moved ahead with an expanded lending program in rural development and we now lend more in this sector than in any other. This is a clear change in emphasis: 50% of all rural-development lending in the history of the Bank has occurred in the last year. We expect to commit $7 billion more in this field over the next five years, and we estimate that these new projects will bring financial benefits to approximately 100 million individuals.

Projects have been devised which combine components from several different sectors—roads, electricity, water, education, family planning, and nutrition—and which integrate these with agricultural inputs into a development package to be applied to an entire region.

Typical of such new-style projects are the following:

- A package of four loans, totalling $86 million, designed to increase the crop production and incomes of subsistence farmers in Nigeria, with the benefits reaching some 2 million individuals. The projects include financing of feeder roads, medium-sized earth dams, water reservoirs, village service centers, seed multiplication farms, training facilities, swamp-land conversion to rice paddies, and extension, credit, and marketing services. The estimated rate of economic return is 25%.

- Two credits totalling $44 million for dairy development in India designed to increase the cash incomes and living standards of some 400,000 households—2.2 million individuals—the majority of whom currently have holdings less than two hectares, or are landless. The projects are expected to boost milk production by 760,000 tons a year, substantially improving nutrition, creating 14,000 new jobs, and yielding a return of 30%.

- A $21 million loan for rural development in Thailand designed to benefit 400,000 low-income farm families—two and a half million individuals. The project will include specialized agricultural extension services, rural electrification, village water supply, access roads, and small-scale irrigation, and yield 16%.

One of the most innovative of the rural development projects is a $10 million credit to assist the Tanzanian government to bolster the productivity and living standards of farm families in the Kigoma region where per capita incomes are among the lowest in the world. The project will channel economic and social services to 250,000 individuals in 135 newly established villages, substantially improving their crop production and doubling their incomes. It will include a credit and marketing system; primary schools, health centers, and improved water supply; cleaning the area of the tsetse fly; regional radio-telephone communications; and a program of adaptive agricultural research. Should the project succeed—and we believe it will—it could serve as a model for new settlements elsewhere.

Though the new rural development projects are innovative, they are designed to provide a substantial economic rate of return at a low investment per individual served so that they can be readily extended to additional areas as additional resources become available.

Overcoming Obstacles

But the closer we get to the core of the problem of poverty in the countryside, the more difficult, complicated, and time-consuming the task becomes. Let me take a moment, then, to describe some of the principal roadblocks we are encountering, and how we propose to deal with them.

One is the issue of appropriate technology. The agricultural methods of the wealthy nations in the temperate zone are frequently unsuited to the environment of many developing countries, where poor farmers are often struggling to subsist on semi-arid, or marginal land. There is a critical need for new agricultural technologies tailored to these conditions. The Bank helps to meet this need through its chairmanship of the Consultative Group for International Agricultural Research, and its shared financing of ten specialized international research institutes around the world, including one specifically for the semi-arid tropics.

In addition to the research work of the international institutes themselves, much more needs to be done by individual governments. The Bank has, therefore, recently agreed to help finance government efforts to consolidate and intensify specialized agricultural research in Indonesia and Malaysia. We anticipate an increasing number of such requests.

One technique we are making increasing use of is satellite remote sensing imagery in the survey and evaluation of potential land and water resources. This new tool is proving valuable in many aspects of project planning, and we are helping a number of our member countries to utilize it—Indonesia, India, Bangladesh, Nepal, and Kenya, among others.

Another problem is the pricing and subsidy policies some governments impose on the rural sector that tend to discourage additional food production. These policies are usually imposed to provide cheap food for the cities. But if prices are kept artificially low in relation to costs, farmers have no incentive to expand production. This is especially true of small farmers who simply have no margin for risk.

What many of us sometimes forget is that just because a man is poor does not mean that he is naive. The truth is that millions of small farmers—even without elaborate inputs—could increase their productivity measurably if they could be given but one simple assurance: that at harvest time they would be able to sell their additional production at a rewarding price.

Moreover, the small farmer is almost always discriminated against by public institutions that tend to favor the larger and more prosperous producers. It is the larger farmer who typically enjoys easy access to public credit, research, water allocations, and scarce supplies of petroleum, pesticides, and fertilizer. And it is the smaller farmer who is left to wait endlessly for the public services he needs far more urgently, but only too rarely receives.

The Bank is intensifying its dialogue with member governments to come to grips with these issues of pricing policy, and to assure more responsive public services specifically shaped to the needs of the poor. There are some signs of movement in this direction, but as yet not nearly enough.

Still another roadblock in implementing complex rural operations is the scarcity of trained technicians. That is why we often include training components in our projects. But much more needs to be done to expand the supply of such personnel, and we are gearing more of our education projects to that end.

Finally, all of us—at every level—have a great deal more to learn about the motivational patterns and behavioral responses of the poor in shifting from traditional subsistence agriculture to cash-crop production. Both the technical and social variables in such a transition are complex. To deal with them effectively calls for continuing feedback and evaluation, sensitivity and respect for indigenous values, and a healthy measure of humility.

Let me, then, conclude this section by summing up the principal points I have made. They are these.

There are some 700 million individuals locked into absolute poverty in the rural areas of the developing world. Their degree of deprivation is so extreme as to be an insult to human dignity —to theirs, because as human beings they deserve better; and to ours, because all of us have had it in our power to do more to help them, and have not.

Two years ago I outlined a strategy for reducing absolute poverty in the countryside. It focuses on the more than one hundred million small subsistence farmers, and their families. And what it proposes is not traditional welfare, but sound investment to assist them to become more productive.

It is a strategy that can succeed. It requires of governments political decisiveness, new policies, and a reallocation of resources. But it can return immense dividends. We in the Bank are developing a whole new program of integrated rural development projects to assist governments. They are projects that package together innovative economic and social components specifically designed to help transform poverty into productivity. We have a long way to go, but the early evidence is clear: it works.

It works because it is an approach that provides the poor with what they really want most of all: a chance to build a better life, through their own efforts, for themselves and their children.

It is an approach that works in the countryside. And it is an approach that we believe can work in the cities as well. I want to turn to a consideration of that now.

V. REDUCING POVERTY IN THE CITIES

We began the assault on poverty in the rural areas because that is where most of the absolute poor currently are. But they live in the cities of the developing world as well. Roughly 200 million are there now. More are coming, and coming soon.

The Bank has been giving increased attention to this issue. It is immensely complex—even more so than the problem of poverty in the countryside. But we believe we are ready now to initiate a much more comprehensive effort to assist governments to reduce urban poverty. What I would like to do today is, first, discuss the scope of the problem; second, analyze its underlying causes; and third, suggest a strategy to deal with it.

The Scope of the Problem

To understand urban poverty in the developing world one must first understand what is happening to the cities themselves. They are growing at a rate unprecedented in history. Twenty-five years ago there were 16 cities in the developing countries with populations of one million or more. Today there are over 60. Twenty-five years from now there will be more than 200.

How has this happened? Fundamentally, of course, it is a function of population growth. But it is more than just that. For though the total population in the developing world is increasing by about 2.5% a year, the urban population is growing at nearly twice that rate. Half the urban growth is due to natural increase, and half is due to migration from the countryside.

What this means is that some 400 million additional people have been absorbed into cities, through birth and migration, in a single generation—something wholly without parallel. In contrast, the developed world urbanized at a leisurely and less pressured pace at a time when its national populations were growing very slowly, at only about half a percent per year.

Latin America is already 60% urbanized, and Asia and Africa about 25%. But by the end of the century, three out of every four Latin Americans will live in a city, and one out of every three Africans and Asians.

Thus, at current trends, over the next 25 years the urban areas will have to absorb another 1.1 billion people, almost all of them poor, in addition to their present population of 700 million.

Life for the urban poor today is unspeakably grim. Though they spend up to 80% of their income on food, they typically suffer from serious malnutrition. It is estimated that half the urban population of India is undernourished. Up to 15% of the children who die in Latin American cities, and up to 25% of those who die in African cities, are needless victims of malnutrition.

Now what do these figures imply?

They make it certain that the cities of the developing world are going to find it incredibly difficult to provide employment, and minimally decent living conditions, for the hundreds of millions of new entrants into urban economies which are already severely strained.

An even more ominous implication is what the penalties for failure may be. Historically, violence and civil upheaval are more common in cities than in the countryside. Frustrations that fester among the urban poor are readily exploited by political extremists. If cities do not begin to deal more constructively with poverty, poverty may well begin to deal more destructively with cities.

It is not a problem that favors political delay.

The Underlying Causes of Urban Poverty

To comprehend the pathology of poverty in the cities, one must begin with an analysis of the employment opportunities of the poor.

Employment in the urban areas of the developing world is a function of an economic dualism that is widespread. Two sectors coexist side by side. One is the organized, modern, formal sector, characterized by capital-intensive technology, relatively high wages, large-scale operations, and corporate and governmental organization.

The other is the unorganized, traditional, informal sector—economic units with the reverse characteristics: labor-intensive, small-scale operations, using traditional methods, and providing modest earnings to the individual or family owner.

In the modern sector, wages are usually protected by labor legislation and trade union activity; in the informal sector, there is easier entry, but less job security and lower earnings.

Though jobs in the modern sector may be more desirable, as a practical matter they are often beyond the reach of the poor. They require literacy, experience, and a level of training the poor find it difficult to acquire; and in a labor-surplus market, employers can afford to insist on exceptional qualifications.

Even more important, the growth of employment in modern manufacturing and distribution lags considerably behind both the growth of its output, and the growth of the urban labor pool: output has increased 5 to 10% per year, but employment rose only 3 to 4%, while the labor pool was growing at a rate of 4 to 5%.

Though it is true that as the formal sector expands it tends to generate some indirect employment in the informal sector, it can also eliminate jobs there on an alarming scale. At the cost of $100,000, for example, a corporation may set up a plastic footwear plant, with only 40 employees, that can displace 5,000 traditional shoemakers and their suppliers.

High population growth rates, and massive migration to the cities, have swollen the urban labor pool. But the capital-intensive nature of the modern sector has kept openings for additional workers down. In some developing countries, manufacturing techniques have already become so mechanized that an investment of $50,000 to $70,000 is often required to create a single new job.

Given, then, the limited potential of the formal sector in most developing countries to absorb labor, it is not surprising that the informal sector is a critical component in urban employment. It provides, for example, nearly half of all the jobs in Lima, more than half in Bombay and Jakarta; and over two-thirds in Belo Horizonte.

And yet, the fact is that governments tend to view the informal sector with little enthusiasm. They consider it backward, inefficient, and a painful reminder of a less sophisticated past.

It is true that economies of scale are important in some activities. But it is not true that all small-scale enterprises are uneconomic. They can frequently operate at acceptable cost levels when costs of labor and capital are measured correctly, and when production operations are broken up into individual processes and products. In the production of many types of food, clothing, and furniture, and in construction, transportation, assembly, packaging, repairing, and service activities, small units can compete effectively.

But government prejudice against the informal sector frequently gets translated into public policies which give undue advantages to big firms: unrealistically low exchange rates for capital imports, special tax exemptions, high minimum wages, underpriced public utilities, and subsidized interest rates. All of these measures favor the large and capital-intensive firm over the small enterprise, and have the net effect of reducing the employment opportunities of the poor.

These discriminations against the poor are compounded by limited access to public services. There are heavy biases in the design, location, pricing, and delivery of such services.

Though most cities, for example, have expensive modern hospitals, the poor usually do not have access to them. They are largely reserved for the rich minority, even though the privileged have less incidence of illness than the poor. Nor is it surprising that the poor are so often ill, considering the squalor in which they must live. Frequently they have no public water supply or sewerage services whatever. And they often have to pay up to 20 times more for water supplied by street vendors than do middle- and upper-income families for water piped by the city into their homes.

But if the poor are denied equitable access to water, sanitation, and health, they fare equally badly with education. Many of their children receive no formal education at all simply because they live beyond a feasible distance to the nearest school. Thus, though half the total population of the capital of one African country lives in the slum areas, all of the schools, with one exception, are located elsewhere in the city. The result is that the primary school enrollment is only 36% in the poor areas, but 90% throughout the rest of the capital.

Children of the urban poor, although often in the majority, very seldom reach secondary school, much less a university, despite the fact that public expenditure per student for secondary and higher education is up to 20 times the expenditure on primary education. This means that education—in theory a powerful force in equalizing opportunity—in fact often reinforces, rather than reduces, existing economic disparities.

In a typical Latin American city, for example, workers with primary education earn 37% more than workers without education, and workers with secondary and higher education earn 40% more than workers with only primary schooling. Denying adequate education to the urban poor, then, is simply synonymous with denying them opportunities for earning higher incomes.

Public transport is another vital service the poor are often without. Their incomes are so low they can rarely afford it. And even if they could afford it, it often does not exist in the peripheral areas of the city where they generally must live.

While the wealthy drive their cars, and the moderate-income workers ride the bus, the poor walk to work—frequently as much as two hours each way. Such distances are a penalty both to their energy and to their earnings. And as the cities grow larger, so their commuting grows longer. Studies indicate that in a city of a million, the poor's average journey to work is three miles; in a city of five million, seven miles.

In city after city of the developing world, the streets are growing congested with private automobiles, and the city councils are pouring over blueprints for elaborate subways or expressways. But little if any of this heavy investment will ever benefit the poor. It will only drain away resources that might be used to help them become more productive.

The deprivation suffered by the poor is nowhere more visible than in the matter of housing. Even the most hardened and unsentimental observer from the developed world is shocked by the squalid slums and ramshackle shantytowns that ring the periphery of every major city. The favelas, the bustees, the bidonvilles have become almost the central symbol of the poverty that pervades two-thirds of the globe. It is the image that is seared into the memory of every visitor.

But there is one thing worse than living in a slum or a squatter settlement—and that is having one's slum or settlement bulldozed away by a government which has no shelter of any sort whatever to offer in its place. When that happens—and it happens often—there remains only the pavement itself, or some rocky hillside or parched plain, where the poor can once again begin to build out of packing crates and signboards and scraps of sheetmetal and cardboard a tiny hovel in which to house their families.

Squatter settlements by definition—and by city ordinance—are illegal. Even the word squatter itself is vaguely obscene, as if somehow being penniless, landless, and homeless were deliberate sins against the canons of proper etiquette. But it is not squatters that are obscene. It is the economic circumstances that make squatter settlements necessary that are obscene.

*   *   *   *

This, then, is the profile of poverty in the cities. It is not the profile of an insignificant minority, nor of a miscellaneous collection of unfortunates, nor of a fringe group of nonconformists —but of 200 million human beings whose aspirations are identical to yours and mine: to lead a productive life, to provide for those they love, and to try to build a better future for their children.

They differ from us in only two respects: in the inhuman burden of their problems; and in the unjust disparity of opportunity they have to solve them. It is development's task to reduce that disparity. Let me, then, suggest at least the broad outlines of a strategy to deal with urban poverty.

A Strategy to Reduce Urban Poverty

Though the dynamics of poverty in the cities differ substantially from those in the countryside, the key to dealing with them both is fundamentally the same. What is required are policies and actions that will assist the poor to increase their productivity. Primarily this calls for measures that will remove barriers to their earning opportunities, and improve their access to public services.

The following are essential steps governments should consider in any comprehensive program:

- Increase earning opportunities in the informal sector;
- Create more jobs in the modern sector;
- Provide equitable access to public utilities, transport, education, and health services;
- And establish realistic housing policies.

The fundamental consideration underlying such a program is the reassessment of the role of the cities in the development process. Let me begin with that, and then turn to the others in sequence.

The Role of Cities in the Development Process

We need to remind ourselves what the role of cities in development really is.

Cities are, of course, many things, but essentially they are an instrument for providing their inhabitants—all their habitants—with a more productive life. They are not primarily collections of elaborate architecture, or of city planners' theories perpetuated in stone. Even less should they be thought of as sanctuaries of the privileged, who wish to put a decent distance between themselves and the masses of the rural poor.

Urban poverty can be cured nowhere in the world unless cities are thought of as absorptive mechanisms for promoting productive employment for all those who need and seek it. In the past 25 years in the developing countries some 200 to 300 million individuals have benefited at least marginally by migration, and since even at their unacceptably low levels of income they have been more productively employed in the cities than they would have been had they remained in the rural areas, the national economy itself has benefited.

This is not to make a case for wholesale migration from the rural areas. It is only to recognize that poverty will persist in the cities until governments determine to increase their capacity not simply to absorb the poor, but to promote their productivity by providing the employment opportunities, the infrastructure, and the services necessary for that purpose.

Now specifically how is this to be done? Our understanding of so complex an issue is limited, but at least it is possible, on the basis of what we do know, to identify policies and actions that could have a significant impact on the problem. The Bank's approach in the urban sector will be different from the strategy we are following in rural areas, although the basic objectives are the same.

The Bank's rural development strategy is focused on the small farmer. The main thrust is to provide the organizational structure and financial resources to increase the supply of essential inputs and raise the productivity of a specific target group. In the urban sector we will retain the emphasis on productivity. But we need a more flexible and diversified approach to match the greater diversity in the nature of the urban environment, the difficulty in identifying a readily accessible target group, and the variety of opportunities arising from the complex linkages in modern economic activity.

Any realistic strategy must place emphasis on increasing the earning opportunities of the poor in the informal sector.

Increasing Earning Opportunities in the Informal Sector

The employment problem in urban areas is not simply "jobs" in the conventional sense but rather the level of productivity and earnings. There is relatively little open unemployment among the urban poor. Without some kind of a job, they simply cannot eat. But they are often prevented from increasing their earnings by a combination of market forces, institutional arrangements, and public policies which confer privileges on the large, well-established firms and which penalize the informal sector.

Governments must take steps to moderate the bias in favor of large-scale, capital-intensive production, and turn their attention more positively to small producers, not only in manufacturing but also in transport, construction, commerce, and other service sectors.

The informal sector offers the most immediate opportunities of greater productivity for the urban poor. It already, of course, provides the livelihood for the vast majority, and though its earnings are considerably less than those in the formal sector, its flexibility and ease of entry are an important asset. What is required is that government policy support it, without attempting to standardize it.

The informal sector's great virtue is its responsiveness to opportunity, its high degree of resourcefulness, and its entrepreneurial originality. The understandable enthusiasm of governments to "modernize" their economies must be restrained in their dealings with the informal sector. The point is not to try to transform it into the formal sector, but to support it without undue insistence on regulating it.

There are a number of ways in which governments can assist the small producer and the self-employed.

They can, for example, assure access to credit facilities on reasonable terms. The informal sector usually has very limited access to government banking and credit services. It must rely largely on the urban moneylender, who, like his village counterpart, is responsive but usurious. What are needed are improved banking policies that will make adequate capital available.

This can be done through rediscounting commercial bank loans to small-scale enterprises by central banks; by government guarantees to cover additional risks in informal-sector loans; and by new specialized institutions designed specifically to finance small enterprises. Like the small farmer, the urban informal-sector businessman is usually starved for credit. He does not need it in large amounts, nor does he need it at unrealistically low interest rates. But he needs it without excessive bureaucratic obstruction, and he needs it without procedural delay.

Further, governments can promote mutually beneficial relationships between the informal and formal sectors by reserving land for small enterprises in the vicinity of industrial developments. One effective technique is to establish industrial estates which will provide space neither exclusively to large nor to small industries, but which will deliberately situate firms of all sizes in close proximity, specifically to encourage economic linkages between them.

Since small enterprises individually have only very limited purchasing and marketing capacity, governments can promote cooperative facilities to lower their costs and increase their efficiency. At the national, regional and municipal levels, government agencies, as well as banks and private firms, can offer technical assistance to the small entrepreneur, analogous to the extension services for small farmers.

Finally, governments can help the informal sector to flourish by the removal of onerous and often outdated licensing and regulatory controls.

Taken together, the removal of biases favoring the modern sector, and the special assistance to the informal sector, can substantially improve the earning opportunities of the urban poor in the informal sector.

Creating More Jobs in the Modern Sector

But the strengthening of the informal sector need not prevent the continued growth of the larger enterprises. On the contrary, special efforts must be made in many countries to turn their manufacturing enterprises away from the relatively small markets associated with import substitution, and toward the much larger opportunities flowing from export promotion. Korea, Taiwan, Mexico and Brazil, which achieved 15 to 20% annual growth in their manufactured exports in the late 1960s and early 1970s, clearly demonstrated the feasibility of bolstering manufacturing employment with this policy.

Further, the gradual reduction, and the ultimate elimination, of capital subsidies to the modern sector, as has been done in Hong Kong and Singapore, can make both production and service activities significantly more labor-intensive. Even in relatively automated modern factories, substantial labor-capital substitution possibilities exist in such activities as materials handling, packaging, and intrafactory transport. When producers have to pay realistic prices for capital, they not only explore more labor-intensive solutions for each process and product, but tend to use the plant's capacity more intensively, thus creating more jobs per unit of capital.

The first element, then, in the strategy to increase the productivity of the urban poor is to remove barriers to their earning opportunities. The second is to provide them with essential public services at standards they can afford.

Assuring Access to Public Services

About one-third of the population in most of the cities of the developing world lives in slums that are either wholly without or very inadequately served by public water, sewerage, transport, education, and housing. These conditions have a seriously detrimental effect on the health, productivity, and incomes of the poor.

The urban poor are frequently denied access to public services, not because they don't exist, but because they have been designed or located largely for middle- and upper-income city dwellers, and are simply beyond the reach of the less privileged.

The whole question of "standards" of urban services works to the disadvantage of the urban poor for they are often written with middle-class or upper-income orientations, and have little relevance to the situation the poor find themselves in.

Standards are important, but they must be formulated to meet realistic and attainable objectives. If the needs of the poor are to be met within a reasonable time span, public utilities and social services will have to be provided at costs which they can afford to pay.

Water and Sewerage Services

The single most important factor in improving the health environment of the poor is to provide clean water and adequate sewerage. A commonly used standard calls for cities to supply 200 liters of water per person per day. Many cities in the developing world simply cannot afford to do that. That is understandable. What is not understandable is that instead of lowering the standard to fit their resources, some cities pipe 200 liters per person per day to individual houses in the affluent and middle-class neighborhoods, but leave 60% of the population—the poor on the periphery of the city—without any piped water at all. The result frequently is endemic cholera among the poor, because they must depend on unclean water from other sources.

Often, all that low-income families can afford are standpipes, but this form of water supply, together with technical assistance in improving sanitation facilities, can have an immensely beneficial impact on their health.

Health and Education Services

Essential health and education services for the poor are also seriously deficient in most of the cities of the developing world. Health care, for example, is frequently confined to modern and expensive hospitals, when what is needed are small clinics located in areas of the city where most health problems begin: in the slums and squatter settlements. Indeed the whole orientation of health care should emphasize low-cost preventive medicine rather than high-cost curative care. The poor are often ill —and their children often die—but the causes are almost always diseases that could have been readily prevented by a more sanitary environment and simple preventive measures.

Inexpensive health delivery systems can be designed around community-based health workers who can provide the poor with a broad spectrum of simple and effective services: immunization, health and nutrition education, and family-planning advice.

The same principle applies to education. What is required are small, inexpensive, and informal basic education units, located in accessible areas, and designed to serve minimum learning needs of both children and adults: literacy and elementary arithmetic, child care, vocational advice, and the knowledge necessary for responsible civic participation.

Transportation

The poor must also be within reach of employment possibilities. This means transport facilities which they can afford. Usually the urban transport available is either too expensive, or does not serve the areas in which the poor live. It is clear that most cities would benefit substantially from a radical reallocation of their transport systems away from domination by the private automobile, and in the direction of public transport that can move large numbers of passengers at low unit costs.

What is needed is a healthy pluralism in transport: buses, jitneys, taxis, motor rickshaws, pedicabs, bicycle paths—whatever is cost-effective and appropriate to the distances involved.

Establishing Realistic Housing Policies

City governments often congratulate themselves on their subsidized blocks of low-income housing, and the physical structures are frequently impressive. What is depressing is that the so-called low-income housing is almost always too expensive for the poor. Surveys indicate that up to 70% of the poor cannot afford even the cheapest housing produced by public agencies.

Slums and squatter settlements are the inevitable result. Authorities typically strongly disapprove of them: they are illegal, they are unsightly, and they are unsanitary. But too often cities have failed to find any solution—short of demolition—to deal with them. The fact is that the upgrading of existing squatter settlements can be a low-cost and practical approach to low-income shelter. Upgrading legalizes the settlement, provides secure tenure, and supplies minimum infrastructure: water, roads, storm drainage, security lighting, and rubbish collection. Education and other community facilities can generally be added.

One of the most interesting features of squatter settlements is that though they are inhabited by the very poor, there is a very strong sense of saving among the residents. Out of their minuscule earnings, they save every cent they can. Their great ambition is to have a better home for their families. But they are prudent men and women: they are unwilling to invest their savings in home improvement until they have tenure. That is why squatter settlements are often so ramshackle. Once upgraded projects provide legal tenure, the poor are not only willing to spend on home improvement, but do so with enthusiasm, and remarkable transformations often take place.

The housing that can be provided by upgrading existing slums and squatter settlements is of course limited. A somewhat more costly, but still practical, alternative is the "sites and services" approach. It can provide the framework for improved housing for vast numbers of the poor, particularly if it is planned with adequate lead time.

The city provides a suitable area of new land, grades and levels it, and furnishes it with essential infrastructure: access roads, drainage, water, sewerage, and electricity. The land is divided into small plots and is leased or sold to the poor, who are supplied with simple house plans, and a low-cost loan with which to purchase inexpensive building materials. The actual construction is made the responsibility of the poor, who build their houses themselves.

And as communities are more than just housing, sites and services projects include schools, health clinics, community halls, day-care centers, and some provision for creating jobs: land, for example, set aside for the establishment of an appropriate small-scale industry.

Sites and services projects, then, stimulate self-help, and make it possible for the poor to house themselves in a viable, cohesive community with a minimum of public expenditure.

But though this is a highly desirable approach, it often suffers from two constraints: the understandable economic constraint of the availability of the land, infrastructure, and building materials; and the less understandable institutional constraint of regulations governing tenure, building codes, and zoning restrictions.

The determination of appropriate standards is critical for the poor family's ability to acquire housing. If, for example, standards relating to land use, floor space, durability of materials, quality of finish, and utilities were modified to meet low-income household budgets, it should be possible for some 80% of the population in the cities of the developing world to afford much improved shelter with no subsidy at all.

It is also important that reasonable user charges and taxes should be levied on the middle- and upper-income consumers of city services of all kinds—housing, utilities, education, health facilities, transport, and others—to generate surpluses which can be used to expand coverage of these services, and give the poor a more equitable opportunity to benefit from them.

*   *   *   *

These, then, are some of the measures that governments should ponder as they confront the growing pressures of urbanization. For the next decade or two—indeed for as far forward as anyone can realistically plan—the urban problem will be a poverty problem.

The urban poor are not simply a statistical inconvenience to planners, a disturbing reminder of what might be possible if they would somehow just go away, a continually disappointing factor in budget allocations because of their chronic inability to pay taxes. That is not what urban poverty is about.

The urban poor are hundreds of millions of human beings who live in cities, but do not really share the good and productive life of cities. Their deprivations exclude them.

It is within the power of governments to change that.

We in the Bank can help, and we propose to do so in the future on a scale far greater than that of the past.

Any serious effort in solving the problems of urban development will clearly involve a number of sensitive and difficult political choices. Those, of course, are for governments to make, not for the Bank. Moreover, the Bank's own lending can finance only a very small proportion of the necessary investments in productive facilities and supporting urban services.

The Bank, however, can play a significant role in pointing out the extent to which governments' present policies, practices, and investment allocations are seriously biased against the poor. And the Bank can expand and redirect its own investments in urban areas to insure that they result in increased earning opportunities and more adequate services for the poor in both the modern and traditional sectors. This will be a major objective of our five-year program for the years FY76-80.

In future years, I will report to you on our progress in helping to achieve the objective of assuring minimum standards of decency for the nearly two billion people who will be living in the cities of the developing world by the end of this century.

VI. SUMMARY AND CONCLUSIONS

Let me now summarize and conclude the central points I have made this morning.

If we survey the global development scene today, it is clear that most of our developing member countries are caught up in a critical situation. The consequences of the continuing world-wide inflation, the sudden surge in the cost of oil, the deterioration of their terms of trade, and the prolonged recession in their export markets have combined to endanger their economic future. The net effect of these external forces has been to reduce their prospective rates of economic growth, while increasing their foreign exchange requirements.

And it is the very poorest countries, countries that collectively contain a billion human beings, which face the bleakest prospects—the prospects of virtually no increase at all in their desperately low per capita incomes for the rest of the decade.

It is important to comprehend what this stagnation really means in the life of an average individual in a poor country. It does not mean inconvenience, or a minor sacrifice of comfort, or the simple postponement of a consumer satisfaction.

It means struggling to survive at the very margin of life itself.

Statistically, the stagnation means that for a billion people, per capita incomes, in constant prices, will grow from $105 in 1970 to $108 in 1980. The comparable figures for the peoples of the developed world are $3,100 in 1970 to $4,000 in 1980.

Over an entire decade, a $3 increase versus a $900 increase.

The 725 million human beings in the middle-income developing countries are also facing a far more difficult situation than we anticipated a year ago. Unless the foreign exchange available to them can be substantially increased, their per capita incomes too will inch forward at a wholly unacceptable pace.

Are those in the developed world going to conclude that they cannot find it within their collective capacity to make a modestly greater effort to help save several hundred million people from a degree of deprivation beyond the power of any set of statistics even remotely to convey?

I cannot believe so.

I cannot believe so because what is involved for the developed nations is not the diminution of their already towering standard of life. All that is required in order to assist these peoples so immensely less privileged is a simple willingness to dedicate a tiny percentage of the additional wealth that will accrue to the developed nations over the next five years.

As for the World Bank, we should at the minimum increase our lending programs not only fully to offset price inflation, but also to increase the flow of capital in real terms, particularly to our poorest member countries. And that is what we propose to do.

Preliminary negotiations for the next replenishment of the International Development Association should start within a few weeks. It is, of course, one of the principal multilateral means available to assist the poorest nations.

It is an instrument that has proved its value through hundreds of carefully designed projects that represent a realistic, tough-minded, unsentimental approach to development.

Whatever other debates there may have been throughout the development community, there never has been serious disagreement over either the principle or the record of the International Development Association.

But even with a generous IDA replenishment, and even with a realistic effort by the governments of the developed world, as well as by those of the capital-surplus OPEC countries, to appropriate sufficient funds for the other forms of Official Development Assistance—even after all this has been done—it is clear that these official flows of external capital, as well as increased private flows, will not be enough to ward off the crisis the developing countries are now confronting.

It is imperative that they generate additional capital both through greater domestic savings, and through expanded export earnings. Both will be difficult. For with such low per capita incomes, only arduous sacrifice can produce significantly greater savings. And though there is an impressive potential for greater export earnings, both the developing and developed countries will have to take major steps to accomplish it.

The current foreign exchange crisis, then, in the developing world—and particularly in the poorest countries—must command the attention of us all. It is an emergency situation. And it requires emergency measures.

But beyond this immediate emergency lies another more profound problem. And in our concern for immediate measures, we must not let our longer-range objective be obscured.

That objective is the central task of development itself: the reduction—and ultimately the elimination—of absolute poverty.

Poverty is a word that has largely lost its power to convey reality. At least that is true among most of those who have never known it in its most abject form.

But if we have not personally endured it—if most of the affluent world has never experienced it—there are 900 million individuals alive today, more than 40% of the total population of our developing member countries, who not only know it, but in their wretched circumstances are living examples of it.

Most of the absolute poor live in the rural areas. And two years ago, in Nairobi, we outlined a strategy—and launched a program within the Bank—designed to reduce that poverty. It is based on the fundamental proposition that the only feasible way to deal with poverty is to help the poor become more productive.

It is a task, of course, primarily for the governments of these countries. The Bank can only assist. But we have evolved a whole new series of multisectored projects to help those governments which are committed to the goals of rural development, and our early experience confirms our initial conviction: it is an approach that can succeed.

But poverty pervades not only the countryside, but the urban centers of the developing world as well. There, the numbers of the poor are smaller. But the natural increase within the cities, combined with the rapid rate of migration from the rural areas, guarantees that the problem will grow to mammoth proportions in the next two decades, if governments do not begin to take appropriate measures to deal with it.

I have tried to suggest today a number of those measures.

We in the Bank are resolved to help our member governments in every feasible way we can to come to grips with the problem.

In the end, cities exist as an expression of man's attempt to achieve his potential.

It is poverty that pollutes that promise.

It is development's task to restore it.

Flow of Official Development Assistance from Development Assistance Committee Members Measured as a Percentage of Gross National Product[a]

	1960	1965	1970	1971	1972	1973	1974	1975	1976	1977	1978	1979	1980 Case I
Australia	.38	.53	.59	.53	.59	.44	.55	.55	.56	.57			
Austria		.11	.07	.07	.09	.15	.18	.16	.16	.16			
Belgium	.88	.60	.46	.50	.55	.51	.49	.55	.57	.59			
Canada	.19	.19	.42	.42	.47	.43	.50	.51	.56	.59			
Denmark	.09	.13	.38	.43	.45	.48	.54	.57	.61	.64			
Finland[b]		.02	.07	.12	.15	.16	.18	.20	.22	.23			
France	1.38	.76	.66	.66	.67	.58	.60	.60	.61	.61			
Germany	.31	.40	.32	.34	.31	.32	.37	.35	.33	.31			
Italy	.22	.10	.16	.18	.09	.14	.14	.14	.14	.13			
Japan	.24	.27	.23	.23	.21	.25	.25	.23	.22	.21			
Netherlands	.31	.36	.61	.58	.67	.54	.62	.72	.76	.76			
New Zealand[c]			.23	.23	.25	.27	.30	.36	.41	.47			
Norway	.11	.16	.32	.33	.43	.42	.57	.61	.65	.69			
Sweden	.05	.19	.38	.44	.48	.56	.72	.75	.78	.81			
Switzerland	.04	.09	.15	.12	.21	.16	.14	.15	.15	.15			
United Kingdom	.56	.47	.37	.41	.39	.34	.38	.33	.30	.30			
United States[d]	.53	.49	.31	.32	.29	.23	.25	.23	.20	.17			
GRAND TOTALS													
—ODA ($b-Nominal Prices)	4.6	5.9	6.8	7.7	8.5	9.4	11.3	12.2	13.5	15.0	16.6	18.6	20.7
—ODA ($b-Constant 1975 Prices)	10.3	12.3	12.6	13.2	13.4	11.5	12.7	12.2	12.3	12.6	12.9	13.4	14.0
—GNP ($t-Nominal Prices)	.9	1.3	2.0	2.2	2.6	3.1	3.4	3.8	4.4	5.0	5.7	6.4	7.3
—ODA as % GNP	.52	.44	.34	.35	.33	.30	.33	.32	.31	.30	.29	.29	.28
—ODA Deflator[e]	.45	.48	.54	.58	.64	.81	.89	1.00	1.10	1.19	1.29	1.38	1.48

[a]Figures for 1974 and earlier years are based on actual data. The projections for 1975-80 are based on OECD and World Bank estimates of growth of GNP, on information on budget appropriations for aid, and on aid policy statements made by governments. Because of the relatively long period of time required to translate legislative authorizations into commitments and later into disbursements, it is possible to project today, with reasonable accuracy, ODA flows (which by definition represent disbursements) by country through 1977 and in total through 1980.

[b]Finland became a member of DAC in January 1975.

[c]New Zealand became a member of DAC in 1973. ODA figures for New Zealand are not available for 1960 and 1965.

[d]In 1949, at the beginning of the Marshall Plan, U.S. Official Development Assistance amounted to 2.79% of GNP.

[e]Includes the effect of parity changes. Figures through 1973 are based on DAC figures (*Statistics for 1973 and Earlier Years*). Projected deflators for 1974-80 are the same as those for GNP.

FIFTEEN

To the
BOARD OF GOVERNORS
MANILA, PHILIPPINES
OCTOBER 4, 1976

I. INTRODUCTION

We meet this year against the background of a growing recognition that equality of opportunity among men, both within nations and between nations, is becoming a critical issue of our time.

The search for greater social justice, and a more equitable economic environment, is evident at both national and international levels.

At the national level it is leading to serious reexamination of earlier growth strategies. It is causing governments to focus more directly on the massive problems of the absolute poor—the hundreds of millions of individuals whose basic human needs go unmet. It is stimulating a search for new development techniques that can combine substantial economic growth with greater equity in income distribution.

At the international level, it is focusing on the immense income disparities between the developed and developing nations, and it is directing attention to the desperate plight of the very poorest countries.

In our meetings in this forum over the past three years, I have discussed the nature and extent of absolute poverty; the maldistribution of income in developing societies; and the immense disparity in wealth between the developing and the industrialized nations. Within the Bank, we have intensified our study of these problems and the weight of the evidence is that they are continuing to worsen rather than improve.

It is, then, these critical issues—issues that are growing more and more insistent—that I want to explore with you further this morning. In particular, I want to answer the question: how can the World Bank respond most effectively to them?

To develop the answer, I shall:

• Review the trend of income growth in the developed and developing countries during the past decade, and project

337

its probable course over the next—distinguishing between the problems of the poorest nations, and of the so-called "middle-income" developing countries.

• Consider in the case of the poorest nations the fundamental reforms required if they are to make even minimal progress against the intolerable conditions of absolute poverty—reforms both in their own internal development policies, and in the international community's development assistance.

• Examine the prospects of the middle-income developing countries, and the internal and external changes that must be made if they are to achieve their growth potential, and moderate the distortion in their income-distribution patterns.

• Point out the contradiction which would result if the operations of the World Bank Group were to be restricted in the face of the demonstrable need of the developing countries for additional external assistance, and the stated intentions of the developed countries—as expressed in the Special Session of the General Assembly, the UNCTAD Meeting in Nairobi, and the North-South Dialogue in Paris—to help provide that assistance.

• And finally, outline the action that will make it possible for the World Bank to contribute to meeting that objective.

These are the issues that all of us must face and deal with if we are to respond to the development task that lies before us.

Let us begin by examining income trends.

II. THE TREND OF INCOME GROWTH IN
DEVELOPED AND DEVELOPING NATIONS

In the decade, 1965-75, the disparity in average incomes between those fortunate enough to live in the developed world and those who, by accident of birth, live elsewhere, remained immense.

Income Disparities Between Nations[a]
(in constant 1975 US$)

	Population (in millions)	Income Per Capita[b]		
		1965	1975	1985[c]
1. Poorest Nations (Below $200 Per Capita)	1,200	130	150	180
2. Middle-Income Developing Countries (Above $200 Per Capita)	900	630	950	1,350
3. Developed Nations	700	4,200	5,500	8,100

Average incomes in the poorest nations, with populations totalling 1.2 billion, grew at an annual rate of only 1.5%—$2 per year—during the period. And for tens of millions of individuals in these countries at the lower end of the income spectrum their already substandard levels of nutrition, housing, health, and literacy deteriorated even further. These societies have been unable to meet even the minimum human needs of the vast majority of their people.

The middle-income[d] developing nations have done considerably better. As a group, they have achieved an overall growth rate for the decade of 6.8%—about 4% in per capita terms. As compared with the poorest nations, they have been able to take advantage of their more favorable endowment in resources, of better market opportunities, and of increased capital flows. Combined with their own vigorous efforts, these factors have made it possible for them to make some progress in reducing malnutrition and unemployment, and in expanding literacy and life expectancy.

[a]Data for centrally planned economies are not published and, therefore, are excluded from the table.

[b]Because the per capita income data in the table are based on official exchange rates rather than purchasing power comparisons, which are unavailable, they represent only broad orders of magnitude.

[c]Long-term projections of economic growth are, of course, highly speculative. They are presented here not as predictions, but only to call attention to problems that may develop if action is not initiated in time to prevent them.

[d]The term "middle-income" can be seriously misleading as applied to these countries. It vaguely suggests "middle-class" as if they were somehow semi-affluent societies enjoying a broad level of prosperity. But that is a dangerous simplification. By any realistic comparison with the developed nations, these countries must contend with serious problems of poverty.

Finally, there is the performance of the developed nations over the decade. It can be summed up very succinctly: whatever their other domestic and international difficulties may have been, the peoples of the developed nations enjoyed per capita incomes, in real terms, over the ten-year period that rose in absolute amounts more than in any comparable period in history.

The Prospects for the Next Decade

What is likely to happen to income trends over the next ten years?

For the poorest countries, the outlook is bleak: a projected per capita growth rate of at best 2% per year. And for tens of millions of human beings that means at most an advance in income of one or two dollars a year. Even if by an extraordinary effort per capita growth rates could be expanded beyond 2%—and that itself is doubtful—it might well mean little or no real alleviation of absolute poverty. Growth in the gross national product, as essential as it is, cannot benefit the poor unless it reaches the poor.

It does not reach most of them now in any meaningful measure.

Could a development strategy be implemented that would reverse that?

It could.

But that would require extensive policy changes within these governments, supported by a comparable effort on the part of the developed nations.

The outlook for the middle-income developing countries is much more favorable. But, penalized by recent declines in their terms of trade and by the worldwide recession, they will not be able to recover their per capita income growth rates of the past decade unless a number of major actions are undertaken.

The governments of these countries must themselves take steps to increase internal savings, expand export earnings, and reduce the severe inequities in income distribution. And the international community must find a feasible way of providing them with additional flows of capital on appropriate terms, and reducing the barriers to their exports, particularly their manufactured goods.

I want to examine these matters now in greater detail. Let us begin with the critical situation in the poorest developing countries.

III. THE PLIGHT OF THE POOREST NATIONS

The past decade for most of the people in the poorest nations has been one of almost unrelieved deprivation. And the future offers little promise of improvement unless substantial shifts in policy are undertaken by both the governments of these nations and the international community itself.

We must try to comprehend what we in fact mean when we speak of poverty in this context. The word itself has become almost incapable of communicating the harshness of the reality. Poverty at the absolute level—which is what literally hundreds of millions of men, women, and most particularly children are suffering from in these countries—is life at the very margin of physical existence.

The absolute poor are severely deprived human beings struggling to survive in a set of squalid and degraded circumstances almost beyond the power of our sophisticated imaginations and privileged circumstances to conceive.

The table below compares conditions of life in the poorest nations and in the developed countries.

	Population (in millions)		Infant Mortality (per 1000)	Life Expectancy (years)	Malnourished (in millions)	Adult Illiteracy
	Total	Absolute Poor				
Poorest Nations	1,200	750	128	50	600	62%
Developed Countries	700	<20	16	72	<20	1%

Compared to those fortunate enough to live in the developed countries, individuals in the poorest nations have:

- An infant mortality rate eight times higher;

- A life expectancy one-third lower;

- An adult literacy rate 60% less;

- A nutritional level, for one out of every two in the population, below minimum acceptable standards; and for millions of infants, less protein than is sufficient to permit optimum development of the brain.

This is what absolute poverty means for some 750 million human beings in these nations. With an average per capita income of less than $100 today, and little more than a faint promise of a miniscule $2 annual increase over the next decade, they are locked into a set of circumstances that they cannot break out of by themselves.

It is not a scene that any one of us here—so favored, so fortunate, so surrounded in our personal lives by privilege and advantage—can contemplate without compassion and resolve.

The blunt truth is that absolute poverty today is a function of neglect—and of our neglect as much as of anyone's. For we here in this hall represent the governments, and the financial resources, and the international institutions best suited to end the curse of absolute poverty in this century.

Poverty tends to perpetuate itself, and unless a deliberate intervention is designed and launched against its internal dynamics, it will persist and grow.

The responsibility for such an effort lies first, of course, with the governments of the poorest countries themselves. Despite the fact that in the past decade they have financed almost 90% of their development investments out of their own meager incomes—a fact not often recognized in the developed world—they must make an even greater effort in the future. They have, after all, invested less than $5 billion annually in agriculture (only 3% of their GNP and only 18% of their total investment program), less than $100 million in population planning, and wholly inadequate amounts in essential public services. And much of what they have spent has benefited only a privileged few.

Yet whatever the degree of neglect the governments in the poorest countries may have been responsible for, it has been more than matched by the failure of the international community to assist them in the development task.

In recent years the poorest nations have received:

- Only 6% of the total capital raised by all developing countries through long-term bonds;

- Only 10% of the total borrowing by all developing countries in the Eurocurrency market;

- Only 45% of the total concessional aid to all developing countries. As a result, the countries of South Asia, for example, received only one-third as much concessional assistance on a per capita basis as all other developing countries.

These instances could be multiplied.

But the central issue is that the plight of the poorest nations can be remedied only by deliberate decisive action, and that action must be taken at both the national and international levels. We must all accept two fundamental points.

The first is that the governments of the poorest nations have to redirect their own efforts to accelerate economic growth and reduce absolute poverty. A reasonable objective for them would be to meet the basic human needs of all of their peoples by the end of the century. They must begin by changing national investment priorities and by putting greater emphasis on assisting the poor to become more productive.

This will involve:

- Intensifying the effort to expand domestic food production;

- Taking more determined action to moderate population growth[a];

- And directing social services more equitably towards the poor.

---

[a]This problem is, of course, of particular urgency, and rather than attempt to deal with it today, I plan to devote a major address to the subject soon.

The second fundamental point is that although nothing can be accomplished unless these governments themselves act, they clearly cannot meet such an objective without outside assistance. Therefore, the international community must help them, help them generously.

There are four principal ways the industrialized nations can make this help available:

- By additional transfers of concessional assistance;
- By reallocation of some of their existing assistance;
- By easing the burden of present and potential debt; and
- By expanding the opportunities of the poorest countries to earn more foreign exchange through exports.

Let us examine each one of these measures in turn.

The Official Development Assistance Target

The external assistance needed by the poorest nations over the past few years to achieve reasonable rates of economic growth, and to move towards meeting the basic human needs of their people, has been within the ability of the wealthy world to supply. And it would have been made available had the developed nations met the target, agreed on in the United Nations in 1970, of contributing 0.7% of their GNP to Official Development Assistance (ODA)—and had 0.2% out of this been earmarked for programs benefiting primarily the absolute poor.

But the target has not been met. Nor is there any present indication that it ever will be met.

In 1975 the flows of concessional assistance from 17 Development Assistance Committee (DAC) nations amounted to only 0.36% of their total gross national product, one-half of the target. There was a wide variation, however, within this group of nations: nine countries provided more than 0.5% of their GNP as ODA; two provided less than 0.5%, but more than 0.3%; and the remaining six were below 0.3%.

This is clearly an unsatisfactory situation, and if the current trends are not reversed, ODA levels, as shown in the table below, are projected to fall to 0.33% by 1980.

Achievement of ODA Targets by OECD Countries
(in billions of constant 1975 US$)

OECD Country Groups[a]	Share in Total DAC GNP	1975 (estimated) ODA	1975 (estimated) % of GNP	1980 (projected) ODA	1980 (projected) % of GNP
I	22.8	5.5	0.64	7.5	0.70
II	17.1	2.6	0.39	2.5	0.31
III	60.1	5.5	0.24	5.9	0.20
Total	100.0	13.6[b]	0.36	15.9	0.33

But ways could be found even now to avoid such a wholly unsatisfactory outcome in 1980. If, for example, the countries that are currently lagging so far behind would agree to increase their flows of concessional assistance by adding to them over the next five years merely a small fraction—no more than 2 to 3%—of the amounts by which their per capita incomes will rise each year, the ODA totals by 1980 would be dramatically larger than shown in the table.

I believe it is time that the industrial nations themselves sat down and candidly reviewed their own record. And I believe they can and ought to come to some firm decisions as to what long-term commitments they are able and willing to make to the poorest nations—to nations whose own development efforts and plans depend so much on a more reasonable resolution of the current aid situation.

[a]Group I: Sweden, Netherlands, Norway, Australia, France, Belgium, Denmark, Canada, and New Zealand.
Group II: Germany, and United Kingdom.
Group III: United States, Japan, Finland, Switzerland, Austria, and Italy.

[b]Since 1974 OPEC members have made available about $5 billion per year in loans to other developing countries, of which approximately one-half could be classified as ODA.

Reallocation of Existing Assistance

It will not be enough simply to increase the level of ODA. Its allocation must be improved as well. ODA should be increasingly directed to the poorest nations and, within them, to programs benefitting the poorest segments of their population. The penalty to the middle-income countries of such an adjustment should be offset by broader trade concessions and greater flows of private capital.

Currently the middle-income countries receive over half the total ODA. In fact, the distribution of concessional assistance on a per capita basis is some 60% higher in middle-income countries than in the poorest nations. If, for example, existing ODA were at least distributed equally between the poorest and middle-income countries on a per capita basis, it would mean an additional $1.5 billion each year for the poorest nations. This could have a very significant impact on the growth of their per capita incomes.

The International Development Association (IDA) is, of course, one of the principal instruments for channeling concessional resources to the poorest nations, and for insuring that these resources are allocated to productive projects benefiting the poorest segments of their societies. In recent years we have pursued a deliberate policy of increasing the share of the poorest nations in the allocation of IDA resources. In FY75 and FY76 these nations received 91% of all IDA commitments. Moreover, IDA resources are increasingly being directed to rural development projects, where they reach large numbers of the absolute poor.

I will return to this point later, when I discuss the replenishment of IDA's resources.

Growing Debt Burden

The dependence of the poorest nations on public as opposed to private sources of external finance is reflected in the table below. In 1975, public sources provided over 80% of the capital flow to these nations, and held over 80% of their outstanding debt.

Debt Status of the Poorest Nations[a]
(in billions of current US$)

	1973	1975	1980
Current Account Deficit before Interest Payments	2.9	7.2	7.1
Interest Payments	.5	.7	1.4
Changes in Reserves and Short-Term Debt	.2	−.7	.7
Total Remaining to be Financed	3.6	7.2	9.2
Financed by Medium- and Long-Term Capital from:			
Public Sources	3.4	6.0	8.6
Private Sources[b]	.2	1.2	.7
Total Net Capital Flows—Current $	3.6	7.2	9.3
—1975 $	5.1	7.2	6.4
Outstanding Medium- and Long-Term Debt			
—Public Sources	18.6	23.6	41.7
—Private Sources	3.1	4.8	7.2
Total—Current $	21.7	28.5	48.9
—1975 $	30.6	28.5	34.2
Debt Service:			
Interest Payments	.5	.7	1.4
Debt Amortization	.9	.9	2.1
Interest Payments as % of GNP	.4	.3	.4
Debt Service as % of Exports	12.7	11.5	12.2
Price Deflator	71	100	143

The table shows that the outstanding debt and the debt service of the poorest nations has risen since 1973, and is likely to rise still further between 1975 and 1980. However, the increases are not large when adjusted for inflation, and they appear still smaller when account is taken of the growth in exports during the same years. Even in 1980, the debt service burden of these nations, in relation to their exports, is likely to be about the same as in 1973.

The real difficulty that the poorest nations face is not the burden of the debt itself, but rather the very low level of capital

[a]Excludes oil exporters.
[b]Includes "Direct Foreign Investment."

flows—a level so low as to seriously limit their economic growth. Their growth was restricted by inadequate capital flows in 1973, and it is being similarly restricted today. Moreover, as the table indicates, these capital flows are likely to remain at a very low level in 1980.

The debt problem of the poorest nations is a long-term one which cannot be solved merely by short-term rescheduling and by further relaxation of already liberal terms. The critical issue here is the need for a substantial real increase in the net flow of capital to the poorest nations, from public sources, beyond the levels which now appear likely.

Some developed countries could contribute to such an increase by enlarging their gross flows and by making future assistance available on grant or grant-like terms. Other countries have more flexibility and could move more directly towards various forms of debt relief. In either case, the principal objective should be a substantial real increase in net capital flows to the poorest nations over the next decade.

Expansion of Exports and Reduction of Imports

Finally, the poorest nations—which have suffered far more than any other group of countries from the deterioration of their terms of trade over the past decade—must move closer to the long-run goal of standing on their own feet by earning, and saving, more foreign exchange. This will require a number of actions on their part, as well as the help of the developed countries. For example:

- Economic policies and governmental procedures should be reshaped to stimulate exports. Such action would result in several billion dollars of additional foreign exchange earnings each year in the poorest countries. This is particularly true of those in South Asia, which have had a declining share in the world's exports of both commodities and manufactured goods in the last ten years.

- An accelerated effort should be made by the industrialized nations to reduce the stiff tariff and nontariff barriers that continue to discriminate against a number of the exports of the poorest nations. If these could be substantially eliminated over the next decade, it would mean, in 1975 dollars, an additional $3 to $4 billion of export earnings annually by 1985.

• The poorest nations must do more to diversify their exports. Some of them rely heavily on earnings from a few weak commodities such as jute, tea, and sisal, which face a very uncertain future in the world market. And yet there are about 15 million families—90 million people—totally dependent on these three crops for their livelihood. These nations need to restructure their patterns of production in order to reduce excessive dependence on weak commodities. They will need financing to help them to initiate such structural adjustments, and to create new sources of employment for the individuals linked to them.

• The poorest nations must reduce their reliance on agricultural imports, particularly foodgrains. By increasing their food production, and by limiting their imports to the present level, they could save $4 billion per year in foreign exchange.

*   *   *   *

These, then, are the key elements in a program to accelerate economic growth and reduce absolute poverty in the poorest nations.

Is there a comparable approach to the problems in the middle-income countries?

Let me turn to that issue now.

IV. PROSPECTS AND PROBLEMS OF THE MIDDLE-INCOME DEVELOPING COUNTRIES[a]

As I have pointed out, the average annual growth rate achieved by the middle-income developing countries exceeded 6.5% over

---

[a] It is obviously a gross oversimplification to consider the approximately 80 countries as one homogeneous group. They are not. Yet despite great differences among themselves, the middle-income developing countries taken as a whole are sufficiently distinct from the poorest developing nations to warrant discussing them as a separate category.

the last decade. In fact, 20 of the fastest developing countries, with 45% of the population of the middle-income group, experienced an average real growth of 8.8% per annum. Their 390 million citizens enjoy by now an average per capita income 75% higher than ten years ago. On the whole, it is fair to say that the middle-income developing countries have begun to establish a promising structure for high economic growth rates.

Given sound economic management at home, and reasonable support by the developed countries, these countries should be able to continue to strengthen their economies. They face, however, two serious problems.

The momentum of the growth of the oil-importing countries has been sharply interrupted since 1973. On a per capita basis, it fell to 1.5% last year as a direct consequence of the recession in their export markets, the increase in their energy costs, the deterioration in their terms of trade, and the persistent worldwide inflation.

Equally disturbing is the fact that in many of these countries there has been a serious neglect of equity in the distribution of employment opportunities, and in the allocation of public services that affect productivity. The inevitable result has been a severely skewed pattern of income distribution.

In some cases this may in part be due to a transitory stage of economic growth. But on the whole, the middle-income developing countries have greater distortions in their income distribution patterns than any growth theory could possibly justify. They have increased their gross national products over the decade, but the benefits of this growth have accrued disproportionately to the already more favored upper-income groups in their societies, and broadened rather than narrowed the gap between the privileged and the deprived.

This has led in a number of these nations to serious economic, social, and political turmoil. It could lead to a great deal more. These countries must devise institutional and policy frameworks within which the benefits of growth can reach the poor and disadvantaged much more equitably than in the past.

Though these countries do enjoy some distinct advantages over the very poorest nations, the fact remains that collectively they, too, contain large numbers of individuals—some 170 million—trapped in absolute poverty.

**Absolute Poor in the Rural and Urban Areas
of Middle-Income Countries**
(1975: in millions)

Region	Absolute Poor			Absolute Poor as % of Population		
	Rural	Urban	Total	Rural	Urban	Total
Middle East and North Africa	10	30	40	25	27	27
Sub-Saharan Africa	32	8	40	29	27	29
East Asia	25	10	35	25	17	22
Latin America	20	35	55	18	18	18
	87	83	170	24	21	23

There are hundreds of millions more in what I have termed "relative poverty"; that is, persons with incomes somewhat above the absolute poverty level, but less than one-third of the national average. These individuals may feel even more frustrated than those in the poorest nations, since they live in an environment of visible economic growth. Their societies are progressing rapidly, but they are not.

A critical prerequisite, then, for continued and stable economic growth in these countries is the formation of an institutional and policy framework that will assure more equitable growth of income for all segments of the society.

But even assuming that effective action is taken by the governments of the middle-income developing countries to moderate these severe income inequities, there are at least three other requirements that must be met to assure long-term sustained growth. The first of these calls for action by the countries themselves, and the other two by both the international community and the countries working together:

- The governments of the middle-income developing nations must place even greater emphasis than in the past on mobilizing internal resources for development;

- The deterioration of the external debt profile must be arrested by more effective debt management, and by longer-term capital assistance;

- And export trade must be expanded.

The Restoration of Economic Growth

To recapture the momentum of growth, there must be a more intensified effort to mobilize internal resources. Over the past decade, investment in the middle-income countries averaged over 20% of their GDP. And nearly 90% of these investments were financed from their own domestic savings. External resource flows, while crucial in supplying the scarce foreign exchange and technical assistance, constituted only 2% of their GDP during the period.

But in the future there must be even greater emphasis on mobilizing and effectively utilizing savings. A prudent limit on the growth of overall consumption is required. And to avoid the anomaly of underutilized capital in a capital-scarce economy, governments will have to devise the kind of price and incentive systems that insure full benefit out of the investments made with such sacrifice. They will need to reassess their exchange rates, interest levels, relative prices, tariff structures, and the associated policies in their economies.

Most of the middle-income countries have demonstrated that they possess the management skill necessary to deal with the purely technical problems of growth. What remains far more uncertain today is the international environment in which they are struggling to recapture their growth momentum. In particular, their debt situation and the continuing protectionist sentiment of the industrialized nations tend to constrain their future prospects.

Debt Management and External Resource Flows

If the middle-income countries do act to restrain the growth of their domestic consumption, and to strengthen internal resource mobilization, they will still confront the problem of a large external debt which is rising rapidly, as is shown in the table below.

Debt Status of the Middle-Income Developing Countries[a]
(in billions of current US$)

	1973	1975	1980
Current Account Deficit before Interest Payments	3.5	26.1	16.4
Interest Payments	2.7	5.2	12.5
Changes in Reserves and Short-Term Debt	7.5	−3.1	1.4
Total Remaining to be Financed	13.7	28.2	30.3
Financed by Medium- and Long-Term Capital from:			
Public Sources	5.2	8.6	10.9
Private Sources[b]	8.5	19.6	19.4
Total Net Capital Flows—Current $	13.7	28.2	30.3
—1975 $	19.3	28.2	21.2
Outstanding Medium- and Long-Term Debt:			
Public Sources	24.5	32.5	64.3
Private Sources	31.1	55.8	113.9
Total—Current $	55.6	88.4	178.2
—1975 $	78.3	88.4	124.6
Debt Service:			
Interest Payments	2.7	5.2	12.5
Debt Amortization	6.2	6.1	22.0
Interest Payments as % of GNP[c]	.6	.8	1.1
Debt Service as % of Exports[c]	18.0	17.0	25.0
Price Deflator	71	100	143

Events of the past three years—persistent inflation, deterioration in the terms of trade, and prolonged recession in the industrialized countries—have, in effect, swept away the progress they had made in reducing their dependence on external capital. All of these conditions have coalesced to increase their current account deficits from $6 billion in 1973 to $31 billion in 1975.

How was this increase of $25 billion financed? Only $3.4 billion came from government loans. A further $10.6 billion came

[a]Excludes oil exporters.

[b]Includes "Direct Foreign Investment."

[c]Based on a sample of 25 countries that account for over 80% of the external debt of the oil-importing middle-income nations.

from shifts in transactions affecting reserves. But the most re-markable element has been the unprecedented growth of private capital flows, which provided the other $11 billion.

Not only is this a large absolute sum, but it represents an increase that few would have thought possible. In 1975, the total net flow of private capital to the middle-income countries is estimated at almost $20 billion, nearly two-and-a-half times the estimated private flows of $8.5 billion in 1973, and more than twice the flows from public sources in 1975.

Most of the increase of private net capital flows has come through the commercial banks of the developed world. They provided a surprisingly large volume of resources, which enabled a number of middle-income countries to continue their economic advance in the face of adverse external conditions. If this flow continues it will help to maintain and even accelerate the pace of development. However, the increased role of the banks in financing the progress of the middle-income countries has created some problems of its own.

The most difficult one is the relatively short-term nature of this commercial lending. The present terms are on average far too short, not only because they discourage the use of such funds for longer-range productive investment, but also because, in the aggregate, these terms exacerbate the debt-service problem of these countries, and erode the creditworthiness which many of them have established over the past decade.

This deterioration in the debt structure of the middle-income countries is contributing to a rapid rise in the debt-service ratio. For 25 of the major borrowers, it is expected to increase from 17% in 1975 to 25% in 1980.

A major cause of the high debt-service ratio is the speed at which the short-term debts need to be rolled over. The interest-rate burden, despite a sharp increase from 1973 to 1980, still remains manageable. But the debt-amortization problem will become increasingly serious. Although in 1975 amortization amounted to only $6 billion, in nominal terms the same as in 1973, by 1980 it will rise to $22 billion.

The dilemma of the middle-income countries can, then, be simply stated. The sharp increase in their current account deficits has not been rolled back. Deficits at high levels are likely to continue for at least the next five to ten years if these countries are to generate the GNP growth rates of 6 to 7%, which are the very foundation for their creditworthiness. But continued heavy reliance on private sources for the financing of such deficits will require very large increases in the outstanding loans held by commercial banks and other financial institutions.[a]

To the extent that a large proportion of such debt is short-term, any temporary foreign-exchange liquidity problem—or even the prospect of one—can too easily be turned into a crisis, or the appearance of one.

This situation calls for a series of actions by national governments, the international commercial banking community, and the international financial institutions.

First, the governments of the middle-income developing countries themselves must recognize the new situation that has arisen. They must increase the current reduced level of savings; adjust relative prices so as to provide adequate incentive to expand both exports and food production; and closely monitor, and where necessary limit, additional external debt.

Second, the international banking community must accept the long-term nature of the financing problems of the developing countries. The most important question facing the lenders is what to do when most of the recent medium-term loans fall due during the next three to five years. This will occur at a time when there is likely to be stronger competing demand for credit from the industrialized nations, the centrally planned economies, and several of the oil-exporting countries.

It would be extremely unfortunate if all the good work that has been accomplished in expanding private flows for develop-

---

[a] If the private lenders are to increase their assistance to developing countries, they need better information. The World Bank itself could help meet that need. We compile and publish debt statistics for our borrowing member countries and for the Eurobond and Eurocredit markets. But these data exclude much private lending and all short-term borrowings. If supported by the international banking community, the Central Banks, and the borrowers, we could go further and assist in the preparation and publication of comprehensive debt reports for each borrowing country.

ment in the recent past were to be undone. But can we really expect extraordinary efforts from the international commercial banking community if the official lenders themselves do not try to improve their own performance? That brings me to actions required by the third group I have mentioned—the international financial institutions.

There is no doubt in my mind—and I have discussed this matter with several bankers heavily involved in lending to middle-income countries—that the confidence of the commercial banking community would be substantially increased were it possible to restore the balance between private lending and official long-term lending to the developing nations. In the case of the middle-income countries, the principal sources of official long-term loans are, of course, institutions such as the World Bank and the Regional Banks. Their role is to serve as financial intermediaries between the world capital markets and these nations.

In view of this unique role, there is a manifest need today for a major expansion in both the capital structure, and lending level, in real terms, of the World Bank and the Regional Banks. I will deal with this issue in more detail a bit later.

Need for Trade Expansion

But larger capital flows, as vital as they are, are not the only ingredient needed in order to restore high GNP growth rates in the middle-income countries. In the long run, trade expansion is even more important.

And yet prospects for the needed expansion are far from encouraging.

A recent World Bank study concluded that the manufactured exports of the middle-income countries are likely to grow by only 10 to 11% a year over the next ten years, as compared to 18% in the decade ending in 1974.

This prospective rate of growth could be increased substantially if the developing countries would act to strengthen and broaden their export programs.

- Only three groups of goods—clothing, textiles, and electrical machinery—account for over 50% of the middle-income countries' manufactured exports to the developed nations. Given the obstacles to the expansion of the first two groups, efforts must be made to diversify into many other products as well.

- To take another example, just six developing countries account for two-thirds of all manufactured exports to the OECD nations. There is ample scope for other developing nations to participate in this trade and they should seek to do so.

The rate of growth of exports from the developing world would increase still more, of course, if the industrial nations were to liberalize access to their own markets. The present barriers to trade have been well documented, and there is no need to repeat them here. But I would emphasize that this is a field in which the interests of the developing countries and those of the consumers in the industrialized world are more complementary than competitive. Dismantling trade barriers, along with appropriate levels of adjustment assistance, will genuinely benefit both sides.

As a target, would it not be reasonable to expect that the remaining trade barriers imposed by the industrialized nations on the exports of the developing countries could be dismantled, or at least very substantially reduced, over the course of the next decade? If this were to be achieved, the potential benefits to the developing countries would exceed by far anything else that the international community could possibly do in the trade field.

Recent World Bank studies suggest that the elimination of tariff and nontariff barriers could increase export earnings of the developing countries by over $30 billion a year by 1985, in 1975 dollars.

Additional Exports Resulting from Elimination of Trade Barriers
($ billion, 1975 prices)

Country Group	Manufactures	Commodities	Total
Poorest Nations	3	1	4
Middle-Income Developing Countries	21	8	29
Total	24	9	33

Much of the support for the remaining protectionism in the developed world understandably springs from the fears of those whose jobs and investments might be displaced. But a ten-year period for the dismantling of trade barriers would allow adequate time for the necessary advance planning and phased adjustments. And unless some such specific timetable is adopted, the political pressures of special-interest groups in affluent nations will prevail over the interests of the majority of ordinary citizens in the rich and poor countries alike.

V. THE NEED FOR A BASIC UNDERSTANDING

Let me now underline one of the major points I have made regarding the prospects of the two groups of developing countries.

Although the formula for economic advance in the middle-income countries differs from that applicable to the poorest nations, the action required is similar in one important respect: both groups of nations need additional support from the developed world if they are to achieve acceptable rates of growth.

It is the recognition of this fact which led to the Special Session of the General Assembly last September in New York; to the formation of the Development Committee composed of Governors of the IMF and the World Bank; to the recent meeting of UNCTAD in Nairobi; and to the North-South Dialogue in Paris. And yet, to date, after more than a year of intense debate, there has been no agreement on the level of additional assistance to be provided to the developing nations.

The reason for the lack of agreement is, I think, obvious: the discussions have focused far too much on details—commodity agreements, buffer stocks, and so forth—rather than on fundamentals.

What is needed, in my view, is a basic understanding among the parties as to:

- The nature and magnitude of the problem;
- The action required to address it;

- The relative responsibilities of the parties for taking such action;

- The costs and benefits to each of doing so.

Such an understanding—a "global compact" if you will— would make clear in overall terms both the additional trade and aid support to be provided by the developed nations and the policy reforms and structural changes to be undertaken by the developing nations. These should have as one of their major objectives the meeting of the basic human needs of the absolute poor in both the poorest and the middle-income countries within a reasonable period of time, say by the end of the century.

Once the broad limits of such an understanding have been established, then the specific form of assistance to be provided by individual developed nations to particular developing countries could be examined. It would then become apparent that it is relatively unimportant whether the assistance is to take the form of commodity agreements, debt relief, trade concessions, bilateral aid, or multilateral financing—or any particular combination of these—provided the overall total is adequate.

Whatever specific form the package of assistance takes, it clearly will need to include additional capital transfers through existing international intermediaries. And it is to that subject that I now want to turn.

VI. THE ROLE OF THE WORLD BANK

I want to consider three fundamental questions:

- First, what the World Bank can and should accomplish in the poorest and the middle-income developing countries in the next several years;

- Second, what problems must be dealt with if the Bank is to carry out that role in these countries;

- And, finally, what actions need to be taken by the Governors to permit these problems to be solved in a timely fashion.

As I have pointed out, the two categories of developing countries each require external assistance, but on different terms. The poorest countries must have increased flows of concessional assistance if they are to attain even minimally acceptable rates of economic growth, and make headway in their efforts to enhance the productivity and income levels of the absolute poor. This is clearly IDA's role. Without an innovative and expanding IDA program, it is virtually inconceivable that the needs of these countries will be met.

The prospects for the middle-income developing countries are brighter, and the range of possible assistance more varied. For many of these countries, in addition to improved trading opportunities, increased flows of long-term capital are particularly important. The IBRD and the Regional Banks can do much to help meet that requirement. The very raison d'être of these institutions is precisely to overcome the reluctance of private capital to invest directly in the long-term debt securities of developing countries.

The uncalled capital subscriptions of these institutions constitute a form of multilateral guarantee, which has proven its acceptability in the market place. They have demonstrated a capacity to mobilize very substantial sums of private capital for development financing, and they have done so without impairing the access of those individual developing countries considered creditworthy by the market.

Moreover, the World Bank, as well as the Regional Banks, provides a great deal more than a simple transfer of resources. Its loans and credits help finance high priority projects essential to development, but for which commercial finance is not normally available.

In particular, both the IBRD and IDA are emphasizing projects designed to raise the productivity of the poor in the developing nations. Before discussing the World Bank as a source of finance, I want to report briefly on the programs I have outlined to you previously that deal directly with these problems in both the rural and urban areas.

Rural Development: Plans and Progress

Three years ago at our meeting in Nairobi I pointed out a series of measures that would be necessary in order to raise the productivity of the rural poor. Within the framework of a comprehensive program we identified several specific goals for the World Bank itself.

I stated our intention to increase lending to agriculture by over 40% in real terms in the five-year period, FY74-78, as compared to the previous five years; and proposed to direct an increasing share of our total lending to programs which directly assist the small farmer to become more productive. Over the FY74-78 period, our target was that 70% of all our agricultural loans should contain a component for the smallholder.

Where do we now stand on implementing this program?

There is every reason to believe that the goal set at Nairobi will in fact be exceeded.

Total lending to agriculture, in constant dollars on an annual basis, was more than twice as high in the last three years, FY74-76, as in the previous five. Because of this very rapid growth, the share of agriculture in World Bank lending has risen from 15% in FY72 to nearly 30% in FY75 and FY76, a major shift in emphasis over the three-year period.

Within this expanding overall agricultural program, there has also been a substantial increase in the proportion of assistance designed expressly for improving the productivity and incomes of the rural poor. Whereas only 27% of agricultural operations —10 per year—were rural development projects in FY69-73, some 55% of the agricultural program in the last three years has focused on the rural poor, including 38 operations approved in FY76 alone.

In weighing the significance of these achievements it is important to consider what they mean in human terms. The operations approved in FY75 and FY76 are expected to benefit directly nearly 5.2 million farm families—or more than 30 million individuals.

Within the five years, FY74-78, we expect to finance projects which have as their objective substantially increasing the incomes—generally by as much as 100%—of 100 million of the poorest people in the developing countries.

Further, the data available for 60 Bank operations approved last year, or scheduled for approval this year, project an increase in rice and wheat production of over 5 million tons—an amount sufficient to meet the nutritional needs of some 25 million people.

Our efforts to assist the rural poor to become more productive are now fully launched, and I outlined to you last year our plans to initiate a comparable program for the cities.

Urban Poverty

The profile of urban poverty differs considerably from that of the rural areas, and there is no simple analog to the small subsistence farmer and his family. But the central strategy remains the same: to help the poor become more productive.

What we are doing is expanding and redirecting our investment in the urban areas in order to insure that it results in increased earning opportunities. I indicated that this would be a major objective of our FY76-80 program. This past year we have taken the first steps toward that objective by translating the agreed-upon goals into operational targets, against which progress can be monitored.

Our new lending targets involve both direct lending for identifiable urbanization projects, and the reorientation of previously programmed lending for industry, development finance companies, and water supply and sewerage projects. Close to 50 new urbanization projects are planned for the five-year period, FY76-80. These will include site and services projects, squatter settlement upgrading programs, small-scale enterprise financing, as well as projects to bring to the poor such productivity-related services as transportation, electricity, and basic education.

But as promising as the rural and urban programs are, the truth is that the Bank is facing serious resource constraints which will severely limit its ability not only to finance these projects, but other forms of economic assistance as well. I want to turn now to this issue, and in particular to the relationship between those constraints and the role the World Bank is to play over the next several years.

Level of World Bank Lending

In FY76, new financial commitments of the Bank Group totalled approximately $7 billion. As the table below indicates, in recent years the Bank Group has increased its lending very substantially.

	Average per Yr. 1964-68	Average per Yr. 1969-73	1974	1975	1976
Financial Commitments:					
Current $ (in billions)	1.2	2.7	4.5	6.1	6.9
Constant $ (FY76 Commitment $)	2.7	4.1	5.1	6.5	6.9
No. of IBRD and IDA Projects	56	129	174	190	214

The role of the World Bank in the international development effort, and the scale of its operations, are further illustrated by the fact that at the end of FY76 it was supervising the completion of over 1,000 projects in 94 developing countries—projects representing a total investment of $65 billion, of which the Bank itself is financing $27 billion.

Yet if steps are not taken—and taken promptly—to relieve the resource constraints facing the Bank, this record of growing assistance to the developing nations will come to an abrupt halt and one of the world's principal sources of development finance could find its scale of operations being steadily eroded in real terms.

Commitments planned for the current fiscal year, FY77, amount to $7.3 billion, including $5.8 billion for IBRD. This is an increase over FY76 of 6% in nominal terms, but virtually no change at all when allowance is made for inflation. Moreover, without additional increases in the capital of IBRD, there can be no increase in future years in annual IBRD commitments in current dollars above the $5.8 billion level. In real terms, therefore, IBRD commitments will actually decline, falling from $5.8 billion in 1977, to $5.5 billion in 1978, $5.0 billion in 1980, and to no more than $3.9 billion in 1985.

It might be argued that such a decline is only to be expected as countries come to rely more heavily on private finance. Yet, with the exception of a handful of nations such as Finland, Israel, Spain, and Greece, which either recently have, or soon will, "graduate" into the developed-member-country category, and can rely primarily upon the private capital markets, the 80 or 90 developing nations now dependent on the World Bank as a major source of external capital will continue to require that assistance for at least the next decade. Indeed, the majority of them will require it for two or three more decades. Clearly, then, we must take these resource constraints seriously, try to understand how they have arisen, and determine what can be done to relieve them.

Resource Constraints

The first constraint I want to examine is that affecting IBRD. As most of you know, there is a ceiling on total IBRD lending that is written into the basic Articles of Agreement. The ceiling requires that the total of loans outstanding at any one time not exceed subscribed capital and retained earnings. Currently the Bank's subscribed capital is about $31 billion, and its retained earnings about $2 billion, constituting a statutory limit of $33 billion.

It may be helpful to put the evolution of the Bank's subscribed capital into historical perspective. When the Bank was founded at Bretton Woods 30 years ago, it was provided a capital base of $10 billion.

The framers of the Articles of Agreement were well aware that if the Bank were successful, it would some day be necessary to expand this capital base. After a little more than a decade of operations that point was reached, and in 1958 the first general review of the Bank's capital structure took place. The outcome of this review was an agreement to double the Bank's capital to a level of $20 billion.

During the 1960s and early 1970s there were no further general reviews of the Bank's capital base, though there were periodic increases on a smaller scale. These minor increases were mainly designed to permit adjustment in the relative positions of individual countries in the Bank in parallel with similar changes negotiated in the IMF.

When the IBRD lending program for FY74-78 was first presented to the Executive Directors in late 1971, there was no men-tion of any requirement to increase the Bank's subscribed capital to permit implementation of that program—and for a good reason. The long-term projections indicated that the statutory ceiling on Bank operations would not be reached until about 1990.

What happened subsequently is a matter of record. The inflation assumptions which seemed reasonable just five years ago —2% per annum—turned out to bear little resemblance to the double-digit inflation that has actually taken place. It is this factor above all others that lies at the root of the IBRD capital problem and which explains why a constraint that once seemed so distant has now become critical to the Bank's role in the immediate future.

The first major revision in the FY74-78 program that took account of the new rates of inflation was presented to the Executive Directors in June 1974. The changes proposed then in the real level of IBRD lending were relatively small, but the changes in nominal commitments, because of the escalating inflation, were large. Whereas earlier IBRD commitments totalling $14 billion for the five-year period had been envisaged, the revised total was over $22 billion.

When allowance was made for the inflation rates expected after FY78, it became apparent that the restrictive effect of the statutory ceiling on Bank lending would be felt before the end of the 1970s. Recognizing the lead time required to negotiate and to obtain legislative approval for a capital increase for the Bank, we announced our intention then, in June 1974, to begin negotiations on the form, size, and timing of such an increase.

In the event, it required two full years to conclude the first step in the recapitalization of the Bank. In May of this year, the Executive Directors recommended to the Board of Governors a Selective Increase in IBRD capital amounting to $8.3 billion. This was a useful and necessary first step.

But the negotiations on the Selective Capital Increase sidestepped the issue of what growth objective would be appropriate for the Bank over the next several years. The Selective Increase was required to permit adjustment in the relative positions of individual countries in the Bank—in parallel with similar changes negotiated in the IMF—and to support continued lending at the modestly higher level planned for FY77, i.e., $5.8 billion. Debate on what positive rate of growth should be sought for future years was deferred. But it can be deferred no longer.

I believe that the discussions of the second step in the recapitalization of the IBRD ought to begin immediately, and ought to seek an early consensus on a desirable growth objective for the Bank over the next decade.

I recognize that support for any program calling for a real rate of growth will carry with it a number of implications that will require careful scrutiny. The associated borrowing requirements will need to be considered against the background of the prospective growth in the Bank's sources of borrowed funds. The staffing implications will have to be examined. And, of course, the capital structure of the Bank will have to be reviewed and the budgetary costs to member governments of supporting an adequate capital increase will have to be weighed. Such costs, it should be emphasized, would not be reflected in national budgets or in payments to the Bank until the mid-1980s.

I hope it will be possible to reach an early consensus in favor of an IBRD that is growing adequately in real terms and is committed to assisting governments in their efforts to improve the productivity of both the rural and urban poor. But I expect no decision, and am requesting no action, on this matter during this meeting. Beginning this fall, we shall present to the Executive Directors a series of papers addressed to the issues I have mentioned. It is then that the discussion of the role of the Bank over the next decade can begin in earnest.

My purpose in bringing these matters to your attention today is to provide—with respect to the World Bank at least—a sharper focus for the continuing debate on what the relations should be between the developed and developing nations. Moreover, a longer-term perspective is helpful in resolving another issue that is of more immediate concern; namely, how to avoid an interim and, in my opinion, most undesirable reduction in the real level of IBRD assistance to the developing countries during the period when the recapitalization of the Bank is being completed.

If we follow the path of least resistance, and merely maintain IBRD lending at its current level of $5800 million until formal agreement is reached on the Bank's recapitalization, I fear that the developing nations will have lost irretrievably several hundred million dollars of badly needed financial assistance, and this at a time of great financial stress for many of our borrowers.

In a period of persistent inflation, a lending program that is frozen in nominal terms inevitably means a steady erosion in real terms.

I do not believe a reduction in the real value of IBRD lending in the next two or three years is an objective desired by any of the Bank's member countries. If we allow it to happen, it will be by default, not by design. There are viable alternatives. Let me suggest, very briefly, three of them for your consideration.

- First, an increase in the level of Bank lending next year could be offset by a further tightening in the repayment terms of IBRD loans. A substantial hardening of repayment terms has already occurred in conjunction with the increase in Bank commitments to $5800 million in FY77. A further hardening is undesirable, but our borrowers would find this alternative preferable to a reduction in the real value of commitments.

- A second alternative would be to increase Bank commitments above the level that could be sustained indefinitely without a further capital increase. The adoption of this alternative would mean that if agreement on a further capital increase were not subsequently achieved, it would be necessary in later years to reduce Bank lending, even in nominal terms, below previous levels. However, so long as this cutback did not have to be so large as to seriously disrupt the work of the institution, it would be consistent with the understanding reached by the Executive Directors earlier this year; that is, the Bank operations and financial plans should not presume a capital increase until it has been approved in principle by member governments.

- A third alternative would be to structure the discussions of the Bank's recapitalization in a way which would permit an agreement by next June that the second step would be at least as large as that required to permit a reasonable real growth for the Bank in the next two or three years.

Under any of these three alternative approaches it would not be necessary to obtain legislative action to complete the recapitalization of the Bank until 1980, and payments would not need to begin until 1983. Nothing I have said is intended to suggest that these intervals should be compressed.

The consensus concerning the future role of the Bank must be based on full discussion of the issues involved. My concern, which I believe many of you share, is that in taking adequate time for these deliberations we should not accept an unintended and avoidable interim reduction in real IBRD assistance. There are practical alternatives. I commend them to your consideration, and urge that a decision among them be made in the very near future.

Replenishment of IDA

Let me move now to the other major constraint on our activities—the availability of IDA funds.

All of us are aware of the crucial importance of expanded concessional assistance to the poorest nations. It would be a tragic irony if in the very midst of the effort to strengthen economic relations between North and South, the international community were to falter in its support for IDA, a proven and effective institution that has become the largest single source of concessional assistance to the poorest of the poor.

Failure to support IDA will be interpreted—and not unreasonably—as a clear indication that the international community's concern for the poor is little more than empty rhetoric.

In my address to you last year, I pointed out that the new replenishment of IDA's resources should be established at a level sufficient both to offset fully the effects of inflation, and to provide an appropriate measure of real growth. I urged support both by the traditional donors, and by the capital-surplus oil-exporting countries, and emphasized that decisive action was required if we were to avoid procedural delays that in the end penalize not the Association, but the poorest countries that all of us are trying to help.

Now, a year later, I must report that progress has been painfully slow. Despite meetings of the Deputies of Finance Ministers in November 1975, and again in February and June of this year, there is as yet no final agreement on the amount of the Fifth Replenishment. Moreover, the burden-sharing arrangements have not yet been negotiated.

The only encouraging point in this otherwise bleak prospect is the forthright support IDA has received from a number of countries. Several governments have explicitly supported a replenishment level of $9 billion for the three-year period. Moreover, the government of Kuwait has indicated its willingness to accept a more than fourfold increase in its share of IDA financing up to a level of 2.5% of the total, provided that the traditional OECD donors make a contribution sufficiently large so that there is no question of Kuwaiti funds merely substituting for OECD efforts.

Many other countries have concluded that contributions of between $7.2 and $7.5 billion seem reasonable for the OECD countries. Contributions from the oil-exporting countries, and certain others, should then bring the total to between $8 and $9 billion. I am optimistic that a replenishment of this general magnitude can be successfully negotiated.

There is now, however, almost no chance that the negotiations will be completed in time to permit legislative ratification by June 1977. Yet IDA's commitment authority will be exhausted by that date. Indeed, mainly because of erosion in the U.S. dollar value of the contributions agreed upon at Nairobi three years ago, IDA's commitment authority in the current fiscal year will have to be substantially less even in nominal terms than the amount committed last year.

There is no practical action available to repair the reduction in IDA commitment authority this year. But we can and must act to prevent a complete hiatus in IDA operations beginning June 30, 1977.

The first step is for the Governors firmly to commit themselves to conclude the negotiations for the Fifth Replenishment of IDA no later than March 31 of next year. There is no reason why such a deadline cannot be met, given the requisite determination. Without an agreement by then, the task of arranging for bridging commitment authority after June 30 will be immeasurably more difficult. Hence, a firm commitment to complete these negotiations at least 90 days before that date is the first priority.

Given such a commitment, and assuming the negotiations can be successfully concluded, the problem then becomes one of permitting IDA operations to continue in the period prior to legislative ratification of the replenishment agreement.

In the past, IDA has managed to avoid major disruption to its operations through the generosity of donors who have been willing to make all or part of their contributions available to the Association in advance of formal ratification of the agreement. Some of these countries are understandably reluctant to see their voluntary acts of generosity become a standard practice to be invoked every three years. However, I hope that these countries will be reassured by recalling that when in the past they made advance contributions, the other donor countries did eventually come forward with matching commitments. And since the latecomers were then called upon to catch up with the earlier contributions, the actual financial sacrifice by the advance contributors was small.

In any event, the essential point is that the gap be bridged. I have asked that the subject of bridging arrangements be added to the agenda of the meeting of your Deputies scheduled for next week in Kyoto.

I hope and expect that with sufficient goodwill the contributing countries can find a way to deal with the risk that the agreement they reach in the spring will be modified subsequently in the course of obtaining legislative approval. I feel sure that none of the donors would wish to make the poorest countries the victims of this risk by allowing a gap in IDA's commitment authority to emerge.

VII. SUMMARY AND CONCLUSIONS

Let me now summarize and conclude the central points I have made this morning.

If we look about the world today realistically, it is evident that the desire for a greater degree of equity—for a more just and reasonable equality of opportunity among individuals, both within nations and between nations—is becoming a major concern of our time.

It is a trend that has been gathering momentum for a century or more. The rise of the labor union movement, the drive against racial discrimination, the expansion of civil rights, the enhancement of the status of women—these and similar movements have all had an ingredient in common: the surge towards greater social justice and more equitable economic opportunity.

This broad thrust is growing more insistent today in all nations. It is searching for new solutions to the intolerable problems of poverty.

The per capita incomes of the more than one billion human beings in the poorest countries have nearly stagnated over the past decade. In statistical terms they have risen only about two dollars a year: from $130 in 1965, to $150 in 1975.

But what is beyond the power of any set of statistics to illustrate is the inhuman degradation the vast majority of these individuals are condemned to because of poverty.

Malnutrition saps their energy, stunts their bodies, and shortens their lives. Illiteracy darkens their minds, and forecloses their futures. Simple, preventable diseases maim and kill their children. Squalor and ugliness pollute and poison their surroundings.

The miraculous gift of life itself, and all its intrinsic potential —so promising and rewarding for us—is eroded and reduced for them to a desperate effort to survive.

The self-perpetuating plight of the absolute poor simply cuts them off from whatever economic progress there may be in their own societies. They remain largely outside the entire development effort, neither able to contribute much to it, nor benefit fairly from it.

Unless specific efforts are made to bring them into the development process, no feasible degree of traditional welfare, or simple redistribution of already inadequate national income, can fundamentally alter the circumstances that impoverish them.

The governments of the poorest countries must, then, reorient their domestic policies so that they will both accelerate economic advance and begin to reach the poor with measures specifically designed to help them to become more productive.

All of this is feasible, but not without greater help from the international community. If poverty is to be reduced, then developed nations must squarely face the fact that current and projected levels of Official Development Assistance for the poorest countries are disgracefully inadequate. On the basis of present plans, not only is there no hope that the ODA target of 0.7% of GNP can be reached but there is a serious possibility that performance may erode even further.

The principal reason for this is that the strongest and wealthiest of the OECD nations—countries whose gross domestic product accounts for two-thirds of the entire combined GNP of the 17-nation Development Assistance Committee group—are substantially below the average of the others in their response to the target. And the contribution of these nations will decline even further unless they act deliberately to reverse their projected ODA trends.

The economies of these nations—already immensely productive—will become even more productive over the next few years. For them—or indeed for any of the other developed nations—increasing their help to the poorest countries would not require them to diminish in the slightest their own high standards of living, but only to devote a miniscule percentage of the additional per capita real income they will earn over the decade.

If the governments of the poorest countries do not take the internal measures they must, and if the developed nations do not help them with the development assistance they so seriously need, then the outlook for three out of every five of the 1.2 billion human beings who live in these disadvantaged countries is unspeakably grim.

The record of the middle-income developing countries over the past decade has been better, but their achievement has been marred by serious inequities in their income-distribution patterns.

Not only do the 170 million absolute poor in their societies suffer the same deprivations as those in the poorest countries, but hundreds of millions more subsist on income levels less than a third of the national average.

These extremes of inequality have contributed to severe political turmoil in a number of these countries, and could easily trigger further violence. Governments must recognize that if the growth rates of the past are to be resumed and sustained, their benefits must be more widely distributed.

As those measures are taken—and are buttressed by greater efforts to mobilize internal resources, expand employment, and broaden the range of exports—the industrial nations must find practical ways to assist by permitting more equitable access to their own markets, and by making available additional development capital on reasonable terms.

All of this, too, is feasible, given a sense of fairness and realism. The dialogue over these issues within the international community is intense, but is often confused and ineffectual because of the tendency to prolong debate over peripheral questions, rather than come to terms first with what is clearly fundamental.

And what is fundamental is that the developing nations must make a strong commitment to internal policy reforms; and the developed nations must, in their turn, make a comparable commitment to provide a more adequate amount of development assistance.

It is less important initially what specific forms that assistance will take than that a general agreement be concluded on two basic points: the overall magnitude of the trade assistance and capital requirements within a given time frame; and the scope of the internal policy reforms that will assure its cost effectiveness.

Once these two fundamental issues have been agreed upon, the specific negotiations will have a pragmatic framework in which to proceed.

Whatever may be decided, it is obvious that our own institutions in the World Bank—IBRD, IDA, and IFC—will be involved. That is why we must move promptly to consider, and to resolve, the resource constraints that face us.

We can no longer afford to defer the discussion over the IBRD's future growth. Either we should accept in principle that it ought to continue—as it has over the past decade—to broaden its response to the critical capital needs of our developing member countries. Or we should decide consciously to let its usefulness decline as the limits of its present capitalization are reached, and as inflation erodes the real value of its commitments.

I believe that the latter course would be extremely unfortunate, particularly since there are a number of practical alternatives to immediate and burdensome budgetary requests. But we must meet the basic issue squarely, and not permit procrastination to drain our opportunities away.

Decisions over the Fifth Replenishment of IDA are even more pressing if a complete hiatus in operations is to be avoided at the end of next June. Surely we cannot contemplate the stark realities of absolute poverty in our poorest member countries, and then turn our backs on the 750 million human beings there who are trapped in it.

IDA has become the international community's primary weapon against the worst forms of poverty. We must not let it grow less effective—or lie unused—through our neglect and failure of purpose.

By any objective standard, absolute poverty is an anachronistic tragedy in our century. A tragedy because it is a condition of life beneath the level of human decency; and anachronistic because there are now at hand the economic and technological means to end it.

But in the final reckoning, it will not be simply economics and technology that end it. It will be people—people who care, people who make sacrifices, people who take practical steps to see the task through.

We are those people.

We have to ask ourselves—each one of us—where we really stand.

Flow of Official Development Assistance from Development Assistance Committee Members Measured as a Percentage of Gross National Product[a]

	1960	1965	1970	1971	1972	1973	1974	1975	1976	1977	1978	1979	1980
Australia	.38	.53	.59	.53	.59	.44	.55	.61	.55	.56	.57	.57	.58
Austria		.11	.07	.07	.09	.15	.18	.17	.16	.16	.17	.17	.18
Belgium	.88	.60	.46	.50	.55	.51	.51	.59	.57	.61	.64	.65	.68
Canada	.19	.19	.42	.42	.47	.43	.50	.57	.58	.61	.65	.68	.70
Denmark	.09	.13	.38	.43	.45	.48	.55	.58	.62	.64	.67	.70	.70
Finland[b]		.02	.07	.12	.15	.16	.17	.18	.20	.22	.24	.27	.29
France	1.38	.76	.66	.66	.67	.58	.59	.62	.61	.59	.60	.61	.62
Germany	.31	.40	.32	.34	.31	.32	.37	.40	.32	.29	.28	.27	.26
Italy	.22	.10	.16	.18	.09	.14	.14	.11	.11	.12	.12	.12	.12
Japan	.24	.27	.23	.23	.21	.25	.25	.24	.23	.22	.22	.21	.20
Netherlands	.31	.36	.61	.58	.67	.54	.63	.75	.85	.88	.89	.88	.88
New Zealand[c]			.23	.23	.25	.27	.31	.52	.42	.41	.44	.46	.47
Norway	.11	.16	.32	.33	.43	.43	.57	.66	.74	.86	.96	.97	.97
Sweden	.05	.19	.38	.44	.48	.56	.72	.82	.86	.89	.92	.96	1.00
Switzerland	.04	.09	.15	.12	.21	.16	.15	.19	.16	.15	.14	.14	.14
United Kingdom	.56	.47	.37	.41	.39	.34	.38	.38	.37	.37	.39	.40	.41
United States[d]	.53	.49	.31	.32	.29	.23	.24	.27	.26	.24	.23	.22	.21
GRAND TOTAL													
ODA ($b-Nominal Prices)	4.6	5.9	6.8	7.7	8.5	9.4	11.3	13.6	14.6	16.2	18.3	20.5	22.8
ODA ($b-Constant 1975 Prices)	11.0	12.3	11.5	12.2	12.1	11.6	12.7	13.6	13.6	14.1	14.6	15.3	15.9
GNP ($t-Nominal Prices)	.9	1.3	2.0	2.2	2.6	3.1	3.4	3.8	4.2	4.8	5.5	6.2	6.9
ODA as % GNP	.52	.44	.34	.35	.33	.30	.33	.36	.35	.34	.34	.33	.33
ODA Deflator[e]	.42	.48	.59	.63	.70	.81	.89	1.00	1.07	1.15	1.25	1.34	1.43

[a]Figures for 1975 and earlier years are based on actual data. Those for 1976-80 are based on OECD and World Bank estimates of growth of GNP, on information on budget appropriations for aid, and on aid policy statements by governments—they are projections, not predictions, of what will occur unless action not now planned takes place.

[b]Finland became a member of DAC in January 1975.

[c]New Zealand became a member of DAC in 1973. ODA figures for New Zealand are not available for 1960 and 1965.

[d]In 1949, at the beginning of the Marshall Plan, U.S. Official Development Assistance amounted to 2.79% of GNP.

[e]Includes the effect of parity changes. Figures through 1975 are based on DAC figures. Deflators for 1976-80 are the same as those for GNP.

SIXTEEN

To the

MASSACHUSETTS INSTITUTE OF TECHNOLOGY

An Address on the Population Problem
(one of a series of lectures at MIT on "World Change and World Security")

CAMBRIDGE, MASSACHUSETTS
APRIL 28, 1977

I. INTRODUCTION[a]

Nearly a dozen years ago, in the city of Montreal, I delivered an address—as the U.S. Secretary of Defense—on the problems of international security.

My central point was that the concept of security itself had become greatly oversimplified. There was an almost universal tendency to think of the security problem as being exclusively a military problem, and to think of the military problem as being exclusively a weapons-system or hardware problem.

"We still tend to conceive of national security," I noted, "almost solely as a state of armed readiness: a vast, awesome arsenal of weaponry."

But, I pointed out, if one ponders the problem more deeply it is clear that force alone does not guarantee security, and that a nation can reach a point at which it does not buy more security for itself simply by buying more military hardware.

That was my view in 1966. It remains my view in 1977.

Let me be precise about this point.

In a volatile, violent world, it is of course necessary for a nation to establish defense forces in order to protect itself. Such forces are always expensive, but if the funds are wisely used there is a reasonable ratio between the amount of money spent and the degree of protection acquired.

One can graph that ratio as a curve. In the initial stages the curve arches upward, and security expands with expenditure. But as the spending grows larger and larger the curve inevitably begins to flatten out.

There is a point at which an additional dollar of defense simply no longer buys an additional dollar's worth of security.

[a] I am indebted to a long list of distinguished scholars and specialists for much of what follows. Their research and insights have assisted me immensely. In particular I want to thank the members of the External Advisory Panel on Population who, at my request, recently reviewed the World Bank's work in the population field. They are: Bernard Berelson, Chairman; Ronald Freedman; Goran Ohlin; Frederick T. Sai; and A. Chandra Sekhar.

379

Expenditures beyond that point are not only wasted on defense but will erode the funds available for other essential sectors.

And by denying that dollar to other essential investment, the process may in the end diminish security rather than bolster it.

Now, if we examine defense expenditures around the world today—and measure them realistically against the full spectrum of components that tend to promote order and stability within and among nations—it is clear that there is a mounting misallocation of resources. We are far out on the flat of the curve.

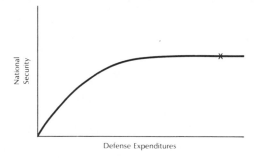

Defense Expenditures

That is true in the industrialized world. It is true as well in many parts of the developing world.

Global defense expenditures have become so large that it is difficult to grasp their full dimensions.

The overall total is now in excess of $350 billion a year.

The United States and the Soviet Union together account for some 60% of that—and for 75% of the world's arms trade. They possess more military power than all the other nations of the world combined.

And yet it is not in the industrialized countries, but in the developing countries that military budgets are rising the fastest.

As a group, the governments in the developing world are now spending as much for military programs as for education and health care combined.

If we are concerned—as all of us must be in this thermonuclear age—about international security, then we would do well to reconsider our present priorities. Do we really believe that we can turn the earth into a less violent place to live by an ever increasing factor of force?

Is the ultimate objective somehow to armor-plate the entire planet?

The question is grotesque. And yet, not any more so than the premise on which much of the world's thinking about security appears to be based.

I want to discuss with you tonight a subject that has nothing whatever to do with military phenomena—but a very great deal to do with global tranquility.

It is the issue of population growth.

Short of thermonuclear war itself, it is the gravest issue the world faces over the decades immediately ahead.

Indeed, in many ways rampant population growth is an even more dangerous and subtle threat to the world than thermonuclear war, for it is intrinsically less subject to rational safeguards, and less amenable to organized control.

The population growth of the planet is not in the exclusive control of a few governments, but rather in the hands of literally hundreds of millions of individual parents who will ultimately determine the outcome.

That is what makes the population threat—even more than the nuclear threat—diffuse and intractable. And that is why it must be faced—like the nuclear threat—for what it inevitably is: both a central determinant of mankind's future, and one requiring far more attention of the world community than it is presently receiving.

What, then, I would like to do this evening is this:

• Examine the background of the population problem;

• Analyze its current trends;

• Evaluate the measures available to deal with it;

• And suggest the actions that governments and others can and must take to help solve it.

Let me turn first to where we now stand.

II. THE POPULATION BACKGROUND

Last year the world's total population passed the four billion mark.

On the face of it, the event was not very dramatic. It marked, of course, the largest number of human beings ever to have been alive simultaneously on the planet—and thus was a record of sorts. But that particular record is broken every year. And will continue to be broken every year long beyond the lifespan of anyone alive today.

Barring a holocaust brought on by man or nature, the world's population tonight—as we sit here—is the smallest it will ever be again.

How did it reach a population of four billion?

For the first 99% of man's existence, surprisingly slowly. For the last 1% of his history, in a great rush.

Table I—The Rate of Growth of the World's Population

Year	Total Population	Rate of Growth Per Year Since Previous Date	Doubling Time
1,000,000 B.C.	a few thousand	—	—
8,000 B.C.	8 million	.0007%	100,000 years
1 A.D.	300 million	.046	1,500
1750	800 million	.06	1,200
1900	1,650 million	.48	150
1970	3,600 million	1.0	70
2000	6,300 million	2.0	35

Man has been on earth for a million years or more. For most of those millenia, his life was largely a search for a secure food supply. During the period that he was without pastoral or agricultural technology, adequate tools, or much protection against a harsh environment, he had a birth rate that only barely kept pace with the death rate.

As a consequence, until the dawn of agriculture around 8000 B.C., the population, after ten thousand centuries, had reached only an estimated eight million. During this immense interval, the average annual rate of increase was only about one additional individual for every 150,000 persons.

With the advent of agriculture and the domestication of animals, the food supply became more dependable, and the eight million population of 8000 B.C. rose to about 300 million by the beginning of the Christian era. This meant an average annual rate of increase of 65 persons for every 150,000—or as demographers would express it today, a growth rate of .046%.

From A.D. 1 to the middle of the eighteenth century, the population ebbed and flowed, gaining in prosperous periods, and falling back sharply in times of trouble. The bubonic plague —the Black Death—struck Europe suddenly in the mid-fourteenth century, and in four years cut down one person in every three. By the year 1400, under the onslaught of further epidemics, the European population had fallen to little more than half what it had been only 50 years earlier.

Thus by 1750, the total had reached only about 800 million. Then, as the industrial revolution gathered momentum, population growth began rapidly to accelerate. By 1900 it had doubled to 1.6 billion; by 1964 it had doubled again to 3.2 billion; and by the end of the century it is projected to double again to about 6.3 billion.

Now these numbers—as abstract as they may seem—illustrate an important point about population dynamics. The doubling time is extremely sensitive to very minor increments in the average annual growth rate.

It took mankind more than a million years to reach a population of one billion. But the second billion required only 120 years; the third billion 32 years; and the fourth billion 15 years. If one postulates that the human race began with a single pair of parents, the population has had to double only 31 times to reach its present huge total.

At the current global growth rate of about 2%, the world's population will add a fifth billion in about 11 years.

But these global totals, of course, obscure wide demographic differences between the developed and developing countries.

During the period from 1750 to 1850, the two groups of countries grew at similar average annual rates: .6% for the developed, .4% for the developing. From 1850 to 1950, the rates were .9% and .6%. From 1950 to 1975 the rates changed dramatically and became, respectively, 1.1% and 2.2%. The recent growth rates in the developing countries are not only twice as great as those in the developed countries today, but exceed by an equally large margin the most rapid growth ever experienced by the developed countries.

Translating these growth trends, and relative population sizes, into absolute numbers of people demonstrates the historical pattern even more graphically. From 1750 to 1850 the developed countries grew annually by 1.5 million people and the developing countries by 3 million; from 1850 to 1950, by 5 million and 7 million respectively; and from 1950 to 1975, by 11 million, and 48 million.

Demographic Dynamics

To grasp fully what is happening here it is helpful to recall the fundamental dynamics of population increase. On the surface they seem simple enough: population growth for any given society is the excess of births over deaths, as modified by migration.

If we disregard, for the moment, the influence of migration, it is apparent that so-called stationary, or steady-state, populations are those in which births and deaths are in balance.

For thousands of centuries the world had something very close to just that.

To achieve a steady-state population there must be a stable age structure and replacement-level fertility: a child must be born to replace each person in the parent generation. That seems obvious enough, but since some females die before or during childbearing age, the average number of children that parents in a given society must have to keep the population stationary is a function of the mortality conditions in the society.

In the Ivory Coast, for example, the death rates in the late 1960s of potential childbearing women were such that 3.5 births per woman would have been required to replace the parent generation; whereas in the United States, where death rates were much lower, only 2.1 births per woman were needed. In actuality, of course, fertility in the Ivory Coast, as in almost all of Africa, is much higher than that; and fertility in the United States has, since 1972, been below the replacement level.

Replacement is measured by the net reproduction rate (NRR), which technically refers to the number of daughters born per woman who could survive to childbearing age, assuming the prevailing levels of fertility and mortality. An NRR of 1.0 is the exact replacement level, and means that on average each woman would have one daughter who could be expected to live to the mean age of reproduction.

When female death rates prior to the end of the reproductive age are high, it clearly requires greater total fertility per woman to maintain a stationary population. When such death rates fall, it requires proportionately less.

We know, too, what are the outer limits of the various female mortality-fertility combinations that can produce a stationary population.

Today in the developed countries over 95% of women survive through childbearing years. Under such conditions, a total fertility rate of only 2.1 children per woman suffices for replacement.

On the other hand, average female life expectancy of 15 is the highest feasible mortality rate any large population could sustain, since in such a case only about 25% of women live to have children, and they would have to have an average of almost 9 children apiece to keep the population from declining. While it is, of course, physiologically possible for individual women to give birth to more than that number, no large grouping has ever been observed with a total fertility rate much higher than 8 to 9 births per woman.

This explains how near-zero growth prevailed in the world's population for thousands of centuries. Life expectancy at birth was very low, probably about 20 years. This meant that only about a third of the females born survived to the mean age of childbearing, and that those who lived to the age of menopause had an average of about 6.5 children; a birth rate of 50 to 55 per 1,000.

Even as late as the eighteenth century, mortality in Europe remained very high. In France, for example, almost a quarter of the population died before they reached their first birthday, and nearly half before the age of 20. By the early 1960s, only 2% died in their first year, and only 4% died before reaching 20. It is these low mortality rates that permit population levels to be maintained with only 2.1 children per female (a crude birth rate of roughly 14 per 1,000). In actual fact, women throughout the developed world today have an average number of children ranging from less than 2 to about 3.

Developing countries today typically have a female life expectancy at birth of about 55; total fertility rates averaging about 5.3 children per woman; and crude birth rates of about 37 per 1,000.[a] This combination results in a growth rate of approximately 2.3%, doubling the population every 30 years. To reach replacement level fertility, at current mortality rates, would require a reduction in the total fertility rate to 2.6, and the crude birth rate to about 20 per 1,000.

But when a net reproduction rate of 1.0—replacement-level fertility—is reached in a society, it does not mean that the population immediately ceases to grow. It will continue increasing for decades. That is a function of the society's age structure.

---

[a]There is, of course, a great range of differences between developing countries. Some have average life expectancies as low as 38; crude birth rates as high as 50 per 1,000; and annual growth rates as much as 3.5%, which double the population every 20 years. Women throughout these countries have an average number of children ranging between four and eight.

The population will continue to grow because the higher birth rates of the past have produced an age distribution with a relatively high proportion of persons currently in, or still to enter, the reproductive ages. This in turn will result in more births than deaths until the population changes to the older age distribution intrinsic in the low birth rate. Thus, even at replacement-level fertility, the population does not become stationary until the age structure stabilizes, which takes 60 to 70 years.

The difference in age distribution between a society that is in a period of high birth rates and falling death rates, and one that has been experiencing low birth rates and low death rates for many years, can be seen by comparing the population profiles of Mexico and Sweden.

Comparison of Mexican and Swedish Age Distributions

MEXICO (1970)   SWEDEN (1970)

Because of Mexico's very young age distribution, even after that country reaches and maintains replacement levels of fertility,[a] approximatey 70 additional years will pass before its age profile will approximate the Swedish pattern. During that entire 70-year period, Mexico's population will continue to increase.

---

[a]Total fertility levels in Mexico now exceed 6.0 children per female, compared to the replacement level of 2.3. Several decades of emphasis on population planning are likely to be required before replacement levels of fertility are reached.

Mexico's case is typical of the developing countries. And therefore the time lag of something like 70 years applies to that entire group of countries. But the 70-year countdown cannot even begin, of course, until the replacement level of fertility is actually reached.

And here we come to a point of immense importance—one that is not well understood, and one that I want strongly to emphasize: the speed at which fertility in the world declines to the replacement level will have a very significant effect on the ultimate size of the stationary population.

For every decade of delay in achieving a net reproduction rate of 1.0—replacement level—the world's ultimate steady-state population will be about 15% greater.

The significance of this statement can be understood by applying it to the present outlook. If current trends in fertility rates continue, i.e., if crude birth rates in developing countries decline by approximately 6 points per decade, it appears that the world might reach a net reproduction rate of 1.0 in about the year 2020. This would lead to a steady-state population of 11 billion some 70 years later.

If the date at which replacement-level fertility is reached could be advanced from 2020 to 2000 (by following, for example, the suggestions made later in this paper), the ultimate population would be approximately 3 billion less, a number equivalent to 75% of today's world total.

This reveals in startling terms the hidden penalties of failing to act, and act immediately, to reduce fertility.

If global replacement levels of fertility were to be reached around the year 2000, with the world ultimately stabilizing at about 8 billion, 90% of the increase over today's levels would be in the developing countries. As shown in the table below it would mean, if each country followed the same general pattern, an India of 1.4 billion; a Brazil of 275 million; a Bangladesh of 245 million; a Nigeria of 200 million; and a Mexico of 175 million.

Table II—The Ultimate Size of Stationary Population in Selected Developing Countries
(in millions)

| Country | Pop. 1975 | Ultimate Stationary Population[a] | | % Increase Caused by Two Decades of Delay |
		NRR of 1.0 Achieved in Year 2000	NRR of 1.0 Achieved in Year 2020	
India	620	1,400	2,000	43
Brazil	110	275	390	42
Bangladesh	76	245	400	63
Nigeria	65	200	320	60
Mexico	62	175	270	54

Source: Frejka, Tomas, *The Future of Population Growth; Alternative Paths to Equilibrium,* Population Council, New York, 1973.

But as I have pointed out, given today's level of complacency in some quarters, and discouragement in others, the more likely scenario is a world stabilized at about 11 billion. Populations in the developing countries would be 40 to 60% greater than indicated above because of two decades of delay in reaching replacement levels of fertility.

We have to try to comprehend what such a world would really be.

We call it stabilized, but what kind of stability would be possible?

Can we assume that the levels of poverty, hunger, stress, crowding, and frustration that such a situation could cause in the developing nations—which by then would contain 9 out of every 10 human beings on earth—would be likely to assure social stability? Or political stability? Or, for that matter, military stability?

It is not a world that anyone wants.

---

[a]The Stationary Population level will be reached about 70 years after the date on which a NRR of 1.0 is realized.

Even in our present world of 4 billion, excessive population growth severely penalizes many of the developing nations.[a]

It drains away resources, dilutes per capita income, and widens inequalities. At the national level, the government must devote more and more investment simply to provide minimal services to an ever-increasing number of children. At the family level, the same needs press in on the parents of large families.

During their early years, most children are primarily consumers rather than producers. For both the government and the family, more children means more expenditure on food, on shelter, on clothing, on health, on education, on every essential social service. And it means correspondingly less expenditure on investment to achieve the very economic growth required to finance these services.

As children reach adulthood, the problem is compounded by mounting unemployment. There are not enough jobs to go round because the government—grappling with the daily demands of the increasing numbers—has been unable to invest enough in job-producing enterprises. Thus the cycle of poverty and overpopulation tightens—each reinforcing the other—and the entire social and economic framework weakens under the weight of too great a dependency ratio.[b]

The sudden global surge in population over the past quarter-century has, of course, been a function of two opposite trends:

---

[a] I should stress that in choosing to speak on population, I do not mean to imply that it is the sole or predominant cause of social injustice and poverty. On several previous occasions, most recently in Manila last October, I have discussed the policy measures that governments of developing countries need to take to tackle poverty in both rural and urban areas. I have also reviewed the role that the developed nations must play through additional stimulus to international trade and higher levels of foreign assistance. To my mind, as later sections of this paper will demonstrate, policies to solve the poverty problem and to reduce the rate of population growth are complementary to each other: an effective attack on poverty is essential if population problems are going to be fully solved; and effective population policies are essential elements in the attack on poverty.

[b] A typical example is the case of Algeria, as contrasted with Sweden. In Algeria, with its high birth rate, every 100 persons of working age in 1970 had to support 98 children under the age of 15. In Sweden, with its low birth rate, every 100 persons of working age had to support only 32 children under 15.

the gradual slowing down of the growth rate in the developed nations, and the rapid acceleration of the growth rate in the developing countries.

The experience of the developed countries gave rise to the theory of the demographic transition.

The Demographic Transition

The theory holds that societies tend to move through three distinct demographic stages:

1. High birth rates, and high death rates, resulting in near stationary populations;

2. High birth rates, but declining death rates, producing growing populations;

3. And finally, low birth rates and low death rates, reestablishing near stationary populations.

If one examines the history of the developed nations, the facts support the theory. Preindustrial societies grew very slowly. Birth rates and death rates generally were both high, and very nearly in balance.

But with the advent of industrialization, more adequate nutrition, and improved public health measures, death rates gradually began to fall, and growth rates to increase.

The process continued in the industrializing societies into our own century until birth rates in turn began to diminish, and growth to level off.[a] Today in all but two or three developed countries fertility rates are near, or at—and in some cases even below—replacement levels. As a consequence, in 1975, the total fertility rate for the developed countries as a group was 2.1, exactly at replacement level.

It has taken the developed world as a whole about 150 years to pass through the demographic transition.

---

[a]Recent research indicates there were some exceptions to the typical pattern of demographic transition. In some cases, the decline in fertility preceded the fall in mortality.

But most of the developing countries remain today in the second stage of the transition. Their birth rates range between 30 and 50 per thousand, and their death rates between 10 and 25 per thousand. The result is that as a group their population is growing at about 2.3% a year, and at that pace it will double in about 30 years.

Now, if the developing countries were to require 150 years to complete the transition, the world's population would grow from its present 4 billion not to 8 or 11, but to 15 or 16 billion.

No one believes it will actually reach that magnitude. But no one is very certain what precisely is going to avert it, short of a major catastrophe brought on by human folly, or by nature's revenge.

The fundamental question is: what, if anything, can rationally and humanely be done to accelerate the demographic transition in the developing world?

Some serious observers say nothing can be done.

I do not share that view.

And to explain why I do not, I want to turn now to a more detailed examination of the current demographic situation in the developing countries.

III. RECENT DEMOGRAPHIC TRENDS

One, as always, must begin with the most recent data.

And one, as always, must begin with cautions about the data.

They are preliminary, they are not very precise, and they are at best only suggestive of trends.

But the trend they suggest is cautiously encouraging.

What appears to have happened in the developing world over the six-year period, 1969-1975 (see Table III) is that the crude birth rate (CBR)—the number of births per thousand of population—has declined 3.9 points. The crude death rate (CDR)—the number of deaths per thousand—during the same period has declined 1.9 points. The result is that the rate of natural increase (NI) declined slightly.

Table III—Birth Rates and Death Rates in Developing and Developed Countries

	Developing Countries[a]			Developed Countries			Total World[b]		
	Crude Birth Rate	Crude Death Rate	Rate of Natural Increase	Crude Birth Rate	Crude Death Rate	Rate of Natural Increase	Crude Birth Rate	Crude Death Rate	Rate of Natural Increase
1969	42.9	17.0	2.6	18.0	9.1	0.9	32.0	13.3	1.9
1975	39.0	15.1	2.4	17.3	9.3	0.8	30.0	12.3	1.8

Source: United Nations, *Selected World Demographic Indicators by Countries, 1950-2000,* May 1975; and Population Council Data Bank.

If we expand the six-year period to a two-decade period, 1955-1974, as in Table IV, the birth rates appear to have declined an average of about 5.6 points in 20 years, or nearly 13%. By major region, the decline has been 6.5 points in Asia; 5.4 points in Latin America; and 2.3 points in Africa.

Table IV—Crude Birth Rate Trends in Developing and Developed Countries

Region	No. of Countries	1975 Pop. (Millions)	Crude Birth Rates (per thousand)				
			1955	1960	1965	1970	1974
Africa	38	366	48.5	48.3	47.9	47.1	46.2
Latin America	21	289	43.0	42.2	40.8	39.4	37.6
Asia[a]	34	1,318	44.6	44.8	43.5	41.9	38.1
Total—LDC[a]	93	1,973	45.1	45.1	44.1	42.4	39.5
Total—DC	35	1,124	22.3	21.3	18.9	17.3	16.6

Source: UN data as revised by Parker Mauldin of the Population Council.

Further, this decline of the CBR was general and widespread. It occurred in 77 of the 88 developing countries for which estimates are available.

---

[a]Excludes People's Republic of China (PRC).
[b]Includes rough estimates of data relating to PRC.

Significantly, the decline appears to be gathering momentum: in the developing countries it is less for the earlier years, and greater for the more recent years as shown in Table V.

**Table V—Trends in the Percentage
Decline in Crude Birth Rates in Developing Countries**

	1955-60	1960-65	1965-70	1970-74
Africa	0.4	0.8	1.7	1.9
Latin America	1.9	3.3	3.4	4.6
Asia[a]	−0.4	2.9	3.7	9.1
Total[a]	0.0	2.2	3.9	6.8

Source: UN data revised by Parker Mauldin of the Population Council.

But even if the higher rates of decline were to continue into the future, it would mean only 6 points off the CBR in a decade. And that is only about half of the generally accepted target of 1 point a year. Thus, though the trend in birth rates is encouraging, its pace is still far too slow.

Moreover, the overall CBR decline obscures wide variations among individual countries as shown in Table VI.

---

[a]Excludes People's Republic of China.

Table VI—Reductions in the Crude Birth Rate in
Selected Developing Countries: 1955-1974

Country	1975 Pop. (in millions)	% Decrease in CBR	CBR in 1974
Group I (over 50 million)			
India	598	17	36
Indonesia	132	13	42
Mexico	60	11	40
Brazil	108	7	39
Pakistan	70	5	47
Bangladesh	79	0	47
Nigeria	63	0	50
Group II (20 to 50 million)			
South Korea	35	30	28
Thailand	42	25	37
Turkey	39	25	33
Colombia	25	25	32
Egypt	37	25	35
Burma	31	5	40
Philippines	42	5	36
Iran	34	5	43
Zaire	25	5	45
Ethiopia	28	5	48
Group III (under 20 million)			
Africa—Mauritius	0.9	37	25
Tunisia	5.6	21	36
Americas—Costa Rica	2.0	42	30
Barbados	0.2	35	21
Chile	10.3	33	23
Trinidad & Tobago	1.1	30	24
Panama	1.7	24	31
Asia—Singapore	2.3	55	18
Taiwan	16.0	47	23
Hong Kong	4.4	44	18
Fiji	0.6	37	28
Sri Lanka	13.6	27	27
Malaysia	10.5	27	30

Source: The Population Council, *Population and Family Planning Programs: A Factbook, 1976*. UN data on birth rates revised by Parker Mauldin of the Population Council.

Among those nations with populations of more than 50 million, India achieved the greatest CBR reduction, possibly as much as 17%; and Indonesia the second best, possibly 13%. Bangladesh, on the other hand, and Nigeria, registered no decline at all.

In countries with populations of 20 to 50 million, several demonstrated very large reductions: Korea, 30%; and Thailand, Turkey, Colombia, and Egypt, 25% each. But the Philippines, Iran, Burma, Zaire, and Ethiopia—all countries with very high birth rates—showed only slight declines of less than 5%.

Finally, among the smaller developing countries, the CBR went down by more than 40% in two, and by more than 20% in all the others listed in Table VI. Most of the larger declines occurred in the last decade, again suggesting the existence of a genuine trend, rather than merely an insignificant statistical aberration.

But, to repeat: statistics in this field are fragmentary, and the situation they describe varies widely from country to country.

It is, then, too soon to be fully certain, but the indications do suggest that crude birth rates in the developing world—outside sub-Saharan Africa—have at last begun to turn downward.

Now, if this conclusion is confirmed by the various censuses scheduled for 1980, then what we are witnessing here is a historic change of immense moment.

Its importance lies in this. Experience illustrates that once fertility turns definitely downward from high levels, it generally does not reverse direction until it has fallen quite low. Further, the higher the level at which it starts down, the more rapid is its descent.

All of this is obviously a welcome development—if it is in fact taking place. And a reasonable interpretation of the admittedly incomplete data indicates that it is. It is welcome particularly because it is far easier to expedite a declining fertility trend once it has really begun, than it is to initiate it in the first place.

But it is essential that we remain realistic. The truth is that at best the current rate of decline in fertility in the developing countries is neither large enough, nor rapid enough, to avoid their ultimately arriving at steady-state populations far in excess of more desirable—and attainable—levels.

And I repeat: for every decade of delay in achieving a net reproduction rate of 1.0—replacement-level fertility—the world's ultimate steady-state population will be approximately 15% greater.[a]

Current trends, as I have noted, point to a finally stabilized global population of about 11 billion. If we accelerate those trends sufficiently to save two decades of time, it would reduce that dangerous pressure on the planet by approximately 3 billion: 75% of the world's current total.

Is that acceleration realistically possible?

It is.

How, then, can we achieve it?

Let me turn to that subject now, and begin by examining the causes and determinants of fertility decline.

IV. CAUSES AND DETERMINANTS OF FERTILITY DECLINE

The task of understanding the factors leading to fertility decline is difficult. The complexities greatly outweigh the certainties. But it is at least possible to draw a number of tentative conclusions from recent research.

We can start with the basic fact that the demographic transition in the industrialized countries demonstrates that socioeconomic development and mortality declines were accompanied by significant reductions in fertility.

That is clear enough. But what is not clear is this: which of the many elements of general development led to that specific result, and with what relative effectiveness? Must the developing countries reach the current levels of income per capita in the developed nations before they reach their fertility rates?

---

[a]As Table II indicates, in many developing countries the effect of a decade of delay in achieving a NRR of 1.0 would not be a 15% increase in the steady-state population, but a 25 or 30% increase.

The question is further complicated by the evidence that certain culturally similar regions—those, for example, with a common language or ethnic background—moved through the fertility transition at the same pace, even though their economic conditions differed substantially. This suggests that in these instances cultural considerations were more decisive than economic advance. Further, there is ample evidence that vastly different fertility rates exist in developing countries with the same income levels, and that rates of change in fertility rates appear to bear little correlation with changes in income per capita.

The truth appears to be that a complicated mix of variables is at work, some economic, some not. Mortality decline, urbanization, educational advance, higher aspirations for one's self and one's children—all these elements appear to be involved in differing combinations.

Though we can learn from the experience of the developed nations, we must recognize that their historical circumstances were quite dissimilar to those in the developing countries today.

The developed nations entered their fertility transition with lower birth rates, lower growth rates, and much more gradual mortality declines. By the time their death rates had fallen substantially, their industrial infrastructure was already in place. Expanding job opportunities were available either in the cities, or in the New World overseas, which received tens of millions of European immigrants. Further, the age of marriage was relatively late, and the literacy rate relatively high.

The developing nations are confronted with a very different set of circumstances, some of them unfavorable, but some of them advantageous.

Their mortality decline has been the most precipitous in history: five times faster than in the developed nations. In the eight years between 1945 and 1953, Sri Lanka, for example, had as great a decline in mortality as had occurred in Sweden in the entire century between 1771 and 1871. That phenomenon has rapidly driven up growth rates all over the developing world. On the other hand, both individual families and government policymakers can directly perceive that the number of surviving children is much greater than in the recent past, and this may well move them to consider a smaller family norm.

Compared to the last century, the means of controlling birth are far more numerous, more effective, and more easily available.

Modern mass communications are both more pervasive, and more influential. The elite in the developing countries, and increasingly the mass of the people as well, are becoming more aware of living standards in the developed world, including smaller family size and less traditional life styles. Exposure to alternate possibilities stirs their imaginations, and affects their aspirations.

Governments have much greater ability now to reach across subnational barriers of linguistic, ethnic, and cultural differences, and can stay in touch with villagers, if they choose to do so.

Debate about education policy continues, but most developing countries regard basic literacy for both males and females as essential for development goals, and greater national unity.

Finally, there are an increasing number of governments in the developing world committed to lowering fertility, and an even larger number supporting family planning programs. In 1969, when as President of the World Bank I spoke on population, at the University of Notre Dame, only about 40 developing countries officially supported family planning, and only 20 of those had specific policies to reduce fertility. By 1975 there were 63 countries with official family planning programs, and 34 with explicit policies to reduce the growth rate.[a]

Now all of this is encouraging.

And in view of it, what are the conclusions we can draw about the linkages between socio-economic development and fertility? More specifically, which are those key elements that can be deliberately managed so as to accelerate fertility reduction?

[a]Mexico, for example, has moved since 1971 from a pro-natalist attitude on population to a vigorous family planning program with explicit demographic objectives.

Linkage of Fertility Decline to Social and Economic Development

We still cannot be as certain as we would like in this matter, but we do know that the following factors are important:

Health: Improving the level of health, particularly of children, insures the survival of a desired minimum of offspring, and provides parents with greater incentive for planning and investment for both their children and themselves. Since 1950, all substantial fertility declines in the developing countries have been preceded by substantial declines in mortality.

Education: Broadening the knowledge of both males and females beyond their familiar and local milieu enables them to learn about and take advantage of new opportunities, and to perceive the future as something worth planning for, including personal family size.

Broadly Distributed Economic Growth: Tangible improvement in the living standards of a significant proportion of the low-income groups in a society provides visible proof that aspirations for a better life can in fact be realized, and that a more compact family size can have economic advantages.

Urbanization: Despite the many problems connected with migration from the countryside to the city, it generally does offer greater accessibility to health services and education; increased familiarity with the more modern economic sector; and new savings and consumption patterns: all of which tends to alter attitudes towards traditional family size.

Enhanced Status of Women: Expanding the social, political, occupational, and economic opportunities of women beyond the traditional roles of motherhood and housekeeping enables them to experience directly the advantages of lowered fertility, and to channel their creative abilities over a much broader spectrum of choice.

Now let me sum up here what we have been discussing.

The central issue is: which are those specific elements of economic and social development that bear most effectively on reducing fertility?

I have suggested several. But how can we be sure they are likely to work?

One way is to examine carefully the available data for any apparent correlations with indicated levels of the crude birth rates.

Table VII—"Correspondence" in 1970 between Crude Birth Rates and Selected Development Indicators[a]

	No. of Countries	CBR Over 45	CBR 40 to 44	CBR 30 to 39	CBR Less Than 30
Health					
Infant mortality (rate per thousand)	34	128	84	61	20
Life expectancy (years)	43	46	57	64	68
Education					
Literacy (percent of population over 15 years of age)	39	33	57	78	80
Urbanization					
Adult male labor in agriculture (percent of total male labor)	46	77	64	45	15

Source: Population Council Data Bank.

The data demonstrate that there are such apparent correlations. What they do not prove conclusively is an ironclad causal connection.

But the figures in Table VII above, and those in Table VIII below, do establish that fertility levels and levels of certain specific socio-economic indices tend to move together.

---

[a]The values shown for the development indicators at each level of CBR are median values for the countries in the sample.

Table VIII—Trends of Crude Birth Rates and Selected Development Indicators: 1960-70

	Number of Countries[a]	Median Value of CBR and Devel. Indicators		Percentage Change
		1960	1970	
Crude birth rate	26	46	42	− 9%
Health				
Crude death rate (per thousand)	22	11.8	9.8	−17
Life expectancy (years)	17	57	61.4	+ 8
Infant mortality rate (per thousand)	15	80	68	−15
Inhabitants per physician	46	7,730	6,212	−20
Nutrition				
Calorie consumption (per capita per day)	34	2,110	2,310	+ 9
Protein consumption (grams per capita per day)	33	55.9	61.3	+10
Education				
Literate as % of population (age 15 and over)	14	61	74	+21
Urbanization				
Adult male labor in agriculture (%)	24	60	54	−11

Thus declining levels of infant mortality, and rising levels of nutrition, literacy, and nonagricultural employment appear to be accompanied by lower birth rates.

In 1970, for example, countries with a crude birth rate greater than 45, had on average an infant mortality rate of 128 per 1,000; an adult literacy rate of 33%; and 77% of the male labor force in agriculture.

Countries with a crude birth rate about 5 points less—a CBR of 40 to 44—had on average an infant mortality rate of 84; a literacy rate of 57%; and 64% of the male labor force in agriculture.

[a]All developing countries for which data are available for both 1960 and 1970. The data are derived from the data banks of the UN Research Institute for Social Development.

But for countries with CBRs in the range of 30 to 39, infant mortality on average had fallen to 61; literacy had climbed to 78%; and only 45% of the male labor force was in agriculture.

Finally, for countries with crude birth rates of less than 30, the infant mortality rate on average was down to 20; literacy was at 80%; and only 15% of the male labor force was in agriculture.

The correspondence in these examples is clear. The higher levels of health and education and nonagricultural employment are associated with lower levels of fertility.

But I want to repeat again. The correlation appears to be with specific elements of development—literacy, for example, and nutrition and infant mortality—rather than with the general level of economic wealth.

Consider the examples of Korea and Mexico.

Both countries have achieved impressive gains in their gross national products: Mexico since 1940, and Korea since the early 1960s. But by 1973, Mexico had reached a GNP per capita of $890, whereas Korea stood at less than half of that, at about $400.

Korea, however, had managed to distribute that much smaller income much more evenly than Mexico. In 1969, the poorest 40% of the households in Korea received 21.4% of total income, whereas the same group in Mexico received only 10.2%.

The infant mortality rate in Korea was at a considerably lower level: in 1970 it was 38, compared to 61 in Mexico.

Adult literacy, in the same year, was greater in Korea: 91% versus 84% in Mexico.

And by 1970, Korea had decisively entered her fertility transition with a crude birth rate of 29; whereas Mexico, with a CBR of 45, had not.

This, then, was a case of substantially higher overall national income failing to correlate with either fertility reduction, or other socially desirable factors.

A similar example is the state of Kerala in India.

In terms of average per capita income, it is one of the poorer Indian states. But its distribution of income is more equal; its literacy rate, particularly for women, is the highest in the country; and its infant mortality rate is the lowest.

In 1974 its crude birth rate was 28: lower than that of any other Indian state.

What these cases, and others, indicate is that gains in overall national economic growth are most related to fertility declines when they are associated with a broad distribution of the fundamental elements of social advance. A study of 40 developing countries revealed that an increase of $10 in the income of the lower 60% of the income strata, carrying with it advances in nutrition, health, and literacy, was associated with a crude birth rate decline of 0.7 per 1,000; but that a $10 increase in the overall average income of everyone was associated with a CBR decline of only 0.3 per 1,000.

If the growth in national income does not result in improvements of the living conditions of the lower income groups, it will not help to reduce fertility throughout the society.

Extrapolating the Data

The correlation, then, in developing countries between certain social changes and fertility reductions is persuasive, and is supported by the trends from 1960 to 1970. During that decade, literacy and education advanced; infant mortality declined; life expectancy increased; and the crude birth rate fell.

Assuming that the social indicators continue to change at the rate of that decade, and that their relation to fertility patterns remains the same, the crude birth rate in the developing countries as a whole would drop approximately half a point per year.

What this means is that without additional intervention, the current population in the developing world is going to continue to grow at rates very substantially in excess of those that would facilitate far more economic and social progress. It is these rates which would lead to an ultimate steady-state population in the world of 11 billion.

That is clearly undesirable.

Governments, then, must intervene. But how precisely? Let us examine the choices available.

V. POSSIBLE INTERVENTIONS TO REDUCE FERTILITY

The range of possible interventions divides into two broad categories:

- Those designed to encourage couples to desire smaller families;

- And those designed to provide parents with the means to implement that desire.

Both approaches are, of course, necessary. The first sets out to alter the social and economic environment that tends to promote high fertility, and by altering it to create among parents a new and smaller norm of family size, and therefore a demand for birth control.

And the second supplies the requisite means that will make that new norm attainable.

Thus family planning services are essential, but in the end can succeed only to the extent that a demand for lower fertility exists.

That demand apparently does not now exist in sufficient strength in most of the developing countries.

There are a number of policy actions that governments can take to help stimulate the demand. None of them is easy to implement. All of them require some reallocation of scarce resources. And some of them are politically sensitive.

But governments must measure those costs against the immeasurably greater costs in store for societies that procrastinate while dangerous population pressures mount.

What, then, are those specific social and economic actions most likely to promote the desire for reduced fertility?

Governments should try to:

- Reduce current infant and child mortality rates sharply.

- Expand basic education and increase the proportion of girls in school.

- Increase the productivity of smallholders in the rural areas, and expand earning opportunities in the cities for low-income groups.

- Put greater stress on more equitable distribution of income and services in the drive for greater economic growth.

- And above all else, raise the status of women socially, economically, and politically.

Let me comment briefly on each of these.

Reducing Infant and Child Mortality

We know from the experience of both the developed and developing countries that a decline in fertility rates can be expected to follow a reduction in infant and child mortality. The current rates in the developing world remain up to 20 times higher than they are in the developed nations.

Over half of all the deaths in Egypt, for example, occur before the age of five. Comparable and even higher rates are common in other developing countries. In Mexico, Cameroon, and Colombia about 30% of all deaths occur in the first year, and 15 to 20% of all deaths in the second through the fourth year. In contrast, in Sweden, the United States, and Japan the deaths of infants and children below the age of 5 make up less than 5% of the total number.

Average rates of infant mortality—deaths per 1,000 in the first year—are 142 in Africa, 121 in Asia, and 60 in Latin America. In the developed countries they average about 20.

Why are they so high in the developing world? Largely because of low nutritional standards, poor hygienic conditions, and inadequate health services.

In most developing countries health expenditures have been excessively devoted to supplying a small urban elite with expensive curative health-care systems—highly skilled doctors and elaborate hospitals — that fail to reach 90% of the people. What are required are less sophisticated, but more effective, preventive health delivery systems that reach the mass of the population.

Even quite poor countries can succeed in this, provided sound policies are pursued. Some 20 years ago, for example, Sri Lanka decided to improve rural health facilities.

The result over the past two decades has been a decline in infant mortality from 78 per 1,000 to 45 per 1,000, an increase in life expectancy from 56 to 69 years, and an associated decline in the crude birth rate from 39 to 29.

Korea has followed a similar policy, with similar results.

But many other countries—countries even with a much higher per capita national income than either Sri Lanka or Korea —have spent as much or more on health, and by failing to stress simple, inexpensive, but effective rural health systems, have reaped much poorer results.

Turkey, for example, had a GNP per capita of $860 in 1975, compared to Korea's $550 and Sri Lanka's $150, but has concentrated on urban health, with conventional facilities, and today has an infant mortality rate of 119 per 1,000, as compared to Korea's 38 per 1,000; life expectancy of 60 years, compared with Korea's 64 years; and a crude birth rate of 39, as compared with Korea's 28.

Infant and child mortality rates can be brought down relatively simply and inexpensively, if the national health policies are carefully designed. The return in lowered fertility, and healthier children, and more equitably served families is clearly worth the effort.

Expanding Basic Education

Education, like health, has often been a casualty of inappropriate policies, and there is wide debate over what ought best to be done. But there is no question that expanding the educational opportunities of females correlates with lowered fertility.

In Latin America, for example, studies indicate that in districts as diverse as Rio de Janeiro, rural Chile, and Buenos Aires, women who have completed primary school average about two children fewer than those who have not.

Schooling tends to delay the age of marriage, for girls, and thus reduces their total possible number of childbearing years.

Further, education facilitates, for both men and women, the acquisition of information on family planning. It increases their exposure to mass media and printed material, and enables them to learn about modern contraceptives and their use.

Schooling, too, clearly enhances a girl's prospects of finding employment outside the home that may compete with raising a large family. In a comparative study of 49 countries, the level of female education in each nation demonstrated a significant impact on the proportion of women earning wages or salaries, which in turn had a strong association with lowered fertility.

While children are in school, they do not contribute much to the support of the family, and thus parents tend to perceive them as having less immediate economic utility, but more long-term earning capacity. Both these factors are likely to lead parents towards a more compact family norm, since a large family is more expensive to educate, and a small, well-educated one will be in a better position to aid parents in later life. Fertility rates are substantially higher in those countries in which children under 15 are economically active, rather than in school.

Parents with an education themselves typically desire an even better education for their children, and realize that if these aspirations are to be achieved, family size will have to be limited.

Education leads to lowered fertility, too, by reducing infant and child mortality. In Northeast Brazil one of the chief motivations for school attendance was found to be the nutritious school lunch program. Further, a parent who has had some schooling is likely to be more careful about basic sanitation, and the value of innoculations and antibiotics. Such a mother is more confident that her own children will survive, and is less likely to want additional children merely as insurance against some dying.

Finally, perhaps the greatest benefit of education to both men and women in heavily traditional environments is that it broadens their view of the opportunities and potential of life, inclines them to think more for themselves, and reduces their suspicion of social change. This creates an intellectual environment in which important questions such as family size and contraceptive practice can be discussed more openly.

There is little likelihood that governments in developing countries—or for that matter, in developed countries—will soon agree over the competing strategies for more effective school systems. But one principle is beyond dispute: in the face of perennial budgetary pressures, it is far better to try to provide a basic minimum of practical and development-oriented education for many, than to opt for an expensive, formal, and overly academic education for a few.

A basic learning package, for both men and women, including functional literacy and numeracy, some choice of relevant vocational skills for productive activity, family planning and health, child care, nutrition, sanitation, and the knowledge required for active civic participation is an investment no nation can afford not to make. The very nature of the educational process imposes a relatively long time lag for the economic return on that investment. But if the basic package is right, the return will be huge. And not the least component of that return will be the benefit of reduced fertility.

Increasing the Productivity of Small Farmers, and Expanding Earning Opportunities in the Cities

As a generality, small farmers in developing countries are among the lowest income groups in the society. Their agricultural productivity is often at bare subsistence levels. Perhaps the only poorer individuals in the countryside are the landless, whose sole source of income is seasonal on-farm employment.

The fertility of both groups is characteristically high.

Typically the smallholders are reluctant to sell their land, but their holdings tend to become even smaller and more fragmented as the land passes through the inheritance process to their surviving sons.

The landless are the most likely candidates for migration to the squatter settlements of the city, since they have no tangible assets to hold them in the rural areas. But, increasingly, the dwindling size of the redivided holdings forces the inheriting sons as well to sell their uneconomic parcels of land, and join the procession to the urban slums in search of a job.

For the small farmers who remain on their land their only hope to escape poverty—with its poverty-related fertility levels —is government policy deliberately designed to assist them to increase their productivity.

There is, in fact, great potential for this, but it requires a comprehensive program of fundamental elements such as land and tenancy reform; better access to credit; assured availability of water; expanded extension of facilities; greater participation in public services; and new forms of rural institutions that can act as effective intermediaries between the appropriate government ministries and the individual subsistence farmers.

I have discussed in detail the essential components of such a program elsewhere,[a] and need not repeat them here, except to point out that our early experience with such rural development projects in the World Bank confirms their feasibility. We have over the last three years initiated 210 such projects, calculated to at least double the incomes of 8 million farm families, or about 50 million individuals.

It is through this increase in income that such farm families will almost certainly experience a beneficial decline in their traditionally high fertility. For the income will give them access to better health and education and living standards, which in turn are likely to lead to smaller families.

There is, then, a sound policy formula that governments can implement for the poor farmer that both reduces poverty, and its attendant fertility.

---

[a]Address to the Board of Governors of The World Bank, Nairobi, 1973.

But what of the growing millions of poor who migrate to the cities, and take their propensity for large families with them?

This is a considerably more complex policy problem since urban socio-economic relationships are by their nature both more varied and more complicated than traditional rural situations.

But the basic principle remains the same.

Policies must be shaped that will assist the urban poor to increase their productivity. In practice this means a comprehensive program designed to increase earning opportunities in both the traditional and the modern sectors, provide equitable access to public utilities, transport, education, and health services; and establish realistic housing policies.

Again, I have dealt with this subject at length in another context[a] and I need not reiterate the issues here. What is clear is that urbanization has usually been associated with low fertility.

In Latin America, for example, studies have indicated that family size in rural areas and small towns is nearly twice as large as those in major urban cities. The correlation has been found in countries as diverse as India, Lebanon, Hungary, the Soviet Union, and Japan.

In the urban setting there are fewer opportunities for children to do useful work, and hence more rationale for them to be in school. In general, cities offer relatively better access to the modern socio-economic system, and its attendant attitudes.

Moreover, migration from the countryside tends to loosen some links with the extended family. If parents cannot expect to dwell with their adult children, there is less incentive for them to have large families for the purpose of support in their old age.

Finally, the very act of leaving the traditional family home may lead to other breaks with tradition, such as the age of marriage and family size.

---

[a]Address to the Board of Governors of The World Bank, Washington, D.C., 1975.

But one must enter a word of caution. From a policy point of view, most governments in the developing world have little practical capacity either to regulate urbanization or to retard it. It simply happens, and it is happening far more rapidly than almost any major city can possibly cope with in an orderly way.

Populations in the countries themselves are doubling every 25 to 30 years, but their large cities are doubling every 10 to 15 years, and the urban slums and shanty towns in these cities every 5 to 7 years. By 1990 Lima, Peru, is expected to have six million inhabitants, 75% of whom will live in what were originally squatter settlements.

Fertility may or may not decrease in such potentially huge and squalid surroundings. And if it does decrease, it may decrease for the wrong reasons: inhuman crowding, unbearable stress, or dysfunctional family relationships. What must be countered in exploding cities is the desperate poverty that fuels them, which is itself, in part, the tragic legacy of rampant population growth in the countryside and city alike.

More Equitable Distribution of Economic Growth

While economic growth is a necessary condition of development in a modernizing society, it is not in itself a sufficient condition. The reason is clear. Economic growth cannot change the lives of the mass of the people unless it reaches the mass of the people.

It is not doing so with sufficient impact in most of the developing countries of the world today. Typically, the upper 20% of the population receives 55% of the national income, and the lowest 20% receives 5%.

In the rural areas, this is reflected in the concentration of landownership. According to an FAO survey, the wealthiest 20% of the landowners in most developing countries own between 50 and 60% of the cropland. In Venezuela they own 82%; in Colombia 56%; in Brazil 53%; in the Philippines, India, and Pakistan about 50%. The roughly 100 million small farms in the developing world—those less than 5 hectares—are concentrated on only 20% of the cropland.

What this means is that the lower 40% of the income strata is neither contributing significantly to economic growth nor sharing equitably in its benefits. They are the poor, and they are virtually outside the entire development process. It largely passes them by.

It is little wonder, then, that national economic growth in itself has had less than optimum effect on the fertility patterns of the vast mass of the population. Their nations have been progressing, but large numbers of the people have advanced at rates far below the average.

Even the conventional measurements that governments have at hand to trace economic progress can be misleading. The growth of the gross national product, for example, is generally regarded as a key index. And it is, for it measures the total value of the goods and services of the economy. But it does not, and cannot, serve as a measure of their distribution.

Since the upper 40% of the population in a developing country typically receives 75% of all income, the growth of the GNP is primarily an index of the progress of these upper-income groups. It tells one very little about what is happening to the poorest 40%, who collectively receive only about 10 or 15% of the total national income.

The implication of much of what was said at the World Population Conference in Bucharest in 1974 was that a sufficient rate of development will solve any population problem in time.

But what precisely is a "sufficient rate of development"? It clearly is not overall average economic growth, which so frequently benefits the few and bypasses the many.

Most countries in Latin America, for example, have considerably higher per capita income than countries in Asia and Africa. And yet fertility rates are not proportionately lower. That, in part, is a function of the serious inequalities in income distribution in the Latin American region.

A study of various characteristics in 64 countries from both the developed and developing areas of the world, for which data are available, confirmed that more equitable income distribution, with the resultant broader distribution of social service, is strongly associated with lower fertility. The analysis suggested that each additional percentage point of total income received by the poorest 40% reduces the general fertility rate by about 3 points.

Governments everywhere in the developing world are, of course, striving to accelerate economic growth. Excessive fertility is itself a serious obstacle to this growth. But unless the benefits of the growth are directed more equitably to the lower 40% of the income groups, where in fact fertility rates are likely to be the highest, then economic growth as such will not move the society forward at an optimum rate of progress.

Enhancing the Status of Women Socially, Economically, and Politically

The importance of enhancing the status of women is critical, and there is a great deal that governments can do in this matter. In some societies even simple legislative changes—such as establishing the legal right of a woman to refuse to marry the mate picked out for her by her parents, or the right to own property herself—are important first steps in improving her position in society.

Of all the aspects of social development, the educational level appears most consistently associated with lower fertility. And it is significant that an increase in the education of women tends to lower fertility to a greater extent than a similar increase in the education of men.

But in most developing societies women do not have equitable access to education. The number of illiterate females is growing faster than of illiterate males. Nearly two-thirds of the world's 800 million illiterates are women, and virtually everywhere males are given preference both for general education and vocational training.

One reason for this is that the prevailing image of women distorts their full contribution to society. Women are esteemed —and are encouraged to esteem themselves—predominantly in their roles as mothers. Their economic contribution, though it is substantial in a number of developing societies, is almost always understated.

The fact is that in subsistence societies women generally do at least 50% of the work connected with agricultural production and processing, as well as take care of the children, and the housekeeping. They rise earlier and retire later than anyone else in the family, often working 18 hours a day.

But despite this contribution, women generally suffer the most malnutrition in poor families. Men are given first claim on such food as is available; children second; and the mother last. This, in itself, tends to lead to high fertility through a self-perpetuating cycle of events.

Malnourished mothers give birth to weak and unhealthy infants, and have problems nursing them adequately. Such infants often die. This leads to frequent pregnancies. The mothers, constantly pregnant or nursing infants, are unable to play a larger role in the outside-the-home work force. This diminishes their occupational and economic status, which in turn reinforces the concept that males are more important. This makes sons more desirable than daughters. When only daughters are born, another pregnancy must ensue in order to try again for a son. Repeated pregnancy not only increases the family size, but exhausts the mother, weakens her health—and thus the whole cycle begins again.

Though governments sometimes recognize that encouraging women to enter the off-farm and urban work force reduces fertility—since it tends to delay the age of marriage, and increase the interval between children—policy makers are often tempted to conclude that this would only exacerbate unemployment among men, and hence diminish family income.

But that objection is a short-term view of the matter. In the longer run, a family with two wage earners, and a smaller number of dependents—due to the related decreased fertility—can contribute more to public revenues through taxes, and more to capital formation through increased savings.

In contrast with a large and poor one-wage-earner family, the smaller two-wage-earner family helps accelerate economic growth, and thus increases the demand for labor, male and female.

The truth is that greater economic opportunity for women—and the greater educational opportunity that undergirds it—would substantially reduce fertility. And in societies in which rapid population growth is draining away resources, expenditure on education and training for boys that is not matched by comparable expenditure for girls will very likely be diminished in the end by the girls' continued high fertility. More education for women in developing countries is a very good buy.

Instruction on nutrition, child care, family planning, and home economics are all, of course, important. But women need market-oriented training and services as well: access to credit, extension services, the skills necessary for participating in a cash economy.

Schools must make the point to young women that the ideal role of a girl is not to be the mother of a large and poor family, but rather to have a double role as mother of a small family, and as a wage earner who contributes to the well-being of her family by economic employment.

Women represent a seriously undervalued potential in the development process. And to prolong inequitable practices that relegate them exclusively to narrow traditional roles not only denies both them and society the benefits of that potential, but very seriously compounds the problem of reducing fertility.

Public Information Programs

Those, then, are the specific socio-economic interventions calculated to encourage smaller families.

They must, of course, be paralleled and supported by a continuing public information program.

There is a need to inform, educate, and persuade people of the benefits of a more compact and manageable family size. This is essential, but it has not been an easy task. The significance of the population problem dawned slowly on an unprepared world. There was not only ignorance and skepticism, but in many instances strong opposition against even discussing the subject.

That is not surprising.

Since reproduction is essential for the survival of society, it is understandable that every society has had strong views about family size.

Norms in this matter have always existed, and there has always been strong group pressure to see that they were followed. Until very recently, childless women in some societies have been regarded with open scorn. And for males not to father a large family has tended to be a reflection on their masculinity.

Norms are patterns of expected behavior, rules of what is appropriate and what is not. And we know, from surveys on desired family size, what those norms are today in various societies. In the developed world the average desired number of children ranges from 2 to 3. In the developing world the average is between 4 and 6, with a majority wanting at least four children.

This is a critical point, since one of the main objects of intervention in population is to create a set of circumstances in which people will change their norm of desired family size.

And there is simply no hope of succeeding at that unless one first clearly understands the reasoning behind their present norms.

To design an effective public information program, to set up a persuasive person-to-person communication scheme, to draft and establish a successful population education plan, it is imperative to comprehend the mind-set that you are attempting to change.

And the reasons for fertility reduction that may be persuasive to planners sitting in distant capitals may not be persuasive at all to parents sitting in remote villages.

Village couples rarely worry about the progress of the gross national product.

What they may well worry about is the progress of a sick child, or how they are going to accumulate enough savings to secure their old age, and whether the signs are auspicious that the next pregnancy will finally give them a second son, rather than a third daughter.

As we have said, it is the poor, as a generality, who have the most children. And it is the poorest countries, as a generality, that have the highest birth rates.

But it is a mistake to think that the poor have children mindlessly, or without purpose, or—in the light of their own personal value systems—irresponsibly.

Quite the contrary.

The poor, by the very fact of their poverty, have little margin for error. The very precariousness of their existence habituates them to be cautious. They may be illiterate. They are seldom foolhardy. To survive at all, they are forced to be shrewd.

What we must grasp is that poverty does not make people unreasonable. What it does do is severely reduce their range of choice. They often do what they do because there is little real opportunity to do otherwise.

Poor people have large families for many reasons. But the point is they do have reasons. Reasons of security for their old age. Reasons about additional help on the land. Reasons concerning the cultural preference for sons. Reasons related to the laws of inheritance. Reasons dictated by traditional religious behavior. And reasons of personal pride.

Demography measures people. It cannot always measure their inner feelings.

And yet understanding poor people—and the narrow range of options that poverty offers them—is the key to assisting them to broaden their choices.

In a good public information program, that is precisely what happens. Alternative choices become evident.

The mass media can be helpful, particularly radio, television, and film since they do not depend exclusively on literacy for comprehension. But all the media can be creatively utilized:

newspapers, signboards, leaflets, exhibits, village posters, songs, and plays.

Communication research concludes that the mass media, while influential with people who are already in general agreement, or at least neutral, can rarely—through direct messages—persuade people to reverse deep-seated convictions, or long-standing behavior.

But what the media can do, and do very well, is help people to change their views indirectly by putting them in contact with another world, expanding their horizons, stimulating their curiosity, and introducing them to new ideas, including the idea of attractive alternative life styles, with fewer, but more advantaged children.

But in the end, no form of media information is as effective as person-to-person communication. Messages can be sent electronically thousands of miles, but it is ultimately people talking to one another in a classroom, on the street, at the village market, or in the village home where the essential questions are discussed, and the essential answers are explored.

Door-to-door field work, discussion groups, study clubs, civic organizations, town and village meetings: all of these are important, and all of them can be made stimulating, informative, and persuasive.

There is a whole spectrum of formal and informal learning situations that can be utilized. Population education as a component of the school curriculum is obvious and essential. Mobile vans visiting villages with films, exhibits, and talks can combine entertainment with instruction. Political leaders, national celebrities, and religious authorities can endorse national population goals in their speeches and public appearances. All of this is possible, given leadership, imagination, and drive. And all of it is very worthwhile.

But beyond these information and educational efforts, there is a whole range of additional measures available to governments that can serve as incentives to postpone the age of marriage, undertake family planning, or adopt new norms of family size and disincentives to retaining inappropriate norms.

Incentives and Disincentives

Housing and job opportunities, maternity benefits, tax deductions, dependency allowances, pension provisions, school admission priorities: these and similar government benefits and policies can be redesigned to encourage parents to have small families, and to dissuade them from having large ones.

Incentives can range from immediate cash payments to family planning acceptors to elaborate programs for future payment, at the end of the childbearing years, for fertility restraint. Disincentives can limit the allocation of various public services on a graduated scale: more to parents with few children, less—or none at all—to parents with many children.[a]

Incentives, of course, widen rather than restrict choice, and are less likely to penalize children, who, through no fault of their own, happen to get born into large families. But the fact is, of course, that disincentives or not, children born into large families in the developing world today are likely to be penalized in any case, simply by the pressures of poverty that the population problem has exacerbated in developing societies.[b]

Experimenting with incentives is still relatively limited, but the prospects are promising. Deferred-payment schemes, which would reward parents financially at the time of retirement, or at the end of the childbearing age, for their fertility restraint are particularly worth exploring.

---

[a]One scheme proposed for Malaysia would make public assistance for the elderly available only for those parents with less than three children. Taiwan is experimenting with a bond system that will provide support for higher education of students in families with no more than three children. Singapore —a high-density island community—has designed a whole series of measures. In 1970, Prime Minister Lee Kuan Yew pointed out: "Beyond three children, the costs of subsidized housing, socialized medicine, and free education should be transferred to the parent."

[b]From a child's point of view there can be few benefits in having many siblings. The close spacing of children and large numbers of children are likely to increase infant and maternal mortality, and to worsen nutritional deficiencies and related health problems. This may in turn reduce a child's opportunity to benefit from whatever educational opportunities he has received. And in matters of inheritance, which in rural areas of some of the land-scarce countries is likely to be of critical importance even among very poor families, children from large families are at an obvious disadvantage.

Such schemes attempt to provide parents with an alternative source of financial security for their old age, in place of the traditional one of large families. And they encourage the creation of a society in which parents can put their resources and energies into providing a small number of children with the best possible start in life, rather than merely hoping to find security in a large number of children—each one of whom must face a proportionately more precarious future.

Promoting a Social Consensus

Governments have considerable capacity, as well, to help create a generalized atmosphere of social consensus in an antinatalist direction. Villages and local communities, just as individual families, can be rewarded by government policies for good performance in fertility restraint. Allocations of central government funds for community improvements—roads, electrification, public works—can be conditioned on evidence of community commitment to new-style family norms.

India, for example, recently adopted a measure which provides that both the political representation of local areas, and their allocation of national financial resources, will no longer increase simply as a function of their population growth. In the future, additional numbers will not automatically mean additional votes or additional claims on tax revenues.

But it is not only the central government in a society that can apply disincentives to high fertility. Community authorities can do the same.

In preindustrial Japan, for example, a strong tradition of social cooperation and consensus at the village level maintained severe constraints on the number of households in the village, often permitting no increase at all. These social pressures were transmitted to heads of households, who in turn exerted authority over individual household members in matters of marriage, divorce, and adoption. This tradition appears to have been a significant influence in holding population increase during the last 150 years of Tokugawa Japan to less than 0.2% a year.

It is obvious that the interest of a local community in the fertility of its membership will be proportional to the social costs of population increase that it is called upon to bear. If schools and other public services are in part locally financed; if pressures on the land lead to local deforestation and erosion; and if local unemployment becomes serious, then communities may well become conscious of the adverse social effects of excessive population growth.

It is clear that there are many different approaches to the task of promoting a new social consensus on population problems within a society, and the choice of one over another—or any particular mix of actions—must, of course, be guided by the cultural context of the society in question.

But the truth is that most of the approaches, and all of the actions, are difficult to implement.

And we must face the reality that if these approaches fail, and population pressures become too great, nations will be driven to more coercive methods.

Coercion

A number of governments are moving in the direction of coercion already. Some have introduced legal sanctions to raise the age of marriage. A few are considering direct legal limitations on family size, and sanctions to enforce them.

No government really wants to resort to coercion in this matter. But neither can any government afford to let population pressures grow so dangerously large that social frustrations finally erupt into irrational violence and civil disintegration.

That would be coercion of a very different order. In effect, it would be nature's response to our own indifference.

Now let me underscore what we have been analyzing here.

We have been discussing those kinds of interventions that governments can make to help stimulate the desire among parents for a smaller family size.

But those efforts must, of course, be accompanied by corresponding interventions that provide parents with readily available means to do so.

Family Planning Services

Governments must improve the access to the modern means of fertility control both qualitatively and quantitatively: more and better services to greater numbers of people.

In practice, that requires:

- Providing a broad selection of the current contraceptives: pills, condoms, IUDs; as well as sterilization, and—where the society desires it—abortion.

- Establishing a broad spectrum of delivery services and informational activities utilizing: physicians in private practice; paramedical workers; professional field workers; community-based local agents; the commercial sector; widespread distribution of contraceptives; sterilization centers; mobile clinics; postpartum arrangements; and the integration of contraceptive services into the maternal and child-health system, the general health system, and the community development system.

- And, finally, improving the acceptability, continuity, and effectiveness of the means of fertility control by accelerating research on such possibilities as: a contraceptive vaccine; a better implant; an IUD free of side effects; a safer and more convenient pill (a once-a-month pill, or a once-a-year pill); a nonsurgical means to terminate pregnancy; or a currently unknown "ideal" contraceptive.

To put the matter succinctly, governments need to provide a broad choice of present contraceptive techniques and services to parents; they need to improve the delivery system by which parents can get the services they wish; and they need to support continuing research for better techniques and services.

The majority of the world's population lives in countries with family planning programs that now have as their explicit objective the reduction of fertility. And yet the programs themselves often do not reflect much political conviction that they can and must succeed.

Many of these programs are small, and rely on foreign sources for much of their finance. All governments, of course, have re-source constraints. But fertility reduction, as a priority, seldom commands even 1% of national budgets. Further, governments have often failed to give the programs the status and national attention that would attract top managerial talent. For these, and related reasons, the world's total family planning acceptors did not measurably increase in the period 1972-1975, despite the increase in the number of national programs.

I listed above a number of actions that governments—both developed and developing—can take to strengthen family planning programs.

One of the most urgent needs is a much greater effort in re-productive biological research and contraceptive technology.

Reproductive Biological Research

The requirement for a substantial expansion in reproductive research is obvious. Though by the early 1970s some 46 million women throughout the world were using the IUD or the pill, this did not begin to meet the need. Of the approximately 500 million women around the globe in their childbearing years, and facing the risk of an unwanted pregnancy, an estimated 70% are using no contraceptive method at all.

The current estimate is that for the world as a whole, one out of every three of four pregnancies ends in abortion, and the vast majority of the women seeking abortion are married. The fact is that abortion, even though it is still illegal in a number of countries—and remains ethically offensive to millions—appears to be the most widespread means of fertility control there is. That is, in itself, a cogent argument for better contraceptive methods.

Cultural, religious, and personal preferences in contraception differ widely, and must, of course, be taken into account if ade-quate levels of acceptability and continuity are to be achieved. While it is true that there may never be an "ideal" contraceptive for all circumstances, it is clear that there should be a broader spectrum of methods which are safer, less discomforting, and more convenient; and which require less complex and costly distribution systems.

Such methods are well within the reach of biomedical science and adaptive technology, but will require sustained investigation and effort. Traditionally, reproductive research has been grossly underfinanced. Worldwide expenditures in 1975 were less than $130 million. Simply to maintain this wholly inadequate level of funding in the face of current inflation would mean approximately $200 million in 1980.

But this is far below what is required. Two to three times that amount is needed, not merely because of the importance of the population issue itself, but because of the intrinsic time lags involved.

There are a number of promising avenues for improved fertility regulation that have emerged from the basic research of the past fifteen years.[a] But even after a potential method has been developed, at least three to five years are required for testing before the method can be practically applied. And a wholly new discovery requires a full decade to reach the stage of a usable product.

What we must understand is that a variety of safe, effective, and acceptable methods of fertility regulation is not just needed now, and ten years from now, but in the years 2000, 2010, 2020 and so on. If new methods are to be available then, the research effort must be expanded now.

And yet the field has been so starved for funds in recent years that more than half the approved grant applications for reproductive biological research have simply failed to be financed. Both the pharmaceutical industry and philanthropic foundations have been active in supporting such research, but they cannot be expected to carry the major funding expansion that is now urgently required. Governments must be prepared to direct substantially more effort in that direction.

The fruits of such research will result not only in better methods of contraception, but in the reduction of many other

[a]Among these are better contraceptive methods for use by males. These could substantially improve the ability to regulate childbearing by giving husbands greater responsibility for contraception. Further, it would make it possible for couples to alternate methods, and thus further reduce the risk of cumulative undesirable medical side effects.

adverse medical and social effects of unwanted or abnormal pregnancy: prematurity, infant mortality, congenital defects, mental retardation, maternal morbidity and mortality—as well as illegitimacy, early marriage, family disruption, educational disadvantage, and the exacerbation of poverty.

The investment in reproductive research is immensely worthwhile. And there is simply no question that more of it is needed.[a]

But, as I have indicated, this expanded research will require years of effort before it can be translated into radically different methods of contraception. Governments cannot afford simply to wait for that. Rather, they must in the meantime take action to improve present family planning programs and make broader use of current contraceptive technology. Such programs are necessary in all countries with rapidly expanding populations, regardless of the particular stage of economic and social development.

Family Planning in Relation to the Stages of Development

In some countries, widespread use of contraception precedes a change in desired family size, and may help it occur. In others, contraception becomes popular only after other factors have reduced family norms. But in either pattern, family planning is important, and indeed ultimately essential to meet the demand of parents for reduced family size.

In the lower-income developing countries, where absolute poverty is endemic, family planning programs should be shaped to service those parents who already desire to reduce their fertility; to urge others to consider that option; to increase local awareness of the damaging consequences of rampant population growth; and to recognize that by improving the health of the local community—and particularly of mothers and children —the program is in fact laying the foundation for a change in fertility norms.

Such an approach ensures that as the demand for family

---

[a]The same need exists for additional social science research in the population field. There is a clear requirement to define more precisely those particular elements of social and economic development that most directly affect fertility.

planning service increases, the supply is there to meet it. In the absence of more fundamental social and economic improvements, one cannot, of course, expect such a program to "solve" the population problem. But it would be equally naive to assume that it can have no effect on fertility whatever.

Indonesia, for example, is a particularly interesting case of a country with strong political commitment to fertility decline, and a vigorous family planning program, that appears to be off to a good start in spite of immense development problems.

In any event, the view that development in and by itself can take care of the fertility problem in the developing world is an unfortunate oversimplification as applied to most of the countries, and a dangerous error as applied to others.

Even for the better-off developing countries, such a "development-only" strategy would be wasteful. The fall in fertility, without a strong family planning program, is likely to come later in the development process than it need to: per capita income would grow more slowly, and the ultimate size of the population would be larger.

But for the lower-income countries, a "development-only" strategy would be disastrous. In these countries it would take a much longer time to reach the socio-economic levels that normally correspond with significantly lower birth rates. Indeed in some of them, it is the very magnitude of the population pressures themselves that is retarding that progress. Were the fertility problem not dealt with directly, the progress would simply be too slow.

At the rate at which literacy has been increased and infant mortality and fertility reduced during the last decade, it would take India, for example, until the year 2010 to reach the literacy levels that normally correspond with crude birth rates of 30; and it would take until the year 2059 to reach the infant mortality levels that correspond with a CBR of 30.

If Nepal were to do nothing about its fertility directly, it would take it 170 years to reach the literacy level associated with a CBR of 30.

India and Nepal—and many other countries—simply do not

have that kind of time to experiment with a "development-only" strategy. And, happily, they have no intention of attempting it.

Whatever the rhetoric at Bucharest in 1974, no country has abandoned the anti-natalist policies it held then, and several have strengthened them.

Competent observers do argue about the relative importance of social development and family planning efforts in reducing fertility rates. Some say the former is too indirect. Others say the latter is too inefficient.

But the truth is that the latest reviews of the experience of individual countries—reviews completed within the past twelve months—clearly support the conclusion that significant reduction of birth rates depends on both social development and family planning.

The reviews suggest that family planning programs have a clear, substantial, and independent effect on country performance.

Virtually all of the countries with reductions of 20% or more in their crude birth rates during the decade 1965-1974 had strong family planning programs.

But the research also confirms what common sense itself would suggest: that the effect of family planning programs is greatest when they are joined to efforts designed to promote related social goals.

Raising Population Consciousness

The real problem—for all of us—is to try to grasp the complexity of the population issue.

Population problems are not simple; they are not straightforward; and they are certainly not very clear. They are like man himself: complicated.

If we are to get down to solutions that really work, we have to try to see the problem in all its ramifications, and in all of its tangled interrelationships.

I recently asked a panel of distinguished experts to review our activities in the population field within the World Bank.

They took a hard look at everything we have been doing since 1969, and they rightly reproached us for a tendency to treat population too much in isolation from our other activities.

They pointed out that we have been prepared to lend for population projects, and were ready to bring specialized analysis to population issues when they were of obvious immediate importance.

But too many of us in the Bank had proceeded as if population issues could be left to specialists, rather than considered automatically in all aspects of our investment and development programs.

In short, they asked us to think about the problem in a more comprehensive way—and deal with it accordingly.

They were right. And that is exactly what we plan to do.

Let me, now, summarize and conclude the central points I have made this evening.

VI. SUMMARY AND CONCLUSIONS

The argument I have made is this.

It now appears that a significant decline in fertility may have at last begun in the developing countries. The data are not yet fully conclusive, but the indications are that the crude birth rates have fallen over the past two decades by an average of about 6 points, or nearly 13%.

By major region, the decline has been 6.5 points in Asia; 5.4 points in Latin America; and 2.3 points in Africa.

Further, the decline appears to have been general and widespread. It has occurred in 77 of the 88 countries for which estimates are available.

If these indications are confirmed by the censuses scheduled for 1980, then what we are seeing here is something of historic importance. It would mean that the period of rapid acceleration in the rate of growth of the world's population has finally reached its peak and is now definitely moving downward towards stabilization.

But as welcome as this is, the fact remains that the current rate of decline in fertility in the developing countries is too slow to avoid their ultimately arriving at stationary populations far in excess of acceptable levels.

Unless governments, through appropriate policy action, can accelerate the reduction in fertility, the global population may not stabilize below 11 billion. That would be a world none of us would want to live in.

But governments can take action, and can accelerate the process, given the resolve and determination to do so.

The critical point is this: for every decade of delay in achieving a net reproduction rate of 1.0—replacement-level fertility—the ultimate steady-state world population will be approximately 15% greater.

Governments, then, must avoid the severe penalties of procrastination, and try to hasten the process forward.

But how?

The causes and determinants of fertility reduction are extremely complex, but it appears likely that there are a number of key linkages between that reduction and certain specific elements of socio-economic development.

The factors that appear to be the most important are: health, education, broadly distributed economic growth, urbanization, and the enhanced status of women.

These factors are at work in the developing world today, but their progress is too slow to be fully effective.

Without additional intervention on the part of governments, the current population in the developing world is going to continue to grow at rates very substantially in excess of those that would permit far more economic and social progress.

There are two broad categories of interventions that governments must undertake: those designed to encourage couples to desire smaller families; and those designed to provide parents with the means to implement that desire.

The first set of interventions sets out to alter the social and economic environment that tends to promote fertility, and by altering it to create a demand among parents for a new and smaller family norm.

And the second set of interventions supplies the requisite means that will make that new norm attainable.

To create the demand for a change in family norm, governments should try to:

- Reduce current infant and child mortality rates sharply.

- Expand basic education and substantially increase the proportion of girls in school.

- Increase the productivity of smallholders in the rural areas, and expand earning opportunities in the cities for low-income groups.

- Put greater stress on more equitable distribution of income and services in the drive for greater economic growth.

- And above all else, raise the status of women socially, economically, and politically.

To satisfy the demand for a change in family norms, governments and the international community should:

- Provide a broad choice of the present contraceptive techniques and services to parents.

- Improve the delivery systems by which parents can get the services they wish.

- And expand present levels of research seeking better techniques and services.

Both categories of interventions are necessary.

Recent studies confirm that the effect of family planning programs is greatest when they are joined to efforts designed to promote related social goals.

We know that eventually the world's population will have to stop growing. That is certain.

What is uncertain is how. And when. At what level. And with what result.

We who are alive today can determine the answers to those questions. By our action—or inaction—we will shape the world for all generations to come.

We can avoid a world of 11 billion, and all the misery that such an impoverished and crowded planet would imply. But we cannot avoid it by continuing into the next quarter century the ineffective approach to the problem of population that has characterized the past twenty-five years.

Man is still young in cosmic terms.

He has been on earth for a million years or so. And our modern ancestor, *Homo sapiens,* for a hundred thousand years.

But the universe of which he is a part is some twenty billion years old.

And if we represent the history of the universe by a line a mile long, then modern man has appeared on that line for only a fraction of an inch.

In that time perspective, he is recent, and tentative, and perhaps even experimental. He makes mistakes. And yet, if he is truly *sapiens*—thinking and wise—then surely there is promise for him.

Problems, yes. But very great promise—if we will but act.

GLOSSARY

Crude Birth Rate (CBR): The number of live births, per year, per 1,000 of population.

Crude Death Rate (CDR): The number of deaths, per year, per 1,000 of population.

Rate of Natural Increase (NI): The difference between the crude birth rate and the crude death rate, usually expressed as a percentage.

Rate of Population Growth: The rate of natural increase, adjusted for migration, and expressed as a percentage of the total population in a given year.

Infant Mortality Rate: The number of deaths, per year, of infants aged 0-12 months, per 1,000 live births.

Life Expectancy at Birth: The average number of years newborn children would live if subject to mortality risks prevalent for the cross section of the population at the time of their birth.

General Fertility Rate: The number of live births per year, per 1,000 women, aged 15-49 years.

Total Fertility Rate (TFR): The number of children an average woman would have if during her lifetime her childbearing behavior were the same as that of the cross-section of women at the time of observation. The TFR often serves as an estimate of the average number of children per family.

Gross Reproduction Rate (GRR): The number of daughters a woman would have under prevailing fertility patterns.

Net Reproduction Rate (NRR): The number of daughters a woman would have, under prevailing fertility and mortality patterns, who would survive to the mean age of childbearing.

Replacement Level Fertility: A level of fertility equivalent to a Net Reproduction Rate of 1.0—the level at which childbearing women, on the average, have enough daughters to replace themselves in the population.

Stationary Population: A population that for a long time has had a constant replacement-level fertility and therefore also has a growth rate equal to zero and a constant age composition.

SEVENTEEN

To the
BOARD OF GOVERNORS
WASHINGTON, D.C.
SEPTEMBER 26, 1977

I. INTRODUCTION

If one surveys what has taken place in the developing world since we last met in this forum, there are, I believe, two important points that emerge.

The first and more obvious one is that the immediate economic outlook, although still clouded, has measurably improved.

You will recall the situation twelve months ago.

The 1975 performance figures for the developing nations were in, and confirmed that their average GNP growth rate did not exceed 3.7%, down sharply from the averages of the 1960s.

The per capita income of the poorest nations—inadequate in the best of years—had simply stagnated.

The middle-income developing nations were faced with mounting external debt, and stubborn problems of adjustment.

And serious difficulties threatened the future operations of the World Bank itself: there were repeated delays in the IDA-V negotiations, and considerable uncertainty over the IBRD capital increase.

It was not a very reassuring situation.

Today, as we meet, the prospects are brighter.

The 1976 performance figures indicate that the average growth rate of the developing countries moved up to 4.7%.

And with the negotiations of IDA-V now successfully concluded, and a broad consensus that there should be both an increase in real terms in the IBRD's lending program, and an expansion of the capital structure, the uncertainties over the World Bank's future financial operations are now largely resolved.

There are, then, discernibly better prospects for the period ahead than there were twelve months ago.

And yet beneath this immediate and short-term improvement in the global development scene—and partially obscured by it—lies a more profound and troubling problem.

437

It is this.

A certain restive and uneasy interlude has followed on the international community's unsuccessful efforts to reach fundamental agreements. There is a pervasive and growing sense of dissatisfaction with the outcome of the lengthy discussions that have taken place over the past two years in various international forums.

The Seventh Special Session of the U.N. General Assembly, the UNCTAD IV Meeting in Nairobi, the protracted North-South Dialogue in Paris, these and a number of other efforts have all come, and gone.

And yet the most urgent issues remain largely unresolved.

Some partial agreements have been reached, some differences have been narrowed, and some willingness to compromise has emerged.

But it is evident that neither the developed nor the developing nations, neither the capital-surplus nor the capital-deficit countries, neither the North nor the South are really satisfied with the outcome. The atmosphere today is at best one of regret and disappointment, and at worst one of frustration and disillusionment.

It is not a promising climate in which to achieve what is needed most of all: a basic understanding of development issues and how to resolve them.

Now, there are two types of actions that can be taken to improve that climate.

One is to prevent the political aspects of the situation from hardening further into stalemate.

That, of course, is essentially a political matter, and as such beyond the mandate of the Bank itself. And it was for this reason that last January I suggested that there be organized a wholly independent, high-level, but deliberately unofficial commission of experienced political leaders—drawn from the developed and developing countries alike—that could assess and recommend feasible alternatives to the current North-South deadlock.

I recommended that someone of the political experience and stature of Willy Brandt, former Chancellor of the Federal Republic of Germany, be the convener and chairman of such a commission.

I continue to hope that Willy Brandt will accept the task, assemble a distinguished group of commissioners, recruit an expert staff, and begin the work.

It would be an important effort to help remove the roadblocks to more effective international development cooperation.

And there is a second type of action that would be useful today: action that would be ongoing and complementary to the political effort.

What is needed is a comprehensive and continuing analysis of development problems: a practical and sustained effort to integrate the diverse components of development experience into a more understandable pattern; an effort to explore and evaluate the critical linkages among such components, linkages that often interact in strongly supportive or seriously disruptive ways not readily apparent; an analysis that would clearly state the costs and benefits to both developed and developing countries of alternative ways of dealing with the central issues.

The truth is that the lack of such systematic, detailed knowledge often makes it difficult for governments to design appropriate long-term development policies with full understanding of their broader impact. The result is that effective international cooperation is hampered.

A good illustration is the population issue. The international community is only now gradually beginning to understand the complicated interrelationships between certain very specific development policies and fertility trends. The critical linkages are there, and have been for years, but even today we have only a dim and tenuous grasp of them. The inevitable result has been piecemeal and inefficient population programs nearly everywhere. And the Bank itself has been no exception to this.

What is true of the population issue is true of many other fundamental problems in development.

The international community today has no fully adequate analytical mechanism for assessing complex development phenomena and hence no fully adequate means of evaluating alternative ways of dealing with them. Nor does it have a satisfactory yardstick by which to measure progress in the cooperative effort.

Earlier this year a number of political leaders of both developed and developing countries proposed that the World Bank should initiate work on such a project—on what might be termed a "World Development Report."

I believe the proposal has merit.

I have discussed it with the Executive Directors of the Bank, with the Chairman of the Development Committee, with the management of the IMF, and with other interested parties.

This morning I want to explore it further with you. But before doing so, I would like to examine some of the fundamental development issues that need to be integrated into such a general framework.

Specifically, I want to:

• Briefly review what we can learn from the past record of development;

• Discuss the elements of an effective strategy to accelerate economic growth in both the poorest and the middle-income developing countries;

• Suggest how the benefits of that growth can be better channeled to meet the basic human needs of the absolute poor;

• Indicate for the near term the projected financial operations of the Bank required to support accelerated growth and the attack on absolute poverty;

• And, finally, outline the initial steps that can be taken to organize the proposed "World Development Report."

Let me begin, then, with what we can learn from the past record.

II. THE PAST RECORD OF DEVELOPMENT[a]

It is a very impressive record.

Indeed, historically, it is without precedent. Never has so large a group of human beings—two billion people—achieved so much economic growth in so short a time.

In the quarter century from 1950 to 1975 the average per capita income of the developing world grew at over 3% a year. The present industrialized countries, at a comparable stage in their own development, required a much longer time to advance as far, and attained an annual per capita income growth of only about 2%.

Nor was the achievement exclusively economic. Important social progress was made as well. Average life expectancy, for example, was expanded from about 40 years to 50 years. Though 50 is still 30% lower than the longevity currently enjoyed in the industrialized nations, it took Western Europe a century to achieve what the developing nations did in 25 years.

So successful were the developing countries in reducing their death rates—by either eradicating or severely reducing a number of major diseases—that as an unintended result, their populations began to grow at unacceptably high rates.

In the period 1950-1975 more people were added to the population of the developing world than the present total population of the developed world. It was the demographic effect, not of expanded birth rates, but of diminished death rates.

Excluding the People's Republic of China, the population of the developing countries increased from 1.1 billion in 1950 to 2 billion in 1975: an annual rate of growth of 2.4%—about double the rate in the developed countries.

That birth rates must come more rapidly into balance with death rates is an urgent imperative of our era, and I have outlined the complex dynamics of this problem in a statement at the Massachusetts Institute of Technology earlier this year.

---

[a] I am indebted to David Morawetz for his perceptive study of this subject.

But the fact remains that it was a staggering feat for the developing world to absorb 900 million people into their population in so short a time, and still effect some improvement in their average standard of living. Had the population growth not been so rapid, the improvement would have been even more impressive.

As it is, despite the immense increase in numbers, marginally more food per person is available there today, on average, than it was a quarter century ago. And during the last ten years in particular, calorie consumption per capita appears to have increased in at least 47 developing countries.

These emerging societies have also succeeded in increasing the literacy of their peoples. Twenty-five years ago 65 million children were in primary school. Today 260 million are. Then, only 7 million were in secondary and higher institutions. Today 65 million are. In 1950 only a third of their adult population could read and write. Today more than a half can.

Much of this social progress was possible because the real per capita income of the developing world, as the table below indicates, had more than doubled during the period.

Table I—Growth of GNP Per Capita in Developing Countries

Region	Population (1975; millions)	GNP Per Capita (1976 dollars)		Annual Growth Rate 1951-1975
		1950	1975	(%)
South Asia	830	85	130	1.8
East Asia	337	170	435	3.9
Sub-Saharan Africa	309	175	285	2.0
Latin America	309	550	1,050	2.6
North Africa and Middle East	158	385	1,300	5.0
Southern Europe	117	555	1,815	4.9
Total	2,060	210	520	3.7

It was, then, in spite of its difficulties, a quarter century of remarkable advance.

And yet, it is very often not perceived as such.

To many people, indeed perhaps to most people in the developed nations, the problems of the developing world seem far more real than its progress.

Nor is that a view shared exclusively by outside observers.

To many within the developing countries themselves, progress seems tortuously slow. And hopes fade and disillusionment grows as the distance between expectation and achievement lengthens.

There are, of course, many reasons for this attitude: some valid, but others quite misleading and unrealistic.

Let me single out two common characterizations that are made about international development today, and briefly examine their validity.

Closing the Gap

The first proposition is that development, despite all the efforts of the past 25 years, has failed to close the gap in per capita incomes between the developed and developing countries—a gap that at its extremes ranges in money terms to more than $8,000 per capita.

The proposition is true. But the conclusion to be drawn from it is not that development efforts have failed, but rather that "closing the gap" was never a realistic objective in the first place. Given the immense differences in the capital and technological base of the industrialized nations as compared with that of the developing countries, it was simply not a feasible goal. Nor is it one today.[a]

---

[a]The algebra of closing the absolute gap in per capita incomes can be summarized as follows: a poor country growing faster than a rich one will not begin to reduce the absolute income gap between them until the inverse ratio of their growth rates is equal to the ratio of their per capita incomes. Thus, if the historical growth rates continue into the future, the present absolute income gap will continue to widen since developed and developing countries have been experiencing similar rates of per capita growth in the last 25 years. Even if the developing countries manage to double their per capita growth rate, while the industrial world maintains its historical growth, it will take nearly a century to close the absolute income gap between them. Among the fastest growing developing countries, only 7 would be able to close the gap within 100 years, and only another 9 within 1,000 years.

As the table below indicates, the relative income gap—despite the high growth rates the developing countries achieved over the 25-year period—widened rather than narrowed, with the single exception of the oil-exporting countries.

Table II—Relative Income Gaps: Developing Country Per Capita Incomes as a Percentage of Developed Country Incomes[a]

Developing Countries:	1950	1960	1975
Poorest[b]	6.1%	4.0%	2.6%
Middle-Income	20.8	18.3	17.0
Oil-Exporting[b]	n.a.	16.1	22.6
All Developing Countries	11.9	9.7	9.2

Income gaps are not unimportant. They tell us a great deal about inequalities in the world, both between nations and within nations. And they make it obvious that the wealthy nations can clearly afford greater financial assistance to the poor nations.

But for the developing nations to make closing the gap their primary development objective is simply a prescription for needless frustration.

What is far more important as an objective is to seek to narrow the gaps between themselves and the developed nations in terms of the quality of life: in nutrition, literacy, life expectancy, and the physical and social environment.

These gaps are already narrowing, and can be narrowed much further in a reasonable period of time. Just how this can be done, I will discuss in a few moments.

Eliminating Poverty

Another characterization of the performance of the developing countries over the past quarter century is that they have

---

[a]The income data used to prepare the table reflect currency conversions at official exchange rates rather than comparative purchasing power. Had purchasing power comparisons been available, they would probably have shown similar income trends, but gaps of lesser magnitude.
[b]Indonesia is included in the "poorest" category.

failed to eliminate, or even significantly reduce the massive poverty in their societies.

Again, the proposition is true, but misleading.

Unlike "closing the gap," reducing poverty is a realistic objective, indeed an absolutely essential one. And it is true that some developing societies have had ineffective policies in this matter. In retrospect, it is clear that too much confidence was based on the belief that rapid economic growth would automatically result in the reduction of poverty—the so-called "trickle down" theory. For several years now the Bank and the countries it serves have been striving to develop effective strategies for dealing directly with the poorest elements in society.

The strategies which are now emerging must, of course, be applied in very different ways for different poverty groups. What is effective for the small farmer with half a hectare of land in the countryside may be irrelevant for the unemployed laborer in the urban slums.

There are ways of dealing with massive poverty effectively, but none of them can completely finish the task in one simple burst of activity, or in one specialized five-year plan, or even in one determined decade of effort.

The time span required depends largely on the institutional structures available through which appropriate policies can be applied. In many of the developing countries those structures are just now coming into place.

There are in the developing world today more trained people, a broader economic and social infrastructure, and a greater practical experience with the development process than these societies have ever enjoyed before. That is a result of their past 25 years of investment and hard work, and it provides the basis for turning the final quarter of the twentieth century into an even more remarkable period.

The characterizations, then, that development has failed because it has not "closed the gap" or "eliminated poverty" are superficial and misleading.

A far more realistic appraisal is that the impressive overall economic growth achieved by the developing world in fact obscures profound differences in the performance of various economic groups. There has been both uneven growth among countries, and misdirected growth within countries.

Uneven Growth Among Countries

Consider the following:

- For 32 poor countries, chiefly in South Asia and Sub-Saharan Africa, the rate of increase in per capita income was 1.5% or less per annum—less than half the average rate. Together these countries contain more than 950 million people: 46% of the total in the developing world.

- Not only have the poorest nations experienced substantially slower growth, but as Table III shows, their growth performance has continued to fall further and further behind from one decade to the next. It fell from 2.6% in the 1950s to 1.8% in the 1960s, and to 1.1% in the first half of the 1970s.

Table III—Per Capita Income Growth Rates[a]

	1950-60	1960-70	1970-75
Developing Countries:			
Poorest	2.6%	1.8%	1.1%
Middle-Income	3.2	3.5	4.2
All Developing Countries	2.9	3.2	3.7
Developed Countries	3.0	3.7	1.9

This decline in the rate of growth of per capita income in the poorest countries is by far the most disturbing trend in the record of development.

Misdirected Growth Within Countries

But it is not merely that the poorest nations have suffered

---

[a]Excludes "Southern Europe." The universe for each group of countries is the same for each period.

unacceptably low growth rates, but that such growth as there has been—both in the poorest and in the middle-income developing countries—has too often bypassed the poorest people in all these societies.

Economic growth is a necessary condition of development in any society, but in itself it is never a sufficient condition. And the reason is clear. Economic growth cannot assist the poor if it does not reach the poor.

The truth is that in every developing country the poor are trapped in a set of circumstances that makes it virtually impossible for them either to contribute to the economic development of their nation, or to share equitably in its benefits.

They are condemned by their situation to remain largely outside the development process. It simply passes them by.

Nor are we talking here about an insignificant minority. We are talking about hundreds of millions of people. They are what I have termed the absolute poor: those trapped in conditions so limited by illiteracy, malnutrition, disease, high infant mortality, and low life expectancy as to be denied the very potential of the genes with which they were born. Their basic human needs are simply not met.

1.2 billion do not have access to safe drinking water or to a public health facility. 700 million are seriously malnourished. 550 million are unable to read or write. 250 million living in urban areas do not have adequate shelter. Hundreds of millions are without sufficient employment.

These are not simply large rounded numbers. They are individual human beings.

Most tragic of all, many of them are children. For of the total of two billion people in the developing countries, some 860 million are under the age of 15.

They are the chief hope of their societies' future. And yet almost half of them suffer from some debilitating disease likely to have long-lasting effects. Well over a third of them are undernourished. 290 million of them are not in school.

That is the profile of absolute poverty in the developing world. And that profile cannot be altered by a development strategy that ignores it.

The problem is not so much that we do not know what to do about all of this.

We do know what to do. We must design an effective overall development strategy that can both:

- Accelerate economic growth;
- And channel more of the benefits of that growth toward meeting the basic human needs of the absolute poor.

The problem is that doing this requires changes in both developed and developing countries which may cut across the personal interests of a privileged minority who are more affluent and more politically influential.

Let me try, then, to analyze the two major elements of such a strategy in more detail.

III. POLICIES FOR ACCELERATING ECONOMIC GROWTH

In view of the global economic turbulence of the last five years, are there actions which the international community can take that will give reasonable assurance of achieving higher rates of economic growth in the developing countries?

I believe there are.

The adjustment processes, as painful as they have been, have not broken down.

The OECD nations are displaying signs of recovery—though it remains slower than had earlier been expected—and growth in the poorest and middle-income developing countries is moving in the direction of more normal historical levels.

The developed nations, in all but a few cases, have resisted the temptation to resort to increased protectionism.

The private capital markets responded well to the emergency needs of the developing countries for credit, and despite a major rise in external debt, the situation has remained manageable.

What is needed now is determination in the international community to assist the developing countries to continue the adjustment process, and to accelerate their present pace of growth.

Let me review with you, briefly, our appraisal of the prospects for growth in the developing countries in the 1977-85 period, and the actions necessary to realize them. We can begin with the poorest countries.

Growth Prospects for the Poorest Countries, 1977-85

An optimistic program for the poorest countries suggests that they may be able to reverse the declining trend of recent years, and achieve an annual growth rate in per capita income, for the 1977-85 period, of about 2%.

This would be a substantial improvement compared to 1970-75, but would do no more than restore their growth to the average level they experienced in the 1950s and 1960s.

In terms of their immense needs, this is disappointing. It would mean an addition of only about $30 to their per capita incomes by 1985.

But we must be realistic. Even this modest advance requires the following difficult actions:

- The poorest countries must save and reinvest at least one-fifth of the small increase in their per capita income;

- They must achieve a 25% increase in efficiency in their capital utilization, through better investment, pricing, and management policies;

- They must double their export growth in relation to the historical trends;

- And there must be a 50% increase, in real terms, in Official Development Assistance flows to the poorest nations between 1976 and 1985.

Now these policy actions are urgent.

Without them, the outlook is dismal. Even with them, the per capita incomes of these already disadvantaged countries would reach only $185ᵃ by 1985. I will return to this matter a bit later on.

Prospects for the Middle-Income Developing Countries, 1977-85

The growth prospects for the middle-income developing nations are more favorable. During the adjustment period from 1973 to 1976 they managed to maintain a per capita growth of almost 3% per year, and now appear to be poised for a major expansion in their exports, particularly of manufactured goods.

If they continue to improve their efforts to mobilize internal resources, and if the recovery quickens in the developed nations, and world trade expands, it would be reasonable to expect that the middle-income countries could achieve during the 1977-85 period an annual increase in per capita income of nearly 4%.

That would mean about a 40% increase in average incomes over current levels. And if these growth rates could be maintained until the end of the century, these countries as a group would achieve an average per capita income then of about $2,100.

But these favorable prospects cannot become a reality unless there is the will to take appropriate policy actions.

Many of these actions, of course, can be taken only by the developing countries themselves: greater mobilization of internal resources; increased efficiency in their use; better incentives for export promotion.

It is their task to fashion and implement these policies, and the Bank will do all that it can to assist them.

ᵃAll per capita income figures in this section and in the following section are expressed in terms of 1976 dollars.

But these actions, as necessary as they are, cannot succeed if the prospects for world trade expansion, and the access to international capital markets, do not improve at the same time.

It is these latter policy actions, both as they relate to the poorest and to the middle-income countries, that I want to examine now.

Trade Expansion

The per capita growth rates of 2% for the poorest countries and 4% for the middle-income nations for the years 1977-85 are based on a continuation of the set of policies that produced the expansion in their export earnings in the last decade.

With such policies we believe the developing countries could increase the volume of primary commodity exports by about 50%, and, more importantly, that they could nearly triple manufactured exports, increasing them from $33 billion in 1975 to about $94 billion by 1985.[a]

To increase exports of manufactured goods at that rate—11% per year—would require a major effort on their part. And the success of this effort assumes a continued tolerance on the part of the developed world to accept such a rapid expansion in imports from the developing countries.

But achievement of the $94 billion level would not exhaust the trade potential of the developing nations. As I pointed out last year in Manila, if the OECD countries were completely to dismantle their trade barriers against the manufactured goods of the developing countries, the latter could, by 1985, earn $24 billion per year beyond the amounts projected above.

And this represents only one part of the additional trading opportunities available to the developing countries. A recent

---

[a]All trade data in this section are expressed in 1975 dollars. The figures for 1985 are not predictions of what will happen. They simply illustrate the trade levels which could be achieved if importers and exporters alike were to pursue certain feasible policies.

Bank study indicates that if these countries themselves were to remove all of their own supply constraints on exportable manufactures, they could earn yet another $21 billion per year by 1985.

In other words, if fully rational policies were pursued by importers and exporters alike, the developing countries' export earnings from manufactured goods would increase by $45 billion per year above the levels which will result from a continuation of past policies.

It is, of course, unrealistic to expect that the developed world, even over a ten-year period, could dismantle all trade barriers, or that the developing countries over the same period, could remove all supply constraints. That would mean that the developed countries would quickly have to shift capital and labor away from those industries that can no longer compete with imports, and the developing countries would quickly have to shift more of their effort from older, less efficient production into the newer export lines.

Now, neither of these adjustments is going to happen immediately, but they do illustrate the immense contribution to development that greater efforts to liberalize trade can bring about. Would it not be a reasonable goal for both the developed and developing nations to try to achieve one-half of that potential by 1985? As Table IV indicates, this goal can be achieved if:

- First, the Tokyo Round of trade negotiations leads to a tariff reduction of 50%. This would add $4 billion to the developing countries' manufactured exports by 1985.

- Second, the non-tariff trade barriers of the industrial countries are partially relaxed. This could add $6 billion per year to these earnings.

- And third, the developing countries exploit at least half of their remaining unused export potential—through greater efficiency and further reduction of supply constraints—and the developed countries pledge not to react by increasing their levels of protection. This would boost export earnings by an additional $10 billion per year.

Table IV—LDC Earnings from Export of Manufactures
($ billion, 1975 prices)

	Poorest Countries	Middle-Income Countries	Total
1965	$ 2.4	$ 7.6	$ 10
1975	3.4	29.6	33
1985—Present Policies	7.3	86.7	94
Possible Additions from:			
• Tokyo Round	.3	3.7	4
• Partial Relaxation of Non-Tariff Barriers	1.0	5.0	6
• Improved LDC Policies	2.5	7.5	10
1985—New Policies	11.1	102.9	114

The truth is, of course, that these policy actions are in the larger interest of both the developed and developing nations.

The increased imports from the developing countries would be matched by increased exports from the developed countries. Thus the expanded trade would benefit both consumers and producers in the industrialized countries, and would expand incomes in the less-advantaged countries.

It would require, however, practical adjustment assistance for those industries affected in the developed nations, adjustment assistance which would shift the burden from the displaced labor and capital to society as a whole. And it would mean that the developing countries must move to a more outward-looking economic stance so as not to inhibit the trade expansion that the international markets are willing to absorb.

In short, it would call for enlightened attitudes on both sides, and a mutual measure of political courage.

Greater Access to Capital

Better, more realistic trade policies are clearly essential. But foreign exchange earnings will supply only part of the financing required for acceptable levels of growth in the developing countries. They must also have continued access to international capital markets.

As Annex I on page 473 indicates, the bulk of the external capital flow to the poorest countries has come from official sources, including the World Bank, rather than commercial banks. It must continue to do so.

The essential problem in these countries is that the resources used to service external debt diminish the already inadequate resources available to support their development efforts. Thus the problem of debt is linked closely to the need for increased transfers of real resources on concessional terms.

Concessional aid from OECD nations has not been increasing in real terms. The final figures for 1976 reveal that total Official Development Assistance (ODA) was 6% below the estimates made a year ago. The 1976 total, in real terms, was actually less than it had been in 1975. The fact is that the ODA level, in real terms, has been essentially stationary for the past ten years. During that time the real income of the OECD nations has increased over 40%. As a result, Official Development Assistance as a percentage of GNP, has fallen from .42 in 1966 to .33 in 1976. The 1976 ratio is, of course, less than one-half of the .7% goal accepted by the U.N. General Assembly in 1970.

The fact that the total for ODA remained more than 50% below the U.N. target is due chiefly to the three largest ODA contributors. In 1976 the ODA to GNP ratio for the U.S. was .26; for the Federal Republic of Germany .31 (down from .40 in 1975); and for Japan .20 (down from .24 in 1975).

Each of these nations within the past six months has stated its intention to increase significantly its level of ODA in future years. On the basis of the statements of government spokesmen, we have projected that ODA in 1980 will amount to .37 of the donors' GNP, an increase of one-third, or $4.9 billion in real terms.[a] The 50% increase in ODA, in real terms, to the poorest nations between 1976 and 1985—on which their modest growth rate will depend—is premised on this action.

The middle-income developing countries, on the other hand, have relied extensively on private external capital sources, as shown in Annex II on page 474.

---

[a]See Annex III on page 475.

As the table indicates, private credits to middle-income countries increased rapidly—by $35 billion—in the 1973-76 period. There has been concern that this dramatic growth in external borrowing—particularly the borrowing from commercial banks—is unsustainable, and that if it is allowed to continue there will eventually be a generalized debt crisis.

A year ago I argued that such a crisis was not inevitable, and could be avoided through a series of interrelated actions to be taken by the developing countries themselves, by the international banking community, and by the international financial institutions. And the record of the past year indicates that corrective action has in fact been taken.

Thus during 1976 the ten nations which account for three-quarters of all the debt owed to private sources by the oil-importing developing countries managed to reduce their total current deficit by more than one-third: from $22.5 billion in 1975, to approximately $14.2 billion in 1976. This improvement exceeded by a substantial margin the Bank's own projections.

Export performance during 1976 was enhanced by unanticipated increases in certain commodity prices—coffee, for example—but this was far from the whole story. Rates of growth of manufactured exports were also higher than expected. Moreover, as a group these ten countries exercised substantial restraint on imports. In several cases, imports were kept constant, or even reduced in real terms.

In addition, the middle-income countries, as a group, raised their real domestic savings last year by 15%.

These impressive overall figures do, of course, tend to obscure the less than satisfactory performance of a few countries. But on balance the adjustment record of the major borrowing countries this past year has been a good one.

Further there is increased public awareness that the debt problem cannot sensibly be measured by simply charting the growth of the developing world's debt. Such global statistics reflect a "money illusion" in the sense that much of the apparent growth is simply a consequence of the high rates of inflation experienced in recent years.

If debt is deflated by the borrowing countries' export price index, the real rate of growth of developing countries' debt was actually slower in the last few years (1973-1976) than in the late 1960s. And as a proportion of export earnings, the disbursed debt of the middle-income developing countries increased only 12% over the last decade: from 84% in 1967 to 96% in 1976.

Based on a series of consultations between World Bank staff and the major international banks in North America and Europe, it appears that the commercial banks anticipate continued growth in their net lending to developing countries, though at a more moderate rate: perhaps 10 to 15% per annum in current dollars, as compared to more than 30% over the last three years. Such a pace in new lending would be consistent with the requirements for private credit which we project for the developing countries over the next few years. And it means, in effect, that the major lending banks and the major borrowing countries are operating on assumptions which are broadly consistent with one another.

Another critical element in the middle-income countries' debt prospects is the outlook for official finance. For the middle-income countries, the major source of long-term official finance is the World Bank and the Regional Banks. A year ago there were major uncertainties about the prospects for future growth in lending from these institutions, particularly for the World Bank itself. Those uncertainties are now largely resolved.

For all these reasons we are even more confident today than we were a year ago that the debt problem is indeed manageable, and need not stand in the way of desirable rates of growth for the developing countries.

But in stating this conclusion, I would not want to create the impression that the debt issue may simply be ignored. It cannot.

Although the adjustment process has been successfully completed by many of the developing countries that are major borrowers in private markets, there are a few cases that clearly need further corrective action. And though the net requirements of the developing countries for private borrowings will not rise much in real terms in the years ahead, large amounts of recent medium-term loans will fall due. In 1980, half of all gross borrowings will be needed for amortization payments.

Past experience suggests that liquidity problems will be encountered by at least a few borrowers in the coming years. The challenge to the international community is to ensure that these isolated occurrences do not undermine the stability of the system as a whole. The IMF's recently approved Supplementary Financing Facility is clearly welcome in this connection.

But the World Bank itself also has a role to play. As I have stressed, there is a need for a better balance between official and private flows over the next few years. This shift should promote greater stability, both by lengthening the debt structure of borrowing countries and by spreading the burden and risk of lending to individual developing countries more broadly throughout the international community.

In summary, then, the goals of expanded trade, and greater access to capital—and the policy actions that will make this possible—are key ingredients of accelerated economic growth in the developing countries.

That growth is absolutely essential to development.

But growth, no matter what its magnitude, cannot assist the hundreds of millions of absolute poor in the developing societies unless it reaches them.

It is not reaching them adequately today, and it is to that issue that I want to turn now.

IV. POLICIES FOR REDIRECTING GROWTH

The aggregate economic growth the developing countries have achieved over the past 25 years—as remarkable as it has been—has not been very effective in reducing poverty.

The poorest countries, as I have noted, participated only modestly in the general trend of rapid growth since 1950. In the last few years, their growth rates have lagged even further behind.

Even in those developing countries that have enjoyed rapid growth, the poorest income groups have not shared in it equitably. Their incomes have risen only one-third as fast as the national average.

Taken together, these two tendencies explain why there has been so little increase in the living standards of the absolute poor throughout the developing world.

It is clear there must be a more equitable and effective sharing of the benefits of growth within both groups of developing countries.

Formulating development objectives in these terms avoids the misconception that because economic growth has not always been effective in increasing the incomes of the poor, it is somehow not really necessary.

It is very necessary.

In the countries with the greatest concentrations of the absolute poor—particularly those in South Asia and Sub-Saharan Africa—economic growth has been particularly slow relative to the growth of population. In these conditions, there is little scope for improving the quality of life through income redistribution alone. The total national income is simply not adequate.

But let us suppose that these poorest nations were now to double the average rate of per capita growth that they experienced in the last 25 years. This is clearly an improbable target, and even if they were able to reach it, their average per capita income, by the end of the century, would only be about $400.

But in the absence of effective government policies to moderate skewed income distribution, such an average level of income in itself cannot effect an extensive reduction in absolute poverty. And that would mean that hundreds of millions of the absolute poor in Asia and Africa have an interminable wait ahead of them before they can begin to lead decent lives in which their basic human needs are met.

The poorest countries, then, must do everything they can to increase per capita income growth, but they must do something else as well. They must fashion ways in which basic human needs can be met earlier in the development process.

Is that feasible?

It is. A number of countries have made progress towards that goal. Not always very effectively, and never without some set-backs. But progress nevertheless.

Even the middle-income developing countries must not rely solely on rising average levels of per capita income to solve problems of absolute poverty. Like the poorest societies, they must attack it directly. They have far more resources with which to do so, and can cut short the time period in which their least-advantaged citizens must wait to have basic needs met.

The strategy we are discussing for attacking absolute poverty applies, therefore, both to the poorest nations and to the middle-income countries. But it obviously applies with much greater force to the poorest nations since they have no other viable alternatives.

What are the components of those basic needs which must be satisfied if absolute poverty is to be overcome? It is not difficult to list them, although the characteristics of each will vary from country to country, from culture to culture, and from society to society. They include:

- Food with sufficient nutritional value to avoid the debilitating effects of malnutrition, and to meet the physical requirements of a productive life;

- Shelter and clothing to ensure reasonable protection against the rigors of climate and environment; and

- Public services that make available the education, clean water, and health care that all members of society need if they are to become fully productive.

The first requirement for meeting these basic needs is that the absolute poor must be able to earn an adequate income with which to purchase on the market such essential goods as the market can supply: food, for example, and shelter.

Enhancing the Productivity of the Poor

Assisting the poorest groups in the society to find earning opportunities and to enhance their own productivity is essential since they are the very groups that are so often bypassed by the traditional development process.

To the extent that the poor possess some tangible assets, however meager—a small farm, a cottage industry, or a small-scale commercial operation in the urban sector—it is possible to help them to become more productive through better access to credit, extension assistance, and production inputs.

The experience of Malaysia, Kenya, Malawi, Taiwan, Korea, Nigeria, and other countries, demonstrates that the productivity of small farms can be significantly enhanced through such programs, and the Bank itself is committed to this objective through its new rural development projects. We have over the last three years initiated projects which will approximately double the incomes of about 40 million individuals living below the poverty line in both the poorest and middle-income countries.

Both the developing countries themselves, and the Bank, have had less experience in creating off-farm earning opportunities and in assisting cottage industries and small-scale entrepreneurs, but it is clearly important to try to do so. Two-thirds of the employment in the industrial sector of the developing world still originates in small-scale enterprises. Their expansion and increased productivity is vital to the overall growth of the economy, and to the incomes of the poor.

We in the Bank are still in the early stages of launching an increased effort to finance such labor-intensive activities— activities that can provide productive employment at low unit capital costs. By 1980 we intend to increase our annual financial commitments to these types of operations to roughly $300 million.[a] We plan to work through and, where necessary, to create local financial institutions for that purpose. Urban and rural development projects will increasingly include such operations as components of the investment plan.

---

[a] In 1976 prices.

This is already being done in projects in Tanzania, India, and Indonesia. In Madras, for example, an urban development project will create 5,000 jobs in cottage industry activities in slum areas at an average investment cost of $225 per job. Thus, the earning capacity of the urban poor will be increased with only a modest investment of scarce capital.

Redesigning Public Services

Equally essential to expanding the capacity of the absolute poor to purchase market goods are the redesign and expansion of public services.

Health care, education, public transportation, water supply, electricity, and similar public services are of course the concern of developing countries everywhere. Over the past 25 years their governments have been faced with increasing pressures to satisfy demand as overall populations have nearly doubled, and urban inhabitants have quadrupled.

Inevitably some mistakes have been made. Wealthy urban and rural families, often constituting a very small but politically influential and elite group, have frequently managed to preempt a disproportionate share of scarce public services.

It is a very old story in human affairs, and far from being an attribute of developing countries only. But wealth and privilege have made their influence felt in these matters, and almost always at the expense of the poor.

Piped water allocation, the availability of electricity, the cost and routing of public transportation, the location of schools, the accessibility of public health facilities — all of these are national and local government decisions that are critical to the living standards of the very poor, who have no margin for alternatives, and no political access to policy makers.

Not only are essential public services often out of financial and geographical reach of the poor, but such facilities as are in place may be so inappropriately designed as to be virtually irrelevant to their needs: impressive four-lane highways, but too few market roads; elaborate curative-care urban hospitals, but too few preventive-care rural clinics; prestigious institutions of higher learning, but too few village literacy programs.

Public services that are not designed modestly and at low cost per unit will almost certainly end by serving the privileged few rather than the deprived many.

To reverse this trend, governments must be prepared to make tough and politically sensitive decisions, and to reallocate scarce resources into less elaborate—but more broadly based— delivery systems that can get the services to the poor, and the poor to the services.

Our own recent experience shows this is clearly possible. For example:

- El Salvador is developing a basic shelter program within the reach of its poorest urban households. The cost per unit in the two projects we have financed is averaging around $1,500. Over 3,000 units have already been built and sold to families with individual incomes below $240 per year. The shelter program is designed to reach as low as the 10th percentile of the population in terms of income, and it is already beginning to do that.

- In Indonesia, the World Bank is helping to finance the Government's Slum Improvement Program that will deliver the basic requirements for a healthier and more productive life —clean water, human and solid waste disposal, and surface drainage—to the massive squatter settlements of Jakarta and Surabaya. The program will benefit over 400,000 people at an investment of $60 per person. At these very low costs, the program is financially replicable on a very large scale.

- Colombia has developed a national health program designed to bring basic health services to an estimated 40% of Colombians who at present have no regular access to health care. The program is organized around community workers, community health posts, and self-help. In only two years of operation, it has reached one million poor. If successful— and the extensive study on which it is based indicates it will be—it will bring basic health services to all of Colombia's poor by 1985 at a yearly cost of less than $4 per person.

- Upper Volta, one of the poorest countries in the world, discovered that even if all its limited fiscal resources were spent on primary education, it could educate only one-half of its children in formal schools. It has, therefore, been experimenting with an alternative non-formal system in rural areas which provides three years of basic education and practical agricultural training for adolescents who have never been to school. The Upper Volta program, assisted by the Bank, now provides training in literacy, numeracy, and practical skills to about 30,000 such young people.

These are only a few instances of what can be done if the governments concerned are prepared to take the necessary decisions. Technically, much is possible. Politically, such decisions can pose difficult choices.

It always comes down to a question of priorities: more foreign exchange for importing private automobiles; or an expanded bus fleet. Elaborate government offices; or squatter settlement upgrading. A new generation of jet fighters for the air force; or a new generation of infants who will live beyond their fifth birthday.

No government can do everything. To govern is to choose. But poverty will persist and grow if the choice too often favors the peripheral extravagance over the critical need.

Basic human needs are by definition critical. And for governments to assist the poor to satisfy them is not public philanthropy, but a wise investment in human capital formation.

It is the poverty itself that is a social liability. Not the people who happen to be poor. They represent immense human potential. Investing in their future productivity—if it is done effectively —is very sound economics.

Certainly what is very unsound economics is to permit a culture of poverty to so expand and grow within a nation that it begins to infect and erode the entire social fabric.

Poverty at its worst is like a virus. It spreads the contagion of bitterness, cynicism, frustration, and despair. And little wonder. Few human experiences are more embittering than the gradual perception of oneself as a trapped victim of gross social injustice.

No government wants to perpetuate poverty. But not all governments are persuaded that there is much that they can really do against so vast a problem.

But there is.

Moving against the roots of poverty; assisting the poor to become more productive, and hence more an integral part of the whole development process; redirecting economic growth and public services more toward meeting basic human needs: these are practical and attainable objectives.

Last year I suggested that developed and developing nations alike establish as one of their major goals the meeting of the basic human needs of the majority of the absolute poor within a reasonable period of time—say, by the end of the century. I continue to believe such a goal is both fundamental and feasible. Moreover, we see more clearly now, than we did then, the means by which it can be achieved.

Should not, then, the developing nations individually, and the world community collectively, formulate the specific actions that must be taken to accomplish such an objective, lay out the time schedule for these actions, and monitor the progress of the program?

Most of the task must, of course, be done by the developing countries themselves. Only they are in a position to adjust their national priorities. Only they can create the necessary economic and political framework in which to reach their own poor. Only they can mobilize the creative energies of their own citizenry.

But the task is too vast for national efforts alone. If it is left exclusively to these countries—if they are refused reasonable outside assistance—either the time period may stretch so far into the future that it outruns the patience of their own people, or they may be confronted with such critical economic strains in the short term that they are forced to give up the longer-term effort.

Surely, the developing societies that make a determined commitment to meeting the basic human needs of all their people deserve broader alternatives than those.

That is why—as I have pointed out—the international community must help in this matter by expanding trading opportunities, and by increasing capital flows. What we all must grasp is that the task itself is neither unrealistic nor naive. Indeed, it is clearly manageable in purely technical and supply terms since the shortfalls are quite modest in comparison to total world production.

It is rather the institutional and political constraints — not physical or technological limits—that are the greatest obstacle.

In this overall effort, the World Bank itself must, of course, do all it can through its own financial operations to be helpful.

Let me discuss with you, briefly, the outlook for those operations.

V. THE FINANCIAL PROGRAM FOR THE WORLD BANK

When I spoke to you last year, it was very far from clear what the future scale of World Bank operations would be.

The negotiations for the Fifth Replenishment of IDA's resources had met with delays, and a discussion on a general capital increase for the IBRD had not yet begun.

Today, as you know, those uncertainties have been largely resolved.

The IDA-V negotiations have been successfully concluded, and—together with the transfer of Bank profits—should enable the Association to commit approximately $8 billion over the next three fiscal years, compared to $4.5 billion over the past three.

Moreover, a consensus has emerged, first at the London Summit Meeting, and subsequently at the CIEC meetings in Paris, in favor of a General Capital Increase for the IBRD that would enable it to maintain real growth in its operations over the next several years.

Finally, the increase in the capital structure of the IFC has now been formally approved.

On the basis of these developments, the World Bank Group is now planning for commitments in the fiscal year ending June 1978 of $8.7 billion—compared to $7.3 billion in the past year—and $9.8 billion in the following year.

It is reasonable to expect that the Bank Group will begin the decade of the 1980s at a level of operations in excess of $10 billion per year.

In terms of current dollars, this represents nearly a tenfold increase over the average achieved in the mid-1960s, and a fourfold increase over the average of the FY69-73 period.

Some of this growth has, of course, simply reflected the high levels of inflation of recent years, but if the figures are adjusted to eliminate that effect and are expressed in real terms, the increases are still substantial.

Table V—World Bank Group New Commitments
(billions of $)

	Avg. per Yr. FY64-68	Avg. per Yr. FY69-73	Avg. per Yr. FY74-78	Preliminary Plan FY79
New Commitments:				
Current $	1.2	2.7	6.7	9.8
Constant FY77 $	2.8	4.3	7.1	8.5
No. of IBRD/IDA Projects	57	129	207	255

Despite the uncertainty regarding the precise level of World Bank commitments in 1979 and in the early 1980s, the level of net capital flows—Bank disbursements less repayments made by our borrowing member countries—can be projected with reasonable accuracy for the next several years.

Table VI—Net Disbursement from IBRD and IDA
to Developing Countries
(billions of current US$)

	FY68	FY73	FY78	FY83[a]		FY64-68	FY69-73	FY74-78	FY79-83[a]
IBRD	0.4	0.7	2.6	5.0		1.7	2.9	9.1	21.6
IDA	0.3	0.5	1.3	2.6		1.3	1.4	5.6	10.5
Total:									
Current $	0.7	1.2	3.9	7.6		3.0	4.3	14.7	32.1
FY77 $	1.4	1.9	3.7	5.0		6.3	7.6	15.4	24.0

As the table indicates, a decade ago net capital flows amounted to $0.7 billion. This year they should be just under $4 billion.

By 1983, the total from the IBRD and IDA combined should reach an annual rate of approximately $7.6 billion.

Thus, over the five-year period ending in 1983—with approximately two-thirds of the funds coming from the IBRD, and one-third from IDA—the Bank should provide to the developing countries between $30 and $35 billion in net financing.

The major expansion in IDA resources in the Fifth Replenishment will enable us to make a significant contribution to the acceleration of the pace of development in the poorest nations, which have suffered a decline in the share of total resource transfers in recent years.

The very substantial sums which the IBRD will be lending to the developing countries in the next four years should help restore a healthier balance between official and private lending. This is particularly true of the middle-income developing countries, in which private lending has grown so dramatically in the recent past.

And finally, we expect that the IFC, with a fourfold increase in its capital, will play an increasingly important catalytic role in stimulating private investment in the developing countries.

---

[a]Preliminary projections.

Now, the future financial operations of the World Bank, as important as they are, will of course be only a part of a much larger effort of the international development community as a whole to pursue the central objectives of development.

The pursuit of these objectives requires substantial mobilization of financial resources. But it requires, as well, a sound conceptual framework, and a clear understanding of the impact on the development process of alternative national and international policies.

One of the obstacles both to public support of development, and to more effective national and international development programs, is the lack of such a framework.

Let me turn to that issue now.

VI. INITIAL STEPS TOWARD A "WORLD DEVELOPMENT REPORT"

As I have noted, a number of policial leaders of both developed and developing countries recommended earlier this year that the World Bank should initiate work on what might be termed a "World Development Report"—that is, a comprehensive analysis of development problems, and of the policies of developed and developing countries that affect them.

The proposal reflects a growing consensus throughout the world that a much more effective approach to the problems of development must be found, and that a prerequisite for this is a better understanding of the impact of internal and external policies on major social and economic issues in countries at different stages of development.

The economic turbulence of the past five years has sensitized every government to the interlocking nature of these issues.

But, understandably, no government has been very certain how best to proceed. More intensive cooperation on the problems of development is obviously necessary. But what kind, how much, at what cost, and with what blend of policies, has been far from obvious.

It is in this context that the Bank plans to initiate an ongoing assessment of development problems. The objective will be to improve the Bank's own understanding of the principal components of the development process and their complex interrelationships, and thus gradually develop a framework that can better assist our member countries to deal with that process more effectively.

As this work proceeds, and as more issues and problems are analyzed, it can provide a continuing basis for reviewing development progress in future years. The report will be revised annually as new data and new knowledge emerge, and it will be available for discussion by governments and in appropriate international forums.

I should stress that there will be no effort in this to duplicate or preempt the work of other development institutions or international bodies. Quite the contrary, our work in the Bank, as it has in the past, will draw on their insights and enlist their assistance.

We will begin modestly, and I would hope that by July of next year we could provide the Directors of the Bank with a draft of the first report. That would allow for discussion in the Board in time for possible consideration by the Development Committee at our next Annual Meeting.

VII. SUMMARY AND CONCLUSIONS

Let me now summarize and conclude the central points I have made this morning.

If one looks objectively at the developing world's economic record during the past quarter century, it is impressive. It surpasses the performance of the present industrialized nations for any comparable period of their own development.

But the unexpectedly high average rate of growth conceals significant differences between groups of countries.

The poorest nations have done only half as well as the middle-income group. Crippled by serious disadvantages, these societies have witnessed their growth gradually diminish. And collectively they contain more than half the total population of the developing world.

In the middle-income countries, the rates of growth have been better, but here too the averages obscure sharply skewed income patterns. Far too many in these societies—as in the poorest nations—have been able neither to contribute much to economic growth, nor to share equitably in its benefits. Development has passed them by.

The tragedy of the absolute poor is that they are trapped in a set of social and economic circumstances that they cannot break out of by their own efforts alone. Hundreds of millions of them cannot read or write; are seriously malnourished; have no access to adequate medical care; are without adequate shelter; and have no meaningful work.

Their basic human needs are simply not met.

For these hundreds of millions, development has failed.

It will continue to fail unless the dynamics of absolute poverty are dealt with directly, and reversed.

There are two essential things that must be done. The rate of economic growth of the developing nations must be accelerated. And more of the benefits of that growth must be channeled towards helping the absolute poor meet their basic human needs.

The task facing the poorest nations of restoring their earlier per capita income growth rates is going to be arduous. Even to return to their average historical level of 2% will require a doubling of their growth in export earnings, and a 50% increase, in real terms, of the current ODA capital flows to them over the next eight years.

Without these two complementary actions, the outlook for the poorest nations—nations that contain well over a billion human beings—is grim indeed.

The middle-income nations have considerably brighter prospects. But they too will be unable to accelerate their present growth rates without greater export earnings, and continued access to capital.

The required increase in export earnings can be realized if the developed countries will make modest concessions in the removal of tariff and non-tariff barriers and if the developing countries reduce their own export constraints.

Economic growth clearly is a necessary condition of development. But it is not in itself a sufficient condition. Little can be done without growth. But much, unfortunately, can be left undone even with growth.

That is what has happened in many of the developing societies over the past 25 years. There has been growth; in some countries very rapid growth. But it has not notably helped the severely disadvantaged break out of their poverty.

What is required, then, is that developing country governments adopt policies that will assist the poor to enhance their own productivity, and that will assure them more equitable access to essential public services.

But the developing countries cannot achieve these immense tasks alone. They will need greater assistance from the developed nations.

The World Bank's contribution to this can at best be only a part of the larger effort of the international community as a whole. But its contribution will not be insignificant. Over the next five years the Bank should be able to provide its member developing countries between $30 and $35 billion in net financing.

Further, the Bank will initiate work on a detailed analysis of major development issues, and of the cost and benefits of alternative policies to deal with them. The objective of this ongoing

"World Development Report" will be both to improve the Bank's own grasp of these complexities, and gradually to develop a framework that can better assist developed and developing nations alike in their own decisions.

In the end, development is always complex and exacting.

None of it is easy. None of it is without cost. And none of it is without some risk.

But the attack on absolute poverty—basic human needs and their satisfaction—cannot be forgotten, cannot be forever delayed, and cannot be finally denied by any global society that hopes tranquilly to endure.

Capital Flows to and Debt Status of the Poorest Nations[a]
(in billions of current US$)

	1973	1975[c]	1976[c]	1980[d]	1985[d]
Current Account Deficit before Interest Payments	1.1	5.6	2.2	4.7	9.2
Interest Payments	.6	.6	.7	1.0	1.8
Changes in Reserves and Short-Term Debt	1.6	−.4	3.6	2.7	5.5
Total to be Financed	3.3	5.8	6.5	8.4	16.5
Financed by Medium- and Long-Term Capital from:					
Public Sources	3.3	6.3	5.5	8.0	15.8
Private Sources[b]	.1	−.5	.9	.4	.7
Total Net Capital Flows: Current $	3.4	5.8	6.4	8.4	16.5
1976 $	6.1	5.8	6.4	6.1	8.6
Outstanding Medium- and Long-Term Debt:					
Public Sources	18.1	23.0	26.4	42.3	79.3
Private Sources	3.0	3.4	4.0	5.2	7.0
Total—Current $	21.1	26.4	30.4	47.5	86.3
—1976 $	37.8	26.2	30.4	34.8	45.1
Debt Service:					
Interest Payments	.6	.6	.7	1.0	1.8
Debt Amortization	1.1	1.5	1.4	1.3	2.1
Interest Payments as % of GNP	.8	.4	.5	.4	.5
Debt Service as % of Exports	16.7	15.2	14.5	9.6	8.7
Price Deflator	55.8	100.7	100.0	136.6	191.5

[a]Excludes oil exporters.

[b]Includes "Direct Foreign Investment."

[c]1975 and 1976 data are based on IMF sources.

[d]The data for 1980 and 1985 are projections of current account deficits and capital flows that are consistent with the income and trade projections referred to earlier. They are not predictions of what may actually happen.

Capital Flows to and Debt Status of the Middle-Income Developing Countries[a]
(in billions of current US$)

	1973	1975[d]	1976[d]	1980[e]	1985[e]
Current Account Deficit before Interest Payments	−1.2	25.4	13.9	14.9	16.0
Interest Payments	3.0	5.8	6.8	14.8	29.6
Changes in Reserves and Short-Term Debt	10.7	−6.7	5.6	8.2	14.6
Total to be Financed	12.5	24.5	26.3	37.9	60.2
Financed by Medium- and Long-Term Capital from:					
Public Sources	4.4	9.8	10.5	15.0	21.8
Private Sources[b]	8.1	14.7	15.8	22.9	38.4
Total Net Capital Flows: Current $	12.5	24.5	26.3	37.9	60.2
1976 $	17.6	24.9	26.3	28.4	32.1
Outstanding Medium- and Long-Term Debt:					
Public Sources	24.2	34.8	42.3	82.6	159.2
Private Sources	35.0	58.7	70.2	128.9	251.1
Total—Current $	59.2	93.5	112.5	211.5	410.3
—1976 $	83.1	94.9	112.5	158.3	218.9
Debt Service: Interest Payments	3.0	5.8	6.8	14.8	29.6
Debt Amortization	10.2	10.8	11.3	27.7	52.9
Interest Payments as % of GNP[c]	0.8	0.8	1.1	1.4	1.3
Debt Service as % of Exports[c]	17.5	17.2	18.8	23.3	19.5
Price Deflator	71.2	98.5	100.0	133.6	187.4

[a]Excludes oil exporters.

[b]Includes "Direct Foreign Investment."

[c]Based on a sample of 26 countries that account for 80% of the external debt of the oil-importing middle-income nations.

[d]1975 and 1976 data are based on IMF sources.

[e]The data for 1980 and 1985 are projections of current account deficits and capital flows that are consistent with the income and trade projections referred to earlier. They are not predictions of what may actually happen.

Flow of Official Development Assistance from Development Assistance Committee Members Measured as a Percentage of Gross National Product[a]

	1960	1965	1970	1971	1972	1973	1974	1975	1976	1977	1978	1979	1980
Australia	.38	.53	.59	.53	.59	.44	.55	.61	.42	.45	.47	.48	.49
Austria		.11	.07	.07	.09	.15	.18	.17	.10	.17	.18	.18	.19
Belgium	.88	.60	.46	.50	.55	.51	.51	.59	.51	.61	.64	.65	.67
Canada	.19	.19	.42	.42	.47	.43	.50	.58	.48	.58	.61	.64	.66
Denmark	.09	.13	.38	.43	.45	.48	.55	.58	.58	.64	.67	.70	.70
Finland[b]		.02	.07	.12	.15	.16	.17	.18	.18	.17	.17	.18	.20
France	1.38	.76	.66	.66	.67	.58	.59	.62	.62	.62	.62	.62	.63
Germany	.31	.40	.32	.34	.31	.32	.37	.40	.31	.32	.32	.32	.31
Italy	.22	.10	.16	.18	.09	.14	.14	.11	.16	.12	.11	.10	.10
Japan	.24	.27	.23	.23	.21	.25	.25	.24	.20	.26	.27	.29	.30
Netherlands	.31	.36	.61	.58	.67	.54	.63	.75	.82	.97	1.00	1.02	1.03
New Zealand[c]			.23	.23	.25	.27	.31	.52	.42	.41	.45	.48	.49
Norway	.11	.16	.32	.33	.43	.43	.57	.66	.71	.87	.96	.97	.98
Sweden	.05	.19	.38	.44	.48	.56	.72	.82	.82	.93	.97	1.00	1.00
Switzerland	.04	.09	.15	.12	.21	.16	.15	.18	.19	.15	.16	.17	.17
United Kingdom	.56	.47	.37	.41	.39	.34	.38	.37	.38	.39	.37	.38	.38
United States[d]	.53	.49	.31	.32	.29	.23	.24	.26	.26	.26	.26	.26	.26

GRAND TOTAL

ODA ($b-Nominal Prices)	4.6	5.9	6.8	7.7	8.5	9.4	11.3	13.6	13.7	16.3	18.8	21.5	24.4
ODA ($b-Constant 1977 Prices)	12.2	14.1	14.4	15.5	15.8	14.3	14.2	15.1	14.8	16.3	17.4	18.6	19.7
GNP ($t-Nominal Prices)	0.9	1.3	2.0	2.2	2.6	3.1	3.4	3.8	4.1	4.6	5.3	5.9	6.6
ODA as % GNP	.52	.44	.34	.35	.33	.30	.33	.36	.33	.35	.35	.36	.37
ODA Deflator[e]	.38	.42	.47	.50	.54	.66	.80	.90	.93	1.00	1.08	1.16	1.24

[a]Figures for 1975 and earlier years are based on actual data. Figures for 1976 are preliminary actuals. Those for 1977-80 are based on OECD and World Bank estimates of growth of GNP, on information on budget appropriations for aid, and on aid policy statements by governments. They are projections, not predictions, of what will occur unless action not now planned takes place.

[b]Finland became a member of DAC in January 1975.

[c]New Zealand became a member of DAC in 1973. ODA figures for New Zealand are not available for 1960 and 1965.

[d]In 1949, at the beginning of the Marshall Plan, U.S. Official Development Assistance amounted to 2.79% of GNP.

[e]Includes the effect of parity changes. Deflators are the same as those for GNP.

EIGHTEEN

To the
BOARD OF GOVERNORS
WASHINGTON, D.C.
SEPTEMBER 25, 1978

I. INTRODUCTION

You will recall that when we met last year I recommended two specific actions designed to improve the climate of international economic development.

To prevent the debate between the developed and developing nations over a whole series of sensitive issues from hardening further into a North-South deadlock, I urged that former Chancellor Willy Brandt form an independent, high-level commission that could search for practical solutions to the growing impasse.

Willy Brandt has, as you know, moved forward vigorously in this matter. He has recruited a distinguished group of commissioners, has gathered an expert staff, and is at work seeking to identify, for the developed and developing nations, areas of mutual interest in an increasingly interdependent world.

All of us are indebted to him, and to his colleagues, for undertaking this complex and difficult task.

The second action I recommended is complementary to the first. I proposed that the Bank should undertake, annually, a comprehensive analysis of economic and social progress in the developing world in order better to assist ourselves, and our member governments, assess the alternatives and make the decisions that confront us all in the development field.

Our goal was to have in your hands, by the time of this meeting, the initial volume in this effort. That we have done. The *World Development Report, 1978* deals with fundamental problems currently facing the developing countries, and explores the relationship of those difficulties to the underlying trends of the international economy.

Many of the conclusions the report reaches are sobering.

One of them is much more than that; it is shocking. Even if the projected—and optimistic—growth rates in the developing world are achieved, some 600 million individuals at the end of the century will remain trapped in absolute poverty.

Absolute poverty is a condition of life so characterized by malnutrition, illiteracy, disease, high infant mortality, and low life expectancy as to be beneath any reasonable definition of human decency.

What I want to do, then, this morning is:

A. Examine with you our current projections for economic growth in the developing countries, and the implications of that growth for the absolute poor.

B. Make clear that in order to achieve even the projected levels of growth, which are short of the optimum, additional effort will be required from both the developed and developing nations. In particular, additional international effort will be needed on three fronts:

- A further expansion of international trade on the basis of long-term comparative advantage and mutual benefit;

- A sharp increase in the level of capital extended to the middle-income developing countries from private sources, together with increased support from the multilateral financial institutions; and

- An increased flow of concessional assistance to the poorest developing countries.

C. Stress that even if the additional international support is achieved, and the projected growth rates are realized, much greater emphasis must be placed on domestic development strategies specifically designed to reduce absolute poverty. We are far from a perfect understanding of the mix of policies required. But within the limits of our present knowledge and experience, a great deal more can—and must—be done.

D. And finally, I want to outline briefly the ways in which the World Bank itself can assist in the achievement of these twin goals of accelerating economic growth, and reducing absolute poverty.

Let me, then, begin by summarizing our projections for economic growth in the developing countries over the next decade, and their implications for absolute poverty at the end of the century.

II. PROJECTED GROWTH IN THE DEVELOPING COUNTRIES, 1975-85, AND ABSOLUTE POVERTY IN THE YEAR 2000

It is important to understand the purpose of these projections. They are not an attempt to predict the future.

Their purpose, rather, is to provide a perspective in which development issues can be examined, and to establish a basis for determining those actions that are necessary if greater social and economic progress is to be achieved.

The pursuit of that progress will, of course, cut across a number of vested interests and require an immense effort from the developing countries themselves.

There must, for example, be a renewed drive to mobilize domestic resources (Table I). It will not be easy for the poorest nations to raise their low savings rate, nor for the middle-income countries to maintain their current high rates, but it is essential that they do so. It will mean reform of taxation policies, more realistic prices for public sector products and services, restraint in low-priority government expenditures, and increased incentives for private savings.

Table I—Developing Countries[a]: Savings and Investment Rates
(Percentage of gross domestic product)

	Gross Domestic Savings			Net Foreign Resource Inflows			Gross Domestic Investment		
	1960	1975	1985	1960	1975	1985	1960	1975	1985
Low-Income Asia	12.6	16.7	20.5	2.1	2.5	2.0	14.8	19.2	22.5
Low-Income Africa	7.0	8.4	11.4	9.0	10.0	7.7	14.0	18.4	19.1
Middle-Income	17.8	22.1	21.8	2.4	4.3	2.6	20.2	26.4	24.4

In addition to strengthening their domestic savings performance, the developing countries must bolster their efforts in two other critical areas.

[a]Throughout the text, developing countries are divided into low-income countries and middle-income countries on the basis of income per capita. Income per capita in low-income countries was below $250 per year in 1976. Country groupings exclude Centrally Planned Economies other than Romania, Yugoslavia, Cambodia, Laos, and Vietnam.

The first is agricultural production. In the low-income countries, action must be initiated to at least double agricultural growth rates from 1.5% to 3.0% a year.

The second is foreign trade. Programs must be launched to increase foreign exchange earnings through export expansion in a larger number of countries.

But as essential as these actions by the developing countries are—and they clearly constitute a formidable agenda in themselves—they simply cannot succeed without a more realistic level of support from the developed nations.

That support must encompass three principal efforts:

- A reversal in the rising tide of protectionism in the developed countries against imports from the developing world;

- A sustained growth in the net financial flows from the world's private capital markets to the middle-income developing countries of about 5% a year in real terms, thus increasing them, in current dollars, from $26 billion in 1975 to $80 billion in 1985; and

- A move away from the virtual stagnation of concessional aid from the OECD countries in recent years to a growth rate of at least 5% a year in real terms, thereby causing it to rise in current dollars from $15 billion in 1977 to $42 billion in 1985.

If one assumes that both the developing and developed nations in fact take these actions, then the projected growth rates are as follows:

Table II—Growth of Gross Domestic Product, 1960-85
(Average annual growth rates, at 1975 prices)

	Per Capita			Total GDP		
	1960-70	1970-75	1975-85	1960-70	1970-75	1975-85
Low-Income Asia	.0	1.5	2.8	2.4	3.9	5.1
Low-Income Africa	1.9	.4	1.5	4.3	2.8	4.1
Middle-Income	4.0	4.1	3.4	6.3	6.4	5.9
All Developing Countries	3.2	3.6	3.3	5.5	5.9	5.7
Industrialized Countries	4.1	2.0	3.5	4.9	2.8	4.2

Because these projected growth rates are predicated on major efforts in both the developing and developed countries, they are—while feasible—very far from certain.

But one thing is certain: there is no reason for the developed nations to believe that the actions suggested for them in this scenario are beyond their capacity. For even if projected growth rates for the developing countries were to be achieved, overall growth in the world would still be heavily skewed in favor of the developed countries, as the table below indicates.

Table III—Distribution of Population and GNP, 1950-1985

Country Group	% of Population	Total GNP (in billions $75)			Share of Incremental Income	
	1975	1950	1975	1985	1950-75	1976-85
Low-Income	43	69	175	286	3	4
Middle-Income	33	208	873	1543	21	25
Total Developing	76	277	1048	1829	24	29
Total Developed	24	1341	3841	5795	76	71
Total	100	1618	4889	7624	100	100

Country Group	% of Population	Income Per Capita (in $75)			Aver. Annual Increase in Income Per Capita (in $75)	
	1975	1950	1975	1985	1950-75	1976-85
Low-Income	43	104	150	195	2	5
Middle-Income	33	454	957	1327	20	37
Total Developing	76					
Total Developed	24	2614	5883	8316	131	243
Total	100					

So far we have been talking about growth rates. What about the poverty issue?

To try to grasp its magnitude at the end of the century, we have projected the growth rates beyond 1985 for another 15 years. Admittedly such projections are subject to large margins of error. But based on what little we do know about the interactions of social and economic factors, and the effect of various patterns of economic growth on the prospects of the poor, the projections point to a global problem of shocking proportions.

The likelihood is that even if the projected growth rates in the developing countries are achieved, some 600 million individual human beings will be living in absolute poverty at the end of the century.

Table IV—Projected Levels of Absolute Poverty, 1975-2000

	Numbers (in millions)			Percent of Total Population		
	1975	1985	2000	1975	1985	2000
Low-Income Countries	630	575	540	52	39	27
Middle-Income Countries	140	140	60	16	12	4
All Developing Countries	770	715	600	37	27	17

I would like to turn now to a more detailed discussion of the actions required from the developed nations if the projected growth rates are to be realized or exceeded. I will then examine what can be done to reduce the projected levels of absolute poverty. And I will conclude with a statement of what the Bank itself can most usefully do to assist in both accelerating growth and reducing poverty.

III. EXPANSION OF INTERNATIONAL TRADE

The scarcity of foreign exchange is, of course, one of the major obstacles to greater economic growth in much of the developing world. Export earnings are the chief source of foreign exchange, and hence the growth rates projected in Table II depend on the achievement of the underlying assumptions of export performance.

What are those assumptions? Can they be realized?

The projections assume that exports from the developing countries will rise marginally from their 5.9% rate of expansion in the 1960-1975 period to 6.4% in the period 1975-1985. While this may seem a modest gain, it depends in fact on manufactured exports—now a quarter of the total—continuing to grow at the rate of approximately 12% per annum, as they have over the past 15 years.

This rate simply cannot be sustained if the protectionist barriers erected by the developed nations against the manufactured exports of the developing countries continue to rise as they have recently.

Even a partial résumé of the new restrictive measures illustrates the severity of the problem.

- Australia, Canada, France, the United Kingdom, the United States, and Sweden have imposed new quotas and so-called "orderly marketing arrangements" on the developing countries' exports of footwear.

- The new protocol of the Multi-Fiber Arrangement, covering the period through 1981, permits the imposition of more severe restrictions on clothing and textiles. Under it, for example, the European Common Market has reduced 1978 quotas for three countries beneath actual 1976 levels, and has severely limited the growth of quotas of other countries, including many that are only beginning to export these products.

- In addition to the EEC, Australia, Canada, Norway, and Sweden have also tightened developing country quotas for textiles and clothing, and the United States, for 1978, has held three of its largest suppliers to 1977 levels. The net effect of all of these restrictive measures will be to limit the growth of developing countries' exports of clothing and textiles to only 5% per annum over the next few years, compared to some 16% per annum in the period 1967-1976.

- The European Community and the United States have introduced special protective measures regarding steel, which pose serious difficulties for those developing countries now emerging as exporters.

- The United Kingdom has imposed quotas on television sets from two developing countries, and similar action is threatened in the United States and elsewhere.

The truth is that throughout the industrialized nations this trend toward protectionism is gathering momentum. There is an increasing readiness for OECD governments to extend assistance to domestic industries at the expense of developing country exports. And producers of a wide variety of products in the industrialized world—ranging from petrochemicals and ships to bicycle tires—are now demanding relief from import competition.

The popular rationale for this protectionist posture in the developed nations is, of course, that the growth in developing country exports eliminates jobs.

But while the impact on jobs in specific firms, or in particular product lines, can sometimes be serious, it is important to recognize that the negative effect of developing country exports on overall employment in the developed world has been negligible.

The fact is that developing countries today supply only a tiny portion of the manufactured goods consumed in developed countries. Less than 2%.

Even in the case of clothing, which contributed the most to developing-country export growth, the ratio of imports to total consumption in 1976 was less than 8% in the United States. In 1974, developing country textiles and clothing together constituted only 8% of the market in Germany, 6% in the United Kingdom, 5% in Canada, 4% in Japan and in the United States, and 2% in France.

These low levels of market penetration have clearly made only a minuscule impact on the overall industrial structure of the importing countries, and the impact on the occupational pattern is even smaller since a number of industries share a common need for specific occupational skills.

Further, the number of workers displaced by imports from developing countries is only a fraction of those displaced by shifts in technology and demand in the industrialized countries themselves.

A number of studies have indicated that within a given industry, the amount of employment lost through import competition is generally much smaller than that lost because of technological advances that increase labor productivity.

A German study, for example, concluded that for manufacturing as a whole during the 1962-1975 period, technological improvements displaced 48 workers in Germany for every one worker displaced by imports from developing countries. Even in clothing, where imports from developing countries grew rapidly, and technology was relatively stable, this ratio was more than three to one.

What the protectionist view overlooks is that the loss of jobs due to imports from the developing countries is outweighed by the increase in jobs due to the growing volume of exports to those same developing countries.

In 1975 the industrialized nations imported $26 billion of manufactures from the developing nations, and exported $123 billion of manufactures to them in return. And that accounted for a full 30% of all their exported manufactures.

If the developing countries are to import even more from the developed nations—and they want to—they must be allowed to export more so that they can earn the foreign exchange necessary to pay for them.

Excessive protectionism is not only unfair. It is self-defeating.

But, as I have noted, though the overall net effect of developing-country imports on employment in the developed nations is beneficial, it is true that problems can arise in individual firms, or in particular product lines, in which comparative advantage lies strongly with the developing countries. In these cases, what are needed are practical adjustment measures, not broadside protectionist barriers that in the end only make reasonable and mutually advantageous adjustment more difficult.

The truth is that the adjustment problem has largely been neglected in the industrialized countries. Too often the effort is merely to keep weak and inefficient industries alive rather than designing effective incentives for labor and capital to shift to more competitive and productive sectors.

Further, with the notable exception of The Netherlands and Norway, there have been very few governments in the developed world that have even studied the need for changes in their industrial structure. As the international economy continues to evolve, and the capacity of the developing countries to export manufactured goods expands, it is essential that there be adequate forward planning to reduce the frictions associated with structural change.

The OECD nations, both individually and collectively, should undertake such studies to identify the problem areas in advance, and explore practical solutions to deal with them.

The primary concern of the industrialized nations today is, of course, greater progress in the recovery of their own domestic economies.

Less restrictive trade with the developing countries can hasten that recovery.

A more liberal import policy, as I have already pointed out, will lead to a more rapid expansion of exports to the developing countries, thus providing a healthy stimulus to demand in the developed nations.

And added to that, imports from developing countries can assist in reducing inflationary pressures. In the United States, for example, while other wholesale prices rose by 66% from 1970 to 1976, those for clothing—due to low-cost imports— rose only 26%.

Adjustment assistance, and economic recovery, are essentially tasks for individual governments. What is needed at the international level—beyond what is accomplished at the Tokyo Round—is a more rational framework of trade relations through which excessive barriers can be more rapidly dismantled, and more explicit criteria can be established governing those barriers which must be imposed to deal with strictly temporary difficulties.

Protectionist measures are, of course, common in developing countries as well. For those societies still at an early stage of industrialization, they are often justified. But for those countries that are well advanced in the development process, the negative effects of industrial protection on efficiency and growth become increasingly apparent.

Such countries will also have to face adjustment problems if they are to increase their competitiveness and diversify their exports. And it is these countries that have the greatest stake in avoiding an increasingly restrictive trading system.

Maintaining the benefits of more liberal trade clearly will demand a cooperative approach, and the success of that approach will be enhanced as the more advanced developing countries—on a reciprocal basis—demonstrate a greater willingness to reduce their own import barriers.

Though developed and developing countries have different interests at different stages of industrialization, given a sense of realism, they can reach practical accommodations that are mutually beneficial.

A realistic agenda for such negotiations should include:

- Assured growth of the developed countries' imports of currently restricted developing-country products;

- Strict rules to prevent new tariff and non-tariff barriers, except for brief periods under agreed criteria and under strict multilateral surveillance;

- Progressive removal of present quantitative import restrictions, and the easing of administrative procedures;

- Greater liberalization of import policies by the more advanced developing countries;

- Gradual reduction of export subsidies, except for the less advanced developing countries with special problems; and

- Agreements facilitating the growth of trade among the developing countries themselves.

By participating more intensively in multilateral trade negotiations, the developing countries—and particularly the
middle-income nations—can counter the growing threat of
discrimination against their exports. This will help ensure a trading environment that better reflects their interests.

Unless this is done, not only will the economies of the developing countries grow at rates less than those projected, but
growth in the developed countries will suffer as well.

In the final analysis, a more rational framework of trade and
adjustment to changing comparative advantage must be the
centerpiece of any long-range international economic strategy
that has any realistic hope of succeeding.

Now let me turn to another facet of this same overall problem: the need for greater capital flows to the middle-income
developing nations.

IV. CAPITAL FLOWS TO THE MIDDLE-INCOME
DEVELOPING COUNTRIES

Over the past five years, the amount of foreign exchange required by the middle-income developing countries to finance
their imports has risen dramatically. This has been in part due
to the steep increases in the cost of oil.

During the same period, the recession in many industrialized
nations reduced in real terms the export earnings available to
the middle-income countries to finance those imports.

Thus these countries faced a dilemma. They could either reduce their imports, thus slowing their own economic growth as
well as that of the industrialized nations. Or they could try to
maintain the level of their imports, and thus protect their growth,
through greater reliance on external borrowing.

They chose to follow the latter course. And as a consequence,
as shown in Table I, their external financing as a percentage of
GDP nearly doubled from 2.4% in 1960 to 4.3% in 1975.

The bulk of these funds, as both the table below and Annex Table II indicate, came from private sources, primarily commercial banks.

Table V—Medium- and Long-Term Capital Flows to Middle-Income Countries[a]
(Billions of current US dollars)

	Net Disbursements			Disbursed Debt Outstanding		
	1970	1975	1985	1970	1975	1985
Grants and Concessional Loans	2.3	8.0	22.0	11.6	24.8	95.5
Loans at Market Terms Multilateral and Government	1.0	3.3	9.2	8.9	19.6	90.8
Private[a]	6.9	26.0	80.0	15.9	83.5	349.8
Total	7.9	29.3	89.2	24.8	103.1	440.6
Total—Current Prices	10.2	37.3	111.2	36.4	127.9	536.1
—1977 Prices	19.0	41.8	63.8	67.7	143.2	307.6

Thus, net flows to middle-income developing countries from private sources increased 30% a year between 1970 and 1975.

Such explosive growth could not, of course, continue indefinitely. And it has already begun to slow down substantially.

In the projections of the future growth of these countries, the assumption is that net flows will grow by 12% a year. As the table shows, even this reduced growth in lending will mean that net flows from private sources will rise, from $26 billion in 1975 to $80 billion in 1985.

That in turn means that outstanding balances would increase from $84 billion in 1975 to $350 billion in 1985.

The question is: can such huge increases in absolute amounts be supported by the private sector?

The projected growth of these balances reflects, of course, inflation: in 1977 prices, the 1985 figures would only be about

[a]Includes "Direct Foreign Investment."

half as large. In real terms the growth in net disbursements is only about 5% a year.

Thus, at this level, net flows will be growing only slightly more rapidly than the GDP in the developed countries, and somewhat less rapidly than the GDP in the middle-income developing countries.

But the fact remains that the magnitude of the increases is immense, and both the governments of the borrowing countries and the commercial lending institutions, and their supervisory agencies, must give the matter very careful thought.

What precisely are the problems involved in this expansion of debt? What are its risks? And what steps ought to be taken to ensure that the debt is managed prudently so as to avoid any sudden disruption in the flow of essential capital to the developing countries?

Two years ago, when the extent of the recent increases in commercial capital flows became apparent, there was considerable anxiety expressed over the prudence of lending on such a scale to developing countries.

We said at that time there was no real cause for alarm. And we believe that today there is a much better understanding of the capacity of the developing countries to manage their debt, even in the context of a less buoyant outlook for international trade.

But if the private lending process is to proceed smoothly, there are three aspects of it that must have continuing attention.

First, there is the problem of the risk for individual developing countries associated with the high volumes of commercial bank loans falling due in the next few years. This quantum leap in maturing debt reflects the typical 5-year maturity of the very large volume of Eurocurrency borrowing which took place in 1974 and 1975.

As long as the outlook for a borrowing country seems bright, the commercial banks are likely to make new loan commitments which not only offset the amounts due for repayment but also provide a substantial inflow of net external finance. But if the outlook for a particular borrowing country is in doubt for any reason, then the entire amount of new loan commitments can be called in question. In such a situation what is at stake is not simply some increment of new funds, but rather the risk of a substantial net outflow of capital.

The nature of the risk can be illustrated with figures for middle-income countries as a group. To meet the projected net disbursement of $68 billion for these countries in 1985, new medium- and long-term loan commitments from private sources would need to reach $160 billion per year by 1985. This is clearly an enormous sum, even allowing for the inflation which may take place over the next few years.

Such a high ratio of gross to net flows is a direct consequence of the relatively short maturity of commercial bank lending. The $160 billion figure assumes an average maturity of five years. Given the rather sharp lengthening of maturities on syndicated loans which has occurred over the past year or so, and given the success of a few middle-income countries in tapping the international bond markets, it would not be surprising if the average maturity were longer than this. But even at an average of 7 years, the gross flows would need to reach $140 billion a year.

There is no doubt that private capital flows of these magnitudes will require a continuing climate of confidence and a supportive framework of public policy in both the developed and developing countries.

Another cause for concern is that much of the international lending is still handled by relatively few banks.

Well over half of all outstanding claims on developing countries are held by about 30 major banks, principally in the United States. How much these banks can increase their lending in developing countries over the next several years depends on the growth in their capital base and the diversification of their portfolios. This is a strong reason for involving more lenders in international development.

Banks in Europe and Japan have been increasingly active in lending to developing countries, and it is important that this trend be accelerated. Diversifying the sources of lending would help dampen excessive volatility in the international capital market. That expansion of private lending can be stimulated by the provision by borrowers to lenders of more adequate information, and by the acceptance of appropriate risk premiums. Expanded cofinancing between official and private lenders can also significantly help the diversification process.

A third area of concern is the high levels of bank exposure to risks in a relatively few countries. While the number of countries that have sizeable borrowings from private markets has grown in recent years, about 70% of outstanding claims are owed by 12 countries.

Debt problems in any one of these countries, even a small one, can affect the willingness of the private market to lend to all developing countries.

While a number of analyses have concluded that there is no general problem of middle-income developing countries being unable to service debt, individual countries may run into liquidity problems. The availability of private capital to a broader range of middle-income developing countries would make the market less sensitive to developments in a restricted few.

In a more general sense, the confidence of private lenders needs to be protected by better arrangements to assist countries in short-term balance of payments difficulties, notably by expanding the resources available to the International Monetary Fund.

The critical flow of private capital to developing countries can be substantially enhanced by expanding the lending capacity of the official lending organizations—both the export credit agencies and the multilateral financial institutions. This is true for three principal reasons.

First, the maturities of official lending are substantially longer than private lending and can effectively assist developing countries in the management of their external debt. Blending official loans at near market terms having maturities of 15 to 25 years with private loans having maturities of 5 to 10 years can lighten the debt service burden on developing countries. It would result in an average maturity of their external debt that is more appropriate to their investment program and balance of payments outlook.

Whether this blending is achieved through cofinancing of the same or different projects is less important than that the volume of funds lent by the official institutions be sufficient to make a significant difference to the average maturities.

Secondly, official lending institutions support the expansion of commercial flows by providing private lenders greater assurance of the quality of economic management in the borrowing country. Through analysis and advice, the multilateral lenders help influence more prudent borrowing and economic management, and the scale of their involvement in individual countries is an important signal to private lenders.

Finally, the lending programs of the official institutions, since they are not subject to short-term changes in liquidity, can provide a less volatile flow of funds, thus adding an important element of stability.

The importance of these factors has been evident in recent years as both official multilateral lending and private lending grew extraordinarily fast, each supporting the other in meeting the capital requirements of developing countries. As I will discuss in more detail when I deal with the World Bank's program, there is a danger that this mutually supportive growth may be weakened by a failure to expand the lending authority of the multilateral financial institutions as rapidly, and as adequately, as is necessary.

Official loans accounted for 36% of developing countries' outstanding debt in 1970—excluding concessional loans—but only 19% in 1975. This share has continued to decline in 1976 and 1977.

It is neither surprising nor undesirable that private lending accelerated. But there can be a problem when the balance shifts as rapidly as it has in recent years, particularly in the case of a few countries that have been exceptionally active borrowers in the private market. The continued health of the current system of international financial intermediation requires that the growth of lending in the next decade be more balanced between official and private lenders.

Maintaining the steady growth of the medium- and long-term capital flow to developing countries, in line with their growing capacity to service external debt, serves their development needs and at the same time is of benefit to the industrialized countries. Such productive investment of a portion of their savings is profitable to their financial institutions and expands the import capacity of the developing countries, and hence the export volume of the developed nations. The additional demand will benefit particularly their machinery and transport-equipment manufacturing sectors, which are likely to account for about half of the increase in the developing countries' imports from the industrialized countries.

As with the growth of trade, strengthening the framework of international capital flows clearly provides important benefits to both developing and developed nations.

Let me turn now to the problem of concessional assistance to the poorest developing countries.

V. CONCESSIONAL ASSISTANCE TO THE LOW-INCOME COUNTRIES

The development strategies of the low-income countries of Asia and Sub-Saharan Africa clearly must give priority to raising agricultural productivity, and to meeting the requirements for essential infrastructure such as roads, health and sanitation facilities, power generating capacity, and schools.

The investment needed to support that strategy is immense. As in the past, and as shown in Table I, the bulk of the funds to finance these investments must come from domestic savings; already they furnish some 80% to 85% of the total.

The domestic savings of these low-income countries have been rising. But they have to be supplemented by external capital flows if the total investment requirements for even modest growth are to be met. And because most of the low-income countries have limited debt-servicing capacity, most of the external capital must be obtained on concessional terms through what is known as Official Development Assistance (ODA).

What is the outlook for such assistance?

As indicated in Annex III, recent trends in ODA from the Development Assistance Committee (DAC) countries are disquieting. In relation to their GNP, it has declined from .52% in 1960 to .31% in 1977.[a]

Since 1970, when the United Nations General Assembly adopted a target of .7% of GNP for concessional aid, it has never exceeded half that level, and there has been a steady deterioration against the objective. The fact is that in 1976 and 1977 the absolute amounts were less in real terms than in 1975, 1972, or 1971.

There have, however, been significant differences within the group of DAC countries. Some of the smaller countries such as The Netherlands, Norway, and Sweden have exceeded the .7% target. Others such as Canada and Denmark have substantially raised their share since 1970.

But among the four largest contributors, only France was close to the .7% objective in 1977. The other three, the United States, Japan, and Germany, all contributed substantially less than half of the target ratio in 1977, and the performance of all three has deteriorated since 1970. Had these countries increased their contributions of ODA in relation to GNP, even up to the average of the other countries, the total supply of ODA in 1977 would have been more than 25% greater.

---

[a] In addition to development assistance from the DAC countries, developing countries since 1975 have received over $5 billion of such aid each year from OPEC nations—the equivalent of about 5% of the GNP of the major donors.

In projecting economic growth in the low-income countries, we have assumed that ODA from DAC members will rise by approximately 5% per year in real terms. The increase in current dollars would be from $15 billion in 1977 to $42 billion in 1985. In relation to recent performance, such increases look formidable.

They are unlikely to be achieved, much less exceeded, unless early action is taken in Japan, Germany, and the United States to increase commitments substantially. There have been statements of intention to increase the flow of aid in all three countries. But these statements have yet to be translated into action.

Today, in September 1978, it is already too late to affect the flow of disbursements significantly by 1980. Unless very substantial increases in commitments—more than sufficient to keep pace with inflation and the real growth of GNP—are undertaken in the next year, and regularly thereafter, even the modest objective we have postulated for 1985 will not be achieved.

In that event, the growth rates we have projected for the low-income countries in Table II will not be realized, and the number of absolute poor projected in Table IV, already intolerably high, will be even greater.

Let me turn now to an examination of that poverty problem.

VI. ABSOLUTE POVERTY IN 1985 AND 2000

The need to give greater attention to the problems of the absolute poor has been increasingly recognized in international discussions. But the intractability of these problems and the scale of efforts needed to reduce the numbers of absolute poor have not been fully appreciated.

In Sections III, IV, and V, I have examined three of the major assumptions—the expansion of international trade, the flow of commercial credit, and the volume of concessional aid—that underlie the projections of economic growth in Table II and of absolute poverty in Table IV.

Because these assumptions are not likely to be achieved without additional action—action that is not now in prospect—I have stressed the need for a number of new initiatives.

But even if such initiatives are undertaken, we will still be confronted by intolerable levels of absolute poverty, as projected in Table IV, and repeated below in Table VI.[a]

Table VI—The Absolute Poor, 1975-2000
(Numbers in millions)

	1975	1985	2000
Low-Income Countries	630	575	540
Middle-Income Countries	140	140	60
All Developing Countries	770	715	600

The projection of 600 million absolute poor in the year 2000 does not assume a lack of progress in the remaining years of the century. The reduction in absolute poverty in any country depends on the growth of its GNP, the extent of improvement in its distribution, and the increase in population. Since the population[b] of the developing countries is projected to increase from 2.1 billion in 1975 to 3.5 billion in 2000, a failure to reduce the proportion living in poverty would result in the number increasing from 770 million in 1975 to 1300 million in 2000. Hence, the projected reduction to 600 million does represent improvement. But it remains unacceptably high.

Now, what can be done to reduce this level of poverty?

The World Bank does not have a full and complete answer to that question, nor do I know of anyone in the world who

---

[a]I should emphasize again that so little is known about the interaction of economic and social structures with development policies that projections of the number of absolute poor are subject to wide margins of error. They provide, nevertheless, sufficient indication of the potential results of existing policies to serve as a basis for the re-examination and assessment of strategy.

[b]The population problem is, of course, a critical issue in itself, and last year, in a detailed statement, I examined its relationship to the overall development task. Cf. Address to the Massachusetts Institute of Technology, Cambridge, April 28, 1977.

does. And that is why I urge that the Brandt Commission, the Development Committee, the UN Overview Committee, UNCTAD, the Development Assistance Committee, and other international groups—and above all the individual developing countries themselves—each give serious and detailed attention to it.

But even though no one yet has a fully comprehensive answer to the problem of absolute poverty, I believe that within the present limits of our knowledge, each of the developing countries can—and should—set specific goals for its own society's direct attack on poverty; and that the international community, in the appropriate forums, should endorse those goals, and pledge the necessary support.

As I have emphasized, such an attack on absolute poverty can only succeed in an environment of growth. And support from the international community—through further expansion of trade and more adequate capital flows—is essential if optimum growth rates are to be achieved.

But though growth is an absolutely necessary condition for reducing poverty, it is not in itself a sufficient condition. For growth cannot help the poor unless it reaches the poor.

It does not reach the poor sufficiently today, and hence the developing countries themselves must both:

- Modify the pattern of growth so as to raise the productivity of the poor; and

- Improve the access of the poor to essential public services.

In most developing countries, growth too often bypasses the absolute poor. They have only tenuous links to the organized market economy. They own few productive assets. They are often illiterate. They are frequently in poor health. And their meager incomes make it almost impossible for them to save and invest.

But though the absolute poor have severe disadvantages, their human potential remains immense. Given a realistic opportunity, they will respond. For no less than anyone else, what they want most from life is an end to despair, a beginning of hope, and the promise of a better future for those they love.

That is why any practical strategy to reduce absolute poverty must begin with the effort to assist the poor to become more productive. If they have land—even if only as tenants—that can be done through a whole range of measures. I have described these in detail elsewhere,[a] and will discuss in a moment what our experience in the Bank has been over the past five years.

If the poor are without land or other productive assets, then the strategy clearly must stress greater employment opportunity, particularly in the more labor-intensive sectors.

It is not so much conventional joblessness that characterizes the lives of the absolute poor in the developing world—though that is bad enough—but rather jobs so grossly underproductive that they yield only minuscule incomes despite long hours of labor.

And not only are the poor without adequate incomes, but they are without equitable access to essential public services: to clean water, to basic education, to preventative medical care, to electricity, to public transportation—to those services fundamental to their health and productivity.

Since most of these services cannot be privately purchased by the poor, they must be expanded through government programs as a key element in a practical strategy to reduce poverty.

Now, I am not suggesting that any of this is easy to do. It is not.

What I am suggesting is that absolute poverty can never be eliminated simply by traditional welfare. And the reason is obvious. No feasible redistribution of already inadequate national income in a developing society is, by itself, going to be enough to wipe out poverty. There must be growth in that income, and the poor must be enabled both to contribute more productively to that growth, and to participate more equitably in its benefits.

---

[a]Address to the Board of Governors of The World Bank, Nairobi, 1973.

The tragedy of the absolute poor in most developing societies is that they remain largely outside the entire development process.

They must be brought more fully into it.

That can only be done by the individual developing countries themselves.

Conditions clearly differ from society to society, but what is essential is that governments:

- Formulate attainable anti-poverty objectives at national, regional, and local levels;

- Define clear operational programs, and institutional policies, for achievement of the objectives within specific time periods; and

- Determine the level of resources required to meet the minimum goals.

Unless such practical steps are taken by the governments in developing societies, the hope to reduce absolute poverty simply cannot be translated into effective action.

Certainly no external development agency—no matter how helpful—can substitute for the internal political resolve necessary to take these steps.

But once that firm resolve is evident, then the international community must support these politically difficult decisions with comparable courage and generosity.

The mandate of the World Bank is, of course, to assist our developing member countries in their overall development tasks—including their attack on absolute poverty—and I would like to turn now to a discussion of the Bank's program.

VII. THE PROGRAM OF THE WORLD BANK

The capacity of the World Bank itself to help accelerate growth and reduce poverty in the developing countries will depend chiefly on two key decisions which our member governments must take in the near future. These concern:

- The General Capital Increase of the IBRD; and

• The Sixth Replenishment of IDA's resources.

The General Capital Increase will determine the scale of IBRD commitments over the next several years.

Without an increase, the IBRD will be forced to cut the lending program planned for the next fiscal year from $7.6 billion to about $6.0 billion.[a] And in future years, new commitments could not exceed $6.0 billion in nominal terms. In real terms, they would, of course, decline by about 6% per year: a major reversal of the 5% per annum increase assumed in the growth projections for the developing countries.

The case for a General Capital Increase is straightforward and compelling. The IBRD is now the largest single source of official development finance. To curtail its lending program in the present circumstances would mean that the developing countries would be faced with a critical dilemma: either they would have to reduce their growth rates, or they would have to increase still further their dependence on potentially volatile private capital flows.

Neither alternative is in the interest of the world community.

A year ago, I reported to you on the consensus which had emerged, first at the London Summit Meeting, and subsequently at the CIEC meetings in Paris. This consensus clearly favored a General Capital Increase sufficiently large to support substantial real growth in IBRD lending for the next several years.

After the meeting of the Governors last year, the Executive Directors held a series of informal discussions on the future role of the IBRD. These discussions revealed broad support for a real rate of growth of lending in the range of 5%—and it is for that reason that such a rate was built into the projections.

While no attempt was made in these informal discussions to reach agreement on a specific figure for the General Capital Increase, the positions taken on the desirable rate of growth,

---

[a]The reduction in lending to a level of $6.0 billion per year would be necessary to ensure that in later years the total amount of loans outstanding would not exceed the total of capital and reserves as required by the Articles of Agreement.

and on other issues affecting capital requirements, implied an increase of between $30 and $40 billion.[a]

Contrary to the hope expressed a year ago, these informal discussions did not lead to a formal agreement in the Board before the end of the fiscal year. Fortunately, the delay in reaching formal agreement has not yet caused any serious penalty to IBRD borrowers. The Executive Directors authorized continued work on the $6.8 billion of IBRD lending previously planned for the present fiscal year, as well as the $7.6 billion planned for FY1980. They did, however, make this approval subject to review at the end of this calendar year.

If agreement on the General Capital Increase has not been reached by, say, January of 1979, it will become very difficult to avoid taking steps which would impose real and lasting penalties on IBRD borrowers. In particular, as I have pointed out, the number of operations and the amount of lending scheduled for FY1980 and FY1981 would have to be reduced.

Such a setback to the progress of our developing member countries can and must be avoided.

The whole range of issues involved in the General Increase has been closely examined and discussed in the two and a half years that have passed since the Executive Directors approved the Selective Increase. And political support for a General Increase has been repeatedly affirmed at the highest levels of government. What remains is to spell out the specifics, and to do so promptly.

I believe it is both realistic and highly desirable to seek formal agreement in the Bank's Board on the size of the General Capital Increase no later than January of next year.

The next few months will also see the start of the negotiations for the Sixth Replenishment of IDA. The first meeting for that purpose should be held before the end of this calendar year.

---

[a]A capital increase of this size would have relatively little budgetary impact on member countries. 90% would be represented by "callable capital," a contingent liability, which we expect would never have to be drawn upon and which serves, in effect, as a guarantee to IBRD's creditors.

Although the funds provided under the Fifth Replenishment will not be fully committed until June 1980, the long lead time required to reach a negotiated agreement, and to secure legislative approval, makes it essential that the negotiating process begin soon.

The precise level of the Sixth Replenishment will, of course, be a matter for negotiation among member governments. I would hope, however, that in view of the critical need of the poorest developing countries for more adequate flows of concessional assistance, all our member governments will support a level that will provide for a substantial increase in IDA's commitment authority in real terms.

Approval of a realistic Sixth Replenishment and General Capital Increase, together with the increase in capital recently authorized for IFC, will give the World Bank a solid financial base for its operations for some years to come.

Before describing the size and wider significance of the World Bank's financial contribution, however, I want to report briefly on where we stand in our efforts to assist in reducing absolute poverty by directing an increasing share of our total lending to projects which directly boost the productivity of the rural and urban poor.

Efforts to Attack Absolute Poverty: Progress Report

Five years ago at our meeting in Nairobi, I outlined a strategy for attacking absolute poverty in the rural areas. This strategy focused on the more than 100 million subsistence farmers and their families.

One element of this strategy was expanded World Bank lending. Our specific goal was to increase agricultural lending by at least 40% in real terms in the five-year period FY74-78 as compared with the previous five years.

Within the context of expanding the overall agricultural program, we proposed to give greater emphasis to projects expressly designed to increase the productivity of low-income farmers, most of whom farm two hectares or less. The target was to have at least 70% of all our Bank agricultural loans contain a specific component for the smallholder.

Each of these goals has been achieved. Not only achieved, but exceeded. In real terms, our lending for agriculture and rural development projects over the five-year period just ended, as compared with the previous five years, was up not merely by 40%—but by 145%.

Further, fully 75% of the 363 agricultural projects approved over the five-year period contained a component specifically addressed to the needs of the small farmer. There were, in fact, over 200 projects in which more than half of the direct benefits were expected to accrue to the rural poor. In total, they will increase the incomes—in most cases, by at least 100%—of over ten million poor families.

The ultimate standard, of course, for judging the success or failure of these efforts is not the benefits projected at the time the loan is approved, but the benefits actually achieved in the field. We have been monitoring these projects very carefully. Because they are designed to produce progressive improvements over a period of years, it is still too early to form definitive judgments on most of them.

They are breaking new ground, and we must expect some failures. But I can attest from personal observation in a number of countries that these "new style" projects can tangibly benefit the lives of literally hundreds of thousands of poor farm families. Our experience with these investments supports the assumption that in low-income countries it should be possible to double the agricultural growth rate, raising it from 1.5% to 3% per annum.

The Bank's efforts to assist the urban poor are at a much earlier stage, and on a much smaller scale. We have very far to go, but we are making progress.

Two years ago at Manila, I expressed the hope that the Bank would be able to finance 50 urban projects during the FY76-80 period. It now looks as though we will meet, or possibly even exceed, that target. During the next two years we expect to process an average of more than 15 such projects per year, as compared with two or three a year in the mid-1970s.

I also pointed out at Manila that we would be expanding and redirecting our investment in other sectors in order to increase earning opportunities in the urban areas. We developed guidelines with the goal that by 1981 at least one-third of the lending we do through industrial development finance institutions should directly benefit the urban poor. That goal, too, now seems within reach.

As we widen our operational experience, we will learn a great deal more about what works best in expanding employment. The traditional labor-intensive sub-sectors of manufacturing— clothing, textiles, leather, light engineering, and certain kinds of machine tools—are obviously important in creating jobs, but they will have to be supplemented by other approaches as well. Recent projects, for example, have been directed at stimulating the construction industry—which can be very labor intensive— as well as artisan activities and cottage industries.

The need for more jobs is critical. The cities of the developing world are expanding at runaway rates. The combination of high natural population growth and accelerating migration from the countryside will add well over a billion people to the urban labor pool by the end of the century.

It is obvious that on any reasonable calculation the developing countries are going to have to make massive investments if these individuals are to find productive employment. It is sometimes argued that the costs will simply be too high; that the world just cannot afford it.

But the truth is really the other way around. What the world cannot afford is procrastination and delay while dangerous social pressures build.

The Bank, for its part, is determined to move forward vigorously in this sector, and to seek new and more effective solutions to the growing urban crisis.

The Bank's effort in this matter is, of course, only one part of its overall financial program, which I would like now briefly to review.

Scale of Operations

Last year I reported that World Bank commitments for the year ending June 1978 were expected to reach $8.7 billion, and that the level of net capital flows—Bank disbursements less repayments by borrowing member countries—was expected to be just under $4 billion.

Our commitments for the year turned out almost precisely as planned though in common with other official sources of finance our actual disbursements fell short of expectations.

Table VII—World Bank Group: Commitments and Disbursements
(Billions of dollars)

	Avg. per Year FY64-68	Avg. per Year FY69-73	Avg. per Year FY74-78	FY78 Actual	FY79 Plan
New Commitments					
IBRD	.9	1.8	4.9	6.1	6.8
IDA	.3	.8	1.6	2.3	2.8
IFC	—	.1	.2	.3	.4
Total—Current $	1.2	2.7	6.7	8.7	10.0
—Constant FY78 $	3.5	4.7	7.5	8.7	9.4
Net Disbursements					
IBRD	.3	.6	1.7	1.9	2.5
IDA	.3	.3	1.1	1.0	1.3
IFC	—	.1	.2	.2	.3
Total—Current $	.6	1.0	3.0	3.1	4.1
—Constant FY78 $	1.6	1.9	3.3	3.1	3.8
No. of New Projects	71	152	242	277	294

The net capital flows from the World Bank are, of course, a relatively small part of the total external capital received by the developing countries. But the World Bank's share in these flows understates its importance for a variety of reasons.

First, and most directly, the Bank has increasingly associated its financing with loans from other sources, both official and private. In the fiscal year just completed, more than 80 IBRD and IDA projects and 35 IFC operations were carried out jointly with other lenders. The total finance committed by these other external sources in FY1978 was approximately $4.4 billion, or nearly three times the volume of just five years ago.

In assessing the full impact of World Bank operations on the flow of external finance, one should also take account of the Bank's non-financial role. The Bank's economic reporting, its assistance in aid coordination, its continuing dialogue with borrowers on sectoral and macroeconomic policies and on the effectiveness of development expenditures—all these activities contribute to a favorable climate for more effective capital flows in general.

As I emphasized earlier, the climate for capital flows is especially important for the private sector, which is now the source for roughly 60% of all medium- and long-term external finance. The commercial banks, in particular, play an indispensable role in channeling savings to the middle-income developing countries.

Governments must be sensitive to the need to provide a supportive environment for these flows, including the expansion of the lending programs of the World Bank, and the Regional Development Banks. And they should be prepared to consider whatever supplementary steps may be necessary in order to assure a more adequate level of such flows.

Let me now summarize and conclude the central points I have made this morning.

VIII. SUMMARY AND CONCLUSIONS

As one surveys the international development scene today, it is clear that there are two fundamental objectives that must command the priorities of us all.

One is to accelerate overall economic growth in the developing countries, and the other is to reduce the massive dimensions of absolute poverty.

In the *World Development Report, 1978,* the initial volume in a new annual series of World Bank analyses of economic and social progress in the developing world, these two issues are examined in detail.

Based on a number of feasible—though admittedly optimistic —assumptions, projections for the period 1975-1985 indicate that the low-income countries could increase their overall growth rate from roughly 4% to about 5%, and that the middle-income countries could sustain their current growth of about 6%.

These are not, however, predictions of what will actually happen. They are prospects which are far from certain. To achieve them, both the developing countries themselves, and the developed nations, must increase their efforts.

The developing countries must, for example, mobilize even greater domestic savings than they do now. This will call for difficult reforms in a number of sensitive areas of public policy.

Further, they must expand their export programs, and their agricultural productivity—which in the case of the low-income countries would mean doubling their current agricultural growth rates, raising them from 1.5% to 3.0% a year: a difficult but attainable goal.

But if the developing countries were to do all of this—as necessary as it is—they simply could not achieve the projected levels of economic growth without substantially greater support from the developed nations.

That support is required, first of all, in the matter of trade. Just as the developing countries have begun to demonstrate their natural comparative advantage in certain labor-intensive manufactures, a new threat of protectionism is gathering momentum in the developed world.

This is both inequitable and shortsighted since it denies the developing countries the only long-range economic strategy that can ultimately decrease their dependence on foreign assistance.

Already the developing world constitutes an important and growing market for the exports of the industrialized nations, stimulating demand and helping to hasten their own economic recovery. But if the developing countries are to import even more goods and services from the OECD nations—which they both need and want to do—then they must be allowed in return to export more to those same nations in order to earn the foreign exchange necessary to do so.

In the end, excessive protectionism is self-defeating for everyone: for consumers, who are denied less expensive, and hence less inflationary, imports; and for producers, who are denied competitive access to expanding markets.

What is required is a more rational framework of international trade that will reduce protectionism on both sides by promoting the dismantling of non-tariff barriers, and by broadening the scope of true comparative advantage. In the industrial countries this will require initiating adjustment procedures that can ease the shift of capital and labor away from marginal industries into more competitive and productive sectors.

The expansion of international trade is, then, essential to the economic growth the developing countries so desperately need.

Another requirement, particularly for the middle-income developing nations, is the continued assurance of adequate capital flows from both the multilateral financial institutions and the private capital markets.

In the recession that followed the economic turbulence of the early 1970s, the middle-income countries had to rely on heavy borrowing abroad to maintain their development momentum. The international development institutions, and the commercial banks, responded to that need, and debt obligations rose swiftly.

This was, on the whole, a very positive phenomenon, and assisted the recovery process in the developed as well as the developing nations. But as the debt grew, there began to be some anxiety that prudent levels might be exceeded.

The World Bank has followed these developments closely and has concluded that the potential dangers lie not so much in the absolute amounts of the debt itself, but rather in a generally burdensome maturity structure and in liquidity problems that will affect a limited number of borrowers.

It is essential that the middle-income developing countries continue to have available adequate flows of capital to finance their high-priority development projects, and prudent borrowing from the private capital markets is an indispensable ingredient in meeting that financial requirement.

Whatever risk is inherent in the debt can be significantly reduced by three measures: lengthening the average maturities of the obligations, in part through more cofinancing between private sources and official development institutions; broadening the number of commercial banks, particularly in Japan and Europe, that engage in developing-world financing; and expanding the number of countries serviced by the private markets, thus diversifying their investment more widely.

The case of the poorest developing countries is quite a different issue. These countries, because of their limited debt-servicing capacity, must of necessity depend on capital at concessional terms, and are in urgent need of greater Official Development Assistance.

If the poorest countries are to attain the very modest economic growth levels projected for the period 1975-1985, there must be an end to the virtual stagnation in ODA flows, and an increase of at least 5% a year in real terms.

Though some of the smaller countries of the Development Assistance Committee have made a strong showing, the overall trend in Official Development Assistance is very disappointing. In relation to combined GNP, ODA has declined from .52% in 1960 to .31% in 1977.

This is due chiefly to the poor performance of three of the most affluent DAC member countries, none of whom has reached even half the United Nations' .7% target, and all of whom have lagged further and further behind since 1970.

All three of these nations have recently pledged to reverse this trend, but these statements—as welcome as they are—have yet to be translated into action. Unless very substantial increases

in commitments—more than sufficient to keep pace with inflation and growth of GNP—are undertaken in the next year, and
regularly thereafter, the poorest nations simply have no chance
to reach their growth prospects.

But increasing economic growth—as essential as it is—is
not the sole objective of the development task. Reducing the
massive and cruel dimensions of absolute poverty is equally
imperative.

And it is here that the *World Development Report* comes to
its most shocking conclusion: that even if the growth rates projected for the developing countries were to be achieved by
1985—which is by no means certain—and even if that growth
were to continue for another 15 years, it seems likely that at the
end of the century there would still remain some 600 million
individuals trapped in absolute poverty.

That is intolerable. And it argues for intensifying our efforts
both to understand the internal dynamics of poverty more
clearly, and to design practical anti-poverty strategies that
will work.

Clearly what will not work is mere traditional welfare—redistribution of an already inadequate national income.

The only feasible hope of reducing poverty is to assist the
poor to become more productive. Each developing society must
formulate specific anti-poverty objectives at national, regional,
and local levels; prepare operational programs to attain those
objectives over a reasonable time; and determine the level of
resources required to meet the minimum goals.

Such programs will, of course, cut across many entrenched
interests in the developing countries, and will require sustained
political courage to implement. If such actions are to succeed,
the developed nations, and the international community, must
exercise comparable political courage in committing generous
assistance to support them.

The experience of the World Bank itself over the past five years
demonstrates that all of this can work. The progress of our new

projects in both the countryside and the cities, designed to enhance the productivity of the poor, is extremely encouraging.

But the Bank's capacity to broaden those particular efforts, as well as to further its overall program of development assistance—and it is now the largest single source of that assistance in the world—will depend on the prompt resolution of two paramount issues.

One is the decision to move ahead with the IBRD's General Capital Increase. The other is the Sixth Replenishment of IDA's resources.

Without an agreement within the next few months to implement the General Capital Increase, IBRD's borrowers will inevitably suffer a real and lasting penalty: the lending program for the next fiscal year will have to be cut sharply from $7.6 billion to $5.9 billion; and in future years new commitments will have to be cut progressively about 6% a year in real terms.

As our developing member countries will readily confirm, their circumstances today do not justify a decline in the World Bank's ability to help them, but rather an increase.

That is true of our IBRD borrowers. And it is true, of course, for our poorest member countries who depend on continuing concessional assistance through IDA.

Approval of the Sixth Replenishment which would allow for substantial growth in commitment authority in real terms, along with the General Capital Increase, will—together with the recent increase in capital for IFC—give the World Bank the financial foundation it will need over the next several years.

Those years will clearly demand a more determined effort from us all if the central goals of development—sustained economic growth, and the reduction of absolute poverty—are to have any realistic chance of succeeding.

We must be candid about the choices that confront us.

There are no easy alternatives.

But to relax in the development effort, to lose momentum, to procrastinate, to let problems fester and grow worse—that choice can benefit neither us, nor those others who must follow after us.

We know who those others are. They are our children.

Will their world be more rational, more compassionate, more peaceful, more human?

That choice is more ours than theirs. For the options are closing, and the inevitable chain of consequences is already underway.

The time, then, to act is now. It is an opportunity that will not return.

Capital Flows to and Debt Status of the Poorest Nations[a]
(In billions of current US$)

	1970	1975	1976[c]	1977[c]	1980[d]	1985[d]
Current Account Deficit before Interest Payments	2.4	6.5	3.3	1.7	8.5	13.1
Interest Payments	.4	.8	1.0	1.3	2.3	3.6
Changes in Reserves, Short-Term Debt and Errors and Omissions	− .1	1.5	3.1	3.3	1.2	4.6
Total to be Financed	2.7	8.8	7.4	6.3	12.0	21.3
Financed by Medium- and Long-Term Capital from:						
Public Sources (including Grants)	2.4	5.8	5.0	5.2	11.6	19.7
Private Sources[b]	.3	3.0	2.4	1.1	.4	1.6
Total Net Capital Flows: Current $	2.7	8.8	7.4	6.3	12.0	21.3
1977 $	5.0	9.9	8.0	6.3	9.7	12.2
Outstanding Medium- and Long-Term Debt:						
Public Sources	14.5	27.0	30.8	35.4	52.8	104.0
Private Sources	1.4	7.2	9.0	9.2	14.0	8.5
Total: Current $	15.9	34.2	39.8	44.6	66.8	112.5
1977 $	29.6	38.3	43.1	44.6	53.8	64.5
Debt Service: Interest Payments	.4	.8	1.0	1.3	2.3	3.6
Debt Amortization	.7	1.5	1.7	2.4	5.1	5.1
Interest Payments as % of GNP	.4	.4	.6	.6	.8	.6
Debt Service as % of Exports	14.5	11.2	11.4	12.7	17.4	11.9
Price Deflator	53.8	89.3	92.3	100.0	124.2	174.3

[a]Countries with 1976 gross national product per person of US$250 and below, mainly in Africa and Asia.

[b]Includes "Direct Foreign Investment."

[c]1976 and 1977 data are based on IMF sources.

[d]The data for 1980 and 1985 are projections of current account deficits and capital flows. They are not predictions of what may actually happen.

Capital Flows to and Debt Status of the Middle-Income Developing Countries[a]
(In billions of current US$)

	1970	1975	1976[c]	1977[c]	1980[d]	1985[d]
Current Account Deficit before Interest Payments	7.9	31.6	17.2	14.0	29.5	70.3
Interest Payments	2.1	7.6	8.5	10.7	18.2	33.7
Changes in Reserves, Short-Term Debt and Errors and Omissions	.2	−1.9	9.4	20.2[e]	2.2	7.2
Total to be Financed	10.2	37.3	35.1	44.9	49.9	111.2
Financed by Medium- and Long-Term Capital from:						
Public Sources (including Grants)	3.3	11.3	10.7	14.0	20.6	31.2
Private Sources[b]	6.9	26.0	24.4	30.9	29.3	80.0
Total Net Capital Flows:						
Current $	10.2	37.3	35.1	44.9	49.9	111.2
1977 $	19.0	41.8	38.0	44.9	40.2	63.8
Outstanding Medium- and Long-Term Debt:						
Public Sources	20.5	44.4	51.4	61.9	99.4	186.3
Private Sources	15.9	83.5	106.0	134.0	169.5	349.8
Total: Current $	36.4	127.9	157.4	195.9	268.9	536.1
1977 $	67.7	143.2	170.5	195.9	216.5	307.6
Debt Service:						
Interest Payments	2.1	7.6	8.5	10.7	18.2	33.7
Debt Amortization	5.3	14.3	16.6	22.7	47.1	102.8
Interest Payments as % of GNP	.7	1.0	1.0	1.1	1.2	1.2
Debt Service as % of Exports	15.6	11.8	11.5	13.3	19.0	22.0
Price Deflator	53.8	89.3	92.3	100.0	124.2	174.3

[a]Developing countries with 1976 gross national product per person above US$250, including Southern European countries and excluding capital surplus oil exporters.

[b]Includes "Direct Foreign Investments."

[c]1976 and 1977 data are based on IMF sources.

[d]The data for 1980 and 1985 are projections of current account deficits and capital flows. They are not predictions of what may actually happen.

[e]Includes an increase in Reserves of $11 billion and a reduction in Short-Term Debt of $0.5 billion.

Flow of Official Development Assistance from Development Assistance Committee Members Measured as a Percentage of Gross National Product[a]

	1960	1965	1970	1975	1976	1977	1978	1979	1980	1981	1982	1983	1984	1985
Australia	.38	.53	.59	.60	.42	.45	.46	.47	.48	.49	.50	.50	.50	.50
Austria		.11	.07	.17	.12	.24	.26	.27	.28	.29	.30	.30	.30	.30
Belgium	.88	.60	.46	.59	.51	.46	.50	.53	.56	.59	.62	.65	.65	.65
Canada	.19	.19	.42	.55	.46	.51	.53	.54	.54	.55	.56	.56	.56	.56
Denmark	.09	.13	.38	.58	.56	.60	.67	.70	.72	.74	.75	.75	.75	.75
Finland[b]		.02	.07	.18	.18	.17	.17	.18	.19	.19	.20	.20	.20	.20
France	1.38	.76	.66	.62	.62	.63	.64	.64	.64	.65	.65	.65	.65	.65
Germany	.31	.40	.32	.40	.31	.27	.30	.30	.31	.32	.33	.33	.33	.33
Italy	.22	.10	.16	.11	.13	.09	.11	.11	.10	.10	.11	.11	.11	.11
Japan	.24	.27	.23	.23	.20	.21	.21	.22	.24	.24	.25	.25	.25	.25
Netherlands	.31	.36	.61	.75	.82	.85	.90	.96	.99	1.00	1.00	1.00	1.00	1.00
New Zealand[c]			.23	.52	.51	.35	.33	.32	.30	.30	.30	.32	.32	.32
Norway	.11	.16	.32	.66	.70	.82	.91	.96	.98	1.00	1.02	1.03	1.03	1.03
Sweden	.05	.19	.38	.82	.82	.99	.97	.99	1.00	1.02	1.03	1.03	1.03	1.03
Switzerland	.04	.09	.15	.19	.19	.19	.18	.19	.19	.19	.20	.20	.20	.20
United Kingdom	.56	.47	.36	.37	.38	.38	.38	.38	.39	.41	.42	.42	.42	.42
United States[d]	.53	.49	.31	.26	.25	.22	.23	.22	.22	.23	.24	.24	.24	.24

GRAND TOTAL

ODA ($b-Nominal Prices)	4.6	5.9	6.8	13.6	13.7	14.8	18.0	20.3	23.0	26.3	30.0	33.6	37.5	41.8
ODA ($b-Constant 1977 Prices)	12.2	14.1	14.4	15.2	14.8	14.8	15.8	16.5	17.5	18.7	19.9	20.8	21.7	22.6
GNP ($t-Nominal Prices)	0.9	1.3	2.0	3.8	4.2	4.7	5.5	6.2	6.9	7.7	8.6	9.6	10.7	11.9
ODA as % GNP	.52	.44	.34	.36	.33	.31	.33	.33	.33	.34	.35	.35	.35	.35
ODA Deflator[e]	.38	.42	.47	.90	.92	1.00	1.14	1.23	1.32	1.41	1.51	1.62	1.73	1.85

[a]Figures for 1977 and earlier years are based on actual data. Those for 1978-85 are based on OECD and World Bank estimates of growth of GNP, on information on budget appropriations for aid, and on aid policy statements by governments. They are projections, not predictions, of what will occur unless action not now planned is taken.

[b]Finland became a member of DAC in January 1975.

[c]New Zealand became a member of DAC in 1973. ODA figures for New Zealand are not available for 1960 and 1965.

[d]In 1949, at the beginning of the Marshall Plan, US Official Development Assistance amounted to 2.79% of GNP.

[e]The deflator series includes the effects of changes in exchange rates. After 1975 deflators are the same as those for GNP.

NINETEEN

To the
UNITED NATIONS
CONFERENCE
ON
TRADE AND DEVELOPMENT

MANILA, PHILIPPINES
MAY 10, 1979

I. INTRODUCTION[a]

It is an exceptionally opportune time for UNCTAD to meet.

Critical decisions affecting the world's economic relationships are being hammered out just now in half a dozen international fora.

In UNCTAD itself work is culminating on the financing of
Commodity Stabilization Agreements and the structure of the
Common Fund; in GATT a new multilateral trade agreement is
nearing completion; the World Bank is moving toward final
decisions on a major capital increase, and the Sixth Replenishment of IDA; the United Nations is formulating a development
strategy for the 1980s and beyond; and the Brandt Commission
is about to draft its overall recommendations.

All of these steps are important. But if we are to accelerate
economic and social advance throughout the world, there are
other steps that must be taken as well.

This meeting of UNCTAD affords us the opportunity to identify them.

Last September I drew the attention of the international community to a shocking conclusion of the "World Development
Report, 1978."

And that was that even if the projected—and optimistic—
growth rates, which the "Report" envisaged, were achieved,
some 600 million individuals at the end of the century would
still remain trapped in absolute poverty.

Now, that clearly is unacceptable.

But, as I pointed out, to attain even these rates of growth, on
which the projections of absolute poverty were based, would
itself demand a greatly intensified effort from both the developed and the developing nations.

---

[a]I am indebted to several distinguished scholars and specialists for their assistance in examining recent trends in international trade, the major subject of
this statement. In particular, I want to thank Mahbub ul Haq, Donald Keesing,
Isaiah Frank, Bela Balassa, Robert Baldwin and Paul Streeten.

In summary, it would require:

- A further expansion of international trade on the basis of long-term comparative advantage and mutual benefit;

- A sharp increase in the level of capital extended to the middle-income developing countries from private sources, together with increased support from the multilateral financial institutions; and

- An increased flow of concessional assistance to the poorest developing countries.

I am encouraged that these three issues figure prominently on the agenda of UNCTAD V. On previous occasions, I have spoken on each of them. This morning, I want to confine my remarks to a more detailed examination of the recent trends in international trade, and their implications for world prosperity.

My view is this. Unless we resist—and roll back—the protectionism that has been gathering momentum over recent years, we risk undermining the progress in development and international cooperation that we have achieved over the past quarter century.

This surge in protectionism is not, of course, an autonomous event. It is the result of pressures brought on by a sluggish growth rate and mounting unemployment in the industrial nations.

But granted the reality of the pressures, what the peoples of these nations do not realize is that trade protection is rarely the right instrument to safeguard income and employment levels. More often it only succeeds in converting potential short-term private costs into long-term social losses.

That is the issue I want to deal with here. In particular, I want to:

- Consider the role of trade in development;

- Illustrate the trend toward greater protectionism, particularly in the period 1976-1979;

- Analyze the penalties of that protectionism for both the developing and developed countries;

- Discuss the policy options available to deal with the problem;

- Comment on the Tokyo Round negotiations, and offer a number of suggestions for further improving the international trade environment.

II. THE ROLE OF TRADE IN DEVELOPMENT

Let me begin with an obvious, but essential, point.

Trade is a means—not the goal itself—of development. The goal of development is to enhance the welfare of everyone, particularly those individuals who have been passed over by earlier efforts. The expansion of trade by itself does not guarantee that poverty will be reduced, but it clearly increases the feasibility of achieving that.

The links between international trade and economic growth are complex. Trade improves the allocation of resources, and hence yields more output, and makes investment more productive. It does this by promoting greater specialization and larger-scale production, and by stimulating innovation and technical change.

There is an important process of mutual causality at work between economic growth and trade liberalization. Rapid economic growth facilitates the liberalization and expansion of trade, both by raising demand and by facilitating improved access to markets. And the rapid expansion of trade contributes to the acceleration of the pace of economic development.

It is this interaction between trade and growth that provides a key to economic progress.

Now, that is what happened between 1960 and 1973.

During those years the total exports of the developing countries rose by nearly 7% per annum, faster than the average annual growth rate of their gross national product. And their manufactured exports increased even more rapidly—at over twice the growth rate of the GNP.

It is true that not every commodity, nor every country, benefited equally from this surge in trade. But for many middle-income countries it provided both the foreign exchange earnings and the market stimulus for accelerated economic growth. And it held out the promise to all developing countries of a rising share in this world trade expansion, provided they could restructure their production and export policies to take advantage of the favorable environment.

It is precisely this favorable trade environment that is now threatened by slow growth, high unemployment levels, and consequent growing protectionism in the developed countries.

The result is that the rate of expansion of total world trade has fallen from 9% a year in the decade 1963-73 to only a little more than 4% in the years 1973-77. For the developing countries, the corresponding rates were 6.5% and 3.6% for the two periods.

There were, of course, a number of factors that led to the major expansion in exports of the developing countries before 1974. These included the creation of new export capacity, together with the utilization of excess capacity created earlier during the import-substitution phase of their industrialization; the increased demand and liberalized trade policies in the developed nations; and the aggressive, export-oriented policies in some of the developing countries.

But it should be remembered that as important as these vigorous export-oriented policies of the developing countries were, they succeeded as well as they did because of the high economic growth rates in the industrial nations, and because of the major liberalization of trade granted by them prior to 1974.

The outlook now is quite different. The slowdown in economic activity in the developed nations, and the consequent rising protectionist pressures of recent years, are seriously compromising the prospects of the developing countries.

The projections in the "World Development Report, 1978" indicate that the developing countries will require some $900 billion worth of imports per year by 1985 in order to achieve the projected modest increase in their GNP growth rates. The expectation of the "Report" is that they would finance $797 billion of that amount from their exports, and would have to finance the balance of $103 billion from other sources.

These export projections were made on conservative assumptions. An annual export growth of 12% was assumed for manufactured goods for the 1975-85 period, as compared to an actual growth rate of 15% during 1970-75.

It is obviously of critical importance to the developing countries that they should in fact be able to achieve these export growth rates. If they do not, they must either add to their already heavy burden of debt, or they must see their development effort cut back.

How can the industrial nations assist the developing countries to earn sufficient foreign exchange through their own efforts?

Their first priority must be to reestablish patterns of steady growth and high levels of employment. If they do not it is going to be increasingly difficult for them to withstand the protectionist pressure groups within their own societies, who are calling for stern measures to solve short-term problems.

At the same time, both the public at large and the decision makers in the industrial countries must be led to see that shortsighted protectionist reactions offer no real solution to their fundamental economic difficulties.

The resort to protectionism may be a politically attractive choice—particularly in the face of difficult structural problems —but it is almost always a poor choice.

Let us examine these choices more closely by taking a hard look at recent protectionist trends, and at the costs they exact from both the developed and developing countries.

Since manufactured goods are the most dynamic element in the developing countries' total exports, and since many of the recent protectionist measures are directed against manufacturers, I will limit my analysis to them, though it should be noted that there are disturbing protectionist tendencies in the agricultural sector as well.

III. THE NEW PROTECTIONISM

Since 1976 there has been a marked increase in protectionism in the industrialized nations, and the pressures for even further restrictive measures are strong.

The pressures stem largely from the continued slow and erratic growth of their economies, and their consequent high levels of unemployment.

They are in part the result of the concentration of the developing countries' export growth in relatively few categories of manufactured products.

In the last analysis, however, they reflect the attempt of organized special-interest groups in the industrialized nations, in a period of slow growth and rising unemployment, to postpone the costs of structural adjustment—and this even if it means penalizing the less organized and less articulate sections of their own society, and the weaker and poorer members of the international community.

The devices utilized to provide such protection have multiplied. In addition to the traditional tariff measures, they now include cartel-like sharing agreements; "voluntary" export restraints; countervailing duties; subsidies and other assistance to domestic industries to sustain levels of production above those warranted by demand; government procurement procedures; and a whole spectrum of administrative, non-tariff barriers.

The intent of these measures is to extend protection to certain declining industries or ailing sectors of the economy without having to undertake the more basic steps necessary to cure the fundamental malaise.

Between 1976 and early 1979 the industrialized nations introduced a large number of new restrictive measures. They can be divided broadly into various forms of non-tariff barriers to trade; government aids to industry; and attempts to establish worldwide restrictive market-sharing agreements. Let me illustrate a number of these.

Non-Tariff Barriers:

- Although the Multi-Fiber Arrangement calls for quotas on clothing and textiles that generally grow at annual rates of 6% or more, starting in late 1977 these provisions did not prevent the imposition of more severe restrictions on the exports of developing countries, particularly by the European Community. The majority of these new EEC quotas limited annual increases of clothing and textiles to between .5 and 4%. Moreover, while the Arrangement calls for quota levels no lower than recent imports, the Community in fact rolled back some quotas on their major suppliers to levels well below those in 1976.

- Contrary to the spirit of the Arrangement, the European Community insisted on applying quota restrictions not only on current suppliers, but also on other low-income countries, such as Indonesia, Bangladesh, and Sri Lanka, which have scarcely begun to enter the export market.

- Australia, Canada, Norway, Sweden, and the United States have also tightened their quotas or imposed new ones to limit developing country exports of textiles and clothing.

The net effect of all these restrictive measures will be to limit the growth of exports of clothing and textiles to industrialized countries to considerably less than 6% per annum. This compares with annual growth rates on the order of 15% in the ten years prior to 1976.

- Australia, Canada, France, the United Kingdom, and the United States have imposed new quotas and so-called "orderly marketing agreements" limiting the developing countries' exports of footwear.

- The United Kingdom imposed quotas on monochrome television sets from Korea and Taiwan, and the United States has arranged for "orderly marketing arrangements" with the same two countries in color sets.

- U.S. countervailing duties have been actively used even in cases in which injury to domestic producers has not been proven.

- The European Community and the United States introduced special protective measures regarding steel which pose serious difficulties for those developing countries now emerging as exporters. The EEC has decided to renew for another year, through 1979, its "anti-crisis" program in steel, including efforts to reach year-by-year export restraint agreements with outside suppliers.

Government Aids to Industry

These take a variety of forms such as direct subsidies and preferential tax and credit arrangements. The latter provide indirect protection by reducing production or sales costs.

- Under the British Temporary Employment Subsidy Scheme, the textile, clothing, and footwear industries received subsidies equivalent to 5 to 10% of total production costs. Other industries have been supported by increasing the former levels of government assistance.

- Very large subsidies are now being given to the shipbuilding industry in a majority of the industrialized countries.

- In France the automobile, data processing, pulp and paper, steel, and watch industries, among others, have all received various forms of government aid.

- The take-over of insolvent firms by the government in industries such as steel and textiles, and the financing of their deficits from public funds, has had protective effects in Belgium, Italy, The Netherlands, and Sweden, among other countries.

International Cartels and Market-Sharing Agreements

- Proposals have been made for international market-sharing agreements in shipbuilding and steel within the framework of the OECD. It is possible that the OECD Steel Committee may in fact turn into a quasi cartel.

While this is only a partial list of some of the trade restrictions in the OECD countries, it illustrates the trend. And to these one could add the government trade policies in the centrally planned economies which directly inhibit the expansion of world trade.

The picture that emerges from all this is not encouraging.

What are the real costs of this growing protectionism to the international community?

It is clearly already paying a high price for these measures. The potential costs could be even higher. And these costs are imposed on developing and developed countries alike.

IV. THE COSTS OF PROTECTIONISM

Let us examine these costs briefly.

Cost to the Developing Countries

Both protection and the threat of protection in the industrialized nations hurt the developing countries in two ways. They hurt them directly by reducing their opportunity to earn foreign exchange, by increasing their unemployment, and by diminishing the rate of growth of their income. And they hurt them indirectly by inhibiting them from adopting investment, production, and trade policies that would improve the allocation of their resources, and their overall development performance.

These adverse effects are felt not only by the established exporters of manufactures, but also by countries that are just beginning to be successful. And it is not only the actual restrictions that hurt, but the threat of them as well, since the threat creates a climate of uncertainty and inhibits long-term investment in export industries.

The fear of future imposition of protectionist measures often discourages governments in the developing world from adopting trade-oriented, outward-looking policies. The result is that they settle for inferior trade and development strategies, and end by strengthening the vested interests in the societies that benefit from producing at high cost for highly protected domestic markets.

No comprehensive studies exist at present quantifying the adverse impact of protectionism on individual developing countries. But such quantification can be made at two levels. A partial analysis would detail losses in export earnings and increases in unemployment on a sectoral basis. And a broader analysis would estimate the damage to the economy as a whole in terms of the denial of opportunities to generate exports, growth retardation, unemployment, low productivity, and increased poverty.

One obvious difficulty in estimating the overall damage done to individual developing countries is that the damage often takes the form of frustrated investment and export opportunities, rather than clearly identifiable foreign exchange losses or unemployment.

In view of the great importance of this subject, it is surprising how little analysis has been carried out thus far on the overall impact of trade protectionism on individual developing countries. I strongly urge that more resources and effort be devoted to this analysis.

Now what about the costs of excessive protectionism to the developed nations? Let us examine that for a moment.

Costs to the Developed Nations

The motivation of a developed nation in extending protection is, of course, to save specific industries or sectors or regions from incurring detrimental economic and human costs. But what is often overlooked is that this does not protect the society from incurring equally real and even larger costs over the longer run.

The desire to resort to trade restrictions to save jobs in dying industries or declining regions is, of course, understandable, particularly when growth is sluggish and unemployment widespread.

And the case for protection—at least for protection against the exports from developing countries—is usually made on the basis of the burden that falls on the low-skilled labor that is displaced.

In the most labor-intensive industries, a large share of the people affected are women who cannot easily move to other regions because of family obligations. Frequently the plants that are threatened are in depressed, low-income areas. Many of the workers released are too old or otherwise disadvantaged to find new jobs easily.

Further, the threat of unemployment falls largely on those workers who are most likely to be displaced by automation and technical improvements, so that even if they are retrained or switched into other low-skilled jobs they are often soon displaced in those jobs as well. At best their incomes are depressed by the weak demand that exists for them in view of the new machines.

Governments on the whole have not been very successful at containing inflation and reducing unemployment at the same time, and hence it is not surprising that they should attempt to save jobs, even at the cost of higher prices, by putting up trade barriers. And affluent societies may believe that they can afford to forgo the further increases in real income that would be derived from a better international division of labor—if protectionism can at least buy them some industrial peace, and save them the costs of structural adjustments.

But what the advocates of protection neglect to say is that the present jobs of these workers may not be saved even under protection. The fact is that protection is often utilized—to the ultimate disappointment of the trade unions that ask for it—as a means of allowing an industry to "adjust" by automating low-skilled jobs out of existence, using the assured higher prices to pay for labor-displacing machinery.

The real choice offered by the protectionists is for society to pay higher prices and transfer income from its more productive citizens, probably on a permanent basis, while at the same time hurting their own consumers, tying up resources in low-priority uses, and adversely affecting export industries, as well as those industries dependent on cheap imports.

It is important that the real costs of protectionism in the industrial countries are fully understood.

The truth is that protectionism is inefficient, counter-productive, and ultimately self-defeating.

It is inefficient because it prevents the restructuring of inefficient traditional industries into modern, high-technology industries for which the advanced countries are best suited, and because it freezes these societies into inefficient production and consumption patterns. By avoiding such adjustments, societies which are dependent on foreign trade may suffer not merely slower growth, but falling living standards as well.

Protectionism is counterproductive because it provokes retaliation by other countries attempting to protect their declining industries, and because it erodes higher incomes and better jobs in export-oriented industries, a large share of whose production goes to the developing countries.

And protectionism is ultimately self-defeating because in the end it penalizes everyone. It makes impossible both the equitable—and the efficient—use of world resources.

In the developed countries protectionism, by walling off low-cost imports, fuels the fires of inflation and often puts the heaviest burden on those in the society least able to bear it.

A survey sponsored by United States retail organizations in 1978 found that goods imported from Asia and Latin America are, on average, sold at retail in the U.S. for 16% less than domestic products of the same quality. These goods are purchased mainly by families with lower incomes, and can make a contribution to moderating the impact of inflation, particularly for the poor.

It has been estimated in a recent study that the effects of protectionist measures imposed by the United States between 1975 and 1977 resulted in a cost to consumers of $660 million in sugar, $1,250 million in carbon steel, $400 to $800 million in meat, $500 million in television sets, and $1,200 million in footwear.

In terms of the short-term gain in jobs, this meant that the consumer cost per-job-protected was more than $50,000 per year.

If protection is seen as a temporary political response to the employment problems created for a small group of workers, then clearly there are less inflationary and less costly forms of income support available.

Protectionism hurts not only consumers, but also growth industries, export industries, and high-productivity industries. It creates vested interests, which once entrenched are difficult to moderate later. And it is contagious. It tends to spread from industry to industry, and from country to country.

Finally, protectionism is self-defeating because it undermines the international system of capital and trade flows on which the successes of the last twenty-five years have been built.

A large proportion of the export surpluses from the industrial countries to the developing countries, on which so many jobs depend, are financed by credits. The only way in which these debts can be serviced is to permit the developing countries to export and earn the foreign exchange to repay these debts.

The present international system of credit and trade will be seriously threatened if protectionist obstacles are put in the way of servicing the sizeable debts which the developing countries have already accumulated, and are continuing to acquire.

But despite these heavy costs of growing protectionism to the industrial countries, the political battle against protectionist pressures is often very difficult. It is difficult because the temporary losers from trade liberalization are visible and vocal, whereas those who gain are generally dispersed and disorganized. Thousands of housewives spread over the whole country often have less voice than a textile worker with a job at stake. But in the long run what is really at stake is not just cheaper shoes, clothes, and bedspreads, but the jobs and living standards of the whole population.

Total Costs

It is difficult to calculate the total costs of protection to the international community as a whole. The GATT Secretariat estimated in 1977 that the application of protectionist measures by the industrial countries in the previous two years had led to restrictions on 3 to 5% of world trade flows, amounting to $30 to $50 billion a year.

But such an estimate fails to convey the full costs to the world community through the loss of total output, jobs, and potential investment.

Estimates may differ about the total cost of protectionism to both developed and developing countries. But it is clear that these costs—to the individuals, to the countries, and to the global society as a whole—are potentially large.

Should the world continue to pay this price?

The answer is obviously no.

The truth is that the present unhappy combination of slow growth, unemployment, and rampant inflation constitutes both a threat and an opportunity.

The threat is that we may decide to engage in even more protectionism, which in the end would inflict severe strains on the world economy, and from which it would take a very long time to recover.

And the opportunity is that we can choose instead to begin to restructure the production patterns in the developed and developing countries, and to establish an international environment which encourages rapid and more equitable growth, at higher levels of employment, in both trade and development.

Let us examine the various options that developing and developed countries face in the present situation.

V. POLICY OPTIONS FOR THE DEVELOPING AND DEVELOPED COUNTRIES

Options for the Developing Countries

A tempting option for the developing countries will be to turn inward, to take greater refuge in highly protected import-substitution industries, and to avoid the struggle for expanding trade.

But this would clearly be a mistake. There are other options which are far more promising, though admittedly they entail a great deal of resolute effort. They include: the creation of efficient export capacity; a larger South-South trade; and a continued effort to roll back the protectionist measures in the industrial nations both within, and beyond, the Tokyo Round trade agreement. Let me briefly discuss each of these options.

Some developing countries have pursued policies that have discriminated against their own expansion of exports. Regardless of the trade environment, these policies were never warranted. The fact is that there are considerable possibilities for the developing countries to increase their exports even under current restrictive conditions, as has been shown by the examples of Korea, Brazil, and Singapore.

For one thing, the developing countries can diversify their exports into products that do not face high trade barriers. For another, those countries that are less advanced should seek to upgrade their export structure in order to take advantage of the export markets being vacated by more advanced developing countries.

As for South-South trade, there are good arguments—on the grounds of comparative advantage—for the developing countries to increase the volume of trade among themselves. Developing nations have already begun to make use of these new channels of trade. There are opportunities for further expansion.

Brazil now trades more with other developing countries than with the United States, and India's exports to developing countries are increasing at a rate higher than that of their trade with the industrialized nations.

But trade among developing countries is no substitute for greater trade with the developed world.

Developing countries' imports continue to be heavily concentrated in machinery and transport equipment, and most of these items are produced by the industrial nations. These products are crucial for the economies of the developing world and they can be supplied only to a very limited extent by the developing countries themselves.

Finally, the developing countries must begin to play a more active role in reshaping the trade environment. Such a role would, of course, involve greater participation in the current and future trade negotiations. I will return to this matter later in my comments on the results of the Tokyo Round negotiations.

Let me turn now to the options that the industrial nations face in the current climate.

Options for the Developed Countries

One must begin by recognizing a fundamental point. And that is that the deterioration in the current world trade environment has not been brought about by the developing countries swamping the markets of the industrialized world. Whatever the protectionists may say, the developed world is not being "flooded by cheap goods."

On the contrary, the developing countries today supply only a miniscule portion of the manufactured goods consumed in the developed countries: less than 2%. The share differs, of course, for different industries, but even in the most successful—textiles and clothing—this share is still low: 5%, for example, in the United States.

The recent deterioration has been caused, rather, by a loss in the economic dynamism of the type prevalent in the 1960s in the developed countries. That dynamism made it possible for the industries in the developed world to make important structural changes—changes that were required both for efficiency and equity.

These changes enhanced efficiency because they allowed the developed countries to make better use of their resources. And they enhanced equity because they permitted the producers in the developing countries to move into kinds of production which they could not have afforded on the basis of their own domestic markets alone.

But the slowdown in the growth of industrial economies has severely hampered this process of dynamic adjustment. And the developed countries have believed that there are essentially two responses to this situation: to limit the entry of goods into their markets from more competitive sources, and/or to undertake adjustment measures.

I have already discussed the long-term costs of restrictions on the imports from the developing countries. Let me now analyze the experience of industrial nations with adjustment measures.

Past experience with adjustment measures has not been very satisfactory in most industrial countries. Often these measures have ended up freezing the existing production patterns and resisting change, rather than encouraging genuine structural improvement by retraining workers and shifting them into industries and regions where they could both be more productive and earn more.

A recent OECD study indicates that even when the policies were vigorously pursued they resulted in greater capital intensity since the government's funds for adjustment were utilized to buy new equipment rather than to retain labor. Attempts, on the other hand, to slow down the process of adjustment and to gain a "breathing space" were utilized to establish permanent protection, and this resulted in turn in raising the price the consumer had to pay for the protected product.

But none of this need happen.

Correctly administered adjustment policies would aim at compensating those adversely affected by increased imports from the developing countries, and would retrain displaced workers and facilitate their move from low-productivity to high-productivity industries.

In order to reduce the political resistance to change and safeguard fairness, adjustment compensation should be reliable and prompt, and should approximate the private costs imposed on those affected. This might well include owners as well as workers, especially in the case of smaller firms, though businessmen cannot, of course, expect the government to relieve them of every possible competitive risk.

A complementary approach would be to assist local communities hit by plant closures or by large lay-offs. Successful programs of this type have been organized in the United States, and in Germany. Such regional relief can both increase the indigenous supply of skilled labor, and help identify new opportunities for relatively unskilled workers. Measures designed to remove obstacles to mobility—better transference of pension rights, for example—are important as well.

But what is most crucial for the success of all these policies is the existence of a high level of aggregate demand and the rapid development of new and dynamic industries. Japan, for example, has been particularly successful in making adjustments well ahead of time and thereby securing its overall momentum of trade and economic activity, rather than delaying and relying on protection to save industries that have already become troubled and inefficient.

Now, what is one to conclude from all this discussion of options?

I believe that in the end the only sensible option that any of us in the international community have is to make a determined effort to improve the trade environment itself.

That was the basic purpose of the Tokyo Round. Let me turn now to an analysis of just where we stand in those negotiations.

VI. THE TOKYO ROUND AND BEYOND

The international community has invested an immense amount of effort over the last five years in negotiating a new framework of rules of conduct governing international trade. This effort began when the Tokyo Round of multilateral trade negotiations was formally launched in September 1973.

These negotiations are now completed, though some details are still to be worked out. However, prior to the formal signing ceremony in the fall, negotiators who have initialed the package agreement must submit it to appropriate government bodies for approval and must introduce the modifications in domestic legislation needed to carry it out. Over the next few months, most developing countries must also decide whether they wish to participate in the various agreements.

It is thus appropriate to ask: what has been achieved so far and what still remains to be done?

The agreements essentially do four things:

- They provide for a series of detailed codes which spell out permissible and non-permissible behavior by governments in imposing non-tariff barriers to trade;

- They establish a framework both for settling disputes which may arise among nations with respect to these non-tariff barriers and for watching over such measures as may be initiated in the future;

- They make special provisions for developing countries; and,

- They include a substantial tariff cut.

Now let me briefly indicate the areas in which I believe the trade agreement is likely to lead to an improvement in the current international trade environment, provided, of course, that it is implemented in a manner that reflects the real spirit and intent of the original Tokyo Declaration.

Areas of Progress

- There will be a substantial further cut—30 to 35%—in average industrial tariff levels in the OECD member countries as a result of an agreed formula which provides for higher cuts in higher duties.

The proposed cuts compare favorably with the Kennedy Round average cut of 35% in import duties for dutiable manufactures. The benefits of these cuts will be automatically extended to developing countries under the most favored nation clause without demanding full reciprocity on their part.

To put the magnitude of these tariff cuts in their proper perspective, of course, it should be remembered that the average tariff level for dutiable manufactured goods in the OECD countries is already quite low—about 10%—and recent fluctuations in exchange rates tend to dwarf the impact of the new cuts, which are to be implemented in a phased manner over an eight-year period.

Further, as I will discuss in a moment, the benefits to developing countries are going to be even more limited because of the numerous exemptions of certain categories of goods, and reductions in their preference margins. But despite these factors, there is no doubt that the proposed tariff cuts do constitute a further move in the right direction.

• As I have pointed out, one of the increasingly preferred protectionist devices in industrial nations today is the practice whereby they enter into various bilateral agreements with other countries—outside the GATT framework—and require those countries to agree to limit "voluntarily" their exports of particular products.

The proposed safeguard code which is still under discussion, attempts to bring the various types of safeguard actions —past, present, and future—back within the GATT framework. It defines the procedures and criteria that have to be met in taking safeguard actions, together with the conditions to which individual safeguard measures should conform. Thus, the code is aimed at preventing arbitrary national action by powerful importing nations.

One of the controversial aspects of this code is the insistence of some of the important industrial nations that a "selectivity clause," which would allow them the right to restrict imports selectively from a few sources, be included. The developing countries are vigorously opposing this.

• The code on subsidies will attempt to control another favorite protectionist measure. It will strengthen the ban on export subsidies on manufactured goods by the developed countries, as well as begin to control domestic subsidy measures that have been increasingly used by the developed countries in recent years.

Further, the United States will no longer be allowed to impose countervailing duties without clearly proving material injury to its domestic producers. If properly implemented, this code represents a potentially significant accomplishment that may enable the international community to control in a realistic manner the trade-distorting effects of domestic and export subsidies.

• There are a number of other codes which, while they may not increase trade significantly, will contribute to reducing many irritations that endanger international cooperation.

The technical codes on standards, customs valuation, and licensing, as well as the proposed agreement on commercial counterfeiting, will help simplify existing procedures; will provide better information to exporters; and will reduce the risk of these provisions being used for protectionist purposes. This will particularly benefit those developing countries which lack adequate information on technical standards and custom valuation procedures.

Another code on government procurement extends the principle of non-discrimination to government purchases, and establishes administrative procedures for providing necessary information and fair treatment to foreign suppliers.

• A major innovation in the trade agreement is that the individual codes also provide for an improved mechanism to facilitate the settlement of disputes. Each code will be administered by a committee of all the signatory nations. These committees are authorized to establish competent panels in each case in which a dispute arises under the code, to make recommendations to the parties concerned, and to take appropriate action — including authorizing countermeasures—if their recommendations are not carried out.

• The trade agreement recognizes the special problems of the developing countries, and makes some special provisions in their favor. It includes an "enabling clause" which provides a legal basis for differential and more favorable treatment to developing countries. They can be granted tariff preferences by the industrial nations, and they can establish preferential arrangements among themselves. Developing country signatories are generally exempted from the ban on export subsidies.

Special provisions are made in various codes to protect the interests of the least developed countries. In return, the developing countries are required to accept the principle of "graduation" in line with the progressive development of their economies and improvement in their trade situation.

All of these provisions constitute progress over the current situation. If the various agreements are fully implemented, there is a possibility that the recent deterioration in the international trading environment may be arrested.

But it is important to face up to two fundamental issues:

- What would the trade agreement really mean in terms of opening up trade opportunities for the developing countries?

- And how should the improvements in the framework of international trade—and the process of trade liberalization itself—be strengthened and continued beyond the Tokyo Round?

Let me suggest that detailed analysis must be undertaken as soon as possible on the full implications of the Tokyo Round for the trade prospects of the developing countries. This should be done by the developing countries themselves, as well as by the industrial nations and the international institutions.

A comprehensive assessment of these implications and of the further action required can only be based on much more detailed and careful analysis than is available at present. There are, however, a few important points that can be made at this stage.

It is quite clear that the multilateral trade agreement does represent some areas of genuine progress for the developing countries, even though the Tokyo Round discussions focused largely on the trade concerns of the developed nations, and despite the fact that the developing countries were often only marginal participants in these negotiations.

There are, for the first time, agreed codes of conduct for most non-tariff barriers, as well as machinery for the settlement of disputes. There is a further — and substantial — tariff cut. And there are other provisions intended specifically to benefit developing countries.

There remain, of course, still many areas of genuine concern to the developing countries, which I will discuss in a moment. But, though they must continue to work for further improvements, I believe that the developing countries do have a strong stake in the implementation of the trade agreement: the original intentions of the Tokyo Declaration must not be frustrated in actual practice, and the new codes must not be used as a cover for legalizing current trade restrictions.

The developing countries can best protect their interests by ultimately becoming signatories to the agreements after their present doubts have been resolved; by participating actively in the implementation and future reviews of the agreements; and by becoming full partners in future trade negotiations both within and outside the framework of the agreements.

Areas of Concern

It must, however, be fully recognized that there are many areas of concern to the developing countries which are not dealt with adequately in the current round of negotiations, and which require further consideration, both during the implementation of the trade agreement and in future trade discussions.

Let me elaborate.

- The trade negotiations did not address the question of reduction in existing quantitative restrictions. Thus, quotas on textiles and clothing, and on footwear, have been left untouched. These quota restrictions are of vital interest to the developing countries, particularly under the Multi-Fiber Arrangement which comes up for formal renewal by the end of 1981.

  A vigorous effort must be made to review, and progressively to eliminate all existing quantitative restrictions, as well as to ensure that no further quota arrangements are negotiated in other products, such as steel. While total elimination of all quotas will take time, steps should be taken to eliminate now at least the quotas for the poorest developing countries. Moreover, the groundwork should begin now for the renegotiation of the Multi-Fiber Arrangement with greatly liberalized quotas.

- The developing countries are concerned over the erosion of preference margins due to the overall reduction in tariff levels. This may, however, turn out to be an unnecessary concern since, according to recent studies, the loss in exports from reduced preferences will be less than one-tenth of the increase in exports that developing countries would enjoy as a result of trade liberalization under the Tokyo Round.

  A more valid concern is the specific exceptions industrial nations have made to the agreed tariff-cutting formula. Duties on some key export products of the developing countries—for example, textiles and footwear—are either not being cut at all, or are being reduced by less than the tariff-reduction formula agreed upon. The inequity of this treatment becomes more obvious when it is recognized that the existing tariffs on these developing country export products are generally higher (15-30%) than the average tariff (10%) in the industrial nations, and when it is recalled that these exports are also subject to quantitative restrictions.

  In future negotiations, the international community must ensure that the tariff rates on the principal exports of the developing countries are lowered progressively by eliminating present exemptions, and by establishing deeper tariff cuts for them.

- Another area of major concern to the developing countries is the insistence by some industrial nations that a "selectivity clause" be included in the proposed code on safeguards. The developing countries are apprehensive—and with good reason—that the most efficient and active exporting developing countries may be singled out for trade restrictions.

Ideally, the selectivity clause should be deleted from the code altogether since it legalizes discriminatory treatment against individual nations. If it is included at all, the criteria for selectivity should specify that this clause will not be invoked against the developing countries, and most especially not against the poorest and least developed countries.

- The developing countries are also worried that the surveillance machinery and the sanction powers remain too weak under the recently negotiated agreements. They are afraid that it will be the weaker and the poorer members of the international community who are most likely to suffer from any violations of the proposed codes of conduct. This is an issue which must be faced candidly since, in the last analysis, a treaty is only as good as the international opinion and enforcement powers behind it.

As I have already pointed out, the developing countries will help their own cause considerably by ultimately becoming signatories to the agreements so that they can obtain representation on the committees charged with the implementation of the individual codes.

In a general sense, then, the Tokyo Round negotiations represent some areas of genuine progress, a few areas of major concern, and an opportunity to build further on the progress already made.

Now, how should we approach this situation? Let me briefly outline my own views.

To begin with, it is essential that the overall trade agreement be rapidly approved. It is, of course, not an "ideal" agreement, nor should the search for further improvements in the international trade framework be abandoned during its implementation. But it does represent another negotiated step in a continued effort to improve the international trade environment. It would be a wise course to accept the progress it already represents, and to chart out a concrete program of action for further improvements, building on its positive features and correcting its negative ones.

A genuine danger is that the industrial nations may be pressured into paying a heavy price to their protectionist lobbies in order to secure the ratification of the trade agreement through their legislatures. Already some government measures are being taken outside of the negotiations—measures such as the "trigger point" scheme for steel, raising the support price for sugar, and the tightening of textile quotas in the United States.

These actions raise apprehensions about the real value of the agreement, and the cost that may have to be paid to achieve its ratification. It is essential to resist vigorously the pressure of the protectionist groups outside of the framework of the trade agreement, and to ensure that the agreement is promptly ratified without having to pay an unacceptable price for legislative approval.

Further, the most important point about the trade agreements is not the careful legal language in which they are expressed, and not even the precise provisions they contain, but rather the environment and the spirit in which they are implemented.

The root causes of protectionist pressures in the industrial nations, as I have pointed out, lie in their slow and erratic economic growth, leading to a combination of unemployment and inflation. These problems are compounded further by the absence of sound structural adjustment policies. Unless these problems are attacked — and attacked systematically — the chances of fully implementing any trade agreement will remain precarious.

There is, at the same time, a great need for broader political awareness, and a more fully informed public opinion, in order to ensure that the right political climate is created to resist violations of the agreement. Many of the codes on non-tariff barriers leave a great deal of room for administrative interpretation and discretion. This discretion can either become a significant ally for trade liberalization or, alternatively, a powerful instrument to defeat the very purpose of the trade agreement. Thus, the task of improving the world's trade environment will not end with the signing of the treaty. It will only begin.

Let me now summarize and conclude the central points I have made this morning, and propose a specific program of action.

VII. A PROGRAM OF ACTION

The argument I have made is this.

It is imperative that we understand the basic causes of the recent protectionist trend, and the heavy costs that it imposes on the developed and developing countries alike.

We must carefully and objectively evaluate the progress made in the Tokyo Round negotiations, as well as the unfinished work that still remains.

And we must determine how best to seek further improvements in the world trade environment, both through the periodic reviews that the agreement itself provides for, as well as through other special negotiations.

In my view, then, the international community's agenda should include the following specific actions:

- The provisions of the Tokyo Round agreements, and the possibilities of further liberalization and expansion of trade, should be analyzed in detail from the point of view of the developing countries, both by the governments concerned, as well as by UNCTAD and GATT. We in the World Bank stand ready to extend full support for such analysis.

- The Tokyo Round agreement provides for a "regular and systematic" review of developments in the international trading system between the contracting parties. This opportunity must be seized—and seized through substantive periodic reviews, not just routine monitoring. GATT and UNCTAD can serve as fora for consultation for these reviews.

- The major concerns of the developing countries should be met through future negotiations both within and outside the framework of the Tokyo Round agreement. Some of these can be met through the periodic reviews of each code by the signatories. But there are others which will require special arrangements for negotiations: the renegotiation, for instance, of existing quota restrictions, and further tariff cuts for developing countries' exports. And there are some concerns which must be addressed in completing the remaining agreements: for example, the deletion of the "selectivity clause" from the proposed code on safeguards.

• There are several areas of trade policy which are not presently covered in the Tokyo Round agreement: trading by state enterprises, for instance; intra-firm trade between multinationals; trade in services, and so forth. These are important omissions.

Some of these items are already under discussion, particularly within the framework of UNCTAD. Others require specific analysis and negotiating machinery. But the main point is that further efforts must be made to cover the presently neglected areas by specifying the negotiating machinery and a reasonable period of time over which the negotiations should be concluded.

• The Tokyo Round will not result in rolling back and dismantling the non-tariff barriers already in force. Obviously, such dismantling can only be undertaken in a gradual, phased manner over a period of time. But there can be no doubt that dismantling of these barriers should be a top priority item on the international agenda and every opportunity should be taken to press this objective.

The Tokyo Round negotiations were conducted and finalized at a time of great economic difficulty for the industrial nations. It is possible that as and when the economic recovery in the OECD countries gains strength, it will become more politically feasible for them to start dismantling these non-tariff barriers. What the international community must consider are the concrete mechanisms and fora through which the objective of progressive reduction and dismantling of existing non-tariff barriers can be successfully pursued.

- In order to benefit fully from an improved trade environment, the developing countries will need to carry out structural adjustments favoring their export sectors. This will require both appropriate domestic policies and adequate external help.

I would urge that the international community consider sympathetically the possibility of additional assistance to developing countries that undertake the needed structural adjustments for export promotion in line with their long-term comparative advantage. I am prepared to recommend to the Executive Directors that the World Bank consider such requests for assistance, and that it make available program lending in appropriate cases.

- As additional measures are taken to protect the legitimate interests of the developing countries, and as they reach progressively higher stages of development themselves, they should, of course, be prepared to moderate their own domestic protectionist measures. The principle of reciprocity should be accepted after a certain stage of development has been reached.

Import policies should be liberalized by the more industrialized developing countries. This would give them a stronger position in their negotiations with the developed countries; it would stimulate their domestic export interests; it would give exports from poorer developing countries a better access to the markets of the more advanced members of the developing world; and it would be in line with the principle that different rules should apply to countries at different stages of economic development.

It is important to recognize that improvements in the framework of international trade are part of a continuous process which did not begin, and should not end, with the Tokyo Round. We should move systematically towards a more liberalized international trading system, and an improved charter for world trade which encompasses those areas which have been neglected in the past. At the same time it should be fully recognized that the fate of the Tokyo Round agreement, and of any further improvements in it, hinges a great deal on the strength and political acceptability of the surveillance and enforcement machinery for the agreement.

There is no simple solution to this issue. Strengthening of the GATT organizational framework and powers would help. So would a greater political awareness of trade issues in developed and developing countries. But, in the final analysis, the only effective sanction powers are those which emerge out of the perceived and enlightened self-interest of nations and which are imposed as a result of their collective consent.

I very much hope that all these issues will receive detailed attention during your deliberations.

Trade problems, of course, are not the only economic issues that trouble our planet. There are many others, and most of them are difficult and complex.

But I remain convinced that a liberal world trade environment is critical to the success of international development.

If we fail to save that environment from the repeated threats of trade protectionism, then the pace of development itself—and the quality of life for hundreds of millions of less advantaged individuals who deserve so much more than the little they have—will remain in jeopardy.

Their hopes lie in our hands.

TWENTY

At the
UNIVERSITY OF CHICAGO
ON
DEVELOPMENT AND THE
ARMS RACE
upon receiving the Albert Pick, Jr. Award

CHICAGO, ILLINOIS
MAY 22, 1979

President Gray, Dr. Harris, Mrs. Pick, and Ladies and Gentlemen:

I am deeply honored and grateful for this award—for the sculpture which accompanies it, and for the generous cash prize of $25,000, which I will contribute to a development-oriented activity.

It seems to me that what the Directors of the Albert Pick, Jr. Fund, and this great university had in mind in establishing this award honoring international understanding was to point out that we need to think more profoundly about the new kind of world that is emerging around us.

The old order is certainly passing. Perhaps the beginning of its breakdown can be dated from that cold December day in 1942 when a few hundred yards from where we are now sitting the first nuclear chain reaction began. The consequences of that event were to transform our whole concept of international security because now Man had the capacity not merely to wage war, but to destroy civilization itself.

If I may on this occasion speak quite personally, I had of course to wrestle with the problem of the fundamental nature of international security during my tenure as U.S. Secretary of Defense, and in 1966 I spoke publicly about it in a speech to the American Society of Newspaper Editors meeting in Montreal.

My central point was that the concept of security itself had become dangerously oversimplified. There had long been an almost universal tendency to think of the security problem as being exclusively a military problem, and to think of the military problem as being primarily a weapons-system or hardware problem.

"We still tend to conceive of national security," I noted, "almost solely as a state of armed readiness: a vast, awesome arsenal of weaponry."

But, I pointed out, if one reflects on the problem more deeply it is clear that force alone does not guarantee security, and that a nation can reach a point at which it does not buy more security for itself simply by buying more military hardware.

553

That was my view then. It remains my view now.

Let me be precise about this point.

No nation can avoid the responsibility of providing an appropriate and reasonable level of defense for its society. In an imperfect world that is necessary. But what is just as necessary is to understand that the concept of security encompasses far more than merely military force, and that a society can reach a point at which additional military expenditure no longer provides additional security.

Indeed, to the extent that such expenditure severely reduces the resources available for other essential sectors and social services—and fuels a futile and reactive arms race—excessive military spending can erode security rather than enhance it.

Many societies today are facing that situation. Certainly the world as a whole is. And any sensible way out of the problem must begin with the realization of the dangers and disproportionate costs that extravagant military spending imposes on human welfare and social progress.

Global defense expenditures have grown so large that it is difficult to grasp their full dimensions.

The overall total is now in excess of $400 billion a year.

An estimated 36 million men are under arms in the world's active regular and paramilitary forces, with another 25 million in the reserves, and some 30 million civilians in military-related occupations.

Public expenditures on weapons research and development now approach $30 billion a year, and mobilize the talents of half a million scientists and engineers throughout the world. That is a greater research effort than is devoted to any other activity on earth, and it consumes more public research money than is spent on the problems of energy, health, education, and food combined.

The United States and the Soviet Union together account for more than half of the world's total defense bill, and for some two-thirds of the world's arms trade.

And yet it is not in the industrialized nations, but in the developing countries that military budgets are rising the fastest.

On average around the world, one tax dollar in six is devoted to military expenditure, and that means that at the present levels of spending the average taxpayer can expect over his lifetime to give up three or four years of his income to the arms race.

And what will he have bought with that?

Greater security?

No. At these exaggerated levels, only greater risk, greater danger, and greater delay in getting on with life's real purposes.

It is imperative that we understand this issue clearly.

The point is not that a nation's security is relatively less important than other considerations. Security is fundamental.

The point is simply that excessive military spending can reduce security rather than strengthen it.

In the matter of military force—as in many other matters in life—more is not necessarily better. Beyond a prudent limit, more can turn out to be very much worse.

And if we examine defense expenditures around the world today—and measure them realistically against the full spectrum of actions that tend to promote order and stability within and among nations—it is obvious that there is a very irrational misallocation of resources.

Is there any way, then, to moderate the mad momentum of a global arms race?

No very easy way, given the degree of suspicion and distrust involved.

But as one who participated in the initial nuclear test ban arrangements, and other arms limitation discussions, I am absolutely convinced that sound workable agreements are attainable.

These matters clearly call for realism. But realism is not a hardened, inflexible, unimaginative attitude. On the contrary, the realistic mind should be a restlessly creative mind—free of naive delusions, but full of practical alternatives.

There are many alternatives available to an arms race. There are many far better ways of contributing to global security. I suggested a number of those ways in my address in Montreal in 1966, pointing out the importance of accelerating economic and social progress in the developing countries. When, two years later, I left the Pentagon for the World Bank this was an aspect of world order with which I was particularly concerned.

Eleven years in the Bank, combined with visits to some 100 of the developing countries, have contributed immeasurably to my international understanding. They have permitted me to explore the whole new world that has come to political independence—in large part over the past quarter century.

I have met the leaders of this new world—their Jeffersons and Washingtons and Franklins—and have sensed their pride and their peoples' pride in their new national independence, and their frustrations at their economic dependence.

I have shared their sense of achievement at the remarkable rate of economic growth which many of them attained, largely by their own efforts. But I have been appalled by the desperate plight of those who did not share in this growth, and whose numbers rose relentlessly with the great tide of population expansion.

There are today more than one billion human beings in the developing countries whose incomes per head have nearly stagnated over the past decade. In statistical terms, and in constant prices, they have risen only about two dollars a year: from $130 in 1965 to $150 in 1975.

But what is beyond the power of any set of statistics to illustrate is the inhuman degradation the vast majority of these individuals are condemned to because of poverty.

Malnutrition saps their energy, stunts their bodies, and shortens their lives. Illiteracy darkens their minds, and forecloses their futures. Preventable diseases maim and kill their children. Squalor and ugliness pollute and poison their surroundings.

The miraculous gift of life itself, and all its intrinsic potential—so promising and rewarding for us—is eroded and reduced for them to a desperate effort to survive.

The self-perpetuating plight of the absolute poor tends to cut them off from the economic progress that takes place elsewhere in their own societies. They remain largely outside the entire development effort, neither able to contribute much to it, nor benefit fairly from it.

And when we reflect on this profile of poverty in the developing world we have to remind ourselves that we are not talking about merely a tiny minority of unfortunates—a miscellaneous collection of the losers in life—a regrettable but insignificant exception to the rule. On the contrary, we are talking about hundreds of millions of human beings—40% of the total population of over 100 countries.

Is the problem of absolute poverty in these nations solvable at all?

It is. And unless there is visible progress towards a solution we shall not have a peaceful world. We cannot build a secure world upon a foundation of human misery.

Now how can we help lift this burden of absolute poverty from off the backs of a billion people? That is a problem we have been dealing with at the World Bank intensively for the past six or seven years.

It is clear that we in the richer countries cannot do it by our own efforts. Nor can they, the masses in the poorest countries, do it by their own efforts alone. There must be a partnership between a comparatively small contribution in money and skills from the developed world, and the developing world's determination both to increase its rate of economic growth, and to channel more of the benefits of that growth to the absolute poor.

Most of the effort must come from the developing countries' own governments. By and large they are making that effort.

In the past decade, the poor nations have financed over 80% of their development investments out of their own meager incomes. But it is true they must make even greater efforts. They have invested too little in agriculture, too little in population planning, too little in essential public services. And too much of what they have invested has benefited only a privileged few.

That calls for policy reforms, and that is, of course, always politically difficult. But when the distribution of land, income, and opportunity becomes distorted to the point of desperation, political leaders must weigh the risk of social reform against social rebellion. "Too little too late" is history's universal epitaph for political regimes that have lost their mandate to the demands of landless, jobless, disenfranchised, and desperate men.

In any event, whatever the degree of neglect the governments in the poor countries have been responsible for, it has been more than matched by the failure of the developed nations to assist them adequately in the development task.

Today, Germany, Japan, and the United States are particularly deficient in the level of their assistance.

The case of the United States is illustrative. It enjoys the largest gross national product in the world. And yet it is currently one of the poorest performers in the matter of Official Development Assistance. Among the developed nations, Sweden, The Netherlands, Norway, Australia, France, Belgium, Denmark, Canada, New Zealand, and even—with all its economic problems—the United Kingdom: all of these nations devote a greater percentage of their GNP to Official Development Assistance than does the U.S.

In 1949, at the beginning of the Marshall Plan, U.S. Official Development Assistance amounted to 2.79% of GNP. Today, it is less than one-tenth of that: .22% of GNP. And this after a quarter century during which the income of the average American, adjusted for inflation, has more than doubled.

There are, of course, many sound reasons for development assistance.

But the fundamental case is, I believe, the moral one. The whole of human history has recognized the principle that the rich and powerful have a moral obligation to assist the poor and the weak. That is what the sense of community is all about—any community: the community of the family, the community of the nation, the community of nations itself.

Moral principles, if they are really sound—and this one clearly is—are also practical ways to proceed. Social justice is not simply an abstract ideal. It is a sensible way of making life more livable for everyone.

Now it is true that the moral argument does not persuade everyone.

Very well. For those who prefer arguments that appeal to self-interest, there are some very strong ones.

Exports provide one out of every eight jobs in U.S. manufacturing, and they take the output of one out of every three acres of U.S. farm land—and roughly one-third of these exports are now going to the developing countries.

Indeed, the U.S. now exports more to the developing countries than it does to Western Europe, Eastern Europe, China, and the Soviet Union combined.

Further, the U.S. now gets increasing quantities of its raw materials from the developing world—more than 50% of its tin, rubber, and manganese plus very substantial amounts of tungsten and cobalt, to say nothing of its oil.

The U.S. economy, then, increasingly depends on the ability of the developing nations both to purchase its exports, and to supply it with important raw materials.

And the same sort of relationship of mutual interdependence exists between the other industrialized countries—the Common Market, and Japan—and the developing world.

Thus, for the developed nations to do more to assist the developing countries is not merely the right thing to do, it is also increasingly the economically advantageous thing to do.

What will it cost the United States and the other industrialized countries to do more?

Far less than most of us imagine.

The truth is that the developed nations would not have to reduce their already immensely high standard of living in the slightest, but only devote a minuscule proportion of the additional per capita income they will earn over the coming decade.

It is not a question of the rich nations diminishing their present wealth in order to help the poor nations. It is only a question of their being willing to share a tiny percentage—perhaps 3%—of their incremental income.

It is true that the developed nations, understandably preoccupied with controlling inflation, and searching for structural solutions to their own economic imbalances, may be tempted to conclude that until these problems are solved, aid considerations must simply be put aside.

But support for development is not a luxury—something desirable when times are easy, and superfluous when times become temporarily troublesome.

It is precisely the opposite. Assistance to the developing countries is a continuing social and moral responsibility, and its need now is greater than ever.

Will we live up to that responsibility?

As I look back over my own generation—a generation that in its university years thought of itself as liberal—I am astonished at the insensitivity that all of us had during those years to the injustice of racial discrimination in our own society.

Will it now take another 50 years before we fully recognize the injustice of massive poverty in the international community?

We cannot let that happen.

Nor will it happen—if we but turn our minds seriously to the fundamental issues involved.

Increasingly the old priorities and the old value judgments are being reexamined in the light of the growing interdependence between nations—and it is right that they should be.

Once they are thought through, it will be evident that international development is one of the most important movements under way in this century.

It may ultimately turn out to be the most important.

Our task, then, is to explore—to explore a turbulent world that is shifting uneasily beneath our feet even as we try to understand it. And to explore our own values and beliefs about what kind of a world we really want it to become.

It was T. S. Eliot, in one of his most pensive moods, who wrote:

> "We shall not cease from exploration
> And the end of all our exploring
> Will be to arrive where we started
> And know the place for the first time."

Thank you, and good evening.

TWENTY-ONE

To the
BOARD OF GOVERNORS
BELGRADE, YUGOSLAVIA
OCTOBER 2, 1979

I. INTRODUCTION

We meet this year as one turbulent decade draws to a close, and what promises to be an even more critical one is about to begin.

We need not be reminded that the economic strains of the 1970s have been more severe than any since the disruption of World War II and the global depression that preceded it. But the truth is that the problems that will confront us all in the 1980s are almost certain to be more difficult. More difficult because with the loss of irrecoverable time the easier solutions to these problems have begun to disappear.

What we will be left with in the decade ahead are increasingly painful dilemmas that can no longer be ignored or postponed. We are going to have to decide—and decide soon—if we can really afford to continue temporizing with severe development problems that are getting worse rather than better.

Various elements in the international community are now at work preparing their proposals for an overall strategy for the Third Development Decade (DDIII).[a]

The time is right to take a realistic look at the development lessons of the Seventies, and decide how we can best apply that experience to the Eighties and beyond.

What I would like to do, then, briefly this morning is:

- Comment on the record of the 1970s, and the implementation of the strategy adopted for the Second Development Decade;

- Identify key problems that the rich and poor countries together are going to have to come to grips with in the 1980s;

---

[a]Work is currently under way in the U.N. Preparatory Committee for the New International Development Strategy on the principal ideas that should be included in that strategy when it is presented to the Eleventh Special Session of the U.N., currently scheduled for May of 1980.

- Suggest what can be done to meet those problems through a new international development strategy based on the realities of interdependence; and

- Indicate how the Bank itself can most effectively assist in that task.

Let me begin with the performance record of the Seventies.

II. LESSONS OF THE SECOND DEVELOPMENT DECADE

In late October of 1970 the UN General Assembly adopted by acclamation the "International Development Strategy for the Second United Nations Development Decade" (DDII).

The chief target of the overall strategy was that the developing countries as a whole should achieve, during the decade, an average annual rate of growth in their Gross Domestic Product (GDP) of at least 6%.

Six subsidiary targets were derived from this main goal. They were: an overall average annual increase in the developing countries of 3.5% in GDP per capita; annual growth rates of 8% in manufacturing, 4% in agricultural production, and 7% in export volume; a domestic savings rate that would reach 20% of GDP by 1980; and annual Official Development Assistance (ODA) from the developed countries reaching .7% of their Gross National Products (GNP) by 1975.

Now, what in fact has happened to these goals?

The performance figures through 1978 are now in and one can project, with reasonable accuracy, the results for the remaining two years of the decade.

The chief target—the 6% growth rate in the combined GDP of all the developing countries—will not be achieved. At best, their growth will not exceed 5.2% per year. This reflects the gradual slowdown in growth throughout the world in the second half of the Seventies.

Further, there were major shortfalls in each of four subsidiary goals. Of particular importance were the deficiencies in agricultural production, with a growth rate of only 2.8%, rather than the targeted 4%; and Official Development Assistance from the developed countries, which averaged less than half the target.

Moreover, these overall average performance statistics obscure as much as they reveal.

For example, the average 5.2% growth rate—although achieved by the developing countries as a whole—obscures the fact that the growth was very uneven among these countries; and that income grew the least where it was needed the most—in the poorest countries with the largest aggregate population.

- The major oil-exporting countries, with less than 10% of the population of all developing nations, enjoyed a GDP growth rate not of 6%, but of 9.5%.

- The middle-income countries that do not export oil, with only 29% of the population, had a growth rate of 6.2%.

- And the poorest countries, with an overwhelming 61% of the population, had a growth rate of only 4%.

The differences are even more pronounced in the case of GDP per capita growth.

- In the middle-income countries that export oil the growth rate was not merely the targeted 3.5%, but nearly twice that: 6.6%.

- Even in the middle-income countries without oil earnings, the growth rate exceeded the goal at 3.6%.

- But in the poorest countries, per capita income grew at only 1.7% a year—in Africa at only .2%. This is virtual stagnation. It means that for hundreds of millions of individuals —already trapped at the bare margin of survival—"growth" in income was two or three dollars a year.

There is little point in establishing overall targets which the poorest countries, with over half the population, have no hope whatever of achieving. These countries, as shown in Table I, have been able to produce only 16% of the developing nations' combined GDP, and less than 10% of their exports. Their average per capita income is only one-seventh that of the middle-income countries.

Table I—Profile of the Developing World[a]

	Population (millions) mid '79	GDP Per Capita $ Amount 1978[b]	GDP Per Capita Growth Rate 1970-80	Literacy 1975	Life Expectancy 1977	As a % of Developing Countries Total Population 1979	As a % of Developing Countries Total GDP[c] 1976	As a % of Developing Countries Total Exports[c][d] 1976
Poorest Countries								
India	656	175	1.4	36	51	28.7	7.9	2.7
Other Asia	455	200	2.7	48	51	19.9	6.1	5.2
Africa	168	175	.2	30	46	7.3	2.1	1.7
Total	1,279	185	1.7	36	50	55.9	16.1	9.6
Middle-Income Countries								
Latin America & Caribbean	346	1,390	2.6	77	63	15.1	32.8	24.2
Sub-Sahara Africa	206	670	1.4	27	48	9.0	9.6	13.2
East Asia & Pacific	174	850	6.2	83	63	7.6	9.3	20.8
Others	283	1,660	2.9	52	60	12.4	32.2	32.2
Total	1,009	1,225	2.9	69	60	44.1	83.9	90.4
All Developing Countries								
Total	2,288	645	2.8	50	54	100.0	100.0	100.0
% of World						76.9	21.0	23.0

These poorest countries have, of course, very severe disadvantages: their populations are less literate, suffer more from malnutrition and illness, and have shorter life expectancies. Their societies have limited domestic resources and desperately need concessional assistance to supplement their own efforts.

[a]Excluding Centrally Planned Economies.
[b]In 1978 prices, preliminary estimates.
[c]In 1975 prices.
[d]Merchandise only.

The middle-income nations, on the other hand, have been able to take advantage of their more favorable endowment in resources, of better market opportunities, and of higher capital inflows. Their prospects are promising provided they can combine sound domestic economic management with continuing expansion of their exports and access to development capital.

The first lesson, then, that one can draw from the experience of the DDII strategy in action is that strategic development planning in the future ought to give greater attention to this diversity, and disaggregate its goals into action proposals that are more specifically tailored to particular conditions. Aggregated goals can serve a useful purpose, but only to the extent that they provide an agreed-upon framework within which detailed national programs for action can be developed.

The second lesson we can learn from DDII is a corollary of the first.

Though the strategic plan spoke of the desirability of "special measures in favor of the least developed among the developing countries," it did not include any time-specific goal of reducing absolute poverty.

The 6% GDP growth target, as desirable as it was, was not identified as a means to a long-term, fundamental social transformation of the developing nations.

There was a great deal of discussion at the time of narrowing the relative income gap between the industrialized nations and the developing countries. That, however, is not only an elusive goal, but one that might bring little relief to the hundreds of millions of absolute poor in the developing world, even if attained.

What is far more important and urgent as a development-strategy objective is to seek to narrow the relative gap between the rich and poor countries in terms of the quality of life: in nutrition, literacy, life expectancy, and the physical and social environment.

Those quality-of-life gaps did narrow during the Seventies, as Table II indicates, and for the poorest countries they narrowed even while their per-capita-income gap with the developed nations widened.

Table II—Indices of Relative Social Progress[a]

	Low-Income			Middle-Income			All Developing Countries		
	1960	1970	1976	1960	1970	1976	1960	1970	1976
Calories as % of Requirements	71	73	73[b]	78	82	83[b]	74	77	77[b]
Life Expectancy	61	63	68[c]	76	80	81[c]	68	71	73[c]
Adult Literacy	30	32	36[c]	52	67	70[c]	39.	47	51[c]
Primary School Enrollment	45	62	72	69	84	90	55	71	81
Income Per Capita	4.7	3.2	2.5[d]	17.2	14.5	16.0[d]	10.2	8.2	8.5[d]

Had the DDII strategy given more direct emphasis to reducing absolute poverty, these and other quality-of-life factors could have improved substantially more than they did.

It is not that income gaps are unimportant. In a struggle for scarce world resources they are immensely relevant. And they illustrate the clear capacity that the rich and powerful have to assist the poor and weak. But this gap is largely irrelevant for determining the long-term objectives of the developing countries themselves.

This is all related to another major problem.

The international development community really has no adequate means to implement agreed-upon development policy.

When, for example, the strategy specifies a production target, such as an agricultural growth rate of 4%, or a financial target, such as Official Development Assistance rising to .7% of the GNP of the Organisation for Economic Co-operation and Development (OECD) nations, these targets are really little more than hopes or aspirations.

---

[a]The value of the indicator is expressed as a percent of the value for the average developed country.

[b]For 1974.

[c]For 1975.

[d]For 1977.

The truth is that there is no united international determination or force behind these targets.

If, then, the formulation of the development strategy is to become genuinely effective, it must do more than just set undifferentiated global targets. It ought to incorporate policy alternatives, and be backed up by sufficient international understanding and agreement among both the advanced and the developing countries to ensure that its broad direction is carried out.

Some of the most important aspects, for example, of the current North-South Dialogue could take concrete shape within the framework of such a development strategy, rather than outside it.

Now that a new strategy for another development decade is being formulated, all of us have the opportunity—and the responsibility—to learn what we can from the record of the past ten years, and to ask ourselves how we can best proceed.

One starting point is to consider some of the critical development problems we are certain to face in the 1980s—problems that carry enormous penalties for procrastination and delay.

III. CRITICAL DEVELOPMENT PROBLEMS IN THE 1980s AND BEYOND

We can begin with the most critical problem of all: population growth.

Population

As I have pointed out elsewhere, short of nuclear war itself it is the gravest issue that the world faces over the decades immediately ahead.

The population growth of the planet is ultimately in the hands not of governments, or institutions, or organizations. It is in the hands of literally hundreds of millions of individual parents who will determine its outcome. That is what makes the population problem so diffuse and intractable. And that is why it must be faced for what it inevitably is: a central determinant of humanity's future, and one requiring far more effective attention than it is currently receiving.

Ironically, one reason the urgency of the problem is under-estimated today is that crude birth rates in the developing world —outside of sub-Saharan Africa—are in fact declining. That in itself is an extremely welcome trend. And it may very well mean that the period of rapid acceleration in the rate of growth of the world's population has finally reached its peak, and is now moving downward towards stabilization.

Table III—Crude Birth Rate Trends in Selected Developing (LDC) and Developed Countries (DC)

Region	No. of Countries	1979 Pop. (Millions)	Crude Birth Rates (per thousand)				
			1955	1960	1965	1970	1975
Africa	50	454	48.1	47.8	47.3	46.5	46.0
Latin America	24	318	42.9	42.1	40.8	39.0	37.6
Asia	36	1,399	43.1	43.8	42.8	40.7	39.3
Total of Above LDCs[a]	110	2,171	44.1	44.4	43.4	41.7	40.5
Total DCs	36	1,172	22.8	21.6	19.7	17.9	16.8

What is misleading about this otherwise encouraging development is that it seems to suggest that the problem of rampant population growth has at last been contained, and that happily it has now become a less urgent matter.

That is a very dangerous misunderstanding.

The current rate of decline in fertility in the developing countries is neither large enough, nor rapid enough, to avoid their ultimately arriving at stabilized populations far in excess of more desirable—and attainable—levels.

If current trends continue, the world as a whole will not reach replacement-level fertility—in effect, an average of two children per family—until about the year 2020. That means that some 70 years later the world's population would finally stabilize at about 10 billion individuals compared to today's 4.3 billion.

---

[a]Excludes People's Republic of China, and certain countries in Southern Europe.

We must try to comprehend what such a world would really be.

We call it stabilized, but what kind of stability would be possible?

Can we assume that the levels of poverty, hunger, stress, crowding, and frustration that such a situation could cause in the developing nations—which by then would contain 9 out of every 10 human beings on earth—would be likely to assure social stability? Or political stability? Or, for that matter, military stability?

It is not a world that any of us would want to live in.

Is such a world inevitable?

It is not, but there are only two possible ways in which a world of 10 billion people can be averted. Either the current birth rates must come down more quickly. Or the current death rates must go up.

There is no other way.

There are, of course, many ways in which the death rates can go up. In a thermonuclear age, war can accomplish it very quickly and decisively. Famine and disease are nature's ancient checks on population growth, and neither one has disappeared from the scene. The World Bank estimates that some 12 million children under the age of five died of malnutrition, or malnutrition-related causes, last year.

But if our choice is for lower birth rates rather than higher death rates—as it must be, for any other choice is inconceivable—then we simply cannot continue the leisurely approach to the population problem that has characterized the past quarter century.

What we must grasp is the time factor involved.

It is a point of immense importance, and yet one that is frequently misunderstood, even by the highest officials in governments.

For every decade of delay in achieving a net reproduction rate (NRR) of 1.0—that is, replacement-level fertility—the world's ultimate stabilized population will be about 11% greater. If, then, the date at which replacement-level fertility will be reached could be advanced from 2020 to 2000, the ultimate global population would be approximately 2 billion less—a number equivalent to nearly half of today's world total.

That demographic fact reveals in startling terms the hidden penalties of failing to act, and act immediately, to reduce fertility. The time lost in temporizing with population problems is simply irrecoverable. It can never be made up.

As it is, if global replacement levels of fertility were to be reached around the year 2000, with the world ultimately stabilizing at about 8 billion, fully 90% of the increase over today's levels would be in the developing countries.

As shown in Table IV, it would mean—if each country followed the same general pattern—an India, for example, of 1.4 billion; an Indonesia of 305 million; a Bangladesh of 215 million; a Nigeria of 225 million; and a Mexico of 170 million. Compared to the current populations of these countries those figures are awesome.

Table IV—The Ultimate Size of Stationary Population in Selected Developing Countries
(In millions)

| Country | Pop. 1979 | Ultimate Stationary Population[a] | | % Increase Caused by Two Decades of Delay |
		NRR of 1.0 Achieved in Yr. 2000	NRR of 1.0 Achieved in Yr. 2020	
India	656	1,375	1,700	24
Indonesia	139	305	380	25
Bangladesh	86	215	290	35
Nigeria	83	225	315	41
Mexico	68	170	230	37

And I am not singling out these particular countries for comment, for most developing countries have comparable problems.

The point is that as large as those figures may seem, they will be 25 to 40% larger if the achievement of replacement-level

---

[a]The stationary population level will be reached about 70 years after the date on which a net reproduction rate of 1.0 is realized.

fertility is delayed for 20 years, and takes place in 2020 rather than 2000.

Governments, then, must avoid the severe penalties of procrastination, and try to hasten the reduction of fertility forward.

But how?

There are two broad categories of interventions that governments can undertake: those designed to encourage couples to desire smaller families; and those designed to provide parents with the means to implement that desire.

The first set of interventions sets out to alter the social and economic environment that tends to promote fertility, and by altering it to create a demand among parents for a new and smaller family norm. And the second set of interventions—effective family-planning services—supplies the requisite means that will make that new norm attainable.

The debate over which efforts in fertility reduction are of the most consequence—socio-economic progress, or family planning programs—is largely irrelevant. Research demonstrates that both are important.

Certainly recent studies confirm that developing countries which rank well in advancing the socio-economic environment *and also* have a strong family-planning program have, on average, much greater declines in fertility than do countries that have one *or* the other, and far more than those countries with neither.

The truth is, of course, that the population problem is an inseparable part of the larger, overall problem of development. But it is more than just that. To put it simply: excessive population growth is the greatest single obstacle to the economic and social advancement of most of the societies in the developing world.

There are other obstacles, of course. Many obstacles. But none is more pervasive, none is more intractable, and none is more punitive in the penalties it exacts for procrastination. For the population problem complicates, and makes more difficult, virtually every other task of development.

Let me illustrate that briefly, now, by turning to three other major development problems that loom before us in the decade of the 1980s and beyond: the problem of jobs, the problem of food, and the issue of absolute poverty.

Employment

As of this final year in the decade of the Seventies there are some 4.3 billion human beings on earth. Next year at this time there will be 74 million more. Tomorrow morning there will be nearly 200,000 more than there are today.

What are the implications of these numbers on the world's employment problem?

The International Labour Organisation (ILO) estimates that over the next two decades the global labor pool will grow by about 750 million people.

Two-thirds of that increase will be in the developing countries, and most of the individuals who will be seeking work in that period have already been born.

They are the legacy of the population growth rates of the recent past, and whatever may be done to moderate those rates over the next 20 years, the developing countries will be faced with an employment problem during the 1980s and beyond that has no parallel in history.

Each year millions of young people will enter a job market that has been able to absorb only a fraction of those who have preceded them.

But open unemployment—as immense as it is in the developing world—is only the visible surface of the job problem. Far more pervasive, and equally serious, is underemployment, with rates averaging an estimated 35% of the total labor force.

Over the past quarter century millions have left the countryside for the city in the search for jobs. The result has been that, while the populations in the developing countries have been doubling every 25 to 30 years, their large cities are doubling every 10 to 15 years, and the urban slums and shantytowns in these cities every 5 to 7 years.

In a single generation these cities have absorbed over 550 million people, roughly half through natural increase, and half through migration. Today a total of some 760 million persons live in these sprawling urban centers.

Over 250 million of them live in slums or squatter settlements, without adequate access to minimal nutrition, clean water, health facilities, primary education, public transport, and other fundamental services. These are the urban absolute poor, and their numbers are growing by 15 million a year.

The pressures on the municipal administrations and the national governments are already enormous. What will the strains become as the cities explode in size over the next two decades? By then, three out of every four Latin Americans will live in a city, and one out of every three Africans and Asians.

Thirty years ago only one city in the developing world had 5 million people living in it. By the year 2000 there will be 40. Eighteen of these cities will have 10 million or more inhabitants. One may well have three times that number.

From a practical point of view, governments in the developing world today have little capacity to control urbanization. It proceeds inexorably, and at present it is happening more rapidly than almost any major city can possibly cope with in an orderly way.

It is clear that the development of greater economic opportunities in the rural areas can slow the process. Here the opportunities are promising, though the task is immense in scope.

It has been demonstrated that when small-scale farmers have equal access to irrigation, improved seeds, fertilizer, credit, and technical advice, they have equal—or greater—productivity per hectare than large-scale farmers. And almost everywhere the small farmer uses more labor per hectare than the large farmer does. Small farms in Colombia, for example, use labor five times as intensively as large farms, and thirteen times as intensively as cattle ranches do.

Land reform, too—as difficult as it is to implement—is a powerful force for greater productivity and employment. Most developing countries that have substantially reduced rural poverty and underemployment have had effective land distribution programs.

But on-farm improvements alone cannot be expected to stem urban migration. The off-farm rural sector is important as well.

Off-farm activities in rural areas are a primary source of employment and earnings for approximately a quarter of the rural labor force in most developing countries, and a significant source of secondary earnings in the slack seasons for both small-scale farmers and landless farm workers. It is this group who supply the bulk of the migrants to the cities. And there are a number of ways in which their employment prospects could be improved in the countryside.

These include:

- Vocational training programs to upgrade skills;
- Banking and credit schemes to provide small amounts of capital to rural entrepreneurs;
- Research and technical assistance services;
- Investment in trading infrastructure to widen markets and improve access to materials and equipment; and
- Selected public works programs in depressed areas to provide short-term employment in the agricultural slack season.

But whatever can be done to increase employment in the countryside both on and off the farm—and a great deal can be done—migration to the city is going to continue, and the massive underemployment problem there must be faced and dealt with directly.

How?

The honest answer is that no one really knows yet.

The usual policy prescriptions—expansion of small enterprises, more appropriate pricing systems, training programs—all have merit, but none of them is going to be adequate in the next decade or two in the face of the stark demographic realities.

We know *what* must be done in the cities. We do not know the most effective way to *do* it.

What must be done is clear enough:

- Productive employment opportunities must be created at much lower capital costs; and

- Programs must be developed to deliver basic public services to the masses of the urban poor on a gigantic scale, and at standards which the economy can afford.

The emphasis on low capital investment per job, and low-cost standard services affordable by poor households is the key to the solution.

The basic concept is to provide the poor with access to productive assets and improved technology by removing the distortions that favor capital-intensive production: very low interest rates, for example, and excessively high wage rates.

The emphasis on affordability of essential services is to ensure that these programs are financially replicable on the large scale that is needed.

And that scale is not merely large. It is massive.

Consider the item of housing alone.

Of the 40 million families among the absolute poverty group in the urban areas, only about half have adequate shelter. At the present pace of urbanization, another 30 million units will be required if decent shelter is to be available to all poor families by the end of the century.

The investment and operating costs for such a goal are enormous: some $215 billion (in current prices) over the next twenty years, even if the standards are kept quite modest.

No government in a developing country can undertake an immense program of public housing lightly. The experience thus far is not very reassuring. Too often such programs are costly and inefficient; too often they turn into a perpetual subsidy; too often they are not adequately maintained and degenerate into slums; and what is most depressing of all, too often so-called low-income public housing is too expensive for the poor and ends up being middle-income housing.

Surveys indicate that up to 70% of the poor cannot afford even the cheapest housing produced by public agencies. Experience suggests that a more effective approach is to upgrade and improve existing slums, and provide basic sites and services for new settlements.

But the problem of housing, and the problem of urban migration, and the overall problem of employment itself do not begin to exhaust the development agenda that lies ahead in the Eighties and beyond.

Let us look for a moment at a related problem—the issue of food.

Food Enough for Everyone

As millions of people in the developing world move from the countryside to the cities, the food production system in these countries will have to undergo a quantum change. It will have to make the transition from a largely subsistence system to a high-productivity system that can yield a significant surplus for the burgeoning cities.

It is, after all, agriculture that makes cities possible in the first place. Cities do not grow food. Countrysides do. And unless countrysides—somewhere—grew a surplus of food, cities would have none.

The countrysides that are growing most of the surplus grain today are not in the developing countries at all. They are in North America, which has recently become the granary of the world.

North America provides fully 80% of all grain exports. But most of this grain is grown under rainfed conditions. A series of poor harvests in North America—always possible given the vagaries of weather—could mean that much of the world might suddenly be in jeopardy.

A major structural change has taken place in the pattern of the world grain trade. It may well result in the poorest developing countries simply being priced out of the market by other grain-deficient nations that are relatively better off financially.

Middle-income developing countries, the Organization of Petroleum Exporting Countries (OPEC), the Soviet Union, and other nations are now the principal customers in the international grain market, and are likely to become even more so in the years to come.

According to detailed analyses currently under way, we estimate that, with a continuation of present trends in agricultural production, the developing countries will not be able to meet their caloric requirements at the end of the century without a tripling of cereal imports to a level of 90-100 million tons per year.

It is problematical whether the food-surplus nations in North America and Oceania could generate exportable surpluses of these magnitudes at suitable prices. And it is questionable whether many of the developing countries could finance a high level of imports.

What do these projections imply?

They imply that developing countries must produce their own food to a much larger extent in the future. There is no other way that they can be sure of adequate supplies.

To achieve that goal, they will have to make more efficient use of resources already available to them. Future increases in food production in the developing world are going to have to come largely from increased yields per acre, rather than from any rapid expansion of land, and this means a significant increase in the supply of agricultural inputs.

Water is by far the most critical resource for agriculture. It has contributed decisively to the increase in agricultural output in the developing countries in the last two decades. But this resource is clearly not available in an unlimited supply. In many areas it is becoming scarce as agriculture becomes more intensive. It must be husbanded carefully, and used efficiently.

By reducing the waste that occurs, the quantum of water available for irrigation could be substantially increased. The vast

Indus River System, for example, loses some 60 billion cubic meters of water every year at the village level through seepage and evaporation. This is more than two-thirds of the entire annual flow of the Nile.

This kind of waste-reduction program would require improved on-farm management of water, and would involve millions of cultivators scattered over thousands of square miles. No new technology is needed for the efficient use of this resource. But what is required are local organizations and capital, a sensible pricing system, and a number of complementary inputs.

According to Bank, and Food and Agriculture Organization (FAO) studies, a program for increasing agricultural output by 3.5% per annum in developing countries would involve:

- An increase of 10% per year in the use of fertilizer;

- Expanding the area under the high-yielding seed varieties from the current 25% of the total cultivated area to at least 50%;

- Increasing the supply of irrigation water by a careful exploitation of available groundwater and the untapped potential of the large river systems;

- Expanding the arable land by no more than 1% a year— as compared to 2% in the past;

- Better research on multiple cropping and rainfed agriculture; and

- A greater effort to bring practical extension service to the small farmer.

Given these efforts, the developing countries could double their agricultural output over the next two decades. In combination with foreign sources of food (annual imports of 90-100 million tons by the end of the century), this could provide a minimally acceptable food supply.

But it must be recognized that such an agricultural production program would also cost a great deal—about $30 to $40 billion per year over the next two decades.

And so while it is true the developing countries will have to take the major initiative in improving their own agriculture, the financial resources required are clearly too large for them to manage alone.

They are going to need help from the international community.

Let me turn now to the issue of poverty.

Absolute Poverty

If we focus on the ultimate objectives of development, it is obvious that an essential one must be the liberation of the 800 million individuals in the developing world who are trapped in absolute poverty—a condition of life so limited by malnutrition, illiteracy, disease, high infant-mortality, and low life-expectancy as to be below any rational definition of human decency.

As I have argued before, this requires that the traditional growth approach be supplemented by a direct concern with the basic needs of the poor.

This is not a prescription for global philanthropy. Nor should it confuse means and ends, and rule out means that may be necessary to achieve the objective—industrialization, for example, or investment for economic infrastructure. Nor should it treat merely the symptoms rather than the causes of poverty.

Such gross oversimplifications can bring the very concept of an attack on poverty into disrepute. And they often have.

To begin with, a poverty-oriented approach must be country-specific; it cannot be global. The areas of intervention will differ country by country. Basic needs may not be met in one society because it is not allocating sufficient resources for their production or importation. They may not be met in another society because it has done little to improve the efficiency of a delivery system.

The relative importance of the areas of policy intervention can be determined only after a careful analysis of specific country situations.

What a poverty-oriented approach offers is not a substitute for economic growth, but an alternative way of achieving that growth through raising the productivity of the poor. The main point is this: a targeted, poverty-oriented approach can eradicate or reduce absolute poverty in a shorter period of time, and with fewer resources, than the more conventional growth-oriented approach.

Very few of the low-income developing countries have the resources, even with external assistance, to meet all the basic needs of the absolute poor in their societies simultaneously. Priorities obviously must be established, and target groups must be identified.

If choices are to be made—as they must be in many poor countries—education, nutrition, and water programs emerge as the high-priority elements in most country studies. And females, and children under five, appear to be the most important target groups in this effort.

But, as always, circumstances do differ in various societies.

What is important is that our collective response to the task of substantially meeting the basic needs of the absolute poor by the turn of this century should be translated into two practical results:

- The attack on absolute poverty should be integrated as a key element into national development plans, with the specified priorities and institutional changes that this requires.

- And the international community should give sustained financial and technical support to these specific efforts.

*   *   *   *

These, then, are some of the major development challenges that are going to confront us all in the Eighties and beyond.

In the final analysis, all of them are linked. And it is clear that to make progress in solving these problems is going to require an environment of economic growth.

It is precisely the relationship between economic growth and these development issues that constitutes the real rationale for establishing economic growth targets, and for examining the factors that affect those targets—particularly capital flows and expansion of international trade.

Let me turn now to a discussion of the outlook for economic growth in the Eighties, and the external support required to achieve that growth.

IV. APPROACHES TO A NEW INTERNATIONAL DEVELOPMENT STRATEGY

What are the growth prospects for the developing countries in the 1980s?

We have examined a number of alternative growth scenarios in the Bank. The point of such projections, of course, is not to attempt to predict statistically what will actually happen, but rather to illustrate the range of policy choices that need to be considered in the effort to accelerate the current pace of development.

Realism dictates that we should begin with the rate of growth that has in fact been achieved over the past decade—roughly 5.2% for the developing countries as a whole—take into account current trends and recent economic events, and in the light of reasonable assumptions, try to determine what an achievable set of goals for the 1980s might be.

The Base Case in Table V exemplifies that. It illustrates a set of projections that appear attainable, but only if a very determined effort is made by the developing and developed countries alike.

If that effort were made—and it is a very considerable one—the annual GDP growth of the developing countries as a group would average 5.6% in the 1980s, up from 5.2% in the 1970s.

5.6% may appear to be an overly modest—even timid—growth projection. It is not. It depends, in fact, on some very bold assumptions: a major economic recovery of the OECD nations; a vigorous mobilization of domestic resources throughout the developing world; a substantial increase in the growth of manufactured exports from developing countries; and rising capital flows from the industrialized nations.

Table V—Development Prospects of the Developing Countries
(Growth rates: percent per annum)

	1970-80 (Estimated Actual)	Projection for 1980-90 (Base Case)
I. Growth Prospects of Developing Countries		
a) GDP		
Low-Income—Africa	3.0	3.8
—Asia	4.2	5.0
—All Low-Income	4.0	4.8
Middle-Income	5.5	5.8
All Developing Countries	5.2	5.6
b) Per Capita GDP		
Low-Income—Africa	0.3	1.0
—Asia	2.0	2.8
—All Low-Income	1.7	2.6
Middle-Income	2.9	3.4
All Developing Countries	2.8	3.3
c) Sectors		
Agriculture	2.7	3.0
Industry	6.2	6.2
Services	5.6	6.0
II. Assumptions about External Environment		
a) GDP of Industrialized Countries	3.4	4.2
b) World Merchandise Trade	5.9	6.0
c) ODA	3.3	3.6
d) Private Capital Flows	7.3	3.9
III. Assumptions about Domestic Action in LDCs		
a) Gross Domestic Investment	6.2	6.5
b) Gross Domestic Saving	5.0	6.7
c) LDC Merchandise Exports	5.7	6.5
Manufactures	10.0	11.1
Primary products	4.2	3.3

To put the matter in sharper perspective, the attainment of 5.6% GDP growth over the next decade would require:

- That the poorest developing countries grow at nearly 5% a year compared to 4% in the previous decade;

- That agricultural production in the developing world increase by at least 3% a year;

- That roughly 27% of the incremental income in the developing countries be saved and reinvested;

- That Official Development Assistance—despite growing restraints on government expenditures in OECD countries —increase, in real terms, at rates higher than in the last decade;

- That recovery in the OECD nations provide an average growth of 4.2% a year over the next decade, as compared with 3.4% in the Seventies, and 2.2% forecast for 1980;

- And that manufactured exports from the developing countries grow at 11.1% a year, despite the short-term adjustment problems and the rising tide of protectionism in many OECD countries.

Now, to achieve all that would obviously require some very major changes in current policies and economic trends, and a return to the more favorable conditions of the 1960s.

Some observers might well argue that such changes are at the outer limits of what is realistically attainable over the next ten years. Clearly, changes of this magnitude raise a number of serious policy questions that the developed and developing countries alike must face candidly if any meaningful international development strategy is to be agreed upon and supported. Policy questions such as these:

- Will the developing countries take the necessary policy actions to accelerate their agricultural growth rate in the 1980s to 3% when it has never averaged higher than 2.7% in the previous two decades, despite both national and international efforts to raise it?

- Will they be able to save and reinvest more than a quarter of their additional output during the 1980s?

- Can the poorest developing countries, containing most of the world's absolute poor, achieve GDP growth rates nearly 25% higher than in the last decade? Can they generate the institutions, mobilize the managerial skill, and motivate the entrepreneurial drive required for such rapid economic growth and the associated structural change?

- Will the OECD nations act to increase Official Development Assistance—in real terms—at a faster pace in the 1980s than they did in the 1970s?

- Will the private capital flows from the developed nations increase in the future at an adequate rate as in the 1970s, despite the growing concern about rising debt service?

- Will world trade, in the face of the continuing threats of recession and trade protectionism, expand in the 1980s at a more rapid rate than in the 1970s, thereby making it possible for the manufactured exports of developing countries to secure a more reasonable share of the market?

- And, finally, can the growth rates of the OECD nations in the 1980s be raised substantially from their present depressed state and thus provide the basis for the necessary expansion of trade and financial assistance?

Simply posing such questions points up the need for serious policy analysis of these issues if the deliberations for a new development strategy are to succeed.

It is clear that the policy assumptions underlying the Base Case—if they can in fact be turned from assumptions into realities in the course of the 1980s—would significantly benefit many of the developing countries.

That is particularly true of those middle-income countries which are well on the way to an efficient and export-oriented industrial sector; which are making serious efforts to limit their population growth; and which have undertaken effective land reform measures.

And yet the fact remains that an overall 5.6% growth target—as arduous an effort as it would require—would still fall far short of what is desirable in terms of results in the developing world: not enough food would be grown; not enough new jobs would be created; and not enough personal income would be generated.

Further, the 5.6% growth target has discouraging implications with respect to reducing poverty significantly by the end of the century.

The projections suggest that some 600 million individuals would remain trapped at the very margin of life in the year 2000.

Now, that is simply not acceptable. And yet, it confronts us all with a serious dilemma. If we were to propose a substantially higher overall growth target for the 1980s—say 6.6%—and if we were to postulate all the necessary assumptions in the international economy that would make that level of growth possible, then we could in fact project a much more acceptable decline in absolute poverty by the end of the century.

Under such a High Growth Case, the projections suggest that the current total of about 800 million absolute poor could decline to some 470 million by the year 2000.

But the dilemma consists in this. It does no good whatever to propose international growth targets—and all their underlying assumptions—that have virtually no possibility at all of being achieved. That merely erodes the credibility of such strategies, and guarantees disillusionment and frustration within the international community, and skepticism and weariness in national legislatures and their constituencies.

Let us be candid. Given current global economic conditions, and the impact of recent events, it is going to be very difficult to achieve even the much more moderate growth assumptions implicit in the so-called Base Case.

Indeed it is entirely possible to visualize a less satisfactory case for the 1980s—with the developing countries as a whole achieving perhaps only 4.8% growth. The impact of such a set of projections, which unhappily are not at all wholly improbable, would yield even less acceptable results in reducing absolute poverty.

As is indicated in Table VI, such projections suggest that as many as 710 million individuals would still be trapped in those deplorable conditions.

**Table VI—Levels of Absolute Poverty Under Alternative
Growth Rates, Year 2000**

	Base Case (5.6% Growth)		High Case (6.6% Growth)		Low Case (4.6% Growth)	
	Millions of Absolute Poor	Percentage of Population	Millions of Absolute Poor	Percentage of Population	Millions of Absolute Poor	Percentage of Population
Low-Income Countries	440	22	340	17	520	26
Middle-Income Countries	160	10	130	8	190	12
All Developing Countries	600	17	470	13	710	20

Now, what are we to do in the face of this dilemma?

The first thing we must do is be realistic.

Absolute poverty is not going to be significantly reduced in an acceptable time frame by the growth rate alone—whatever that rate may turn out to be.

Growth is absolutely essential, and every effort must be made to increase it in the developing societies. But while a necessary condition for reducing poverty, growth is not in itself a sufficient condition. It is naive to assume in any society that absolute poverty will automatically melt away simply because the gross national product is rising.

What is important to understand is that the growth rates by themselves—even the most ambitious ones—cannot possibly reduce absolute poverty as rapidly as it should be.

That requires, in addition to growth, specific and targeted programs. Throughout the Seventies, in a series of UN sponsored world conferences, the international community committed itself politically to improving the quality of life in the developing societies by providing to every individual primary education, basic health care, clean water, sanitation, and adequate nutrition.

The development efforts of the Eighties must turn these now agreed-upon political commitments into practical programs of action.

Within the international framework of a development strategy for the Eighties, individual developing countries must develop their own plans of action to provide specific improvements in the standard of life of the absolute poor in their societies in a stated planning period of 5, 10, or 15 years.

It is only such concrete programs on the national level that can translate international intent into actual improvements in the lives of individuals, and that can provide the realistic basis for assessing the type and volume of external assistance required.

Most of this effort will, of course, have to come from the developing countries themselves. In dealing with the critical development problems, it is clear that no amount of outside assistance from the international community can substitute for determined internal efforts by individual developing societies.

Those efforts are absolutely essential. Nothing can be achieved without them.

But it is also true that these internal efforts must be matched by greater assistance from the international community if the development task is to succeed.

That assistance will be required in a number of interconnected actions. Let me consider briefly some of the principal ones.

Official Development Assistance

To achieve GDP growth rates in the poorest developing countries in the 1980s higher than those in the Base Case, ODA must increase at a rate faster than GNP growth in the OECD nations. The High Case assumes ODA growth at 6.7% per year, which is double the present growth rate. At that rate, by 1990 ODA would amount to .39% of OECD GNP, as compared with .33% at present. But this, of course, cannot be realized—and hence the accelerated economic growth in these countries cannot be achieved—unless the major donors substantially increase their contributions: especially the United States (presently at .22% of GNP), Japan (at .25%), and Germany (at .32%).

As shown in Annex I, the current indications are that in relation to GNP, the United States will not increase its contributions at all during the period covered by the projection (1979-85), and that Japan and Germany will increase theirs by only three one-hundredths of a percentage point.

Private Capital Flows

It is equally essential to the development prospects of the middle-income countries that private capital flows increase in the 1980s at rates close to those of the 1970s. But it is far from certain that this will happen.

There will be increased competition for private funds from the OECD countries as their economic recovery gains momentum. And even more important, the private banks, already heavily committed in a number of developing countries, may be reluctant to expand further at the rate required to support the growth which these countries are capable of achieving.

What may be needed are new institutional arrangements for dealing with unexpected liquidity crises; a broader role for the International Monetary Fund in dealing with short-term balance of payments emergencies; and greater flexibility for the World Bank in providing long-term finance. These were the subjects of yesterday's Development Committee meeting, and they must continue to receive our attention.

World Trade Expansion

Further, as I have noted earlier, any improved growth pattern is going to require a continued healthy expansion both in world trade at large and especially in the manufactured exports of developing countries.

This clearly cannot happen unless the OECD countries succeed in reestablishing patterns of steady growth and high levels of employment, and unless the current surge of protectionism is effectively opposed.

I addressed this issue in detail at the United Nations Conference on Trade and Development (UNCTAD) in Manila earlier this year, and pointed out the heavy economic penalties that trade protectionism imposes on the developed and developing countries alike. But as I emphasized then—and want to reiterate here —the task of improving the world's trade environment will not end with the signing of the Tokyo Round treaty. It will only begin.

There is an unfinished agenda that needs serious attention. The developing countries still have a number of legitimate and urgent concerns.

These include:

- Rolling back and dismantling the non-tariff barriers already in force, especially the existing quotas on textiles and footwear;
- Further tariff cuts for LDC exports that are being exempted from average cuts in the current round; and
- The coverage of items excluded from the Tokyo Round discussions, such as intra-firm trading of multinational corporations, trading between state-owned enterprises, and trade in services.

The point is that the liberalization of the world trade environment must be a continuous process.

We must consider how we can move more quickly and systematically towards a more equitable international trading system, and a more open charter for world trade.

Growth in OECD Nations

The Base Case assumes a major recovery of the momentum of growth in the OECD nations. Without it the prospects of the developing countries themselves are severely limited.

The truth of the matter is that the economic fortunes of the developed and developing countries are more and more intertwined in our increasingly interdependent world.

The growth of the developed countries will be restrained if the incomes—and hence the markets—of the developing countries fail to expand.

And if economic growth and employment levels continue to be depressed in the industrialized nations, these societies will be reluctant to open up their markets, and to offer greater assistance to the developing countries.

During the coming decade the industrialized nations may face much the same choices as they did during the depression era of the 1930s: either to turn fearfully inward in self-defeating efforts to preserve narrow privilege, or to look courageously outward and assist both themselves and the less advantaged to become productive partners in an expanding international system.

As I have pointed out, the realities of interdependence are inevitably forging a new world order, but the institutional arrangements and policy actions to deal with it lag far behind.

Finally, we must remind ourselves that there is no special magic connected with any aggregated economic growth target for the developing countries, be it 5.6%, or any other number.

International consideration of such targets is valuable only to the extent that it leads to a policy dialogue on the issues and assumptions that underlie it.

That is the sort of dialogue that we need, and at a minimum that analysis ought to deal with the development tasks for the 1980s that are clearly fundamental: population growth, employment creation, food production, reduction in absolute poverty, the energy issue, and the necessary structural changes both within the developing countries, and between them and the industrialized nations.

Every one of these problems is urgent, and every one of them currently suffers from various degrees of postponement, temporizing, or delay.

This does not make their solution easier. It only makes it more difficult. Options close. Complications mount. Costs rise. And the penalties of procrastination multiply.

We must, then, get on with these tasks.

If an international strategy is to be at all operationally useful, it must provide a framework within which national programs for action can be developed. No matter how specific the strategy is—and at the international level it can never be very detailed— its ultimate success or failure depends entirely on the extent to which it provides useful guidance for feasible national action-oriented programs.

*   *   *   *

To summarize this section, then, the formulation of a development strategy for the Eighties offers the international community a valuable opportunity to reconsider the fundamental objectives of development itself.

One of the principal frustrations of the North-South Dialogue thus far has been that it has become so bogged down in arguments over means that it has tended to lose sight of ends.

As I have pointed out before, what is needed most of all is a basic understanding among the parties as to:

- The nature and magnitude of the current development problems;

- The action required to address them;

- The relative responsibilities of the parties for taking such actions;

- And the costs and benefits to each of doing so.

The preparations for the new international development strategy—which will benefit from the Report of the Brandt Commission scheduled for the end of this year—provide a context to pursue that basic understanding.

Such an understanding is all the more necessary because we simply do not yet possess the same instruments of implementation at the international level which are available—and taken for granted—at the national level.

There is obviously no global planning system, no world treasury based on international taxation, and no central budgeting machinery to allocate governmental financial resources.

It is possible—even likely—that some of these institutions will eventually evolve. Certainly the realities of our increasing interdependence ought to move us all towards less arbitrary and hopefully more rational management of global resources.

In the interim we must shape and improve the institutions and the system we have as wisely as we can.

Let me, then, turn to a consideration of how the Bank itself can best assist the international community in coping with the development problems of the 1980s.

V. THE WORLD BANK IN THE 1980s

The Bank enters the 1980s with a solid financial base for planning its operations in the years ahead. During the current fiscal year over 300 operations are expected to be approved involving total Bank Group commitments of about $11.5 billion. Disbursements should reach nearly $6 billion. Although the scale of operations in subsequent years remains, tentative, and is subject to possible revision as circumstances change, the following figures indicate the dimensions of our current work plans for the five-year period FY79-83, as compared to actual results for previous five-year intervals.

**Table VII—World Bank: New Financial Commitments and
Net Disbursements by Five-Year Period**
(Billions of dollars)

	FY64-68	FY69-73	FY74-78	Working Plan FY79-83
New Commitments				
IBRD	4.3	8.9	24.4	42.5
IDA	1.3	3.9	7.9	19.0
IFC	0.2	0.6	1.2	2.6
Total—Current $	5.8	13.4	33.5	64.1
—Constant FY79$	21.0	28.2	40.9	56.7
Net Disbursements				
IBRD	1.7	2.9	8.4	18.6
IDA	1.3	1.4	5.3	10.1
IFC	0.1	0.3	0.8	1.5
Total—Current $	3.1	4.6	14.5	30.2
—Constant FY79$	10.0	11.8	19.5	26.4

These plans reflect the fact that in late June the Executive Directors agreed to recommend to the Governors a $40 billion general increase in the International Bank for Reconstruction and Development's (IBRD) capital, thus providing an assured basis for continued real growth in lending over the next several years.

Further, I am optimistic that during our meeting here in Belgrade there will be agreement on the Sixth Replenishment of the International Development Association (IDA) sufficient in size to ensure a substantial real increase in commitment authority over the next three years.

There is, of course, an important agenda still to be completed in these two matters. But as an institution we are moving into the difficult decade of the Eighties, confident that we can build on our experience and the progress achieved in the Seventies, and that we can continue to innovate and adapt our policies to the tasks that lie ahead.

Before I discuss those tasks in more detail, let me stress a general point. Increasingly the developing countries are looking to the Bank as their main source of external assistance. I believe, therefore, that over the next two years we ought thoroughly to reexamine our role in the development process in order to ensure that the Bank is meeting the evolving needs of our members, and to see if we can better provide the full range of services implicit in our mandate. In such a reexamination, none of our programs or policies ought to be regarded as carved in stone. It is our mandate to promote development which is permanent, not the tools we use to implement it.

Now let me turn to what the Bank is doing—and plans to do— to help solve some of the problems that I have been describing.

Let me begin with the issue of population.

Population
The World Bank has been responding to the population issue in the developing member countries in three broad ways: by fostering an awareness of the critical importance of realistic

population planning; by financing activities that directly and indirectly lower fertility; and by supporting research to better understand the determinants of fertility.

Population sector studies providing general guidance for country programs have now been completed for 15 countries, containing one-third of the population of the developing world. Over the next five years an additional 11 countries, with 20% of the population, will be covered.

The population projects financed by the Bank provide a broad range of support for national population programs. They include such components as organizational and administrative assistance to strengthen institutions; population education; motivational programs promoting smaller family size; integrated health and family-planning systems; and many others. Over the next five years we plan to finance at least twice as many population projects as in the past five-year period.

We recognize, of course, that family-planning efforts need to be supplemented by actions which promote socio-economic progress. The Bank has long been committed to the support of projects which directly improve the productivity, and hence the welfare, of the poor. Such investments have been concentrated in the agricultural sector and are, of course, also of critical importance in meeting the food requirements of member countries.

Food

The Bank now is by far the largest single source of external funding for agriculture in the developing world, particularly for food production. We currently make available over 40% of all official external assistance to the sector.

Over the past five years the Bank has directly provided about $12 billion for agricultural development, financing projects with a total cost of about $30 billion, and representing 15 to 20% of the total public investment in agriculture.

Over 75% of this investment has been directed towards increasing food production.

We expect that in the early 1980s Bank-financed projects will contribute up to a fifth of the annual increase in food production in our developing member countries.

In accord with this emphasis on agriculture and expanded food output, the Bank over the past five years has:

- Provided about $1.5 billion of technical and financial support for fertilizer manufacturing projects—projects which will account for a third of all incremental fertilizer production in developing countries in the 1980-85 period;
- Invested approximately $6 billion in irrigation systems, which represents one-fourth of the total worldwide public investment in irrigation in developing countries;
- Financed nearly a fifth of the total investment in rural road networks—in effect, building a rural road network larger than the entire interstate highway system of the United States; and
- Chaired and given financial support to the Consultative Group for International Agricultural Research, which provides the funding for the international agricultural research system; and in addition invested $160 million in the development of 13 national research programs.

The next decade will require a continued strengthening of these programs.

We estimate that the Bank will provide $20 to $25 billion for agricultural investment during FY79-83, and that this will support a total of over $50 billion worth of projects and programs.

Thus, the Bank's projects will continue to provide at least 15 to 20% of total public agricultural investment in the developing countries during the 1980s.

The Bank will also be prepared to provide technical and financial support to governments that seek to develop specific national plans to overcome their food problems.

In addition to this direct assistance for increasing food production in the developing countries, the Bank is considering how food security programs, based on decentralized storage systems, can be designed to assure adequate prices to farmers, to reduce the substantial amounts of post-harvest losses, and to strengthen the internal distribution systems against the threat of adverse weather conditions.

Reducing Absolute Poverty

The investments the Bank has helped to finance in the rural sector over the past five years are expected to raise the incomes of some 60 million of the poorest individuals in the developing world. That has been the central thrust of the Bank's effort to help reduce absolute poverty—and will continue to be so.

Today, however, I want to emphasize the important complementary activities undertaken by the Bank which reinforce our direct efforts to increase productivity. And I want to cite two important sectors in particular: water supply, and health.

The Bank began to lend for water supply and waste disposal in the early 1960s, but prior to 1970 such projects were directed almost exclusively toward meeting the water supply requirements of major cities—often the capitals—in the developing countries. In the early 1970s, in accord with the strategic considerations spelled out in my address at our meeting in Nairobi, this lending began to be shaped not only as an important contribution to infrastructure, but as a vital public service which if directed toward the absolute poor could have a major impact on their lives. In the past four years, therefore, over half of the water-supply loans have included funds for such purposes.

The linkages to productivity and better standards of living are immediate. In the past the productive potential of poor households, and particularly of the women in these families, has been severely reduced by the time and energy spent in obtaining sufficient quantities of water to meet essential needs. In many rural areas, drawers of water—mostly women—have to walk one to five miles to reach the nearest source. And unclean water and inadequate waste disposal are among the chief causes of illness and death, particularly among infants.

Strategies to assist the poor to improve their health are critical both to their quality of life and to their enhanced productivity.

Over the past four years, the Bank has experimented with the financing of health components in projects in other sectors.

On the basis of that experience, it has now been agreed the Bank should initiate a full program of technical assistance and lending in the health sector itself.

While dealing with these fundamental development problems—population, food production, and the alleviation of absolute poverty—the Bank must, of course, take account of those changes in the world economic environment that can have a major impact on the ability of the developing countries to sustain reasonable rates of economic growth. In the decade of the Seventies, no single issue has loomed larger than the sharp increase in the relative price of energy.

Meeting Energy Needs

The oil import bill of developing countries rose from $4 billion in 1972 to $26 billion in 1978, and we estimate it will be about $42 billion in 1980. This has dramatically affected the economics of energy supply, increasing the incentives for exploiting known energy resources in developing countries and for intensifying resource exploration and pre-investment activity.

In view of this situation we examined the prospects of 78 non-OPEC developing countries with a potential for oil and gas production. Only 23 of these are now in production and in most cases the output is small. Provided that sufficient resources can be made available—on the order of $12 billion per year—these 78 countries should be able to increase their oil production by some 3 million barrels per day, and their gas production by some 1.2 million barrels per day oil equivalent by the end of the 1980s, thereby saving some $30 billion in import costs.

This, in addition to the planned trebling of their hydroelectric generation and a doubling of their coal production during the same period, would constitute an important contribution to the expansion of global energy supplies.

The question is: will the necessary financing be available?

To help ensure that it will be, the Bank has recently launched a five-year energy program.

Our tentative plans are to:

- Gradually expand our petroleum lending to $1.2 billion per year by FY1983—financing, annually, oil and gas exploration and production projects with a total cost of over $4 billion, and representing roughly a third of the total investment requirements of our developing member countries in this sector;

- 60% of this lending program for oil and gas will be in the poorer countries;

- 40% of this lending program for oil and gas will be for such activities as surveys, exploratory drilling, and project preparation;

- Assist up to 40 countries during FY78-83 in evaluating and updating data from earlier geological surveys, or in commissioning new surveys; and

- Undertake sector work in about 15 developing countries each year to help establish their energy requirements and production potential, and to assist in preparing national energy plans.

Of course, our role in this field is to be a catalyst: the bulk of external funding must come from other sources. But the response of the Bank in this difficult area illustrates the kind of flexibility that we must ensure in our policies if we are to help meet the changing needs of the developing world.

Financing Structural Change and the Adjustment Process

The increase in energy prices is only one example of the changes in world economic conditions that affect the external financing prospects of the developing countries. As I emphasized earlier, the deteriorating outlook for growth in the industrial nations threatens to compound the problems facing the developing societies. It puts an additional premium on the rapid adjustment of each country's pattern of production to its evolving comparative advantage.

As a group, the developing countries need to increase their manufactured exports by 11 to 13% a year in the 1980s in order to be able to finance reasonable GDP growth rates. This will call for difficult structural adjustment internally, especially given the prospects of slower growth and the threat of rising protectionism in the developed nations.

These difficulties are going to be compounded by the recent increases in oil prices which will add about $14 billion to the current account deficits of the oil-importing developing countries in 1980.[a] The necessary adjustments will take time and countries willing to take hard decisions will need external help to support the adjustment process.

In my address to UNCTAD this year, I urged the international community to consider sympathetically additional assistance to developing countries that undertake the necessary structural adjustments. I indicated that I was prepared to recommend to the Executive Directors that the Bank consider such requests for assistance, and that it make available additional program lending in appropriate cases. Particular attention needs to be given to the possibility of providing assistance to countries before they get into acute balance of payments difficulties.

Supporting Private Capital Flows

As in the case of energy financing—where the Bank's role is essentially catalytic—the direct assistance we can make available from our own resources to member countries which face mounting external capital requirements is, of course, limited. The bulk of the external finance, especially for the rapidly industrializing middle-income countries, must continue to come from commercial banks and private direct investors.

Over the next few years the financing requirements of the developing countries can be met—in a manner consistent with reasonable rates of growth—only if the private markets succeed in recycling funds to these countries on a scale even larger than in the past. These needs simply cannot be met by Official Flows

---

[a]The current account deficits of the oil-importing developing countries are estimated to total approximately $50 billion in 1980, compared to $23 billion in 1978 and $5 billion in 1972.

alone. And there is considerable uncertainty about the ability of the commercial banks to supply the necessary funds. Their very success in the recycling job of the past few years has greatly increased their holdings of developing country debt, and it is unclear whether those holdings can be further increased sufficiently to meet the new requirements.

The Bank has sought to support flows of private capital on reasonable terms through its own direct lending, through co-financing operations with commercial banks and—perhaps most importantly—through its efforts to promote in individual countries strategies of development which are realistic and sustainable. And because major uncertainties cloud the outlook for the future volume of commercial bank lending to the developing countries, we will monitor closely the level of total financial flows and, if they appear inadequate, we will work with the International Monetary Fund and other agencies to devise new approaches.

Contribution to the North-South Dialogue

Let me touch, finally, on the Bank's expanding role in preparing analyses of international issues affecting the developing countries.

Because of the more than 30 years of experience that the Bank has acquired in economic work in developing countries, and the resources of its international staff, it has a unique capacity to analyze in an objective fashion the implications of the growing interdependence between developed and developing countries. In Manila earlier this year, I addressed certain aspects of interdependence in trade in manufactured goods. The type of analysis presented there can be, and will be, extended and deepened in the period ahead. But—and this is the point I want to stress—there are many other aspects of interdependence that require careful, professional analysis.

As you know, we have already undertaken the preparation of the World Development Report on an annual basis. The first two Reports have analyzed the development prospects and problems of low-income and middle-income countries on the basis of alternative assumptions of their own domestic efforts, and of the international environment.

In addition to continuing to assess the growth prospects of the developing countries, each Report will concentrate on an analysis of one or two priority policy issues on the international agenda.

We hope through these means to make a useful contribution to the understanding of global development issues, and to the ongoing North-South Dialogue.

The World Bank is a major financial institution charged with the task of financial intermediation. But we are also a development agency with a vital role to play in assuring that adequate consideration be given to alternative policies for accelerating economic and social advance in the developing world.

This institution came to birth in a burst of innovation in 1944—at a time of unparalleled global disruption—with a bold belief in the creative principle of international collaboration.

The demands that the 1980s make on us may turn out to be even greater than those of the critical mid-1940s.

We need to be ready. I am confident that we will be.

Let me now summarize and conclude the central points I have made this morning.

VI. SUMMARY AND CONCLUSIONS

As the Seventies draw to a close it is important to try to learn what lessons we can from a period that has been so unexpectedly turbulent.

The principal goal adopted nine years ago by the international community in its official strategy for the Second Development Decade—the average 6% rate of growth target for the developing countries as a group—will not be achieved. At best, growth will not exceed 5.2% a year.

Further, there will be serious shortfalls in the subsidiary targets, particularly in LDC agricultural production, and in the level of Official Development Assistance from the OECD nations.

Moreover, the overall performance statistics obscure very significant differences between various groups of countries.

Income grew the least where it was needed the most: in the poorest countries, containing over half the population of the developing world. The economies of most of these nations, with hundreds of millions of their people already trapped in absolute poverty, scarcely advanced at all.

Now the international community is considering what sort of proposals it ought to adopt in its official strategy for the Third Development Decade.

Should it once again draw up a series of specific statistical targets for overall average performance by the developing countries, or should it approach the whole question of goals in some other way?

In the end, effective development strategies revolve essentially around policy choices. Quantitative targets may be useful to monitor progress once fundamental policy decisions have been taken, but targets themselves do not guarantee that the policies are appropriate.

It seems to me, therefore, that a more practical approach for DDIII planning would be to consider in detail the hard policy choices that the developing and developed countries alike are going to have to confront in the Eighties and beyond if fundamental development objectives are to be realized.

These policy choices will inevitably revolve around such immense and complicated problems as population growth, food production, employment creation, urbanization, reducing absolute poverty, and expanding international trade and financial flows.

All these problems are interconnected.

But our experience with them is beginning to reveal that the measures of the past are simply not going to be adequate in the decades that lie immediately ahead.

The truth is that structural changes of immense magnitude are going to be necessary if we are to make any significant headway against such problems.

In a way that is what the dialogue between the North and the South is fundamentally about, and I believe that the dialogue ought to involve itself fully with the formulation of any new agreed-upon strategy.

For its own part, the Bank is, of course, deeply engaged in all these fundamental development issues, but there is a great deal more it can and should do to assist its member countries to deal effectively with them.

Our recent initiative in the energy field—a sector we will give high-priority attention to in the coming decade—is an example of the flexibility we need in order to respond quickly and effectively to the changing needs of our developing member countries.

The Bank, together with all of the international development community, should look to the new interdependent world order that will inevitably evolve in the Eighties and beyond with the vision and courage and boldness that history is clearly asking of us all.

The options are closing, the easy answers are disappearing, the hard choices are becoming more insistent.

Procrastination and delay and inadequate effort in the face of these momentous issues can only bring the most severe penalties to those in the next century who will have to live with the consequences of the decisions we must take—and take soon.

It is an era in which we are learning that our natural resources must not be prodigally wasted.

But our most irrecoverable resource of all is time.

We must use the time we have. And we must use it now.

It will never return.

INSERT FOR PAGE 596, PREPARED AFTER THE TEXT WAS PRINTED IN SEPTEMBER 1979

When I drafted my address for today, and released the text to the printers, I stated at the outset of Section V—the section that deals with the work of the World Bank itself—that the Bank is entering the 1980s with a solid financial base.

And I want to emphasize that a great deal of progress has been made in this matter recently. On June 28 the Executive Directors approved the $40 billion General Capital Increase and recommended it to the Governors, and the negotiations for the Sixth Replenishment of the International Development Association have been going very well.

But after the text of my address was printed, the U.S. House of Representatives passed an amendment to the legislation appropriating funds for the Fifth Replenishment of IDA that precludes the use of U.S. funds for certain purposes—specifically, for loans to Viet Nam, and a number of other countries.

Under these circumstances, our Articles of Agreement would prohibit the Bank from accepting the funds. And in the absence of the U.S. contribution the Bank is specifically prohibited by the terms of the IDA agreement from using funds of any other donor. In such a situation the Bank would be forced to stop IDA operations immediately.

The blunt truth is that if this amendment is finally enacted into law, the Congress literally will have destroyed the largest single source of economic assistance to the one and one quarter billion people living in the poorest developing nations.

I cannot believe that the United States—itself the principal founder of the International Development Association—wants to do that.

But the fact is that it is on the way to being done.

And the only relevant question now is: how do we deal with this crisis?

It is clear that we must have the support of all our donor countries in this issue. I am grateful to President Carter for his assurances that the U.S. Administration will do all that it can to assist in the solution of the problem. And I will be giving my priority attention to this matter until it is solved.

Certainly for the sake of those who suffer the greatest deprivations of all, the problem must be solved. I repeat: I cannot believe—I do not believe—that the United States wants to turn its back on the more than one billion people in the poorest countries of the developing world.

Flow of Official Development Assistance from Development Assistance Committee Members Measured as a Percentage of Gross National Product[a]

	1965	1970	1975	1976	1977	1978	1979	1980	1981	1982	1983	1984	1985
Australia	.53	.59	.60	.42	.45	.45	.45	.46	.47	.47	.48	.49	.50
Austria	.11	.07	.17	.12	.24	.27	.28	.29	.29	.30	.30	.31	.32
Belgium	.60	.46	.59	.51	.46	.55	.54	.58	.60	.62	.65	.67	.70
Canada	.19	.42	.55	.46	.50	.52	.46	.47	.47	.48	.50	.50	.50
Denmark	.13	.38	.58	.56	.60	.75	.69	.70	.70	.71	.71	.72	.72
Finland[b]	.02	.07	.18	.18	.17	.18	.20	.21	.21	.22	.23	.24	.25
France	.76	.66	.62	.62	.60	.57	.57	.57	.58	.58	.59	.60	.61
Germany	.40	.32	.40	.31	.27	.31	.32	.33	.33	.34	.34	.35	.35
Italy	.10	.16	.11	.13	.10	.06	.10	.10	.09	.13	.11	.10	.11
Japan	.27	.23	.23	.20	.21	.23	.25	.26	.26	.27	.28	.28	.28
Netherlands	.36	.61	.75	.82	.85	.82	.90	.93	.93	.93	.94	.95	.97
New Zealand[c]		.23	.52	.41	.39	.34	.30	.27	.27	.27	.29	.31	.33
Norway	.16	.32	.66	.70	.83	.90	.92	.94	.96	.97	.98	.99	1.00
Sweden	.19	.38	.82	.82	.99	.90	.93	.94	.95	.96	.98	.98	1.00
Switzerland	.09	.15	.19	.19	.19	.20	.21	.21	.22	.23	.23	.24	.25
United Kingdom	.47	.36	.37	.38	.37	.40	.39	.39	.40	.40	.40	.41	.41
United States[d]	.49	.31	.26	.25	.22	.23	.22	.22	.22	.22	.22	.22	.22

GRAND TOTAL

ODA ($b-Nominal Prices)	5.9	6.8	13.6	13.7	14.7	18.3	20.7	23.0	25.7	29.0	32.7	36.7	41.3
ODA ($b-Constant 1979 Prices)	16.7	15.9	19.2	18.8	18.6	20.0	20.7	21.5	22.4	23.7	25.0	26.1	27.5
GNP ($t-Nominal Prices)	1.3	2.0	3.8	4.2	4.7	5.6	6.3	7.0	7.7	8.6	9.5	10.6	11.9
ODA as % of GNP	.44	.34	.35	.33	.31	.32	.33	.33	.33	.33	.34	.34	.35
Price Deflator[e]	.36	.43	.71	.73	.79	.91	1.00	1.07	1.15	1.23	1.31	1.40	1.50

[a]Historical figures through 1977 and preliminary estimates for 1978 are from OECD. Those for 1979-85 are based on OECD and World Bank estimates of growth of GNP, on information on budget appropriations for aid, and on aid policy statements by governments. They are projections, not predictions, of what will occur unless action not now planned takes place.

[b]Finland became a member of DAC in January 1975.

[c]New Zealand became a member of DAC in 1973, ODA figures for New Zealand are not available for 1965.

[d]In 1949, at the beginning of the Marshall Plan, U.S. Official Development Assistance amounted to 2.79% of GNP.

[e]The deflator is the US$ GNP deflator which includes the effects of changes in exchange rates.

TWENTY-TWO

To the
BOARD OF GOVERNORS
WASHINGTON, D.C.
SEPTEMBER 30, 1980

I. INTRODUCTION

This is the thirteenth, and final, address that I will have the privilege of making in this forum.

The occasion, I believe, places on me a special responsibility, and hence what I have to say this morning will be particularly frank and candid, especially as it relates to the future role of the World Bank.

During the past 18 months the external environment affecting economic growth in the oil-importing developing countries—and thus their rate of social advance—has become substantially more difficult.

The new surge in oil prices, and the downturn in trade with the developed nations, have imposed on these countries huge and potentially unsustainable current account deficits. The result is that their critical development tasks, never easy in the past, are now seriously threatened.

Meanwhile, the industrialized nations continue to grapple with problems of inflation, unemployment, and recession. Governments are searching for politically feasible ways to reduce public expenditures. And though Official Development Assistance remains a miniscule and insignificant fraction of gross national product—and is, in fact, wholly inadequate to the urgent needs at hand—there is little legislative initiative to increase it.

Further, the global financial system as a whole, still trying to cope with past imbalances, must now find a way to recycle to appropriate recipients over $100 billion a year of additional surpluses being earned by the capital-surplus oil-exporting countries.

The cumulative effect of all of this is a climate of apprehension in which the temptation will be strong for both the developed and developing nations to react unwisely.

The developing countries will be tempted to postpone the internal policy changes required to adjust to the new external

613

conditions. And the developed nations will be tempted to turn to shortsighted protectionist and restrictive measures that in the end can only delay economic recovery for the rich and poor nations alike.

These temptations are very real. And they are very dangerous. They lead precisely in the wrong direction.

What we need are measures that lead in the right direction. They are available, but like almost everything else worthwhile in life they are going to demand courage and effort and vision.

I want to explore those measures with you this morning.

Specifically, I want to examine:

- The prospects for economic growth and social advance in the oil-importing developing countries throughout the 1980s;

- The actions the developing societies themselves, as well as the industrialized nations and the OPEC countries, can take to maximize that growth;

- The need to accelerate the attack on absolute poverty; and finally

- The role the World Bank itself ought to play in all of this in the decade ahead.

Let me begin with the current economic outlook.

II. ECONOMIC PROSPECTS FOR THE DEVELOPING COUNTRIES

Global economic prospects have seriously deteriorated since we met last year in Belgrade. The outlook now is that the oil-importing developing countries in the years immediately ahead are going to have a very difficult time. The Bank is currently projecting, for the decade of the 1980s, lower levels of economic growth in those countries than it did twelve months ago.

TABLE I—GROWTH OF GNP PER CAPITA, 1960-85

	1980		Average Annual Percentage Growth Rates		
	Population (millions)	GNP Per Capita 1980 dollars[a]	1960-70	1970-80	1980-85
OIL-IMPORTING DEVELOPING COUNTRIES					
Low-Income:					
Sub-Saharan Africa	141	239	1.6	0.2	−0.3
Asia	992	212	1.6	1.1	1.1
Sub-Total	1,133	216	1.6	0.9	1.0
Middle-Income	701	1,638	3.6	3.1	2.0
Total	1,834	751	3.1	2.7	1.8
OIL-EXPORTING DEVELOPING COUNTRIES	456	968	2.8	3.5	3.0
Industrialized Countries	671	9,684	3.9	2.4	2.5
Centrally Planned Economies[b]	1,386	1,720	—	3.8	3.3

The most probable outcome for at least the next five years is that the annual average per capita growth of the oil-importing developing countries—which was 3.1% in the 1960s, and 2.7% in the 1970s—will drop in 1980-85 to 1.8%.

More depressing still is the outlook for the 1.1 billion people who live in the poorest countries. Their already desperately low per capita income, less than $220 per annum, is likely to grow by no more than 1% a year—an average of only two or three dollars per individual. There would even be negative growth for the 141 million people in the low-income countries of sub-Saharan Africa.

There are two principal causes. The new surge in oil prices has more than doubled the cost of imported energy for the oil-importing developing countries. And the continuing recession in the industrialized nations, which comprise their most important markets, is severely limiting demand for their exports.

In 1973 the oil-import bill of these developing countries (in

[a]Preliminary estimates.
[b]Including China.

current dollars) was $7 billion. In 1980 it is likely to be $67 billion. The price of oil is not going to come down—on the contrary it is likely to continue to rise in real terms by perhaps 3% a year. The projection for 1985, therefore, is $124 billion, and by 1990—even assuming these countries more than double their own domestic energy production, and make a considerable effort at conservation—the bill is projected to be nearly $230 billion (see Table II).

TABLE II—PETROLEUM IMPORTS OF THE OIL-IMPORTING DEVELOPING COUNTRIES
(Billions of current US dollars)

	1973	1978	1980	1985	1990
Cost of Petroleum Imports					
Low-Income	1	2	6	13	23
Middle-Income	6	30	61	111	206
Total	7	32	67	124	229
MEMO ITEMS:					
Price per Barrel (c.i.f., U.S.$)					
Current Dollars	4.20	13.70	29.80	50.30	78.30
1980 Dollars	8.88	17.13	29.80	35.10	40.85
Volume of Net Imports (million barrels per day)	4.6	6.4	6.2	6.8	8.0
Volume of Domestic Production[a]	5.7	7.3	8.5	12.7	18.5

Meanwhile, as I indicated, the continuing sluggishness in the growth rate of the industrialized nations will pose additional problems for these developing countries. The expansion of their principal export markets will decline, and an already unfavorable situation could be seriously compounded by additional deflationary policies and a resort to greater protectionism in the developed world.

Reflecting the effect of these two factors, the current account deficits of the oil-importing countries have increased sharply.

---

[a]All forms of energy production translated into the equivalent of million barrels of oil per day.

In 1980 they are expected to constitute nearly 4% of their GNP (see Table III).

TABLE III—CURRENT ACCOUNT DEFICITS OF OIL-IMPORTING DEVELOPING COUNTRIES
(Billions of current US dollars)

	1973	1975	1978	1980
Current Account Deficits[a]				
Low-Income	2.3	5.4	5.7	10.0
Middle-Income	4.4	34.2	21.4	51.0
Total	6.7	39.6	27.1	61.0
Current Account Deficits as a Percentage of GNP				
Low-Income	2.2	3.8	2.7	3.6
Middle-Income	0.9	5.3	2.2	4.0
Total	1.1	5.1	2.3	3.9

III. A PROGRAM OF STRUCTURAL ADJUSTMENT

Persistent deficits of the magnitude reflected in Table III cannot be sustained indefinitely. In the short run the deficits can be, and are being, financed by additional external borrowing. But in the longer run this will not suffice since at the levels involved the mounting burden of debt service would soon become unsupportable.

The countries will, therefore, have to make those structural changes in their economies that can enable them to pay from their own resources for increasingly more expensive, but necessary, oil. This can only be done by expanding their exports, or by reducing their non-oil imports, or by some combination of the two.

Now, since there is no other way to do this, these internal adjustments will in fact take place sooner or later. And they will take place whether or not there is external financial assistance available to help get it done.

But the point is that it will make a very great deal of difference

---

[a]Excludes official transfers.

to these countries' economic and social advance—that is, to their development progress—whether these adjustments are made sooner rather than later, and with external financial assistance rather than without it.

For if the action in a given country is delayed, or if the external financial assistance available to it is inadequate, then the adjustment process will have to take place in an internal environment of low or negative growth, of little or no social advance, and of almost certain political disorder—a very heavy and unnecessary penalty for that society to have to pay.

But if, on the other hand, the required structural changes are initiated before a crisis situation develops, and scheduled over a reasonable period of time—say, five to eight years—and if during that adjustment period the country is assisted in maintaining a reasonable level of imports by an expansion of the external financial resources available to it, then the negative impact of the adjustment process on the country's economic growth and social advance will be substantially less.

This would permit growth rates in the developing countries to recover to more satisfactory levels in 1985-90, possibly exceeding even the rates achieved in the 1960s and early 1970s.

But such a reversal in fortunes will not be easy to achieve.

To begin with, there are significant differences between the present adjustment situation, and that of the 1974-78 period:

- The real cost of oil actually declined from 1974 to 1978 by about 23%. Since 1978 it has risen sharply, and is now expected to continue to rise during the 1980s.

- The commercial banks rapidly expanded their claims on oil-importing developing countries in the previous period: from $33 billion in 1974 to an estimated $133 billion in 1978. But now their capital to risk-asset ratios have worsened, and some feel overexposed in certain of these countries.

- Some of the middle-income developing countries, which borrowed extensively in the past, are regarded by the commercial banks as being less creditworthy today than they were then. Increased spreads on new lending and a slower rate of growth in such lending are both likely.

- Considerable financing became available to cushion the impact of higher energy costs during the 1974-1978 period from bilateral aid programs and from international financial institutions. Neither source now seems likely to expand as rapidly in the future as it did in the past.

- The debt-servicing burden was considerably reduced in the 1970s by negative real interest rates, whereas the developing countries have recently been borrowing large amounts at positive real interest rates.

- Many developing countries have already carried out a major pruning of their import, investment, and consumption levels so that the scope for further retrenchment is now considerably less.

- The oil-exporting nations that are currently accumulating surpluses are likely to have them longer this time—thus prolonging the recycling task—since their imports are not expected to expand as quickly as they did in the previous period, nor are the workers' remittances from these countries likely to accelerate as fast.

- And finally, the possibility of a prolonged recession in the industrialized nations, particularly if it is accompanied by restrictive measures applied to trade or capital flows, will make the adjustment task of the developing countries that much harder this time.

It is well to remind ourselves of this comparison between the present and past. The sense of relief over the relatively successful adjustment in the earlier period should not be allowed to lead to a feeling of complacency now.

The truth is that even in the earlier period there was a considerable erosion of economic growth. Both new jobs and new income were simply lost in most of the developing countries. Their political and economic systems are already under serious strain. And there are limits to how much more they can restrict their domestic consumption levels.

Further, this new adjustment problem is caused by a permanent change in the world economy, not by some temporary phenomenon which will later automatically reverse itself. Hence the longer the developing countries postpone adjustment policies, the more intractable their problems will become.

Many governments failed to recognize this in the 1970s. They looked instead to short-term finance as the answer to what they regarded as essentially a passing problem. But such finance merely borrowed time; it could not, and did not, substitute for basic adjustment policies.

Countries that recognized the long-term nature of the problem expanded their exports, reduced their imports through efficient domestic production, used borrowing to support investment and structural adjustment, and restored their growth momentum after a relatively brief decline. Those countries, on the other hand, that perceived it as a short-term problem did not use their external borrowing to carry out fundamental structural adjustments, and as a consequence merely accumulated more debt and a much greater problem for the future.

The point I want to stress here is the necessity of using external finance in support of structural adjustments, and not as a substitute for them. In the developing countries' interests, and in the interests of the world community as a whole, there is no other viable alternative.

Obviously it is desirable that these adjustment policies be implemented in a framework of vigorous development activity, rather than at depressed levels of investment and effort. What is needed is not just a new balance-of-payments equilibrium, but that this equilibrium be reached at the highest feasible level of economic growth. Indeed a key lesson of the 1970s is that success in adjustment should be measured not just by the reduction of current account deficits to present levels, but by the growth achieved during and following the adjustment period.

That is vital to these countries' future, and it is all the more necessary if they are not to lose ground in the most fundamental struggle of all: the attack on absolute poverty in their societies.

Now let me turn to certain of the specific actions required if the prospective balance-of-payments deficits are to be reduced to a manageable level within a reasonable period of time, say during the next five or six years, while preserving as much growth momentum in the developing countries as is possible.

There will have to be major adjustments in both national and international policies, and a sustained, collective effort on the part of the world community, including:

- A sharp increase in the savings rate of the oil-importing low-income countries, and the reinvestment of over 25% of the increment in their GNP during the 1980-90 period;

- A significant rise in net resource flows to these countries, from $9 billion in 1980 to $19 billion in 1985, and $33 billion in 1990;

- A substantial increase in private capital flows to middle-income countries;

- A faster rate of growth in the exports of oil-importing developing countries during the Eighties than in the Seventies;

- A more than doubling of domestic energy production in these countries between 1980 and 1990, implying import substitution in the energy sector of over $280 billion a year by 1990; and

- Much greater efficiency in the domestic use of capital.

These are clearly a demanding set of actions and policy changes. What is essential is that the early years of this decade be used to establish the necessary framework of adjustment so that a vigorous economic recovery can take place in the later years.

Each country will, of course, have to design its own specific plan of action for this purpose. If exports are the dynamic sector in a given economy, the promising strategy would obviously be to stress further export expansion. If good possibilities exist for import substitution—as they clearly do in domestic energy production—these ought to be pursued.

Let me comment briefly on this issue of domestic energy production in oil-importing developing countries.

Domestic Energy Production

It can make a very substantial contribution to the entire adjustment process.

To understand that, one need only reflect that even if their domestic energy production expands in the future at the rate of recent years (6.7% per annum), their oil-import bill in 1990 will be over $280 billion—a level that would be difficult to finance by any conceivable expansion of exports, or increase in external borrowing.

Although the sharp rise in the world price of oil has put considerable strain on the balance of payments of the developing countries, it has also changed the economies of domestic energy production dramatically.

At current and prospective oil prices, many oil-importing developing countries can now turn what were previously regarded as marginal energy reserves of oil, gas, coal, hydroelectric, and forest resources into commercial propositions. If they maximize energy production between now and the end of the decade, and pursue a vigorous program of energy conservation, we estimate that these countries could by then cut their annual oil-import bill by more than $50 billion.

But if they are to achieve this substantial saving they will have to adjust their domestic prices, incentives, and investment priorities so as to give much greater emphasis than at present to internal energy production. In all too many countries, governments have kept domestic prices of petroleum products artificially low compared to world prices, with the result that there has been little incentive for consumers to conserve, or for producers to invest.

What we propose is this: the oil-importing developing countries should establish efficient import substitution in energy as one of their principal tasks for the 1980s. They should draw up concrete national energy plans, and formulate specific domestic investment programs. These, in turn, should be backed by newly mobilized domestic resources and by additional external assistance, including assistance from the World Bank which I will discuss in a moment.

External Financial Requirements of Low-Income Countries

As I indicated earlier, there is an urgent need for more external funds if the developing countries are to manage the adjustment process, including the expansion of domestic energy production, without avoidable and hence unnecessary penalties to their economic growth and social progress. Let me turn to that subject now, dealing first with the requirements of the low-income countries.

A major expansion in concessional flows to these countries is required in the 1980s to support their adjustment programs. What we have to remember is that they will benefit only marginally from world trade expansion, and will have limited access to international capital markets. Their financial requirements are likely to increase by $5 to $8 billion in 1980 over 1978 due chiefly to their declining terms of trade, to the sluggish growth in the OECD nations, and to the investments now required to adjust their economies to the changed international environment.

These are also the very countries that can least afford to cut back on their programs directed at reducing poverty. And yet they find themselves suddenly caught in a new and painful squeeze on their resources. They are clearly the priority case for a significant increase in concessional assistance.

But what are the prospects for this?

Total Official Development Assistance flows, including those from OPEC countries, did not increase in the 1977-79 period. In real terms they declined, and the outlook for the future is not bright.

Recent actions give cause for concern. The aid cuts announced by the British Government will cause their ODA to fall to .38% of GNP by 1985, from the .49% average for 1977-79. Aid bills continue to face difficulties in the U.S. Congress, suggesting that support from the largest donor is likely to remain the lowest, relative to GNP, of all major industrial nations. Germany and Japan have indicated their intention to continue to improve their aid flows, but most donors have not committed themselves to increasing the share of GNP allocated to concessional assistance.

What is even more disappointing, the portion of these ODA flows that were allocated to the low-income countries—which, of course, needed them most—was shockingly small in both absolute and relative terms. It amounted to less than one-half of the total (see Annex II). On a per capita basis, the low-income countries receive less concessional assistance than the middle- and high-income nations.

In view of the penalties the new global economic situation imposes on these poorest countries—a situation they themselves neither caused nor can do much to influence—the donors, both OECD and OPEC, ought to indicate clearly how much, if at all, they are prepared to help. The needs of the poorest countries are well known. It is not a time to temporize with the problem. It is a time to act.

The OECD nations should consider the following course of action:

- At the very minimum, each country should maintain its Official Development Assistance at the same percentage of its GNP as it did in 1978, and thus should increase the real level of its ODA as quickly as its GNP increases.

- Those countries which are well below the present OECD average of .34%—in particular, the United States and Japan —should consider increasing their real ODA flows faster than their GNP growth. The former Secretary of State of the United States called the U.S. performance "disgraceful"— and I agree with him.

- In view of the particularly difficult prospects the poorest countries face in the 1980s, the OECD nations should increase the share that these countries will receive in their individual ODA allocations. As Annex II indicates, in 1978 these countries received less than one-half of the total ODA that DAC provided: in the case of Austria and New Zealand it was less than one-fifth; and for Australia, France, and the U.S. no more than one-third.

- The OECD nations in 1978 supported a retroactive adjustment of terms in respect to the past debt of poor and least-developed countries. However, only about $5 billion of past debts have so far been cancelled or rescheduled—out of a potential total of about $26 billion—and it is far from certain that this debt relief constituted additional assistance. Full cancellation or rescheduling would be equivalent to a substantial increase in concessional flows, particularly if it were extended to include all low-income countries.

A major responsibility rests as well on the capital-surplus oil-exporting nations.

Since 1973 the level of the ODA contributions of these countries—Saudi Arabia, Kuwait, Iraq, the United Arab Emirates, Libya, and Qatar—has been remarkable: they contributed 4.0% of their combined GNP during the 1974-79 period (see Table IV).

TABLE IV—ODA FLOWS FROM CAPITAL-SURPLUS OIL EXPORTERS TO DEVELOPING COUNTRIES[a]

	1973		1974		1975		1976		1977		1978		1979	
	$m.	% of GNP	$m.	% of GNP	$m.	% of GNP	$m.	% of GNP	$m.	% of GNP	$m.	% of GNP	$m.	% of GNP
Saudi Arabia	305	4.0	1,029	4.5	1,997	5.4	2,407	5.7	2,410	4.3	1,470	2.8	1,970	3.1
Kuwait	345	5.7	622	5.7	976	8.1	615	4.4	1,518	10.6	1,268	6.4	1,099	5.1
Iraq	11	.2	423	4.0	218	1.7	232	1.4	61	.3	172	.8	861	2.9
U.A.E.	289	16.0	511	7.6	1,046	14.1	1,060	11.0	1,177	10.2	690	5.6	207	1.6
Libya	215	3.3	147	1.2	261	2.3	94	.6	115	.7	169	.9	146	.6
Qatar	94	15.6	185	9.3	339	15.6	195	8.0	197	7.9	106	3.7	251	5.6
Total	1,259	4.5	2,917	4.5	4,837	5.8	4,603	4.6	5,478	4.5	3,875	3.0	4,534	2.9
Memo Item: Current a/c Surplus—in billion US$	7		43		31		36		34		20		56	

[a]Data for 1978 and 1979 are provisional.

The issue now is over future trends in their ODA. If the OPEC capital-surplus countries begin increasing their concessional assistance flows after the recent and hopefully temporary decline, this can make a major contribution to easing the adjustment problem of the poorest nations. Though they have a number of plans under active consideration, what the situation needs now are some firm decisions in order to meet the most urgent requirements of these low-income countries.

- In 1980 the current account surplus of the capital-surplus oil-exporting countries is expected to increase by about $100 billion over the levels of 1978. As already noted, they have provided 4.0% of their GNP in the form of ODA during 1974-79. The question is: can they continue to do so in the future, and can it be provided in the form of quick-disbursing assistance to a large number of the low-income countries in order to meet their immediate needs?

- Iraq, Venezuela, and Mexico have proposed that they compensate the poorest countries importing their oil for the recent oil-price increases by granting them long-term, low-interest loans. If this initiative is adopted by other oil exporters, it will have the immediate and beneficial impact of easing the balance-of-payments deficits of the poorest countries.

- The Long-Term Strategy Committee of OPEC has recently endorsed the proposal of Algeria and Venezuela to convert the OPEC Fund into a development agency with an authorized capital of $20 billion. If implemented soon, this initiative, too, could be of substantial help to the low-income developing countries.

The contribution of the Soviet Union, and the other industrialized countries with centrally planned economies, to Official Development Assistance is so small as to be scarcely measurable —only .04% of their GNP. Surely they, too, ought to do more.

External Financial Requirements of Middle-Income Countries

I want to turn now to the external financial requirements of the middle-income oil-importing countries. As Table III indicates, between 1978 and 1980 these requirements will have more than doubled in absolute terms (from $21.4 billion to $51.0 billion) and nearly doubled relative to GNP (from 2.2% to 4.0%).

Commercial banks, of course, constituted by far the most dynamic element of capital flows to middle-income developing countries in the 1970s (see Table V).

TABLE V—BORROWINGS OF THE MIDDLE-INCOME DEVELOPING COUNTRIES FROM THE WORLD'S PRIVATE BANKING SYSTEM[a]
(US$ billions)

	1970	1971	1972	1973	1974	1975	1976	1977	1978	1979
Claims of the Private Banks on LDCs— End Yr.[b]	30	37	44	53	72	92	110	151	204	251
Increase in Banks' Claims on LDCs[b]			7	7	9	19	20	18	41	53	47

The chief anxiety today is that the commercial banks may not be able to play a similar role in the 1980s. There are several reasons for this:

- As noted earlier, there is likely to be tough competition for funds between the developing countries on the one hand and the industrialized nations and centrally planned economies on the other;

- Two-thirds of the commercial banks' credits were concentrated in only 10 middle-income developing countries. These have now acquired sizable commercial debts, and some of the banks are concerned over their own portfolio limits; and

- There is an increasing tendency on the part of national regulatory agencies to restrict the activities of the commercial banks in developing countries.

---

[a]Includes small amounts loaned to Low-Income countries which could not be separated out of total.

[b]1970-75 and 1979 World Bank estimates. For other years, BIS data.

This does not mean that the commercial flows to developing countries will not expand in the 1980s. They will. But the key question is this: will they expand enough to permit the adjustment process in these countries to take place at relatively high —rather than at unacceptably low—growth rates? In all probability they will in 1980, and perhaps even in 1981. But beyond 1981 they well may not. Already leading commercial bankers in both Western Europe and North America have expressed their doubts.

It is not too early, therefore, to discuss actions to supplement and facilitate the role of the commercial banks if these doubts materialize. This should be a major focus of the work of the Development Committee and of the Boards of the International Monetary Fund and the World Bank in the year to come.

If the task of recycling to the developing countries a portion of the surplus of the capital-surplus oil exporters is to be tackled efficiently and equitably in the 1980s, there is not the slightest doubt that the financial intermediation by the Bretton Woods institutions, as well as by other international institutions, should increase substantially above previously planned levels in order to supplement the role of the commercial banks.

Financial intermediation was, in fact, one of the main reasons for setting up these institutions: to stand ready to step in as last-resort intermediaries to help recycle funds from those countries that are in surplus to those countries that need them most, whether for short-term balance-of-payments support, or longer-term development needs.

The 1980s, then, call for a major reexamination of the function of the Bretton Woods institutions in the recycling of financial flows. And I will comment in a moment on a possible role for the World Bank in all of this.

Before turning to that, however, I want to reemphasize an underlying issue, which is in danger today of being obscured by the anxiety over the global adjustment problem. And that is the most fundamental development issue of all: the drive against absolute poverty.

IV. THE DRIVE AGAINST POVERTY

Over the past decade I have drawn attention repeatedly in this forum—sometimes at the risk of tedium—to the principal goals of development. They are: to accelerate economic growth, and to eradicate what I have termed absolute poverty.

Economic growth, of course, is obvious enough. And once one has been in contact with developing societies, so is absolute poverty: it is a condition of life so limited by malnutrition, illiteracy, disease, high infant mortality, and low life expectancy as to be beneath any rational definition of human decency.

The two goals are intrinsically related, though governments are often tempted to pursue one without adequate attention to the other. But from a development point of view that approach always fails in the end. The pursuit of growth without a reasonable concern for equity is ultimately socially destabilizing, and often violently so. And the pursuit of equity without a reasonable concern for growth merely tends to redistribute economic stagnation.

Neither pursuit, taken by itself, can lead to sustained, successful development.

When we met together here in 1972, I began a discussion of these issues with you. I pointed out that all too little of the benefits of economic growth was reaching the bottom 40% of the population in the developing world. For 800 million individuals, their countries were moving ahead in gross economic terms, but their own individual lives were standing still in human terms, locked in poverty.

As our analysis of growth and equity continued in these meetings in subsequent years, we outlined a number of specific actions designed to deal directly with that problem in the context of overall development planning. It was clear that any successful effort to combat poverty would have to do two basic things:

• Assist the poor to increase their productivity; and

• Assure their access to essential public services.

In our meeting in Nairobi in 1973, I proposed a major program for the rural areas,where the vast majority of the absolute poor are concentrated. The strategy focuses on a target group of roughly 100 million subsistence farmers and their families, most of whom farm two hectares or less. It is directed towards raising their agricultural productivity, and thus their incomes, as well as providing them with more equitable access to the services they need.

Two years later, at our meeting in 1975, I outlined a comparable program for the urban areas. Though the circumstances of the some 200 million absolute poor in the cities differ from those in the countryside, the strategy is fundamentally the same: remove the barriers to their greater earning opportunities, broaden their access to basic public services, and help them more fully achieve their productive potential.

In each of the following years our discussion has pursued these issues further.

But now, as I have pointed out this morning, most of the developing countries are facing a new, an unanticipated, and what is certain to be—for at least the next several years—a very difficult situation.

Their rates of growth are going to be low. Their capital requirements are going to be high. And there are going to be severe pressures on their governments to adopt austere budget allocations for every activity that is not considered of immediate priority.

In these circumstances the temptation will be strong to push aside and postpone anti-poverty programs. The argument will be that poverty is a long-term problem, and that the current account deficits are a short-term emergency: that poverty can wait, but that deficits can't.

It is a very specious argument.

Mounting deficits cannot be indefinitely sustained, and, as we have seen, the necessary solution lies in structural adjustment. Efforts to get that basic adjustment in place must not, indeed, be delayed.

But absolute poverty in a society cannot be indefinitely sustained either. To ignore it, to temporize with it, to downgrade its urgency under the convenient excuse that its solution is "long-term"—and that there are other immediate problems that preempt its priority—is dangerous self-deception.

To reduce and eliminate massive absolute poverty lies at the very core of development itself. It is critical to the survival of any decent society.

Development is clearly not simply economic progress measured in terms of gross national product. It is something much more basic. It is essentially human development; that is, the individual's realization of his or her own inherent potential.

Absolute poverty, on the other hand, is a set of penalizing circumstances that severely impair the individual's pursuit of that very potential. It is the direct denial of the benefits of development.

But it is more than just that. It is an open insult to the human dignity of us all: to the poor themselves, because simply as human beings they have deserved better; and to all of us in this room, for we have collectively had it in our power to do more to fight poverty, and we have failed to do so.

Now that both the developing countries and the developed nations are under the sting of hard times, are we going to do still less?

Let us be clear about one point. Sustaining the attack on poverty is not an economic luxury—something affordable when times are easy, and superfluous when times become troublesome.

It is precisely the opposite. It is a continuing social and moral responsibility, and an economic imperative—its need now is greater than ever. It is true that sluggish economic growth in both the developing and developed nations in the early years of the 1980s may mean that the privileged and affluent in most societies will have to accept slower rates of advance or even some selective reduction in their already favored standard of living. If they have to, they can absorb such inconveniences.

But for the 800 million absolute poor such a downward adjustment is a very different matter. For them downward does not mean inconvenience, but appalling deprivation. They have little margin for austerity. They lie at the very edge of survival already.

What we must remember is that absolute poverty is not a simple function of inadequate personal income. Though the poor have too little income, and desperately need more, their plight is not exclusively related to that.

Their deprivations go beyond income. And in many cases, even if their income were higher—which it must become— they could not by that fact alone free themselves from their difficulties.

The reason is that absolute poverty is a complicated web of circumstances, all of them punitive, that reinforce and strengthen one another.

And lest we become insensitive to the magnitude of those circumstances in the developing countries, it is worth reminding ourselves of their scope:

- 600 million of their adults—100 million more than in 1950 —can neither read nor write, and only 4 out of every 10 of their children complete more than 3 years of primary school.

- Of every 10 children born into poverty, 2 die within a year; another dies before the age of 5; only 5 survive to the age of 40.

- Common childhood diseases—measles, diphtheria, whooping cough, and polio—which have either been eliminated or reduced to minor nuisances in the developed nations, are frequently fatal in the developing world. A case of measles is 200 times more likely to kill a child there than here.

- Though all four of those diseases can be prevented by a simple vaccination, fewer than 10% of the children born each year in the developing world are now being protected.

- Malnutrition afflicts hundreds of millions of individuals, reducing their energy and motivation, undermining their performance in school and at work, reducing their resistance to illness, and often penalizing their physical and mental development.

- In the low-income developing countries, average life expectancy for their 1.3 billion people is 50 years. It is nearly 75 in the industrialized nations.

- In short, compared to those fortunate enough to live in the developed nations, individuals in the poorest countries have an infant mortality rate eight times higher; a life expectancy one-third lower; an adult literacy rate 60% less; a nutritional level, for one out of every two in the population, below minimum acceptable standards; and for millions of infants, less protein than is sufficient to permit optimum development of the brain.

Now, these impersonal rounded numbers are not simply statistics on some economist's computer. They represent individual human beings. Most tragic of all, so many of them are children. Of the total of two and a quarter billion people in the over 100 developing countries that the Bank has served, some 900 million are under the age of 15.

They are the chief hope of their society's future. And yet almost half of them suffer from debilitating disease likely to have long-lasting effects. Well over a third of them are undernourished. A third of primary school-age children are not in school.

All of this illustrates the tragic waste of poverty. If millions of a country's citizens are uneducated, malnourished, and ill, how can they possibly make a reasonable contribution to their nation's economic growth and social advance? The poverty they are immersed in, through no fault of their own, simply denies them that.

As I have pointed out before, it is the poverty itself that is the liability. Not the individuals who happen to be poor. They represent immense human potential.

It used to be said that lack of capital was the chief obstacle to economic growth. But we now know that capital formation explains less than one-third of the variation in growth rates among developing countries. Human resource development explains a great deal more.

Investment in the human potential of the poor, then, is not only morally right; it is very sound economics.

Certainly what is very unsound economics is to permit a culture of poverty to so develop within a nation that it begins to infect and erode the entire social and political fabric.

No government wants to perpetuate poverty. But not all governments, at a time of depressed economic growth, are persuaded that there is much that they can really do against so vast a problem.

But there is.

A number of avenues of attack deserve attention. Today I want to emphasize two that reflect our research of the past year. Both of these are concerned with human resource development. They are: the redesign of social programs to reduce their per capita cost while expanding their coverage; and the restructuring of the total set of social sector programs to establish priorities that take advantage of the linkages and complementarities between them, thereby reducing their overall cost. Unless essential services are both redesigned and reorganized to complement each other, governments will not be able to afford them on the scale required, particularly in periods of austerity.

Our studies confirm the synergistic effects on productivity of actions designed to meet basic needs in each of the five core areas: education, health care, clean water, nutrition, and shelter. Each has linkages to the others. Advance in one contributes to advance in the others, and all contribute to higher output.

Reducing, for example, the incidence of gastrointestinal disease and parasitic infection—through education, cleaner water, and health and sanitation programs—considerably increases the nutritional value to be gained from any given quantity of food.

This improvement in nutrition, in turn, can expand students' learning capacity, and hence the benefits that they will receive from education, including enhanced productivity and incomes.

Studies in many countries have demonstrated that small farmers with a primary education are more productive than those without it. They are quicker to adopt innovations, and are more receptive to the advice of extension agents.

Research has also confirmed the beneficial linkage between primary education and the reduction of infant mortality. Studies in Bangladesh, Kenya, and Colombia have shown that children are less likely to die the more educated their mothers are, even allowing for differences in income among families.

In Sri Lanka, widespread basic education has to a degree compensated for the poor quality of water because villagers have been taught to boil it in order to eliminate contamination. And health and nutrition everywhere in the developing world affects how well children do in school, how long they remain, or indeed whether they enroll at all.

Urban employment, particularly in the modern sector, is not only often dependent on the degree of education, but on health and nutrition as well. Workers who are easily fatigued and have low resistance to chronic illness are inefficient, and add substantially to the accident rate, absenteeism, and unnecessary medical expenditure. More serious still, to the extent that their mental capacity has been impaired by malnutrition in childhood, their ability to perform technical tasks is reduced. Dexterity, alertness, and initiative have been drained away.

And yet not only are essential public services often out of reach of the poor, but such facilities as are in place may be so inappropriately designed as to be virtually irrelevant to their needs: impressive four-lane highways, but too few market roads; elaborate curative-care urban hospitals, but too few preventive-care rural clinics; prestigious institutions of higher learning, but too few primary schools and village literacy programs.

Public services that are not designed modestly and at low

cost per unit will almost certainly end by serving the privileged few rather than the deprived many.

To reverse this trend, governments must be prepared to make tough and politically sensitive decisions, and to reallocate scarce resources into less elaborate—but more broadly based—delivery systems that can get the services to the poor, and the poor to the services.

The developing countries do not, of course, have the financial and administrative resources at hand today to eliminate rapidly all the inadequacies in education, health, and other public services that penalize the poor. They must—out of very real necessity—be selective in determining where to concentrate their efforts.

All the more reason, then, that they should analyze the most important linkages and complementarities between the various public services since utilizing them in combination can lead to substantial reduction in the cost of individual services, and hence in the total cost of the ongoing poverty program.

It has been estimated, for example, that in Egypt the full use of such complementarities among sectors, together with redesigned programs within sectors, would decrease by more than a third the resources required to reduce, and ultimately to eliminate, absolute poverty.

If choices have to be made—and they do—what are the most promising ones?

That will differ, of course, in various societies, but in the case of most developing countries two deserve particular attention. One is primary education, and most particularly for girls. And the other is primary health care.

Primary Education

School enrollments throughout the developing world still fall far below the objective of universal primary education for both boys and girls, and this picture is made even worse by dropout rates which are often over 50%.

Research makes it clear that economic returns on primary education for boys are high. This is not always recognized. But I want to emphasize today something much less recognized and understood. And that is the immensely beneficial impact on reducing poverty that results from educating girls.

In most developing societies women simply do not have equitable access to education. The number of illiterate females is growing faster than illiterate males. Nearly two-thirds of the world's illiterates are women, and virtually everywhere males are given preference both for general education and vocational training.

One reason for this is that the prevailing image of women distorts their full contribution to society. Women are esteemed —and are encouraged to esteem themselves—predominantly in their roles as mothers. Their economic contribution, though it is substantial in a number of developing societies, is almost always understated.

The fact is that in subsistence societies women generally do at least 50% of the work connected with agricultural production and processing, as well as take care of the children and the housekeeping.

Schooling clearly enhances a girl's prospects of finding employment outside the home. In a comparative study of 49 countries, the level of female education in each nation demonstrated a significant impact on the proportion of women earning wages or salaries.

Greater educational opportunity for women will also substantially reduce fertility. In Latin America, for example, studies indicate that in districts as diverse as Rio de Janeiro, rural Chile, and Buenos Aires, women who have completed primary school average about two children fewer than those who have not.

Of all the aspects of social development, the educational level appears most consistently associated with lower fertility. And it is significant that an increase in the education of women tends to lower fertility to a greater extent than a similar increase in the education of men. In societies in which rapid population growth is draining away resources, expenditure on education and training for boys that is not matched by comparable expenditure for girls will very likely be diminished in the end by the girls' continued high fertility.

Women represent a seriously undervalued potential in the development process. And to prolong inequitable practices that relegate them exclusively to narrow traditional roles not only denies both them and society the benefits of that potential, but very seriously compounds the problem of reducing poverty.

Primary Health Care

In the health sector, as well, carefully designed and sharply focused efforts can contribute immensely to an overall anti-poverty program.

In most developing countries health expenditures have been heavily concentrated on supplying a small urban elite with expensive curative-care systems—highly skilled doctors and elaborate hospitals—that fail to reach 90% of the people. What are required are less sophisticated, less costly, but more effective preventive-care delivery systems that reach the mass of the population.

Even quite poor countries can succeed in this, provided sound policies are pursued. Some 25 years ago, for example, Sri Lanka decided to improve rural health facilities. As a result of its efforts in health care, along with those in education and in nutrition, there has been over the past two decades a decline in infant mortality to 47 per 1,000, an increase in life expectancy to 69 years, and an associated decline in the crude birth rate to 26.

But many other countries—countries with a much higher per capita national income than Sri Lanka—have spent as much or more on health, and by failing to stress simple, inexpensive, but effective primary care systems, have reaped much poorer results.

Turkey, for example, had a GNP per capita of $1,200 in 1978, compared to Sri Lanka's $190, but has concentrated on urban health, with conventional facilities, and today has an infant mortality rate of 118 per 1,000, life expectancy of 61 years, and a crude birth rate of 32—all far short of Sri Lanka's accomplishments.

As part of their preventive-care programs, governments should make a special effort to reduce sharply current infant and child mortality rates. Average rates of infant mortality—deaths per 1,000 in the first year—are well above 140 in Africa, and roughly 120 in Asia and 60 in Latin America. In the developed countries they average only about 13.

Why are they so high in the developing world? Largely because of low nutritional standards, and poor hygiene, health practices and services. But infant and child mortality rates can be brought down relatively quickly with a combination of redesigned and reoriented health, education, and nutrition policies. And the return in lowered fertility, healthier children, and increased productivity is clearly worth the effort and costs.

The truth is that a basic learning package for both males and females—and particularly for females—and a carefully designed program of primary health care for both the countryside and the cities are investments that no developing country can afford to neglect.

The economic return will be huge. And the same is true of other investments in the immense untapped human potential of the absolute poor. Even in a period of austerity—indeed, especially in a period of austerity—those investments must be accelerated.

I want to turn now to the role the World Bank itself can play in the 1980s. And to establish the background against which this must be viewed, let me briefly summarize the principal points that emerged earlier in our discussion.

V. THE ROLE OF THE WORLD BANK IN THE 1980s

The current account deficits of the oil-importing developing countries have risen dramatically. The increase in these deficits is the mirror image of a portion of the rise in the surpluses of the oil-exporting nations. A major objective of the world's intermediation effort to deal with these surpluses must be to assure that appropriate portions of them flow, directly or indirectly, back to these developing countries.

The assistance the developing societies will need in the 1980s —both to alleviate their burden of absolute poverty, and to facilitate the structural changes in their economies required by the changes in the external environment—is much larger than was projected before the events of the past 18 months.

The developing countries, already financing 90% of their own development efforts, will now have to mobilize substantial additional resources. But they cannot succeed in this enormous task by their own efforts alone. That is why all previously planned programs of international assistance, including that of the Bank, must be reexamined in order to determine how the most urgent needs of the developing world can be met.

It is in this perspective that the future level of World Bank lending, and the nature of its operating policies, should be reviewed. The Bank clearly cannot do everything. Nor should it try to. But neither can it be allowed to fail in its basic responsibility toward its developing member countries.

Let us examine for a moment the role the Bank has undertaken over the last decade.

During the past twelve years, the World Bank Group has expanded dramatically its level of financial assistance to the developing world (see Table VI).

TABLE VI—WORLD BANK GROUP: NEW FINANCIAL COMMITMENTS AND NET DISBURSEMENTS
(US$ billions)

	Annual Average Per Period					Working Plan[a]				
	FY64 -68	FY69 -73	FY74 -78	FY79	FY80	FY81	FY82	FY83	FY84	FY85
New Loans										
IBRD	.9	1.8	4.9	7.0	7.6	8.6	9.6	10.7	11.9	13.2
IDA	.3	.8	1.6	3.0	3.8	3.6	4.1	4.7	5.0	5.3
IFC	—	.1	.2	.4	.7	.6	.7	.8	.9	1.1
Total—Current $	1.2	2.7	6.7	10.4	12.1	12.8	14.4	16.2	17.8	19.6
—Constant FY80 $	5.0	6.8	9.5	11.2	12.1	11.9	12.6	13.3	13.8	14.3
Disbursements										
IBRD	.5	.9	2.2	3.6	4.4	5.2	6.3	7.4	8.3	9.2
IDA	.3	.3	1.1	1.2	1.4	1.8	2.2	2.7	3.5	4.1
IFC	—	.1	.2	.2	.3	.3	.5	.7	.8	.9
Total—Current $	.8	1.3	3.5	5.0	6.1	7.3	9.0	10.8	12.6	14.2
—Constant FY80 $	3.1	3.5	5.3	5.5	6.1	6.7	7.6	8.6	9.4	9.9

But our objective during these years was not principally the size of the Bank's operations. We did not simply want to do more. Rather, we wanted to do more of what would contribute most to our member countries' evolving development needs.

Thus, over the past decade there has been a major qualitative change in the Bank's lending, and in its development policies. That change arose out of the understanding that if the absolute poor had to wait for the benefits of overall economic growth to trickle down to them, their incomes and welfare would inch forward at an intolerably slow pace.

It became clear that developing countries needed to devise policies and investment programs to assist the poor in their societies to become more productive, and to assure an equitable distribution of basic services to them.

---

[a]The Working Plan is subject to annual review by the Executive Directors and is based on the assumption that necessary legislative action on the General Capital Increase and IDA VI replenishment will be completed according to schedule.

Throughout the 1970s the Bank made a determined effort to help its member countries to devise such policies, and to finance and implement such projects. It has devoted to this objective a high proportion of its intellectual resources, and a growing share of its expanded lending. In the FY64-68 period such loans, on average, amounted to only $60 million per year, and accounted for less than 5% of total lending. In FY80 they had grown to $3,565 million, and accounted for over 30% of total lending. In that year alone the Bank approved agricultural and rural development projects to raise the productivity, and thereby the incomes, of 29 million people, including 18 million of the world's poorest—and to increase food production by 6 million tons per annum.

Highways, electric power, and other traditional infrastructure and production investments remain, of course, vital to development. They are basic to strengthening the foundations of growth, and to expanding employment opportunities and enhancing the incomes of all members of society. While the Bank reduced the share of its lending to these sectors, it substantially increased its absolute volume. Bank lending for traditional infrastructure projects grew from an annual average of $700 million in 1964-68 to $4.4 billion in 1980; and for traditional production projects, from $350 million to $3.5 billion.

Only by raising its overall level of lending was the Bank able to meet its member countries' new development needs without neglecting their traditional requirements.

This clearly remains the path for the future. The Bank must be in a position to respond to new needs which have already appeared. And it will certainly be called upon again and again to help meet needs which we cannot yet foresee. It must be able to do so without disrupting other programs for which developing countries are counting upon its assistance.

Is the Bank in such a position now?

Last year I reported to you that we were making progress in laying a foundation for further expansion of the Bank Group's lending program in the 1980s. Let me summarize the steps that have been taken over the past twelve months, and where we stand today.

The General Capital Increase in the Bank's authorized capital, from $45 billion to $85 billion, was approved by the Board of Governors in January 1980. Some countries, including the United States, will need legislative approval before they can subscribe to the additional shares.

Negotiations for a sixth replenishment of the International Development Association (IDA) were successfully concluded last December, and the basis for the replenishment was approved by the Governors in March 1980. The replenishment itself, however, is still not effective because a few countries, and in particular the United States, have not been able yet to complete the necessary legislation.

Other donor countries have agreed to make voluntary contributions to prevent an extended hiatus in IDA's lending program. But I want to emphasize the importance of early action by all governments to make the sixth replenishment effective, and the severe penalties for the poorest nations of the world that will result from prolonged delay and uncertainty.

Let us assume, however, that all the necessary legislative actions for the General Capital Increase and for the IDA VI replenishment will be completed soon.

Will the lending program summarized in Table VI, which the General Capital Increase and IDA VI are intended to support, be adequate for the role the Bank Group must play in the 1980s to assist its developing country members? Will it allow the Bank to meet these countries' needs in even the limited way that we hoped it would when the program was prepared?

The answer is clearly no.

The lending program for FY81-85 reflects the Bank's assessment of the future financial requirements of the developing countries as they appeared early in 1977, when the plan was prepared. In the light of that assessment we believed the planned level of lending would permit the Bank to increase its new commitments each year by 5% in real terms, and that this projected growth would allow the Bank to make an adequate contribution to its member countries' priority development needs.

That assessment is no longer tenable. Four events have intervened in the meantime that invalidate its underlying assumptions.

A rampant and unexpected rate of inflation has reduced the real value of the commitments permitted by the General Capital Increase and the IDA VI agreements. In planning the program in 1977, the Bank had assumed a world inflation rate of 7.5% for FY79. It turned out to be 13.3%. And we now project inflation in future years will taper off more slowly than we had previously expected. As a result, the real value of the lending program planned for 1981-85 will fall 10.5% below what was projected. In today's dollars this represents a loss of over $5.6 billion.

Quite apart from this, our developing member countries' needs for Bank assistance have increased for three other reasons:

- First, as I have emphasized, the sharp rise in the oil price has raised the cost of their imports, while recession in the industrial countries has depressed their export prospects. They must react to these events by carrying out the far-reaching structural adjustments in their economies, discussed earlier, and yet do so without reducing their growth to totally unacceptable levels during the transition period.

- Second, as part of that process, in their own interest as well as that of the world community, they should step up substantially their investment in energy development.

- And third, the change in the representation of China has increased by 45% the number of people who now need, who now desire, and who are now entitled to have World Bank Group lending.

Let me briefly discuss the effect on the Bank of each of these three points in turn.

First the financing required for the much larger than anticipated current account deficit:

Let me sum up the key points of the argument put forward earlier.

As compared to 1978, the oil-import bills of developing countries have increased by $35 billion. And even if the industrialized nations resist domestic protectionist pressures, as they must, their continuing problems of recession and slow growth have already reduced the export prospects of the developing world.

The problem is not that developing countries will be left with deficits they cannot finance. If deficits cannot be financed, they will disappear. But if they disappear because adequate financing cannot be found, this will seriously cripple their development programs.

If that were to happen, the rest of the world could not be cushioned from the deflationary pressures generated by such a collapse. Even the narrowest self-interest of the industrialized nations requires that these essential financing needs should be met.

Adequate financing of imports is not a substitute for structural adjustment to the new external circumstances. Rather, it is a prerequisite for such adjustment: it permits the developing countries to adapt sensibly their production, trade, investment, and savings patterns to new needs. Without adequate financing of their imports they will be forced to adopt "quick-fix" remedies—such as blanket controls on imports or arbitrary cutbacks in public investment programs—which are in no one's long-term interest.

Nor is the financing of structural adjustment a substitute for the financing of other development needs. The magnitude of the other investments required to make at least a minimally acceptable impact on absolute poverty has not diminished. The cost and urgency of raising the productivity of the world's poor and of providing them with equitable access to the essential public services they desperately need remain high.

Should not the Bank, then, shoulder part of the burden of financing its developing member countries' structural adjustment? In doing so it would clearly not be substituting for the private-market mechanisms to recycle surpluses. On the contrary, it would be helping to underpin private flows, and by closely supporting the adjustment process it would improve the creditworthiness of the recipients.

Nor would the Bank be substituting for appropriate action by the IMF. Rather, it would be complementing such action by bringing its resources and its expertise to bear on the longer-term development aspects of structural adjustment.

To help meet these requirements, the Bank introduced structural adjustment lending several months ago, and is tentatively planning to commit $600-800 million for that purpose in the current fiscal year. In FY82 or FY83, such lending might amount to $1,500 million, and in subsequent years to more.

At present, however, such structural adjustment loans have to be fitted into the previously planned lending program. But these new and unanticipated needs are clearly additional to the requirements identified in 1977, which the current lending program was designed to meet. The Bank needs, therefore, to expand the current program to respond to them. If it fails to do so, it simply will not be contributing to the solution of the world's intermediation problem.

Let me move now to the second point: the financing required for energy development.

Beyond their immediate impact on import costs, the higher energy prices present both long-term challenges and opportunities for the oil-importing developing countries.

Our studies indicate that at the new price levels there are highly profitable investment opportunities in these countries which are additional to current plans and which, taken together with vigorous conservation measures, would reduce oil imports by 3 million barrels of oil per day—150 million tons per year— by 1990. This would have obvious benefits for all producing and consuming nations. But the exploitation of these opportunities will require substantial investment over the next five years.

Total investment needs for energy development in oil-import-ing developing countries, in the period 1981-1985, will amount to about $185 billion in constant 1980 prices, as against $80 billion devoted to energy investment in these countries over the past five years. Most of these needs will be financed by their own savings, and by external sources other than the Bank.

The Bank, however, should help by expanding its previously planned energy development program, both in order to serve as a catalyst for other funds, particularly from private sources, and in order to finance those needs for which such funds are not likely to be available. To assist in this vital role, we now estimate that the Bank should lend an additional $12 billion above the $13 billion planned for energy development in the 1981-85 period.

Finally, let me turn to the matter of China.

The change in the representation of China in the Bank has increased by nearly a billion the number of people who now have a claim on the Bank's resources. That claim is no less com-pelling, and their needs are no less urgent than those of the Bank's other members. It will take time to translate these needs into specific Bank projects, but when that has been done it is clear that they will amount to several billion dollars per year.

If we had to accommodate these needs within the lending program planned earlier, we would have to reduce sharply our lending to other member countries. This would seriously dis-rupt their development programs, and this we must not do. An addition to the lending program is clearly required.

The inescapable conclusion of all these considerations is this: the Bank Group must mobilize substantial additional resources if it is effectively to assist its developing member countries through the critical years of the 1980s. But it must do this in a manner that takes full account of the current budgetary con-straints faced by the governments of the developed nations.

What we need to do now is to reach broad agreement on the following objective.

The Bank should:

- Increase its lending program in order to offset fully the higher-than-anticipated inflation levels;

- Finance structural adjustment, but not at the cost of reducing the development finance already planned for the oil-importing developing countries;

- Assist in financing an expanded energy development program, but not at the cost of cutting its assistance to other equally vital programs; and

- Respond to the development needs of China, but not at the cost of its other borrowers.

If we agree on this objective—and I believe we can—then our task is to find the means for financing the expansion in lending without imposing undue burdens on the budgets of our member governments.

Several approaches to that seemingly impossible task are worthy of consideration. Let me refer to them briefly.

It is through payments for capital subscriptions that the International Bank for Reconstruction and Development (IBRD) places demands on the budgets of our member governments. Those budgets are tight, and the equity capital that they finance is, therefore, a scarce resource. Loan funds, on the other hand, are available, and even abundant on the world's financial markets.

The issue facing the Bank today is whether we are making the best possible use of that very scarce resource, our equity capital, in order to mobilize those other more abundant funds. The question is: could we increase our borrowings in the private financial markets without imposing additional claims on scarce funds from governments?

Throughout its history, the World Bank has gradually improved the use it has made of its equity base.

Twenty years ago, for example, the Bank concluded that it had only barely begun to utilize the full financial power of that base in support of its borrowing. At that time, in 1960, the Bank's callable capital of $17.3 billion—essentially member government guarantees of its borrowings—plus its paid-in capital and reserves of $2.5 billion, a total capital base of $19.8 billion, supported borrowing of only $2.1 billion and loans of $2.8 billion. To increase the efficiency with which its paid-in capital was being used, in 1960 the Bank doubled its subscribed capital without any increase in the amount of capital paid in. And yet even in 1970, when paid-in capital and reserves had risen to $3.9 billion, and callable capital amounted to $20.8 billion, borrowings totalled only $4.6 billion and loans $6.0 billion. We were an under-leveraged institution.

During the 1970s the Bank began to use its equity base to mobilize much larger amounts of borrowed funds for investment in its developing member countries. Borrowings and outstanding loans had increased to $30 billion and $27 billion respectively by the end of FY1980. Meanwhile, the Bank's paid-in capital and reserves rose to $7 billion—of which over half came from retained earnings—and callable capital rose to $36 billion. Moreover, the Governors, having reduced the amount of the paid-in portion of the 1960 capital subscription from 20% to 10%, have now reduced the paid-in portion of the new General Capital Increase from 10% to 7.5%.

When the General Capital Increase is completed, the Bank will have total subscribed capital of $85 billion. About $7.5 billion will then have been paid in. This will be augmented by reserves and retained earnings that amount to about $3.4 billion today, and are growing fast. This means that if it fully uses the authority provided by the General Capital Increase, the Bank's own paid-in equity and reserves will finance about 15% of outstanding loans. When callable capital is included, every single dollar of outstanding loans will be backed by a dollar of capital or reserves.

These ratios contrast with the standard practice of large commercial banks, whose capital to risk-asset ratios run to less than 6%. And yet none of these banks has the IBRD's repayment record; none of them relies on such long-term sources of funds; and none has such a strong liquidity position.

The World Bank, then, should continue to improve the efficiency with which it uses its immensely broad and uniquely guaranteed financial base. It must begin to use the demonstrated strength of its loan portfolio that reflects the prudent lending policies that it has followed for over thirty years. This is essential if it is to meet more fully the needs of the developing countries without imposing additional burdens on the budgets of other governments in a period when the domestic demands of many are particularly pressing.

The question is how can this best be done, while at the same time fully safeguarding the strength and integrity of the Bank's financial structure?

There are at least three actions that should be considered.

The relationship between the Bank's loans—and hence its outstanding debt—and its equity base could be changed.

The Articles of Agreement, drafted over 35 years ago in immensely different financial circumstances, provide that the Bank's total disbursed and outstanding loans cannot exceed its total subscribed capital and reserves.

The question the Brandt Commission, investment bankers, and other financial experts have been asking us in the Bank is this: in the circumstances of today, as contrasted with those of 1944, does it still make financial sense to limit any increase whatever in the Bank's lending authority to an equal increase in its capital?

The tentative answer appears to be that the 1 to 1 ratio, established at Bretton Woods in the closing months of World War II, is no longer really relevant to the Bank's financial condition or to the economic situation of its principal shareholders, and that the result now is an unnecessary underutilization of the Bank's capital base.

It is obvious that any action to change the ratio should not be construed as a substitute for the completion of the General Capital Increase. On the contrary, it should be viewed as a necessary additional step. The General Capital Increase was agreed to prior to the more recent events that have now substantially enlarged the financial requirements of our developing member countries. The change in the ratio would make it possible for the Bank to respond to these new requirements through a more effective use of the increase in its capital base which has already been authorized.

A second possibility would be the organization of a separately capitalized energy affiliate.

As I remarked earlier, the need and the potential for developing new energy resources present a major challenge, as well as a major opportunity, to the developing countries, and to the world community at large. To meet that challenge, and to exploit that opportunity, there is now an international consensus, reflected most notably in the decisions of the Venice Economic Summit and the meetings of the OPEC ministers, that measures must be taken to assist the developing countries in the development of their energy resources. More specifically, the World Bank has been asked to examine the possibility of setting up an energy affiliate to assist in this effort. Such an affiliate would serve both as a direct source of finance itself, and as a catalyst for other public and private funds.

The equity capital of such an institution could come from IBRD profits, and from contributions by member governments: not necessarily by all member governments, and not in the same proportion as their contribution to the Bank's capital. Such an equity base would be utilized to underpin borrowing and lending that could ultimately amount to a multiple of the scarce equity funds.

A third approach would be to raise the Bank's lending and borrowing authority again, as was done in 1960, by increasing subscribed stock, but without the necessity of additional paid-in capital.

Any one of these three actions, or a combination of them, would make it possible for the Bank to be more responsive to the urgent needs of its developing member countries which were not anticipated when the General Capital Increase was put forward. The variety of means available to equip the Bank to be more responsive should encourage those who, like myself, believe that the current climate of budgetary constraint in the developed nations need not stand in the way of necessary action.

While these measures are being studied, because of the urgent need to expand the Bank's lending program for FY82-86, we should consider drawing forward a portion of the lending presently planned for later years to the nearer term. In this way we could increase IBRD loans over the next five critical years by a total of $10 billion.

Implementing these various proposals would allow the IBRD to expand its lending program. Yet that would not by itself help the Bank's poorest member countries, which require highly concessional financing of very long maturity. As I have indicated, the needs of these low-income countries have also greatly increased. And the IDA VI replenishment, while it is generous, will fall far short of meeting them.

Just as we need to find a way to exploit more fully IBRD's equity base, so we must also increase the leverage of scarce IDA resources. The creditworthiness of a number of countries which have in the past received IDA credits has now markedly improved. This is most notably the case for oil exporters such as Indonesia and Egypt. But others too have increased their ability to service debt on intermediate terms.

Some of these countries could shift in the future to IBRD loans only, or to a blend of IBRD and IDA loans less concessional than had been necessary earlier. This would permit an increase in IDA lending to those countries whose financial requirements have expanded but which are not yet creditworthy for IBRD loans.

It should go without saying that making additional IDA funds available to the poorest countries by shifting some countries from IDA to IBRD borrowing will be possible only if IBRD itself is enabled to meet these additional claims on its resources. And it should be unnecessary to add that a truly adequate response to the poorest countries' needs would require additional resources, raised perhaps by such new means as those suggested by the Brandt Commission.

In this discussion of the role of the Bank in the 1980s, I have focused on only one aspect of its work: its loans to developing countries, and the means of financing them. In the short run, this must have first claim on our attention. But in the longer run, as both Executive Directors and Ministers from developing countries have emphasized so often in recent months, it is the non-financial assistance of the Bank that is of even greater value than its financial support, indispensable as that is.

In the 1970s the Bank's policy advice and technical assistance were directed toward the twin goals of accelerating economic growth and reducing absolute poverty. These must continue to be our objectives in the 1980s. But the environment in which those goals will be pursued will be so different, and so difficult, as to require a major shift of emphasis within the Bank:

- Population growth, although decelerating, will place increasingly heavy burdens on the resources of most developing countries;

- Labor forces growing at explosive rates, reflecting past levels of population growth, will place a premium on job creation;

- Migration from the countryside will burden metropolitan areas grown larger than most in the developed world;

- Widespread malnutrition, if it is to be overcome, will require substantial increases in food production per hectare because opportunities for putting land under cultivation in the developing countries are sharply reduced; and

- External payments imbalances will require acceleration of industrialization and expansion of exports in the face of slower growth in world trade and rising tides of protectionism.

It is shocking to reflect that in spite of the progress of the past quarter century and the advances that are likely in the next two decades, it is probable that at the end of this century 600 million human beings in the developing countries will continue to live in absolute poverty.

Clearly there will be an immense intellectual and technical effort required from the Bank in the 1980s—in addition to its financial contribution—if it is effectively to assist the developing countries to address their fundamental social and economic problems.

Let me now summarize and conclude the central points I have made this morning.

VI. SUMMARY AND CONCLUSIONS

Global economic conditions over the past 18 months have become substantially more difficult, and the prospects for growth in the oil-importing developing countries during the decade of the 1980s now appear less promising.

The sharp new rise in oil prices has more than doubled these countries' cost of imported energy, and the continuing recession in the industrialized nations will seriously limit demand for their exports.

As a result, their current account deficits have increased rapidly, and now constitute on average 4% of their gross national product—and for many countries substantially more. Though they can continue to finance these deficits in the short term by additional external borrowing, in the longer term their mounting debt service would become unsupportable. The deficits must be reduced. What is needed are fundamental structural adjustments in their economies.

If these difficult changes are undertaken soon, and can be completed over the next five to eight years, growth rates in the oil-importing developing countries should recover to more satisfactory levels during the second half of the decade.

This, however, will require financial assistance in the interim, beyond what is now in prospect, if severe reductions in the level of their development activity are to be avoided. If this financial assistance is not available, or if the developing countries delay initiating the necessary structural changes, their development progress will be seriously compromised throughout the decade.

The current adjustment process is likely to be more difficult than the earlier one in the 1974-1978 period. One of the most important actions the oil-importing developing countries can take to moderate its damaging effects is to adopt efficient import substitution policies in energy.

At present and prospective oil prices, many of these countries can turn what were previously regarded as marginal energy reserves of oil, gas, coal, hydroelectric, and forest resources into profitable investments. This will require their mobilizing additional domestic and external finance, but would permit them by the end of the decade to reduce their annual oil-import bill—projected by then to amount to some $230 billion—by more than $50 billion.

The current global economic situation has imposed particularly severe penalties on the poorest developing countries. They desperately need additional Official Development Assistance to get through the adjustment period. But total ODA flows declined in real terms from 1977 through 1979, and that portion of the flows allocated to the poorest countries was shockingly small in both relative and absolute amounts.

Both the OECD nations, and the capital-surplus members of OPEC, should now consider what measures they can take to increase concessional assistance to the poorest nations who continue to be damaged by a global economic situation they neither caused, nor can do much to influence.

The middle-income developing countries will continue to depend on external capital flows from commercial banks throughout the decade, though it is questionable whether the volume will be sufficient from these sources to meet the additional requirements imposed by the new adjustment difficulties.

If the task of recycling to the developing countries a portion of the more than $100 billion a year of additional surpluses now being earned by the oil-exporting countries is to be tackled in the 1980s efficiently and equitably, there is no doubt that the financial intermediation of the World Bank, and other international institutions, should increase substantially above previously planned levels.

During the 1980s the Bank should:

- Increase its lending program in order to offset fully the higher-than-anticipated inflation levels;

- Finance structural adjustment, but not at the cost of reducing the development finance already planned for the oil-importing developing countries;

- Assist in financing the expanded energy development program called for at the Venice Economic Summit meeting, but not at the cost of cutting its assistance to other vital programs; and

- Respond to the development needs of China, but not at the cost of its other borrowers.

All of this can be done—and in a manner that takes full account of the current budgetary constraints faced by the governments of the developed nations—provided we make full use of the potential of the Bank's capital base, and facilitate the use of the large private resources available for sound investment opportunities.

The 1980s are likely to be a turbulent decade, preoccupied with a whole new range of financial difficulties.

But underlying the immediate financial concern, more fundamental problems persist.

The most fundamental of all is the persistence of widespread absolute poverty.

Development itself comprises a twofold task: to accelerate economic growth, and to eradicate absolute poverty.

These two goals are related, though governments are sometimes tempted to pursue one without adequate attention to the other. In the end, that approach fails from a development point of view. The pursuit of growth without a reasonable concern for equity is ultimately socially destabilizing. And the pursuit of equity without a reasonable concern for growth merely tends to redistribute the deprivation of economic stagnation.

In our meetings throughout the 1970s we have examined the

various requirements of these two goals. This morning I have stressed both the critical need and the economic good sense of developing those human resources who have been inequitably passed over by the modernization process.

None of us, of course, can pretend that our understanding of the complexities of the poverty problem is complete. We are all still learning. But I believe we can take a measure of satisfaction that many governments and institutions throughout the international development community, including this Bank, are beginning to think about poverty in a more thoughtful way than they did a decade ago. And they are beginning to ask themselves how they can reshape their own efforts to deal with it more effectively.

That should be encouraging to everyone in this room.

Due to your support, and that of the governments you represent, the World Bank over the past ten years has become by far the world's largest and most influential development institution.

That is important.

But what is far more important is what has transpired throughout the developing world in the millions of individual lives that this institution has touched.

What these countless millions of the poor need and want is what each of us needs and wants: the well-being of those they love; a better future for their children; an end to injustice; and a beginning of hope.

We do not see their faces, we do not know their names, we cannot count their number. But they are there. And their lives have been touched by us.

And ours by them.

PERSONAL NOTE, PREPARED AFTER THE TEXT WAS PRINTED IN SEPTEMBER 1980

And now—if I may—let me add a purely personal note.

These past 13 years have been the most stimulating of my life. I wouldn't have traded them for anything.

And I want to say to all of you how deeply grateful I am for the privilege of having served with you throughout these years.

This World Bank—born out of the ruins of World War II— has grown into one of the world's most constructive instruments of human aspiration and progress.

And yet, it has only barely begun to develop its full potential for service and assistance.

There is so much more it can do, so much more it ought to do to assist those who need its help.

Each one of us here can help make that happen.

And how can we begin?

We must begin—as the founders of this great institution began—with vision. With clear, strong, bold vision.

George Bernard Shaw put it perfectly:

"You see things, and say why? But I dream things that never were, and I say why not?"

Thank you, and good morning.

ANNEX I

FLOW OF OFFICIAL DEVELOPMENT ASSISTANCE FROM DEVELOPMENT ASSISTANCE COMMITTEE MEMBERS TO DEVELOPING COUNTRIES AND MULTILATERAL INSTITUTIONS[a]
(Percent of Gross National Product)

	1965	1970	1975	1976	1977	1978	1979	1980	1981	1982	1983	1984	1985
Australia	.53	.59	.59	.41	.42	.54	.52	.51	.50	.50	.50	.51	.51
Austria	.11	.07	.17	.12	.24	.29	.19	.23	.25	.27	.28	.29	.30
Belgium	.60	.46	.59	.51	.46	.55	.56	.59	.60	.61	.63	.65	.67
Canada	.19	.41	.52	.39	.48	.52	.47	.46	.45	.45	.45	.44	.44
Denmark	.13	.38	.58	.56	.60	.75	.75	.67	.70	.70	.70	.70	.70
Finland[b]	.02	.06	.18	.17	.16	.17	.22	.22	.23	.24	.26	.27	.28
France	.76	.66	.62	.62	.60	.57	.59	.59	.59	.59	.60	.60	.60
Germany	.40	.32	.40	.36	.33	.37	.44	.44	.44	.44	.45	.46	.46
Italy	.10	.16	.11	.13	.10	.14	.09	.09	.10	.10	.11	.11	.11
Japan	.27	.23	.23	.20	.21	.23	.26	.27	.27	.28	.28	.29	.30
Netherlands	.36	.61	.75	.83	.86	.82	.93	.94	.94	.96	.97	.98	.99
New Zealand[c]		.23	.52	.41	.39	.34	.30	.30	.30	.30	.30	.30	.30
Norway	.16	.32	.66	.70	.83	.90	.93	.95	.96	.97	.98	.99	1.00
Sweden	.19	.38	.82	.82	.99	.90	.94	.95	.95	.95	.95	.95	.95
Switzerland	.09	.15	.19	.19	.19	.20	.21	.22	.25	.26	.26	.27	.28
United Kingdom	.47	.41	.39	.40	.46	.48	.52	.52	.49	.45	.42	.40	.38
United States[d]	.58	.32	.27	.26	.25	.27	.19	.18	.22	.22	.22	.22	.22
GRAND TOTAL													
ODA ($b-Nominal Prices)	6.5	7.0	13.8	13.8	15.7	20.0	22.3	24.6	28.7	32.1	35.7	39.7	44.1
ODA ($b-Constant 1980 Prices)	20.3	18.0	21.9	20.9	22.1	24.4	24.5	24.6	26.3	27.2	28.3	29.4	30.8
GNP ($t-Nominal Prices)	1.3	2.0	3.8	4.2	4.7	5.6	6.5	7.2	8.0	9.0	9.9	11.0	12.1
ODA as % of GNP	.49	.34	.36	.33	.33	.35	.34	.34	.36	.36	.36	.36	.36
Price Deflator[e]	.32	.39	.63	.66	.71	.82	.91	1.00	1.09	1.18	1.26	1.35	1.43

[a]Historical figures through 1979 are on note deposit basis as reported from OECD/DAC. Those for 1980-85 are based on OECD and World Bank estimates of growth of GNP, on information on budget appropriations for aid, and on aid policy statements by governments. They are projections, not predictions, of what will occur unless action not now planned takes place.

[b]Finland became a member of DAC in January 1975.

[c]New Zealand became a member of DAC in 1973. ODA figures for New Zealand are not available for 1965.

[d]In 1949, at the beginning of the Marshall Plan, U.S. Official Development Assistance amounted to 2.79% of GNP.

[e]The deflator is the US$ GNP deflator which excludes the effects of changes in exchange rates.

DISTRIBUTION OF ODA FROM OECD COUNTRIES IN 1978 BY DEVELOPING COUNTRY INCOME GROUP
(Amounts in millions of dollars)

	To Low-Income Countries[a]			To Middle- and High-Income Countries[a]			Total ODA	
	Amt.	Percent of Total ODA	Percent of GNP	Amt.	Percent of Total ODA	Percent of GNP	Amt.	Percent of GNP
Australia	198	34	.18	390	66	.36	588	.54
Austria	31	19	.06	135	81	.23	166	.29
Belgium	384	72	.40	152	28	.15	536	.55
Canada	564	53	.28	496	47	.24	1,060	.52
Denmark	254	66	.50	129	34	.25	383	.75
Finland	30	56	.10	24	44	.07	54	.17
France	768	28	.16	1,937	72	.41	2,705	.57
Germany	1,171	50	.19	1,176	50	.19	2,347	.37
Italy	247	66	.09	128	34	.05	375	.14
Japan	1,136	51	.12	1,079	49	.11	2,215	.23
Netherlands	606	56	.46	468	44	.36	1,074	.82
New Zealand	7	13	.04	48	87	.30	55	.34
Norway	237	67	.60	118	33	.30	355	.90
Sweden	508	65	.59	275	35	.31	783	.90
Switzerland	91	53	.11	82	47	.09	173	.20
United Kingdom	897	62	.29	559	38	.19	1,456	.48
United States	2,078	37	.10	3,586	63	.15	5,664	.27
Total	9,207	46	.16	10,783	54	.18	19,990	.34

[a]1978 is the latest year for which available information permits distribution of ODA as between "Low-Income" and "Middle- and High-Income" countries. Low-Income countries have a total population of 1.3 billion with per capita incomes averaging $200 per year. The populations of Middle- and High-Income countries total 900 million with per capita incomes averaging $1,250 per year. The distribution includes bilateral ODA contributions and allocable shares of contributions to multilateral development assistance institutions.

INDEX

Absolute poverty: explanation of, 238-39, 268, 341-42; extent of, 242, 314, 557, 632-33; individual country approach to, 583-84, 591; levels of, 590; projected, 484, 498-99; public services to reduce, 459, 461-63, 634-36; social and moral responsibility to reduce, 560, 631-32; strategy to combat, 297, 308-09, 459-65, 500-02, 505-10, 513, 557, 584-85; World Bank efforts to reduce, *1980s,* 600-01. *See also* Poorest developing countries; Poverty

Abu Dhabi Development Fund, 287

Africa: family planning in, 125; illiteracy in, 10; infant mortality in, 639; inflation effect on Sahel countries of, 280-81; loans to, 8-9, 72, 235; per capita income growth in, 4; poverty in, 309; school dropout rate in, 76

African Development Bank, 93

Agriculture: green revolution in, 11-12, 47-48, 57, 78, 132, 153-55, 218; industrialization at expense of, 87; investments for development of, 10, 12, 77, 257-58, 270, 505; land and tenancy reforms for, 251; Latin American, 24-25; need for expanded production in, 63, 116, 282-83, 581-83; need to increase productivity of small-scale, 165, 246, 247-49, 259, 269, 505; *1969* and *1970* projects for, 113; potential social revolution in, 132; research in, 11, 79-80, 116, 153; status of small farms in, 154-55, 218, 313-14;

technologies for, 312-13; World Bank investment projects for, *1980s,* 599-600. *See also* Rural areas

Algeria, birth rate in, 390n

Alliance for Progress, 19, 28

Animal and plant diseases, research in, 79-80

Appraisal, of projects for investment, 62

Asia: absolute poverty in, 309; family planning in, 125; food grain yield increase in, 47-48, 57, 152-53; illiteracy in, 10; infant mortality in, 639; loans to, 8; school dropout rate in, 76; urbanization in, 316. *See also* East Asia; South Asia

Asian Development Bank, 93

Australia: agricultural research in, 153; development aid by, 177, 558; protectionist measures of, 485, 527

Austria, development aid by, 177

Balance of payments: developing country difficulties, 7-8; economic growth and equilibrium in, 620-21; Germany's surplus in its, 60; OPEC countries' surplus, 275. *See also* Current account

Bangladesh: inflation effect on, 280; projected stationary population in, 388-89

Barbados, family-planning program in, 49

Basic human needs, 320, 459-64, 470, 631

Belgium: development aid by, 558;

663